Christopher Lloyd's
GARDEN FLOWERS

Christopher Lloyd's
GARDEN
FLOWERS

PERENNIALS ❧ BULBS ❧ GRASSES ❧ FERNS

CASSELL&CO

First published in the United Kingdom by Cassell & Co.
Wellington House
175 Strand
London WC2R 0BB

ISBN 0-304-35427-9

A CIP catalogue record for this book is available from the
British Library

A **Domino** book. No part of this publication may be reproduced,
stored in a retrieval system or transmitted in any form or by any
means, without permission from Domino Books Ltd., 7 Bond
Street, St Helier, Jersey

Printed in Great Britain by Butler and Tanner Ltd., Frome

CONTENTS

Introduction 9

Contents

Contents

Contents

INTRODUCTION

The main difference between this book and the all-embracing encyclopaedia lies in its offering not simply descriptions of plants, but personal assessments of them – their good points and their less good. All the plants included have come within my experience during a long life of gardening, and most I have grown myself at some time. Others, not suited to my conditions in Sussex, I know from other peoples' gardens. So for good or ill, here you have the voice of an individual rather than the omniscience of a faceless team of contributors. I am afraid that I will certainly have omitted some plants which you may want to look up. But then, we all need more than one work of reference, and I suppose that what I most hope for is that those who consult this tome may actually enjoy it. I love plants: at least that must be clear – perhaps even infectious.

WHAT ARE PERENNIALS?

Taken literally, the word would refer to any plant that carries on living over a period of years as an individual. This would include shrubs and trees, which would clearly be unhelpful. We gardeners generally imply *herbaceous* perennials.

Herbaceous is a term that has had a long innings and the herbaceous border (not, as my one-time botany teacher told us, to be confused with the vegetarian lodger) has been a popular concept since Gertrude Jekyll's time at the turn of the nineteenth and twentieth centuries – though she herself referred to her principal mixed border as just that, not as specifically herbaceous at all. But the word herbaceous is tiresome to add and hardly beautiful, so it has gradually been dropped. The word perennials, as now generally understood, refers to non-woody plants which live from year to year but disappear from sight at certain periods when the climate does not favour growth. In high latitudes, this will be in winter, the plants going into hibernation, but in warm temperate regions it is often during the intense heat and drought of summer; such plants aestivate. The majority of bulbs belong to this group. Bulbs, corms and tuberous-rooted plants should all be included within the definition of perennials.

Perennials, while ostensibly dormant, continue their existence beneath or at soil level, by some sort of fleshy, nutrient-storing organism. Annuals maintain themselves through their seeds, while the actual seed-producing plant dies at the end of the growing season. Shrubs and trees store much of their energy in sap-retaining woody tissue and in above-ground dormant growth buds.

But we define these categories for our own convenience. The plants themselves have been given no choice in the matter and often fail to conform. And so, in writing a work on perennials, the author has to make choices, where borderline cases arise. Should penstemons be included or not? I said no; they are woody. My editor said yes; they are treated very much as unquestioned perennials. To please him (and myself, as I like them) they have been included. But I have not included *Echium*, as he wished. *E. plantagineum* is an out-and-out annual; *E. vulgare* is an out-and-out biennial; *E. fastuosum* is an out-and-out shrub. The rest of those I know are monocarpic, dying after flowering but taking a few years to reach the flowering condition. One way or another, I have decided to displease my editor in this case and in a few others.

THE POINT OF PERENNIALS

By disappearing at the end of their growing season, perennials give us, as well as themselves, a rest. When they reappear, all their growth is fresh and pristine. Their response to spring (or, in some cases, to rain) changes from day to day and this is a source of excitement and joy to us. Evergreens in spring are looking their worst – thoroughly battered, in most cases, but the perennials escape all that and their reappearance in better times is proof of how wise (to be anthropomorphic) they were.

But a less obvious point that needs to be made is that the seasonal disappearance from view of perennials may give us the opportunity for a side-bet. The vacated surface area of ground is an invitation to make use of it, with plants which have a different season of rest. Thus we gain a succession and the garden totally changes its aspect through these different seasons.

A couple of examples are easily given. When the white Californian tree poppy, *Romneya coulteri*, which flowers in high summer, goes to rest in the autumn, we can cut it to the ground and interplant its fleshy roots with winter aconites, winter-flowering bulbous irises, crocuses, scillas – a range of winter- and early spring-flowering bulbous plants, in fact, which will flower for us in late winter but will have completed their growth cycle before the romneya stretches itself and makes ready for a new summer season. These bulbous plants, once given a start, will increase and carpet the area by their own efforts, none being required of us after the initiation of our bright idea.

Then consider the giant fennel, *Ferula communis*. That starts into growth before winter's end, in the British climate, or at winter's end, where winters are more severe. It unfolds voluptuous fans and platforms of huge but minutely divided leaves which are a feast in themselves, even in those years when no flowering stem shoots up to 3m/10ft and opens stately umbels of tiny yellow flowers. When these excitements are at an end, the plant, in early summer, rapidly goes to rest for the next six months or more. Meantime, the gardener has worked the situation out to his best advantage. The mossy green platforms were interplanted, in the previous autumn, with tall, red tulips ('Halcro' is one of my favourites for the purpose), which will flower while the fennel is at its freshest. When these and the fennel have gone to rest, the space can be occupied for the rest of the summer and early autumn with annuals – for instance cosmos of your choice, sown in late spring. Thus, our garden economy has allowed us to grow two different perennials and one annual to give a succession of interest from the same piece of ground through the four seasons.

Perennials, at the cost of comparatively little effort, offer us the choice of an unlimited range of flower colour from which to choose and over a long season. The majority of those suited to border conditions flower in the warm months of the year when the temperature, at least for quite a slice of the day, encourages us to linger in the garden anyway. For it is pleasant to be able to consider the garden as a seasonal out-of-doors room.

Many perennials have handsome foliage and the particular value of this is in its generally being larger, bolder and more persistent than are most flowers. It is quite logical to think of many perennials in terms of foliage first, their flowers being a welcome, if short-term, bonus. Quite a large section of perennials die gracefully and leave us with sightly skeletons which it is a pleasure to allow to remain untouched through the winter months. If they become broken or bedraggled, it is easy enough to cut them down, especially when the sap has been withdrawn from their stems and most of their weight has been lost.

FLEXIBILITY AND CHOICE

The huge range of different perennials available to us might seem daunting, at first, but it is generally wise to choose those which will flourish in the conditions we can easily offer them without unremitting effort on our part. You might be entranced by a sparkling blue gentian seen on your holidays in the Alps, but, for a quiet life, it will be more sensible to retain that ideal setting and occasion in your mind's eye or to revisit it when opportunity allows, rather than try to grow it under totally alien garden conditions.

Himalayan poppies of the genus *Meconopsis* can be grown and flowered in the gardens of south-east England, but if you are not constantly serving their needs they will quickly disappear. Whereas, even 500 miles or so north, in Scotland, they will, given a good start in suitable soil and shelter from gale-force winds, grow like cabbages without undue effort on your part. They will be undeterred by winter frosts and will benefit from the generally cooler ambient air, whether the sun is shining or not. I have myself been surprised, in approaching the many genera discussed here, how large a number of them are naturally happier in Scotland than in my part of southern England. This should not so much be the cause of envy as of rejoicing, encouraging us to travel north at the best season, but to live gratefully in the south for much of the rest of the year.

There are, within our own garden boundaries, vital factors to be considered, possibly to be modified, of perennials' preference for sun or shade, for light soil or heavy, for dry conditions or water-retentive. The less modification that is necessary, the easier our lives will be. But some will generally be advisable. Bad drainage suits few plants. This may go along with heavy soil and that can be modified once and for all by the introduction of grit, which is generally ground up shingle or gravel, supplied by builders' merchants. Unduly light, easily drying soil can be modified by the addition of humus, which retains moisture and provides a well-aerated medium conducive to healthy root action.

When all such improvements have been taken account of, the fact remains that a great many perennials are extraordinarily tolerant of a wide range of growing conditions. If a lover of shade and moist soil will grow healthily alongside an equally healthy sun- and free-drainage-lover, there is no moral issue that need detain us, seeing that the whole concept of gardening (as of man's proliferation over the face of the earth) is artificial anyway. The main question, after the plants' welfare, is whether they look pleasing together. Do they compose well? Gardening is an art form, albeit ephemeral. We should always be aware of the picture we are creating.

LIMITATIONS

Perennials cannot be expected to be stars in every role. If wonderful for colour, they are likely to be weak on structure. By and large, the fact of their making all their growth in the short space of a few months means that their framework is flimsy. What about acanthus, you will say, immediately homing in on an obvious exception. Yes, but I only want a very limited amount of acanthus in my garden and there must be reasons for that, too. Their rectitude is overpowering (you must know people like that) and their dress is in appallingly good taste, with off-whites and murky purples.

With the permanence of their framework, there are shrubs (among which I include bamboos), which can supply this missing structure. And, given sensible selection, these shrubs will prevent a border from looking a desolate waste-land in winter (if you belong to the autumn-cut-down school for all your perennials).

Even at its peak, in high summer, an all-herbaceous border generally seems to be lacking in body. Swags of climbing roses, trained on supports, would work wonders.

Annuals and biennials also have a part to play which perennials cannot emulate. They are even more flexible and can be moved in and out over a large part of the year, so they are inestimable gap fillers. Again, the immediacy of their display, even if short-lived, has a gladness and charm that touch your heart. I would not dispense with annuals, nor biennials, in any border.

Look at a biennial *Verbascum* like *V. olympicum*, for instance. You can plant it in the autumn or you can depend on self-sowns, which will provide the unpremeditated joy of appearing in different places in different years. In June-July they will soar to 8ft, branching near the top to a symmetrical candelabrum of yellow blossom which lasts for many weeks. And yet this imposing plant is as suitable near the margin of a border as it is at its centre or back, because its habit is such as not to block your view. See-through and see-past plants are invaluable for precluding the stodginess of a border (most often seen in institutional gardens) that is carefully graded for height from back to front.

Self-sowers such as this, as teasels, forget-me-nots, purple orach (*Atriplex hortensis*, an annual) and *Verbena bonariensis* (which is perennial but short-lived), can create a running theme through your border and play a unifying role among otherwise disparate ingredients.

My message here is, go for the mixed border, where all types of plant are permissible if they seem to suit the circumstances. Segregation of different types of plant may make for simplicity and is easier to plan and visualise, but in the long run, a readiness to accept the widest range of plants will produce the most adult and original gardening results.

BEST FEATURES

A few aspects I look out for choosing some perennials for border use in preference to others.

A long flowering season is an asset if the plant continues to look presentable all through it. Geums and herbaceous potentillas often start flowering in May and run on till late summer, but their habit becomes increasingly weedy, stemmy and diffuse. Sometimes this can be corrected by cutting the whole colony hard back in mid-season, as with the geranium 'A. T. Johnson'. Better still, however, is the hybrid geranium (cranesbill) 'Ann Folkard'. Its young foliage, in April, is an attractive shade of lime green and the leaves have a pleasingly jagged outline. It starts flowering in May – brightest purple, almost magenta, with a near-to-black 'eye'. Its shoots are of indefinite growth, ever increasing their range (you must provide either support in a vertical direction, or abundant horizontal space) and continuously making new flower buds so that its season lasts well into autumn. There are several other geraniums with this habit, where *Geranium himalayense*, by contrast, flowers for a couple of weeks in June but has nothing more on offer, apart from fresh foliage arising from the centre of the plant. That is admittedly better than nothing.

These cranesbills highlight another virtue in certain perennials, an intertwining habit which ignores gaps between plantings of different species but creates a tapestry effect, their growth and flowers appearing where not originally intended. Many violas and the less darkened pansies also have this capacity of intertwangling (to borrow a friend's coined description).

Equally, if a plant disappears from sight soon after flowering, like certain aroids (*Arum creticum* and *Dracunculus vulgaris* come to mind), you can take advantage of the vacated space by interplanting with an annual or bedding plant – begonias, for instance. The most tedious kind of perennial under border conditions where no falling off is wanted, is the kind that flowers in April or May, but is then a passenger, refusing to disappear from the scene, but a boring obstruction for the rest of the growing season.

Oriental poppies are good, because they don't mind being cut to the ground in late June, and they can then be interplanted – with marigolds or whatever. Herbaceous peonies, by contrast, flower briefly in early summer and then, if they behave with you as they do with me, their foliage, albeit necessary to them, becomes increasingly sleazy and is a pain to contemplate. In some gardens it keeps its health and produces some fine autumn colour. Herbaceous lupins are rarely much to look at after the end of June and are extremely prone to mildew in late summer, which is the reason for my treating them as biennials (see main entry).

Freedom from disease-proneness is an important consideration. Since the conditions that we offer most of our plants, in close proximity and possibly in stuffy, sheltered surroundings, are sure to promote certain diseases, this is something which, up to a point, we have to live with. Some plants will be less susceptible than others and we may be prepared to give the others some protective spraying. The alternative of growing only low plants in an open, wind-swept site will not be conducive to the humans' full enjoyment of their garden.

Avoidance of specialisation is a great help. If you herd a collection of closely related plants together, any pest or pathogen will have a field day in building up trouble for you and them. Variety should be the watchword.

Do not be ashamed of growing some plants entirely for their delightful foliage. It will hold you in good stead for a long, long time. Ferns, whether evergreen or deciduous, are the shining example. Most benefit from light shade to prevent them 'burning', but polypodies are pretty reliable anywhere, sun or shade, dry or damp.

The worst visual feature that a plant can have, within my canon (but I do not expect you to agree with me) is insignificance. If you have to be within inches of a flower before you can distinguish its features, then it is not a good garden plant, although it may be botanically interesting. Take *Geranium phaeum* 'Mourning Widow'. It is one of the least significant cranesbills. Tall plant, weedy habit, tiny flower and so dark that it doesn't show up at all. Forget it. But it has many devotees, partly because its flowers are so near to black, which seems currently to be a popular attraction; partly because of its curious shape, with prominent 'beak' and laid back petals. A plant has no business to be dull in company – same with humans.

COLOUR AND IMPACT

Many perennials are naturally of bright colouring; it is among their great assets and we should value it as such, not bend over backwards to gentrify it – for instance by growing oriental poppies only if they have pastel shades or by emasculating the brilliant magenta of *Geranium psilostemon* with the more acceptably timid 'Bressingham Flair' or of *Lychnis coronaria* with miserably watered down versions like the Oculata group – white with a pale pink eye.

After long emphasis on polite colours and shades, it is becoming more generally accepted that all colours (if not all shades – some are unacceptably muddy) have their place in the scheme of things. But while red, orange and bright yellow are no longer taboo, we are now into colour theming, previously known as colour harmonies, whereby you plant all your red-flowered (or orange-flowered or yellow-flowered) plants together, thus putting all the emphasis on differences (if any) in shape.

This, alas, misses out on the thrilling opportunities presented by colour contrasts. But these make timid gardeners nervous. They keep looking over their shoulder and wondering what criticism they will arouse from some supposed expert in this field. Stop worrying; experiment and develop your own value judgements. Look at some of the amazing juxtapositions of colour that you often see in textiles – in women's summer wear, for instance. They work and they also work with flowers. And foliage, one should add, as green leaves often have a dominant influence, not necessarily soothing at all.

PERENNIALS AMONG TREES

This is commonly known as woodland gardening. Few of us have a wood but even the gathering of a few trees can provide an opportunity for woodland planting. It will suit the needs and preferences of a range of perennials which would not always fit into border life.

Most perennials benefiting from a modicum of shade are adapted to flowering in spring, before tree foliage has darkened the ground beneath them. But a little shade is very different from a heavy canopy of foliage. Your woodland plants will suffer if the overhead canopy is heavy. Furthermore, the more trees there are, the more tree roots. These can be devastatingly greedy and thirsty. Dry shade provides the most difficult kind of gardening. It may often be both dignified and sensible not to make the attempt. Bare ground is not necessarily an admission of defeat. It can be covered with mosses in winter. In early spring, while there is still light and moisture, it can sustain colonies of winter aconites and crocuses. For the summer, you can enjoy a clear view of the tree's trunk.

However, in the ideal manifestation of woodland gardening, you will drastically thin the trees, so that a good deal of light reaches the floor at all seasons. Your preparatory cultivations should be deep and thorough, incorporating a great deal of humus – leaf mould, rotted bark, garden compost and the like. And, really, you should be prepared to come to the rescue with irrigation in time of summer drought. Even in the cool moist climate of Scotland, drought does sometimes develop.

Having attended to all these requirements, you are likely to succeed with many delights such as hardy orchids, arisaemas, *Dicentra macrantha*, *Meconopsis*, the trickier primulas, *Nomocharis* and *Lilium duchartrei*, trilliums, *Glaucidium palmatum* and many more perennials that would be unable to cope with normal mixed border conditions.

Most such plants will be flowering before the end of June, but in autumn, nearly all the colchicums will be happy and *Cyclamen hederifolium*, *Saxifraga fortunei*, *Kirengeshoma* and the fruits of actaeas. *Sinacalia*, *Gentiana asclepiadea* (the willow gentian) and Japanese anemones themselves all enjoy such an environment. But still, do not allow the darkness before leaf-fall to be heavy. A tree canopy is easily overdone.

A few paragraphs on the mechanics of looking after perennials may not come amiss.

PLANTING

Container-grown perennials can be planted at any time of the year when soil conditions allow. Avoid frozen or waterlogged ground. Bare-root plants are best moved when dormant or, in the case of those with fleshy roots, when just coming out of dormancy. These types, whose roots are easily damaged, can repair the damage if they are becoming active but if just becoming dormant, in autumn, the damage may set up irreparable rotting in the remaining roots.

However, there are many perennials which are better moved and established in autumn than in spring. These include most of those that will flower in the first half of the year, or whose growth starts up early in the year, as with aconitums.

This said, you should always accept a valuable gift when it is offered, rather than wait for 'the right time', which is easily forgotten. And if you have to move gardens at the wrong time, do not be deterred but cut the leafy plant hard back, so that its roots do not have to undergo undue strain. By the same token, water heavily the day before lifting an active plant and heavily again when re-planting it.

Prepare the soil well and to root-depth, before planting. When planting, always make a large hole. 'Fit the hole to the plant, not the plant to the hole'. Many gardeners who have made too small a hole, will twist the roots around in a spiral, so as to get them in, rather than increase the hole's size, allowing the plant's roots to spread out naturally. Bad.

After planting, firm the ground around the plant by leaning on it with your knuckles. Don't pummel a plant in, however, and if the soil is ultra-wet, don't firm at all. But remember that frost action after autumn plantings may lift the smaller plants, so they may need a firming come the spring. Water in thoroughly, at most times. This will wash soil into the large air spaces that are likely to be present after planting. If you are planting in droughty weather, puddle the plant in. I do this by holding the plant in its ready-made hole with one hand while I tip enough water from an up-turned can into the hole to fill it. Just as the last of this is about to drain away, fill in the hole with the soil you have excavated.

A surprisingly large number of perennials can be transferred from a reserve area where they are in full growth in the open ground, to positions in a border where they are required to make a display in later summer or autumn. Such would include chrysanthemums, michaelmas daisies, herbaceous lobelias and many more with fibrous roots. The method is to soak them heavily the day before the move and again as the move has just taken place. Spray their foliage morning and evening, until it stops flagging in the sun. It helps if the weather is dull, but this is not essential.

Reverse moves work in the same way. If you have had a spring display of doronicums, cut them right down after flowering, water and move them into a damp reserve area for the summer, watering again. Same treatment, but at the end of June, with pyrethrums.

REPLANTING

How much attention they require depends partly on the plant and partly on the ambition combined with energy of the gardener. Many perennials ask no better than to be left undisturbed for many years. These usually have deep, tenacious roots. I have not replanted my first colony of cardoons in fifty years. A colony of *Eryngium* × *oliverianum* even longer than that. Kniphofias and Hemerocallis might flower more freely if re-planted, say, once in seven years. That is not too demanding. Hosta are generally considered to be entirely labour-saving ground cover, if they like their situation. Personally I think their foliage quality may fall off if the crowns are unduly overcrowded. Flowering, as also with begonias, may be confined, after a while, to the margins of a colony, but there is no imperative to get busy, here.

Looking at it another way, however, there are rewards for the active gardener, who is ambitious for best possible results from his/her perennials, and who may, in order to attain these, be happy to split and replant frequently; to offer support where called for, rather than resort to growing the darkened form, which will have less personality. Who will water in times of drought and feed with organic manures on an annual basis. Perennials are very responsive.

SUPPORT

We soon get to know which plants will collapse if we do not support them. The answer is to anticipate and to provide that support before they have collapsed. Once keeled over, their stems, hitherto straight, will bend up to the vertical at the tips and a kink results. You can never get rid of that kink and it looks dreadful.

In giving support, you should never draw the stems together so that they appear like a trussed up bundle. They should not be drawn in at all but given their support in the positions where they naturally grew.

A single stake and tie is sometimes enough; or, if there are a number of stems a couple of stakes, sometimes more. I use bamboo canes most of the time. A cane was once part of a growing plant and it always has a thicker and a thinner end. Both for stability and for appearances, always make sure that it is the thick end which goes into the ground. Also, get your stakes in upright. They look drunken if leaning this way and that. Be self-critical.

If only a single tie is needed, make a clove hitch (which will never slip down) at the required height. Pass the string's free end around the stem, then back round itself before returning to the starting point and finishing the job with a reef knot. If several stems and canes are required, as where you are dealing with a group, start in the same way but with a long free string end. Take this round the stems that are placed between the first cane and the next, then, on reaching the latter, make another clove hitch before proceeding around more stems and canes, finally ending where you started with the reef knot. If the group is really large, you may need one or more canes in its centre as well as around its perimeter. In that case the progress of the string's free end will describe a sort of cat's cradle (occasionally doubling back on itself). It may not be necessary to make a tie around every stem, just a selection of key ones, leaving the rest to be supported in the limited gaps within the cradle.

The string used should be soft but tough enough to last a season and of neutral colouring. I use fillis, which is undyed hemp, either 2-ply or 5-ply, but this is none too easily found from retail sources. For really heavy work, like the stems of cardoons, we use chestnut stakes and insulated telephone wire.

When you have finished, cut off any projecting cane ends. They don't look pretty. The best work is utterly concealed, within a very short period. As a substitute to canes, link stakes or others of durable metal doing a similar job, also work well and are discreet. I don't like the circular wire supports on one or two struts. They are inflexible in their adaptability and they usually show. They might just be tolerable for peony stems.

If you can get it, brushwood (peasticks) is very effective for multi-stemmed plants like *Clematis recta*. In these cases, it is most important to anticipate the plant's eventual height so that the framework of sticks is long enough to do the job when the plant becomes top-heavy with blossom. *C. recta*, in the strain I grow, needs brushwood to reach 2m/6ft above ground level. *Aster sedifolius* 1m/3ft and plenty of it. Brushwood becomes too brittle to use in a second season. Hornbeam, hazel and birch are all good, being twiggy. You may need to sharpen the ends of your pieces of brushwood and it makes life easier if you use them while the ground is still soft.

DEAD-HEADING

The main purpose of removing the faded blooms or developing seed pods from flowered plants, is for appearances. It may also save the plant from using up misdirected energy (from our point of view) and this may by the same token encourage it to flower a second time. A bird that loses its first clutch of eggs will quickly lay a second.

For the sake of appearances, don't just pull off the faded blooms, leaving behind a forest of stem ends. Use a knife or secateurs and make your cuts back to where you can see an incipient side-shoot (as in *Helenium* 'Moerheim Beauty'). If there isn't one, then back to a leaf or (as in the case of border phloxes) pair of leaves. Sometimes, as with certain cranesbills, *Alchemilla mollis* and doronicums, it pays to cut the entire plant right to the ground. It will soon make new leaves and will look fresh for the rest of the season.

This does have a slightly weakening effect, which may or may not matter. In the case of the early-summer-flowering *Hemerocallis flava*, the foliage looks dreadfully slovenly by July and, in a passion, I often cut the plant entirely down. It soon makes new leaves which remain fresh till the autumn and there may even be some late flowers. But its performance the next year is not so good. One has to make the choice. If I were really on the ball, I should have plants in front of the Hemerocallis which came late into growth but concealed it by the time it needed to be out of sight. Or I could move some plants in, ready-grown. We never stop learning

FAMILIES

The botanists have been busy re-naming them. They have sometimes broken up established families, so that the new names give no points of reference. Thus, *Hosta* is now in a new family of its own, Hostaceae, *Hyacinthus* in Hyacinthaceae, *Veratrum* in Melanthiaceae, and so on. These new family names no longer inform you of the familiar floral attributes which formerly placed these and many others within Liliaceae, distinguishing them from Iridaceae and Amaryllidaceae.

Furthermore, the botanists have decided that all family names must terminate in aceae. This has led them to rename a number of familiars which have entered the English language. We talk about labiates, umbellifers, composites, legumes, crucifers, taking these definitions from Labiatae, Umbelliferae, Compositae, Leguminosae and Cruciferae. But these unruly suffixes are no longer acceptable to the current generation of rule-makers, who don't in the least mind making our lives difficult in a good cause. Those families have become Lamiaceae, Apiaceae, Asteraceae, Papilionaceae and Brassicaceae.

Where the names have recently changed, I have therefore given the new ones first as accepted by *The RHS Plant Finder*, followed by the older familiar ones, and leave readers to chose for themselves.

Acanthus

ACANTHACEAE

Most Acanthaceae are too tender to be treated as hardy plants in temperate climates. Acanthus is the chief exception. It is the bold habit and form of the species that makes them noteworthy. In all, the flowers are in some shade of off-white and very off-purple, neither elevating to the spirits nor sufficiently depressing to warrant any sort of a gasp.

All have fleshy roots, pieces of which, when broken, readily make new plants. This means that acanthus are often a nuisance in mixed company and are best treated as solo, landscape features (perhaps in the company of some other large-leaved perennial), where the strength of their large, deeply divided leaves and the statuesque nature of their stiff flower spires can be best appreciated.

A. spinosus (1.2m/4ft) is the best all-round species, free-flowering, good in partial shade as well as in full sun, the leaves deeply and sharply divided, but variable in this respect as also in its vigour. In some variants, the flowering spikes will rise to 1.8-2.4m/6-8ft.

Neither is there any hard and fast division between *A. spinosus* and Spinosissimus group.

A. mollis (1-1.2m/3-4ft) has limp, soft leaves, outstandingly broad in the Latifolius group. They remain a feature through most of winter. But flowering can be shy or failed, unless the previous summer was hot, and a position in full sun is needed, despite the flabbiness of the foliage in torrid weather. 'Fielding's Gold' and 'Holland's Gold' are striking in spring for their bright yellow-green young foliage. This species in particular has been seriously afflicted by powdery mildew, of recent years.

A. hungaricus (1m/3ft) has suffered tiresome name changes, including *A. longifolius* and *A. balcanicus*. It is less handsome than the two species already described, since the leaves (which are yellowish when young) are only once (though deeply) divided. It is reliably free-flowering but sets abundant seed and if this is allowed to self-sow, control of a colony is soon lost. The seeds are ejected to some distance from their source.

Achillea

ASTERACEAE/COMPOSITAE

This genus has come up in the world since I first knew it. From earliest childhood, there was sneezewort, **Achillea ptarmica**, which I first discovered as a wilding in the Lake District, later in my own parish. In its double forms, variously known as 'The Pearl', 'Perry's White' and then, so mixed up did they become, the Pearl group, this was in our garden as far back as I can remember. Flattish heads of pure white flowers on lanky, collapsible stems, but admirable for cutting. Height 60cm/2ft. This is a plant of weedy habit and habits, its thin, white rhizomes invading groups of neighbouring plants. Not a clubbable border ingredient, therefore.

A. filipendulina reached our garden in the 1930s (as *A. eupatorium*), the selection being known as 'Gold Plate'. With its substantial, flattish (though slightly domed) corymbs, it has a strongly architectural presence in the border. Being bright, English-mustard-yellow as it comes into flower in late June, it contrasts strongly, effectively but crudely with the spikes of rich blue delphiniums. Height 1.5m/5ft and support, with string passed between canes among the flowering stems, is necessary.

As with mustard, the colour changes, with age, to a tired, brownish yellow, but if gathered in youth, the flower heads retain much of their brightness and are popular in dried flower arrangements, where they may gather dust and cobwebs for many years.

At half this height, 'Coronation Gold' is a more convenient plant for smaller borders, barely requiring support. In Scotland, where habitually grey skies demand compensating brightness wherever it may be found, I have seen it combined with the magenta *Geranium psilostemon* and the reddest red astilbe. With plenty of mauve and purple flowers around them and grey foliage, this was surprisingly acceptable.

The palest and most dazzling grey foliage is found in the foot-tall **A. clypeolata**, with bright yellow flower heads. But in my garden it was regularly defoliated by house sparrows for nesting material, and anyway needs frequent replanting. So, if the truth be told, do many achilleas. 'Moonshine' (45cm/18in) has pleasingly grey foliage and considerably paler (though still bright) flowers, but if not divided and replanted every second year, becomes a virtually non-flowering foliage plant. I have always preferred 'Taygetea', though this name is now said to be invalid. It is a really soft, pale yellow. At 45cm/18in it makes an admirable companion, in June-July, for

27 *

---

* References to photographs. Figures in the margins refer to the colour photographs so numbered throughout the book. These may illustrate particular species and varieties, or general groups such as cannas and day-lilies, or wider views of plants used in combination.

the purple spikes of *Salvia nemorosa* 'Ostfriesland' ('East Friesland'). It is weaker growing than 'Moonshine', needing good soil and frequent re-planting.

However, it has lately mutated, in my garden, to a much stronger-growing, self-supporting, 1m/3ft plant, which I have named 'Lucky Break'. With its delightfully soft yellow colouring, this is just what many of us have been waiting for.

Our other native species, the ubiquitous yarrow, **A. millefolium**, has ferny leaves and is a weed of lawns which, however, remains green through any drought. In meadow areas, its heads of white flowers are welcome enough and, even in the wild, the colouring often tends towards pink. The best known cultivar for border usage is 'Cerise Queen', whose colour is good at first, but fades nastily, while its weedy habit has for long excluded it from my garden. That, also, is the case with 'Schwefelblüte' ('Flowers of Sulphur'), which is an old variety, clearly of *A. millefolium* origins.

'Anthea', however, is a clumpy plant, 45cm/18in tall and of a nice sulphur yellow. It should be divided frequently. Many new 60-75cm/2-2½ft achilleas have appeared of recent years, a high proportion of them bred by Ernst Pagels, in his north German nursery. On the whole, I find them extremely disagreeable. Each flower is often in two contrasting colours, which makes for a confusing blur in the mass; and although the colours may start clean, they fade disastrously, so that old flower heads mixed up with new become a problem.

Often they cash in on the tastes of the soft-pastel shades brigade (haters of flowers that are bright yellow, scarlet or orange). One nursery's Modern Hybrids is a horribly muddy mix. This is akin to the Summer Pastels group.

'Lachsschönheit' ('Salmon Beauty') and 'Apfelblüte' ('Apple Blossom') clearly have their following, to judge by the number of nurseries offering them, but at the least I hope the Germans should not be touchy about the English-speaking world translating their, to us, tongue-twisting names into anglicized equivalents.

Acidanthera — see Gladiolus

Aciphylla

APIACEAE/UMBELLIFERAE

A genus of New Zealand evergreen perennials which either fascinate or repel. Known here as speargrass, the Maori name Kurikuri is more often used in New Zealand. The normally stiff, divided leaves are extremely sharply pointed and arranged in mounded rosettes. But I was interested in one species, **Aciphylla divisa** (15cm/6in), in the Southern Alps, which, growing under the continuous spray of a small river, had perfectly soft, bright green leaves. Flowers on male plants (the whole genus is dioecious) were sulphur yellow. When flowering, male plants are always showier than female.

More typical is the subalpine **A. aurea** (60cm/2ft), which makes hummocks of yellow-green leaves, brightest at the margins (you see it with colonies of the yellow-spiked *Bulbinella angustifolia*). This flowers freely and although the flowered rosette subsequently dies, others that have remained vegetative take over. **A. squarrosa** (45cm/1½ft when flowering), with hummocks of stiff, grey leaves, is in cultivation and seems reasonably hardy. Rather surprisingly (although like *Celmisia*), aciphyllas seem more at home in the Scottish climate than in the south of England.

King of them all (from the Southern Alps) is **A. scott-thomsonii**, which reaches 2m/6ft when flowering and the yellow-flowered males are tremendously handsome. That does well in Scotland, though I have never seen the two sexes together there, so seed (which should be sown fresh) is never produced.

Aconitum

RANUNCULACEAE

The aconites might, in their name, be confused with the winter aconite of the same Family. They are also popularly known as monkshoods – from the hooded, asymmetric flower.

Aconites are poisonous – pretty well all the Ranunculaceae are to some degree. But aconites are the chosen favourite of do-gooders who insist that they should always be labelled as poisonous in gardens that are open to the public and should always be mentioned as poisonous in every gardening article or entry where they feature. But who is going to be tempted to nibble aconites, anyway? And if we did, wouldn't we quickly spit out the disagreeable contents of our mouths? This insistence on designating every poisonous plant has spread like a leprosy, wasting a lot of time, space and effort. I suppose we shall be expected to label our poisonous weeds, soon.

Within Ranunculaceae, aconites most closely resemble delphiniums, having irregular flowers and pleasingly incised, palmate leaves. But, as John Raven remarked in *A Botanist's Garden*, 'their colour always strikes me as dingy and lifeless' compared with delphiniums or veronicas. Another appropriate comment is that aconites all look in need of a good wash. However, they are very hardy and easily grown perennials of which we should not like to be deprived. They thrive in sun or in shade. In the wild, they tend to grow on the margins of woodland or in open glades.

Their rootstock is a tuber – one tuber being formed below each stem. Some varieties easily become over-congested, which prevents flowering. These should be divided and replanted every year or two. Autumn is the time for this, as monkshoods are remarkably early on the move, new foliage being made as early as late January. That applies even to the autumn-flowerers; so they have a long growing season.

To date, only four aconites have received the RHS Award of Garden Merit. That seems a fair assessment, to me. Among the earliest in bloom, May-June, is ***Aconitum napellus*** (1m/3ft). It need not detain us. A fault in many aconites is the dominance of the central spike. Side-growths may comprise the bulk of flowering potential, but these are later in flower and their impact is marred by the central spike having already run to seed. The early summer-flowering 'Bressingham Spire' (1m/3ft) is of this kind, though imposing and a good if murky blue.

One of my favourites, though I have never grown it, is the July-flowering ***A.* × cammarum** 'Bicolor' (1.2m/4ft), usually known as 'Bicolor' *tout court*. The hoods are a mixture of blue and white and show up well, notably in a shady situation. That is July-flowering. So, and well into August, is 'Spark's Variety' (1m/3ft). Its branching, indigo-blue inflorescence has no strong central spike to detract from the equally important laterals, when they come out. I grow this with mauve border phloxes but also, for contrast, with the bright yellow sunflower, *Helianthus* 'Capenoch Star' (1.2m/4ft).

In autumn, we are well served by ***A. carmichaelii*** – always a telling shade of blue, though it varies a good deal in its different forms. ***A. fischeri*** (1m/3ft) was the name of the typical cultivar grown in gardens, for many years. Truly, a no-trouble plant guaranteed to keep down weeds and requiring no attention. It does not flower till October, by which time its leaves are yellowing, which seems a bit incongruous as accompaniment to a newly opening flower spike, but I got used to it in time and rather liked the contrast.

A. c. 'Wilsonii' is described as a group. Often 2m/6ft tall, it would combine well, in its autumn season and in a rather moist, shady place, with the white cones of *Hydrangea paniculata* 'Tardiva' (also 2m/6ft or more) and the pyramids of spidery, yellow flowers of *Senecio tanguticus* (2m/6ft), now *Sinacalia tangutica* (senecios have been mercilessly split by the systematic botanists). This is a colonising plant.

Best in the Wilsonii group, is 'Kelmscott' (1.3m/4½ft), with a long inflorescence, and a long autumn-flowering season. I sometimes use its strong blue behind bronze chrysanthemums, bedded out in August.

Apart from indigo and blue aconites, some are muted yellow, like **A. lycoctonum** (1.2m/4ft, self-collapsing). I have no time for this. Nor have I done well with 'Ivorine' (60cm/2ft), which is ivory white but so quickly becomes congested and non-flowering that you need to be thinking about replanting every year; an attention it hardly deserves.

Not to be omitted is the climbing, herbaceous **A. hemsleyanum**, (syn. *A. volubile*). This is easily raised from seed but can be an unacceptably weak and washy mauve. On the other hand it can be quite a telling 'blue', and then looks well intertwining with the yellow lanterns of *Clematis tangutica*. Probably the wisest course is to buy a plant specifically advertised as 'dark blue'.

Acorus

ARACEAE

Acorus calamus (1m/3ft), sweet flag, grows in shallow water and is naturalised in Britain, especially in Norfolk and the fens. It has iris-like leaves, with crimped margins but shows its aroid identity when flowering, in early summer. 'Variegatus' is a handsome variegated form with a broad, cream stripe along the side of each leaf. The spadix seems to appear fairly low down from the side of a leaf, though this 'leaf' is in fact a leaf-like spathe. The spadix is a narrow cone, packed with fertile, cream-coloured flowers. Seed is not ripened in Europe.

The whole plant is sweet-smelling when bruised or dried and an essential oil is extracted from the rhizome, which is also powdered and has been used like cinnamon or nutmeg. The foliage used to be strewn on the floors of churches and private houses, instead of rushes. Although I have grown 'Variegatus' in my natural pond for many years, it has never thrived, perhaps because of a high fish population creating too much turbulence.

Actaea

RANUNCULACEAE

Actaeas are hardy herbs, unusual in being grown more for the handsome appearance of their fruits (invariably poisonous, however; hence the common name Baneberry) than for their over-discreet, fluffy white flowers. They are all good in shade.

Herb Christopher, **Actaea spicata**, is locally a British native but is little grown in gardens. Its berries are black. The other species are North American. **A. alba** (1m/3ft) (syn. *A. pachypoda*) has white berries with distinctively inflated reddish pedicels. The other white-berried baneberry most likely to be encountered, but with normal pedicels, is *A. rubra* f. *neglecta*. **A. rubra** (1m/3ft) itself has spikes of closely set, bright red berries, ripening (as do the others) in late summer. All flourish better in Scotland than in south-east England.

Adiantum

ADIANTACEAE

We have one native Maidenhair fern, **Adiantum capillus-veneris**. It grows in limestone pavement clefts, as close as possible to the sea, and is a great thrill to find, but is a tender plant.

There are two hardy species. **A. pedatum** (30cm/1ft) has a wide geographic range in North America and the Far East. A deciduous plant of the greatest delicacy, in appearance, it is really quite tough, though liable to scorch if too exposed. In nature it grows in open woodland. The stems are black and wiry subtending an arc of almost horizontal pinnules (the leaflets), palest green in spring. The rootstock becomes tough and dense and it is easier to split young plants than old, though spores germinate readily. The variety that has been known as var. **aleuticum**, actually var. **subpumilum**, is less than half the height and I don't think worth bothering about.

On woodland fringes in Kashmir, but with a wide Far Eastern distribution, I saw **A. venustum** (15cm/6in), which is an easy garden plant, spreading into a carpet, more or less deciduous, the old fronds taking on a pleasingly rufous colouring in winter. The new fronds begin to unfurl in early March. This is a splendid filler – for instance among hydrangeas – and easily divided as growth is being resumed in spring. The much divided fronds are roughly triangular in overall outline.

Aegopodium

APIACEAE/UMBELLIFERAE

The redoubtable ground elder, or bishop weed, as it is known in America, is **Aegopodium podograria**. It is a deep-rooted, rhizomatous perennial, difficult to get rid of if entangled in the roots of other perennials or in box hedging. However, as a cheerful foliage plant, 'Variegata' is undeniably attractive, with plenty of bright, creamy variegation which is no less bright if the plant is colonised under trees.

Sometimes (and I have personal experience of this) the variegated form, which is far less vigorous than the all-green type-plant, reverts to type, which is a dastardly trick to play. But there are different clones and that most seen in the USA seems to be pretty reliable. It is popular, there, and I can see why. If you know what to expect and site accordingly, the variegated ground elder has its place, especially if it is a difficult spot for most other plants.

Agapanthus

ALLIACEAE/LILIACEAE

Agapanthus are fleshy-rooted South African perennials, the more tender kinds evergreen, the more hardy, deciduous. In general they are late summer flowerers and a blue colouring is their main strength, though there are a number of albinos (particularly attractive when the anthers are black) and some are purple. The strap leaves are apt to be boring when plants are out of flower, and the season of any one kind is seldom longer than four weeks.

One of the main faults in agapanthus is imposed upon them by mindless admirers, who tend to mass them. The overall effect is monotonous.

The flowers are massed in umbels above naked scapes. The umbel is often globular, sometimes flattened on the underside. The range available has greatly increased in the past 50 years, but as division of crowns is a comparatively slow process, there is always the temptation to raise stock from seed, which gives mixed and often inferior results. This has been particularly evident in unnamed Headbourne hybrids, originally raised by Lewis Palmer and notably hardy. Those that have retained their cultivar names and were at one time trialled by the RHS at Wisley, are still excellent.

The old evergreen and somewhat tender *Agapanthus* that has long been a favourite for tub culture, being wheeled under cover in winter, was known as *A. umbellatus*, but **A. praecox** subsp. **orientalis** (1m/3ft) is the name currently favoured by the experts. Congestion of the crowns favours free flowering, but generally breaks the tubs or pots containing them. Agapanthus need splitting and replanting from time to time but do not flower freely again immediately thereafter.

The flower is generally funnel-shaped, but may open wider than that or may, on the contrary, be tubular for most of its length. The latter is the case in the late-flowering *A. inapertus* subsp. *pendulus* (1.2m/4ft), whose deep colouring is indigo. Graham Thomas suggests the bright pink *Nerine bowdenii* (60cm/2ft) as a companion, which sounds excellent to me.

With 'Loch Hope' (1m/3ft), which is a late-flowering, rich blue Headbourne hybrid, I have associated the bright orange *Crocosmia* × *crocosmiiflora* 'Star of the East', which is light orange.

A. campanulatus (60cm/2ft) is small-flowered, deciduous and hardy, usually of a quite intense shade of blue. I have long grown the cultivar 'Isis', which flowers freely, but I have never used it to notable effect. There is plenty of room for experiment, for those who are not too easily satisfied.

Agastache

Lamiaceae/Labiatae

Highly aromatic labiates, the smell is generally too rank to be pleasing, but then you don't have to roll in the plant. Many have spikes of flowers of a somewhat dirty colouring: whitish, purplish, bluish, reddish – and I avoid these.

Years ago, I grew **Agastache mexicana** (60cm/2ft), sometimes known as *Brittonastrum mexicanum*; a short-lived perennial but easily replaced from seed, the seedlings flowering in their first summer. It bore broad, shortish spikes of rose-red flowers. Then, under the same name, I found that I was being sold seed of something entirely different, with dense spikes of murky purple flowers, and I gave up.

Then came 'Firebird' (38cm/15in), sometimes listed under **A. barberi**, which is a splendid bedding plant, flowering for three months from early July. It is of a spreading habit, making an open bush, with small greyish leaves and narrow spikes of salmon flowers. Salmon, in my experience, is a difficult colour to get right, with a tendency to being insipid, but this agastache gets away with it (just about). Like many long-flowering perennials, this one tends to be short-lived, though reasonably hardy (most agastaches are on the borderlines of hardiness). It is easily raised from autumn-struck cuttings, however, which can be overwintered under cold glass. It goes well with the broad grey leaves of the tender, shrubby *Plectranthus argentatus* to back it up.

69

11, 55

Seen on a seedsman's trial ground but not yet grown by me, I liked **A. cana** (1m/3ft), which again flowers in its first year and from July to September. Of upright habit, it carries long reddish-purple flower spikes.

Ajuga

Lamiaceae/Labiatae

Bugle, **Ajuga reptans** (15cm/6in), is a widespread native of open woodland or of woodland glades, which makes colonies by stoloniferous runners, flowering in spring, with chunky, deep blue candle spikes. I see it in my mind's eye on the Kentish North Downs, in May, when besieged by Pearl-bordered Fritillary butterflies, as it was in the 1950s – perhaps still is.

I like it best, in my garden, in paving cracks, where it can run to its heart's content. But it has been selected for many variants, having differently coloured leaves, sometimes variegated. A number of these have received the AGM, among them 'Catlin's Giant' (23cm/9in). At its best, this has leaves twice the normal size, purple, glossy and light-reflecting in shady places. On flowering, the leaves become much smaller. It is a plant that should not be allowed to become congested, but be frequently replanted. In fact, this is the best treatment for most of the cultivars with classy foliage.

John Raven, in *A Botanist's Garden*, described how, in a wildish part of his garden, he had a carpet of a purple-leaved version of *A. reptans*, through which, first *Anemone × fulgens* and then *Tulipa sprengeri* were able to penetrate and flower at a higher level, both being a strong shade of pure red. I can picture that in my mind's eye and the additional likelihood of blue flowers in the bugle, during part of the display.

I do not want to discourage any enthusiast, but I have given all of them up. They are incorrigible infiltrators and do not suit mixed border conditions. After flowering, they self-sow and all sorts of bastards are the result. Furthermore, they are subject to powdery mildew.

Ajuga pyramidalis (23cm/9in) is another native but highly localised in the north and west, preferring (as John Raven tells us in *Mountain Flowers*) rather dry, stony conditions where juniper and bearberry are its frequent associates. It makes a compact, non-stoloniferous plant and is extremely handsome in spring with numerous spikes of rich, deep blue flower spikes. They go well with the grey-leaved, luminous yellow buttercup, *Ranunculus gramineus*.

Alcea

The hollyhocks that we treasure as cottage garden plants and that we loved as children, the flowers being easily converted into fairies with glamorous, ready-made skirts, have been lifted out of the genus *Althaea* and told to get on with it in future as *Alcea*.

12   ***Alcea rosea*** (2.4m/8ft) is therefore the multi-talented hollyhock, which includes every colour except purple and blue, can be single or a fully double rosette and can be treated as perennial, biennial or, in some strains, annual. The last sounds a good option, but in my experience the flowers are too deeply buried, along their spikes, among over-large leaves.

Many colour strains can be raised from seed and among the most popular is 'Nigra', whose deep maroon passes for black. However, like other 'black' flowers, you cannot see it except on a sunny day and at close range.

Hollyhocks should stand like sentinels at your cottage door (some tactful support is generally needed) and there should be paving cracks at hand into which they can self-sow.

The bane of hollyhock cultivation (already written about by Miss Jekyll in the 19th century) is rust disease, which not only looks horrible but seriously weakens the host. As you know that it will reappear every year, the obvious and effective precaution should be taken of spraying with a protective fungicide *before* the trouble appears – say in early May, in the northern hemisphere, and to repeat the treatment a couple of times during the summer.

Since Roy Lancaster re-introduced ***A. rugosa*** (1.5m/5ft) from the Caucasus, some years ago now, this has become a popular garden plant. The leaves (still subject to rust, though seldom cripplingly) are more lobed than in most hollyhocks and the flowers are an agreeable pale yellow, with a long summer season. It comes true from seed and a flowering plant will be obtained in the second year from sowing.

Alchemilla

Although not seen in many gardens when I was young, ***Alchemilla mollis*** (30cm/1ft) is ubiquitous today. At its best, it is not only a beautiful plant but incredibly obliging, sowing itself into paving cracks, placing itself beneath garden seats and, in general, giving a comfortable and settled look, in early summer, to gardens which may become a bit of a shambles before summer has ended.

The scalloped leaves are softly hairy and retain light-reflecting water drops, after rain or dew, to look like quicksilver. The inflorescence is a loose spray of small, pale green flowers. Its looseness becomes something of a hazard after heavy rain, for it flops over to one side and is easily bruised by being trodden on. From late July on, the plant becomes shabby and it should be cut hard back so that not a leaf or stem remains. It will quickly refurnish and will regain pristine freshness by September, when it is nice to have clumps of *Colchicum* flowering between alchemilla colonies.

The alchemilla's rootstock is tough and woody, as in the majority of non-shrubby Rosaceae. Self-seeding should be forestalled, if possible, but if seedlings do need to be weeded out, catch them young and before they become toughly resistant.

A. erythropoda (15cm/6in) is a smaller species but still strong enough for a marginal border position, preferably in full sun so as to bring out the glaucous colouring of its foliage. It makes a pleasant change.

Allium

ALLIACEAE/LILIACEAE

Alliums and onions are synonymous, but we distinguish food for the soul, alliums, from food for the stomach, onions and leeks. In passing, leeks (not to mention chives) do present a mild overlap. If allowed to flower, which they do in the second year from seed at a height of 2m/6ft, their globes are admirable for drying.

It is the arrangement of their flowers, in simple umbels, generally of globular outline, that makes alliums so distinctive a feature in the garden. Their smell is also distinctive, and shared by so few other genera that we feel suspicious of the botanists' classification which separates those from *Allium*. A notorious example is *A. siculum*, which must now be sought under *Nectaroscordum*.

Some alliums are bulbous, with a marked dormant season when they may be harvested and sold in a dried-off condition. Others are clumpy perennials, with only slightly enlarged and fleshy leaf bases to carry them through the winter. These cannot be dried.

In many of the earlier-flowering alliums, the leaves are dying off before they flower. This is a point that the gardener should not be blind to (but often is). The taller kinds can be sited so that other plants are masking their leaves, which are always close to the ground, by the time they are in flower.

1

2

1   The upright thrust of red-hot-poker, *Kniphofia uvaria* 'Nobilis', gives focus to less dominant *Crocosmia* 'Late Lucifer' (front) and purple orach, *Atriplex hortensis* var. *rubra*, a self-sown annual.

2   Shelter, sunlight and warmth promote luxuriance, with cannas and dahlias in the lead for floral display in late summer and early autumn.

3   The tender, climbing *Tropaeolum tricolorum* flowers in spring from dormant tubers potted in late summer and overwintered under barely frost-free glass.

4   Summer luxuriance largely created by foliage: *Phormium* 'Sundowner', centre; *Miscanthus sinensis* 'Variegatus', behind; *Tetrapanax papyrifera*, left; *Rhus glabra* 'Laciniata', right.

5

5   From North American mixed woodland comes the ultra-hardy, spring-flowering *Uvularia grandiflora*.

6   Traditional spring bedding but informally used: the lily-flowered tulip, 'Ballerina' above a carpet of forget-me-nots.

7   The spring-flowering *Gladiolus tristis* (delicously night-scented) needs mild winters to survive outside. Here it has sown itself in the middle of a plant of *Rhodanthemum hosmariense*. ▷

Alliums are widely distributed throughout the northern hemisphere and you only need to go for a walk in some wildish spot in spring or early summer to become aware of their prevalence and of the overwhelming ordinariness of many species. Some are ferocious weeds, under cultivation, but may gain entry into our gardens by dint of a pleasing appearance. As with humans, these are the most dangerous of all, the con-men of the vegetable world.

One of the most difficult to eradicate is **Allium triquetrum** (30cm/1ft). My neighbour, quite innocently I feel sure, planted it on his boundary with mine and I have been trying to eradicate it, with the help of Roundup (glyphosate), for the past ten years. It spreads both by seed and by bulbils. Its fresh white, nodding flowers are borne in May. You see it naturalised in much of Cornwall and the south-west where, on roadside banks, it makes a pretty feature with bluebells and pink campion (*Silene dioica*).

Another beautiful stinker is **A. roseum** var. **bulbiferum** (38cm/15in). It carries heads of soft pink flowers, in May, and I first admired it in a meadow area at Kew, in lilac time. I still think it has a place as a meadow ingredient, but the bulbils formed within the flower head are devastatingly prolific.

Alliums cover a wide colour range: white, pink, purple, blue, mauve and yellow. Their foliage can be exciting, too, notably in **A. karataviense** (23cm/9in), in spring, when two broad, purple-streaked, glaucous leaves unfold, enclosing the budded flowering stem. By the time it is in (not very exciting, mauve) flower, the leaves are withering. Other than by removing them, there is nothing to be done about this, as the plant is so short.

With **A. hollandicum** – far better known as **A. aflatunense** – (75cm/2½ft), it is easy, when it flowers in May, to whisk over and remove the more obtrusive of the dying leaf tips, which are well below the inflorescence. This species has bold, mauve globes and I have seen it looking particularly well in a Perthshire garden in June (things are later there), in the company of the mauve, cow-parsley-like *Chaerophyllum hirsutum* 'Roseum', each self-sowing, on equal terms, into the other. Another telling use is beneath the laburnum tunnel in Rosemary Verey's garden at Barnsley, Gloucestershire. 'Purple Sensation' is an even more effective clone, of richer colouring. I use these two as bedding plants – they look well among and above a carpet of the double pink campion, *Silene dioica* 'Flore Pleno'.

Comparable, though shorter and with much larger globes, is the mauve **A. cristophii** (also known as *A. albopilosum*) (45cm/1½ft). This is June-flowering and can be allowed to self-sow in mixed borders, being especially useful among the developing foliage of Japanese anemones. It adds a dimension to the sites where they will

32

29, 48

later dominate. (Tulips will do the same, a few weeks earlier.) The allium's perianth segments are stiff and persistent, so their globes remain sightly through most of summer. If required for drying, however, they should be gathered while newly expanded and fresh, and hung upside-down till sere.

A. neapolitanum (30cm/1ft), which is leafy in winter and ends its growing season by flowering in May-June, has flower heads of pearly whiteness. Its incontinent seeding is easily prevented by grabbing all stems and foliage in a clump (for it makes clumps), with both hands and tugging. Everything breaks cleanly away from the bulbs, which can then be inter- and overplanted for the summer. *A. n.* Cowanii group is larger-flowered but less thrifty, being on the borderlines of hardiness.

In a deep shade of pink, the May-flowering **A. oreophilum** (syn. *A. ostrowskianum*) (15cm/6in), is easily grown but easily overlaid under normal border conditions. Give it an open site. **A. unifolium** (syn. *A. murrayanum*) (23cm/9in) is a little bit stronger, spreading to form a small colony, with clean pink flower heads in May-June. It goes dormant after that, but a neighbour like *Geranium wallichianum* will soon fill the vacuum.

26 The cheerful, bright yellow, June-flowering **A. moly** (23cm/9in), remains undemanding of attention for at least 60 years at a time. Tennyson's Lotos-Eaters, 'propt on beds of amaranth and moly', presumably had a weak sense of smell. The clone 'Jeannine' seems exactly the same as the undifferentiated species that I have always grown. **A. flavum** (30cm/1ft) has glaucous leaves and flowers of a muted yellow shade. It needs an open, undisputed site. July.

I could wish to grow **A. sphaerocephalon** (1m/3ft, but usually leaning) better than I do. It makes plenty of spawn around its bulbs and also seeds, if you are patient enough to allow for rather late ripening. Flowering in July-August, the oval heads are rich, reddish purple (contrasting well with red penstemons). In the wild state, it looked handsome under meadow conditions near Lake Balaton in Hungary, flowering a good month earlier there. I should like to establish it in my own meadow – somewhere that we didn't give its annual cut until well into autumn.

In a class of its own, because it is difficult to please and none too hardy, but a flower arranger's dream come true, is **A. schubertii** (60cm/2ft). It has globes as large as or larger than *A. cristophii*, but instead of the globe being perfect, with units all of the same length, they are all different lengths, resembling the sparks of a firework in action. Marvellous for drying. Purplish in flower.

A. giganteum (1.3m/4½ft) has beautiful, glaucous foliage early on but this has died off by the time its imposing, rosy-lilac globes come into bloom in June. So site it in the middle of a border. It stands up well to wind, but is slow of increase on heavy soil and never ripens seed. *A. altissimum* (2m/6ft) has small mauve globes but could be useful, at that height. There are several other tall and imposing alliums with clonal names. All are mauve. 'Beau Regard' (1.2m/4ft) is very strong and has broad leaves. 'Globemaster' (1.2m/4ft) is another strong grower with good foliage. 'Gladiator' (1.2m/4ft) multiplies quite fast and is a good shade of mauve, but even deeper is 'Lucy Ball' (1m/3ft), May-June-flowering, as are the others.

So far I have dealt only with bulb-forming alliums. I now come to clump-formers without proper bulbs. Such is chives, *Allium schoenoprasum* (23cm/9in), of which (since it self-sows freely) there are a great many clones, so it is worth starting out with the best, having sizeable, scabious-like heads of definite colouring. Then, when it self-sows, the progeny, while slightly different (which is rather nice), will still be worthwhile. Recommended for their pink, rather than mauve colouring, are 'Pink Perfection' and 'Black Isle Blush'.

Any chives are excellent for culinary purposes, in salads and soups and to mix with cream cheese for sandwiches. They start into new growth as early as late January in mild winters, the peak of their flowering being in May. Slashed to ground level with a strong knife at that stage, they are leafy again within a week, flower again a little and the same performance can be enacted yet again before autumn. Clumps should be divided frequently and replanted in improved soil.

Chinese chives, *A. tuberosum* (38cm/15in) is the last in flower, August-September, and will make a self-sowing fringe, requiring no attention, at a border's margin. Its seed heads look pleasing through the winter. The flowers are white.

A. angulosum (syn. *A. pyrenaicum*) (30cm/1ft), has tufts of bright, shiny green leaves; heads of mauve flowers. It may not start a flame in your heart, but I like it. Long summer season.

Sometimes disappointing, sometimes good (it has a wide geographical range), you need to choose *A. cernuum* (30cm/1ft) carefully. Its generous clusters of pinky-mauve-purple flowers are hung on curved pedicels in June. Nice with old-fashioned laced pinks. The clone called 'Hidcote' has an AGM.

A. carinatum subsp. *pulchellum* (better known as *A. pulchellum*) (45cm/1½ft), makes clumps of small, pinky-mauve, July-flowering bells on slender scapes with a top-knot of whiskery bracts. It is endearing and its rather free self-sowing habits can be turned to our advantage by allowing it to colonise in paving cracks and at the foot of dry-walling, where it can do no harm whatsoever. It combines well with white-flowered 'Album'.

A. cyaneum (30cm/1ft) has long been known as *A. beesianum* in the horticultural world. Its bell-like flowers in July-August are a pleasing mid-blue shade. But no need to go overboard about it, as there is, I believe, for my last offering: *A*. *senescens* subsp. *montanum* var. *glaucum* (23cm/9in), if that lot doesn't put you off. It is the best in the species. A low, clump-former with swirls of glaucous foliage, it flowers August-September; pinky-mauve globes, popular with butterflies. It needs and deserves an open site without competition from neighbours.

Alopecurus

Poaceae/Graminae

Meadow Foxtail, *Alopecurus pratensis* (60cm/2ft) is a constituent of most mixed meadows and one of the earliest grasses to flower, from late April on. When the dark, cylindrical inflorescence first emerges, we enjoyed, as children (and I still do), pulling it from its sheath and nibbling the sweet and succulent lowest tip.

For use in more civilised parts of the garden, the green-and-yellow-striped clone, 'Aureovariegatus' is a charmer, in spring, and contrasts nicely with forget-me-nots or a blue *Omphalodes*. But self-sowns come plain green and are a nuisance.

Alstroemeria

Alstroemeriaceae/Liliaceae

Still sometimes known as Peruvian lilies, though in fact Chile is the heart of alstroemeria-land. Most bloom at the height of summer, with umbels of lily-like, open-funnel flowers. Their fleshy white roots are covered with the finest hairs, which it is difficult not to damage if you wish to transplant them. This operation is not impossible (best performed immediately after flowering), but it is risky. Root damage is responsible for the myth that alstroemerias always remain dormant for a year after planting. If pot-grown plants are set out carefully, for preference in spring, they will never look back and are quite likely to produce some blooms in the autumn of the same year.

With the named hybrids, which are generally sterile, division is the only possible propagating method. The popular **Ligtu hybrids** (1m/3ft), originating from accidental crosses between *Alstroemeria ligtu* and *A. haemantha*, produce plenty of seed and are usually raised in that way. It is best to sow several seeds to a pot in March,

36

and to germinate them in a cold frame where the temperatures will range from warm in the day to freezing at night. Germination will then be assured, taking about a month to become apparent and giving rise to some flowering in the same year. If seed is given uniformly high temperatures, it will not germinate. Likewise, if you sow in May or later, germination may be delayed till the following autumn or spring, even with the pots being kept outside.

The hardiness of alstroemerias has been much disputed, mainly because of inadequate tests. New growth is sometimes made dangerously early in the year and may be frosted. By and large, however, the Ligtu hybrids are hardy in Britain, once established. The new large-flowered florists' hybrids vary somewhat in this respect, but most of them appear to be pretty hardy also. All are exceptionally good cut flowers, lasting for 3 weeks in water, even in the hottest weather of the year.

Ligtu hybrids seem mainly to be in shades of pink nowadays. This used not to be so; they included carmine red, biscuit, cream – everything except orange and strong yellow. In a way, they seem to have been outclassed by the showier, larger-flowered, though coarser modern hybrids, which originated in Holland as closely guarded florists' glasshouse plants for the cut-flower trade, none being allowed to be distributed to the general public. All that has changed and we are now experimenting in our gardens with the exciting new range that has become available.

Some of these have an exceptionally long flowering season, which is particularly useful if they are required for cutting. It may, in some cases, dilute their impact as border plants. Except for the shortest, all need support, and as they are thin-textured plants, this needs to be done discreetly for borders. In good soil, some of the new hybrids will reach a height of 1.5m/5ft, though 1.2m/4ft is more usual.

Of those that I noted on the Wisley trial ground and which were given the AGM 'Orange Gem' (1.5m/5ft) is sturdy, even coarse, There is a tinge of pink in its wings. 'Flaming Star' (1.2m/4ft) is a strong, bright orange combined with crocus yellow and has a long season. There are many good yellows. 'Friendship' (1.2m/4ft) is pale and luminous, while 'Yellow Friendship' (1m/3ft) is a slightly stronger shade, with a pink flush. 'Golden Delight' (1m/3ft) is luminous yellow with a touch of orange and very free flowering. 'Apollo' (1m/3ft) is white, flushed with orange and yellow (the colourings and markings in alstroemerias are often quite complex). 'Mars' (1m/3ft) is red, as you would expect. It did not win an AGM but I thought it effective.

'Coronet' (1m/3ft) is salmon; 'Solent Rose' (1m/3ft), deep pink with a yellowish centre. It is at its best in August, which could be usefully late, seeing that our borders are tending to be on the wane by then. 'Solent Crest' (60-90cm/2-3ft) is also late, and unusual with its mauve and white colouring. At a mere 30cm/1ft, 'Princess

Mira' is bright, rosy purple and might look well at a border's margin. 'Princess Carmina' (30cm/1ft), is a warm brick colour and that flowers late.

The June-July-flowering types can become unsightly later on. As their roots go deep, you can yank out the flowered stems – they break off cleanly – and over-plant with some quick-developing bedder, to fill the gap for the rest of the season.

The alstroemeria that originally became common in our gardens is **A. aurea**, known till recently as *A. aurantiaca*. The colour is deep yellow. It is so fast-spreading as easily to become a weed in a mixed or herbaceous border, and many of its shoots come blind, which is an additional insult. To get rid of it, you may need to resort to Roundup. All that said, it can be just what you need in an open woodland setting and among spring-flowering azaleas and other shrubs, giving a new lease of life to a garden feature that may otherwise turn dull in July. But you would do better to start off with one of the improved clones, such as 'Dover Orange'.

Some of the other species are fun. **A. pulchella** (75cm/2½ft) is charming in green and red. **A. psittacina** is so named because of its parrot-like colouring in green, red, brown and more besides.

Amaryllis

AMARYLLIDACEAE

Amaryllis is such a beautiful name that other genera, notably *Hippeastrum*, have attempted to muscle in on it. But the only true amaryllis likely to be encountered as a garden plant is the South African bulb, **A. belladonna** (60cm/2ft) (the two names together are irresistible).

It is autumn-flowering and will be free in any sunny position in Cornwall, but needs the sunniest possible wall to radiate heat from behind it in most other British gardens. It also needs good, deep soil. This often means that you see it in front of the red brick footings of a greenhouse, where the colour clash does not help the flower. This is pink (paler within), trumpet shaped and borne in a terminal whorl above a purple scape. The scent is of cheap sweets. No leaves are present at flowering and it is not very easy to think of suitable companions to set the amaryllis off. The best I have seen was in Cornwall, where amaryllis clumps alternated with the hardy, pink-and-blue fuchsia, 'Chillerton Beauty', which makes about 60cm/2ft of summer growth if cut down in winter.

The strap-shaped amaryllis leaves appear soon after midwinter and are vulnerable to hard frost. A number of clones of richer flower colouring have been named, but the type-plant is good enough for me.

Amicia

PAPILIONACEAE/LEGUMINOSAE

Amicia zygomeris (2m/6ft plus) is really a shrub, but if you can overwinter it in the garden at all, will be treated as a herbaceous perennial. We grow it as a foliage plant, the pinnate leaves having a few, broad, blunt-ended leaflets of great presence. It is a plant that visitors notice without having it pointed out, the more so as the young leaves have a couple of large, foliar stipules at the base, rounded and bloodshot. They persist for several weeks before being shed. The leaves close back on themselves at night, as with many legumes. Sometimes, sizeable dusky yellow pea flowers are produced, two at a time, from the leaf axils. This may happen at any time of the year and is a bonus, without amounting to much.

The plant grows fast and gives a feeling of summer luxuriance. There is one against Nigel Nicolson's house at Sissinghurst that has been there for many years and is enormous, but we lift our stock in autumn, cut it back for convenience, pot it up and overwinter under heated glass. We also take cuttings of side-shoots, which root easily.

Amsonia

APOCYNACEAE

There are three species for consideration, here, both about 60cm/2ft tall, with lance leaves and loose heads of small, wishy-washy blue flowers, in summer. *Amsonia tabernaemontana* is from eastern North America. *A. orientalis* (syn. *Rhazya orientalis*), from Greece and Turkey has more personality and looks well, I'm told, with the magenta *Geranium psilostemon* as a neighbour. I can believe that. *A. hubrichii* was new to me on a recent visit to the eastern USA, where it is widely grown. It flowers in May with fairly tight terminal panicles of soft, white, narrow-petalled flowers. The 'blue' perennial cornflower, *Centaurea montana*, should make a good alliance.

These plants will elicit curiosity from any gardener hitherto unfamiliar with them, because they look unusual and yet, in a kind of way, familiar. This is because of their recognisable affinity with *Vinca*, the periwinkles, but amsonias are the poor relations.

Anaphalis

ASTERACEAE/COMPOSITAE

A group of grey-green-leaved perennials with heads of small, papery white 'everlasting' flowers. They spread into thick colonies by means of rhizomes and are lacking in personality but ideal as no-trouble ingredients for traditional grey and white gardens. The amount of pubescence on the leaves varies a good deal. They are usually green on the upper surface with marginal hairs, but white-felted underneath. Unlike most greys, they enjoy good soil and plenty of moisture in summer. Good for cutting, fresh or dried, though their stems kink easily.

Best is the tallest, **Anaphalis margaritacea** var. **yedoensis** (syn. *A. yedoensis*) (75cm/2½ft), late summer and autumn-flowering, with wide flower heads. This has some presence and although it is easily knocked sideways, this doesn't seem to matter much. **A. margaritacea** (45cm/1½ft) is a worthy bore; **A. triplinervis** (60cm/2ft) is better.

Anchusa

BORAGINACEAE

The popular old cottage garden plant, **Anchusa azurea** (syn. *A. italica*) (1.2-2m/4-6ft) is at its best in May-June, becoming straggling and serpentine thereafter. Although perennial, it is never so good after its first year of flowering, and is best treated as a biennial. It can be raised from seed but seed strains need improving as to colour. Of the named cultivars, 'Opal' is pale blue and 'Loddon Royalist' deeper, richer.

The roots are fleshy. Before planting young stock in their flowering sites, in autumn, cut off terminal pieces of root some 10cm/4in long, bundle them up and plunge them upright, topside uppermost, in grit, outside, so that they are only just covered. In spring, when they are sprouting, line them out in a reserve plot, 45cm/18in apart, and they will provide strong plants for bedding out that autumn. Discard at the end of June and replace with dahlias, cannas or tall annuals.

Each plant will require a stake, with a tie around each main stem, just as flowering commences. The flowers (like related borage) are edible and nice for decorating a green salad at the last moment, after it has been dressed.

Anemone

RANUNCULACEAE

A vast, unwieldy genus, horticulturally important but in a constant state of flux and confusion in respect of nomenclature. *Pulsatilla* has been hived off (q.v.). *Anemone* – windflower – has roots that are tuberous, rhizomatous or tough and woody.

A. nemorosa (15cm/6in) is our native wood anemone. It is immensely variable and has given rise to a wide range of selected, named cultivars. The roots make a mat of thin rhizomes and may need dividing from time to time, to keep them flowering freely. Although generally a woodlander, flowering is always most prolific after a wood has been coppiced, thereby admitting extra light. Shade-loving is a relative term. Moisture and humus are more important factors. Flowering starts in early March. Typically, the flower is blush-white but often changes (like many white flowers) to pink as it fades. In the west of Britain and notably in Ireland, the wildings are often pronouncedly blue (though always tinged with mauve). One of the best known selections of these is 'Robinsoniana' (23cm/9in), robust and large-flowered. I prefer 'Lismore Blue' (15cm/6in) (from the Duke of Devonshire's estate in south-east Ireland), neater in habit and in flower shape, flowering into May. It colonises well in quite dense turf. 'Allenii' (15cm/6in) is the best known name among the blues, but stock is tremendously mixed up. Best to buy what you can see in flower.

'Vestal' (15cm/6in), one of the latest flowering nemorosas, is pure white with an outer ring of petals (or tepals) and an inner, dense cushion of petaloid stamens. This condition is referred to as anemone-centred in many other flowers.

The European **A. ranunculoides** (23cm/9in) is of similar habit but bright yellow, easily grown, indispensable. 'Pleniflora' is a double form and not a bit clumsy. The above two species have a hybrid, **A. × lipsiensis** (syn. *A. × seemannii*) (10cm/4in), with flowers that are pale (though definite) yellow. March-flowering and well worth having.

A. apennina (23cm/9in) is similar to *A. nemorosa*, but slightly larger-flowered and with narrower petals, but more of them. It copes well with dense turf and self-sows, but the colouring is apt to be wan. There are good pale blues around.

A. blanda (12.5cm/5in) is similar, making a somewhat smaller plant. I do not find that it naturalises in my turf; but it does in some gardens, notably those with light, alkaline soil. A selected cultivar should be chosen. 'Ingramii' is intense blue, 'Radar' bright, rather vulgar pink – most enlivening in its early spring season – while the rather later 'White Splendour' is large-flowered and robust.

The tuberous-rooted *A. coronaria* (23cm/9in) from the eastern Mediterranean, has given rise to the florists' anemones that are readily and cheaply available cut flowers in winter as well as spring (and summer and autumn), which is the reason for so many amateur artists, without gardens of their own, choosing them to paint. Their colours range from purple to red and the central knob is black. The De Caen group is single flowered, while the St. Brigid group has several rows of narrow petals. All are easily raised from seed but there are also named cultivars.

A. hortensis, from southern France and Italy, is similar but smaller flowered. As a garden plant, I do not keep it for long but it is easy in pans, the colour varying from purple, through mauve to dark red and salmon. Crossed with *A. pavonina* (a species which I should not care to define), this gave rise to the brilliant scarlet, April-May-flowering *A.* × *fulgens* (23cm/9in). This looks marvellous when planted among hummocks of acid lime greeny yellow *Euphorbia polychroma*. 'Multipetala' has numerous narrow petals that do not improve the flower. The St. Bavo group comes in here, but the colours are mixed. All these are worth propagating from your own-saved seed, sown fresh. Rust disease sometimes overtakes the anemones I have so far written of, but this is not transmitted through the seed.

Of the many odd anemones that fall into no special category and flower in late spring or early summer, I have seen *A. canadensis* (30cm/1ft) only in the wild, near Chicago, making delightful colonies beside a sluggish river, the pure white flowers borne singly. In cultivation, it is something of a runner. *A. rivularis* (45cm/1½ft) is a sound woodlander, freely self-sowing, with branching candelabrums of pale bluish-white flowers.

From high summer onwards, Japanese anemones dominate the scene, deservedly among the most popular of late-flowering hardy perennials. They have a woody, but running rootstock. Generally propagated from cuttings made of thin year-old roots, they should be pot-grown and will then take a year to settle down when planted out. After that there is no holding them.

It is sometimes levelled as a criticism of the most invasive that this militates against them as border plants. So it may, but there is a place in many gardens where a beautiful take-over perennial is just what's required. They are good in moist shade and good in sun and most flower for two and a half months, which is more than can be claimed for many perennials. Plant height varies greatly with growing conditions. If rich and moist, 2m/6ft will be reached by many cultivars but they will need support. Otherwise, seldom.

An RHS trial of Japanese anemones at Wisley threw up a great many problems of identification, only partially solved.

The plant we knew as *Anemone japonica* is now *A. × hybrida* and the pure white we simply knew as 'Alba' is 'Honorine Jobert' (1.2m/4ft). It is far and away the best white Japanese anemone, with two rows of broad petals, which set off the green central knob and circle of yellow stamens to perfection. Flowering is from the third week in July to mid-October. As growth is slow to pick up speed, in spring, you can interplant your colonies with vigorous bulbs, such as *Allium cristophii*.

'Louise Uhink' has quite a large number of narrow, white petals, which it sometimes fails to shed before they turn brown. 'Whirlwind' is another such. 'Géante des Blanches' (75cm/2½ft) is nice but blush rather than white.

Among avowedly single pinks, *A. hupehensis* 'Bowles's Pink' (1.2m/4ft), is a good deep colour. Quite a spreader. 'Hadspen Abundance' (1m/3ft) is variable as offered but should be a deep pink, often deepest on the outer petals. Very free. I like it intermingled or in front of the glaucous foliage of *Melianthus major*; also beneath fruiting branches of *Rosa glauca*, pruned so as not to become too dense.

Of semi-double pinks, there are a number of contenders. I would give top marks to *A. × hybrida* 'Pamina' (1m/3ft), neatly double and a deep shade. *A. hupehensis* var. *japonica* 'Prinz Heinrich' (1m/3ft) (also on offer as 'Bressingham Glow' and 'Bodnant Burgundy': heaven help you if you are offered Burgundy of this colour) is deep mauve-pink with lots of showy blossom.

Rather different from the above is *A. tomentosa* 'Robustissima' (1.5m/5ft) which probably failed to gain an award on account of its extreme vigour, which filled the judging panel with visions of horror. Its smallish mauve flowers are abundant, start blooming in June but continue well into October.

Another cultivar that won few friends but delighted me, though as a foliage, not a flowering, plant, was entered by R.D. Plants, who had the better clone, as 'Crispa', but has since been defined as 'Lady Gilmour' (1m/3ft). The pale, bright green leaves are pleated and crested, making a good display from early June. The mauve flowers are distorted but could easily be removed if they worried you.

Anisotome

APIACEAE/UMBELLIFERAE

There is considerable scope for the wider appreciation of umbellifers in this country and a huge number are just waiting to be introduced and distributed, once the penny has dropped. *Anisotome* come from New Zealand, mainly from the Southern Alps. The larger species are handsome with good foliage, often twice or more pinnate. They are perennial, with deep, woody roots and I suspect that they would prefer conditions in the west of Scotland to any other part of the British Isles.

A. lyallii is the name I was given for the one I had from the Ventnor Botanical Garden. It has come through several winters (with umbels of white flowers in late spring) and actually looks its happiest in winter, being evergreen. In the heat of summer, it seems to be under stress. A few sources offer stock of one species or another and they are worth following up.

Anomatheca

IRIDACEAE

Anomatheca laxa (syn. *Lapeirousia laxa*, *Anomatheca cruenta*) (30cm/1ft or less) is a South African cormous plant clearly related to *Crocosmia* and *Gladiolus*. It flowers in summer and autumn and is happy in sun or in shade, so long as not too dry. Hardiness is generally no problem. It has rather flattened flowers of a soft red colouring with a deeper blotch near to the centre. There is also an equally charming white variety, *alba*, which comes true from seed.

Seed, in slightly inflated capsules, is liberally ripened and is itself deep red. Self-sowing is free. This is a most obliging filler and I like to have it as a takeover from a colony of *Cyclamen hederifolium*, when that goes dormant in summer. But whereas the cyclamen will tolerate drought at that time, anomatheca will not. I also enjoy it colonising under my greenhouse benches, together with *Begonia grandis* subsp. *evansiana* and *B. sutherlandii*. All three look after and spread themselves.

Anthemis

ASTERACEAE/COMPOSITAE

Three species of Anthemis enter strongly into my garden life.

A. punctata subsp. *cupaniana* (38cm/15in), better known just as *A. cupaniana*, is a loose mat of a plant with grey-green, pinnate leaves. It is there all winter but, like many fast-growing plants, tends to be short-lived, especially on heavy soils. It is the kind of plant to grow in, or on the edge of, gravel, where it can sprawl to its heart's content – or appear to do so. In fact, as usual in gardening, it still needs to be kept tidy.

Its pure white, yellow-centred daisies are out in their fullest force in May. After that, a rather tedious dead-heading should be practised. Follow the sprays of spent blooms, and the branched shoots on which they grow, back to the crown of the plant, and sever them there. Starting from the outside of the mat, this always takes you awkwardly underneath the freshest growth, which is located near the centre. A worthwhile scattering of blooms will be borne throughout the summer.

As I learned from the experimental Brian Halliwell, who was for years in charge of the bedding-out at Kew, this makes a splendid carpeter under spring bulbs, notably late-flowering tulips. Those of orange or yellow colouring combine best with the yellow disc and white rays of the anthemis. For bedding purposes, cuttings of young shoots should be taken late in July or in early August. When rooted, pot individually and plant out in October. The plants may look a bit thin at first, but soon do the job required of them.

A. sancti-johannis (1m/3ft), so called because it flowers around St. John's Day, 24 June, grows wild in Hungary, and has a large disc and short rays. In cultivation, it is a showier plant, better balanced for having longer rays. The colour is pure, uncompromising orange – very exciting in the June garden. You have to raise it from seed (which it never seems to set in England) and treat it as a biennial, since it normally flowers itself to death like an operatic heroine. We normally sow it in a pot in April, pot the seedlings individually, line them out for the summer and plant them in their flowering positions in the autumn. They resent this final move, which should be accompanied with a large ball of soil. Alternatively, as with pyrethrums, wait till February, when they are growing again, and move them more safely then.

They flower for a month and can then be replaced with something like dahlias for the rest of the season. They contrast brilliantly with the purple spikes of *Salvia nemorosa* 'Ostfriesland' ('East Friesland'), in front, or with a loose 'blue' carpet of *Geranium himalayense* underneath.

25   The best known species is *A. tinctoria* (60-150cm/2-5ft), a stalwart of the old herbaceous border, at the height of its flowering season in July. The daisies are, according to variety, strong yellow ('Grallach Gold, 'Pride of Grallach'), cool yellow ('Wargrave'), cream ('E.C. Buxton') or white ('Alba'). 'Wargrave' and 'E.C. Buxton' are often interchangeable and I cannot tell you which should be which.

My favourite is the cool yellow, which is 'Wargrave' to me. Cultivation of this species needs understanding. To overwinter, it makes, in autumn, a cushion of bright green, mossy leaf shoots, which will carry next year's blossom. If the plant is exhausted, through too much flowering and because no light has reached the bottom of the plant at the end of its flowering season, it will die. Old plants, even if full of life, are not too satisfactory, however. They grow awkwardly tall, even to 2m/6ft if drawn up in a border, need thorough staking and are prone to powdery mildew. They flower the once and that's it.

But young plants, made from cuttings of the basal, leafy shoots at any time in winter, can be planted out from April onwards. They will start flowering in the last days of June and, given a dead-heading mid-season, will carry on non-stop into late autumn, so they can be treated as summer bedding, reaching no higher than 60cm/2ft. Each plant, having only the one shoot, needs but a single tie to a shortish stake. Dead-heading, back to vestigial buds, is tiresome, as the knob-like flower heads catch in one another. That may make you impatient, with disastrous results. Reserve your impatience for humans. In gardening, patience is essential.

This anthemis is an example of the flower that shuts down at night, reflexing its ray petals, rather than the more usual practice of shutting up.

Anthericum

ANTHERICACEAE/LILIACEAE

St Bernard's Lily, **Anthericum liliago** (1m/3ft) is an old-fashioned, May-flowering perennial that seems always to have been around. It makes clumps of coarse grassy foliage, above which stand numerous racemes of white, starry flowers. (In **A. ramosum** (1m/3ft) these are smaller but more numerous.) It contributes nothing for 49 weeks of the year and is best grown where it will not get in the way, along with other early perennials.

Anthriscus

APIACEAE/UMBELLIFERAE

Anthriscus sylvestris (1m/3ft) is known in Britain as cow parsley or, if you are being polite, Queen Anne's lace (the latter name, in America, is generally applied to carrot, *Daucus carota*). It is a widespread weed of coarse turf, vying with stinging nettles and docks in conditions that ideally comprise rather rich soil and some shade. Its umbels of white flowers are at their peak in April-May and have a strong, sickly-sweet fragrance. It is often the despair of those who wish to practise meadow gardening, as it chokes out smaller and more desirable plants. But then meadows conducive to the success of a large number of species should be on poor land, where *A. sylvestris* will cease to be a menace, making quite small, weak plants.

Its popularity has been greatly heightened by the appearance of a dark, purple-leaved form called 'Ravenswing', against the foliage of which the usual white flowers show up admirably. However, with much of the ordinary type-plant in my garden, I find it hard to keep the two separate.

Aquilegia

RANUNCULACEAE

In common parlance, the old English name, columbine, has of late tended to drop out in favour of aquilegia. These flowers of early summer can be used in many ways. Some, the granny's bonnet kinds, are good beneath trees in a woodland setting. The long-spurred hybrids are better in sunshine and they combine well, for instance, with shrub roses like *Rosa rugosa* hybrids. They are also good bedders for a May-June display and are raised from seed for this purpose. Sow under glass no later than March, as seedlings are slow to develop. But if brought on without check, being lined out in well nourished soil for the summer, they will be ready for bedding out in the autumn, flowering the following year. More often, the inattentive gardener will find that it takes two years to get a good, fat plant.

Although perennial, the long-spurred types of columbine are rather unpredictable in terms of longevity. Some die out after a couple of seasons. Others continue robustly for many years. Under mixed border conditions, it is a good plan to cut the plants down flush with the ground after flowering. They will quickly refurnish with young foliage.

The long-spurred types are the most elegant, the spurs being the calyx, which takes in most of the colours of the rainbow. The corolla is nearly always white or yellow. Long-spurred mixtures are less effective in the garden than single-colour strains. I find no great advantage in F^1 hybrids and where they aim at dwarfness, this in itself is generally undesirable. The plant is more graceful at 60-100cm/2-3ft. Taller than that and support will be required, as it often is in fat soil.

The parents of the long-spurred hybrids derive from North American species.

Aquilegia chrysantha (1m/3ft) is a beautiful soft yellow throughout and well worth grouping on its own. *A. longissima* is similar but with even longer and more attenuated spurs. It has a not–long–for–this–world air, which does not belie it.

The habitats of *A. canadensis* (1m/3ft) and *A. formosa* overlap in the western halves of Canada and the USA and they are commonly seen by roadsides, both being red, the latter more of a coral shade and the more beautiful species. They are easily grown but generally fairly short-lived in cultivation.

A. fragrans (the fragrance is nothing to boast of) (75cm/2½ft) is the species that you see a lot of in Kashmir, in July, with largeish flowers that are creamy-white throughout. The sepals are broad and petal-like while the spurs are small. Seed is available but I have not grown it.

The European *A. vulgaris* (1m/3ft) is a British native, which I have seen in chalky downland, but have been unable to establish in turf myself. It is particularly good in shade, however, self-sowing almost too freely. This is the archetypal granny's bonnet, a cosy name for it that was not used when I was young. The spurs are short, the flower chunky and the colour range fairly limited, mostly around bluish mauve, dusky old rose and purple. A particularly good strain called 'Magpie' has got around of recent years, with a very deep purple calyx and a white corolla. It looks good in a border with seakale (*Crambe maritima*) in flower.

A. vulgaris Vervaeneana group, of which 'Woodside' is an example, is grown for its boldly variegated foliage. The flowers are nothing special. After flowering, you cut it down and the new crop of foliage will totally rejuvenate its appearance.

'Nora Barlow' is the name given to another range of *A. vulgaris*, in which the petals are narrow and numerous, but short and the spurs are entirely absent. Seedlings come more or less true and although a pinkish coloration is normal, there is considerable variation. It is an ugly flower but different.

Aralia

Araliaceae

Like all members of the ivy family, aralias have distinction. Their pinnate leaves are a principal feature, but whereas some species are woody, others are herbs. They are poisonous.

Best known of the shrubs is *Aralia elata* (3m/10ft). In horticultural terms, *A. chinensis* is the same thing. This is an upright, suckering shrub with straight, sparse stems thickly covered with tough prickles. Thus, devil's walking-stick. It is crowned with loose rosettes of long, pinnate leaves and, in autumn, these enclose a froth of tiny white blossom. From the underside, you see little of this but from a terrace or the top of a steep slope with an aralia colony beneath you, it can be a great and unusual sight.

25   There are two variegated forms: 'Variegata' (or 'Albomarginata') (2.4m/8ft) in white, and 'Aureovariegata' (2.4m/8ft) in yellow. Both are equally striking and in great demand. But they have to be grafted on to the type-plant (this is nearly always done in Holland), which makes them very expensive; the more so when your plant dies at an early age, which not infrequently happens without the advantage of a suicide note by way of explanation. Another trap is when the plant takes to suckering, which it will from any area where the roots have been wounded. The suckers will be plain green. But at their best these are splendid and enviable plants.

Of the herbaceous species, the one I know best and grow is **A. cachemirica** (2m/6ft or more). It makes a bold clump, suitable as a solo feature, if desired. The compound panicles of tiny flowers, borne distinctively in umbels, are quickly followed by near black berries, which are supported by purple pedicels.

This plant likes good moisture-retaining soil, otherwise it is apt to scorch in time of drought. As it covers a good deal of ground, use can be made of this with early-flowering bulbs, like snowdrops or winter aconites.

Arisaema

ARACEAE

A strange and exciting genus, closely allied to *Arum*. Because of their strange appearance, arisaemas are thought to be difficult or tender, but so long as they have cool, leafy soil, there seem to be no problems and as most come from quite cold areas of Asia, hardiness is often assured. I know of a cold garden in central Scotland, where they flourish better than anywhere I have met them.

Propagation and hence availability tends to restrict their distribution and there is a particular danger that the stock you buy may be wild-collected. They are tuberous plants and in your own garden will increase at a quite reasonable speed. The tubers tend to quest in a rhizomatous manner.

Best known and most widely available is **Arisaema candidissima** (45cm/1½ft in leaf). Dormancy continues until late June or even later and is then broken by the appearance of its flowers, these being quickly submerged by young foliage. If you are not watching, you may miss this flowering altogether. The stems are short; the spathe makes a white impression but is generally streaked on the inside with pink; it comes to a shortish point at the top. Big trifoliate leaves are extremely handsome and long-lasting, so this is primarily a foliage plant. The tubers are quite large and can be divided.

The only other species that I grow is **A. consanguineum** (up to 60cm/2ft). This has purple-mottled stems and palmate leaves that are divided into long, lanceolate segments. The flowers are borne at the same height as the leaves and are striped purple and green. The spathe ends in a long tail – a feature in many species. It is a ravishing plant. One could easily become an arisaema addict.

Artemisia

ASTERACEAE/COMPOSITAE

Even easier to become an **Artemisia absinthium** addict, absinth being many an alcoholic's primary stimulant, refuge and downfall. Still, as most of us appreciate, alcohol is good for us in reasonable quantities, so why not a Pernod, or one of its many equivalents? The plant is known as wormwood and is described by John Raven (*A Botanist's Garden*) as 'a dowdy dweller on derelict dumps'. But selected cultivars such as 'Lambrook Silver' (1m/3ft) are good foliage plants, and it is for their grey foliage first, their aroma second, that artemisias are courted by gardeners. Like many another, 'Lambrook Silver' loses much of its appeal once it runs up to flower.

There is a tendency to shrubbiness in many species, most pronounced in the herb garden favourite, **A. abrotanum** (1m/3ft), variously known as ladslove, southernwood and old man. The leaves are green and finely dissected, with a strong and, for most of us, agreeable aroma. The plant easily becomes scrawny and is best cut hard back each spring. This also delays flowering, which is a good thing.

A. arborescens (1.2m/4ft or more against a wall) is one of the most scintillating of grey foliage plants – very pale silvery grey, with dissect leaves. This is a distinctly tender shrub of quick growth and loose habit. It can be trained against a sunny wall, giving it increased hardiness. The foliage, in spring, is particularly attractive to house sparrows for nesting material, so plants may need black-cottoning.

This species crossed with *A. absinthium* is the probable parentage of 'Powis Castle' (60cm/2ft pruned), a highly valued foliage shrub with the advantage of never running to flower, so that it remains pristine to the end of autumn. It straggles if not annually given a hard cut-back in spring, but this should be delayed until tiny shoots make their appearance low down on the old wood, otherwise plants are apt not to respond and rejuvenate. With this artemisia and *A. arborescens*, keep a watchful eye open during the height of their growing season, for attacks on their juicy young shoots by black aphids, and spray against these betimes.

Lower down the height scale, **A. stelleriana** (38cm/15in) has pale, well felted leaves and a slightly running habit. 'Boughton Silver' is a good clone, but has several synonyms. **A. alba** 'Canescens' (syn. *A. canescens*, *A. splendens*) (30cm/1ft) is a wiry tangle of pale, linearly-divided leaves and makes a beautiful background to *Crocosmia* 'Solfaterre'. Cut hard back each spring. **A. caucasica** (syn. *A. pedemontana*) (15cm/6in) is basically shrubby and apt to sprawl. Its soft, finely divided leaves put it in the same category as the more upright and superior **A. schmidtiana** 'Nana' (for long masquerading as *A. schmidtii nana*) (15cm/6in). Cut hard back annually, this makes perfect domes of finest, softest, pale grey filigree. You will mistakenly think that winter has killed it if sparrows peck out all the young basal shoot buds in spring.

A. pontica (30cm/1ft) is truly herbaceous, making a dense forest of upright shoots with grey, finely divided leaves. With a mildly invasive habit, it is a no-trouble plant for the no-trouble gardener in herb or grey garden.

A. ludoviciana (1m/3ft) has some excellent cultivars with silvery, lobed foliage. 'Silver Queen' gives good value – I have it alongside the pink spikelets of *Hebe* 'Watson's Pink' (1.2m/4ft) – but it becomes floppy as it runs to flower. It also makes a fine substrate into which the magenta *Geranium* 'Russell Prichard' can weave. 'Valerie Finnis' has the broadest leaves; they are lobed and felted. This also runs to flower but if cut to the ground, mid-season, then makes a second, quite low display of young foliage which really sees it at its best for the year.

All-important tarragon, **A. dracunculus** (1m/3ft) has no pretensions to beauty and should be tucked away, but handily for the kitchen. As its shoots run to flower, cut about half of them back so as to have young foliage coming along for the autumn. Replant in spring, in improved soil, every third year or so. Colonies can die out.

The only species grown expressly for its flowers is, on heavy, moisture-retaining soil, one of the most valued of all herbaceous perennials for late summer. **A. lactiflora** (2m/6ft) is entirely self-supporting. From very dark green leaves, it throws up plumes of small, creamy flowers. They contrast well with fiery *Kniphofia uvaria* 'Nobilis' and much else. But on dry soils *A. lactiflora* is hopeless. The Guizhou group has purplish young foliage and a more widely branching habit. I didn't get along with this but it can be good.

Arum

ARACEAE

Our native species, of woodland and shady hedge bottoms, is **Arum maculatum** (30cm/1ft), called lords and ladies, or cuckoo pint. It is a common weed in gardens, making clumps of its L-shaped tubers, which are none too easy to dig out, as they easily break at the angle of the L, leaving the business end to grow again. The glossy, hastate leaves are sometimes purple-spotted. As Gertrude Jekyll pointed out, you can grasp a sheaf of these low down and pull them cleanly away from the base, using them to arrange indoors with yellow trumpet daffodils, but it is as well to give this fleshy foliage a deep drink before using it.

The most popular garden arum is **A. italicum**, a species of wide distribution in the Mediterranean and thus having many subspecies. In one (or more) of these, the leaf veins are white, creating a beautiful marbled effect. This has long been known as *A. italicum* 'Pictum', but the currently favoured terminology is *A. italicum* subsp. *italicum* 'Marmoratum' (30cm/1ft). It is fairly hardy but, with its foliage appearing in autumn, is apt to be damaged in winter, but new leaves will be made in spring. From June, the plant is dormant apart from an array of berries on club-shaped spikes. They are scarlet and make a fine display in August, if not immediately devoured by birds. Flowering is inconspicuous.

This arum comes fairly true from seed (though particularly well marked forms can easily be selected and some are quite inferior); the seedlings do not generally show their markings for the first year or two (awkward for the salesman to impulse buyers). Birds spread seedlings over the garden and they appear in most unlikely places, such as the crutch of an old fig tree. The leaves are excellent to pick for many months and look well associated with snowdrops.

A. creticum (30cm/1ft), like the last, grows through the winter and can be frost-damaged. The leaves are of smart, sharp outline. At flowering, the spathes are held horizontally, the yellow spadix, upright. In nature, the spathe is most often cream-coloured, but there is a yellow form which is the one most cultivated and it makes a great show for a few days in late April or early May. The plant makes tubers which can be separated during the dormant period, from June to September. Grow in moist, humus-rich soil, in partial shade.

There are many more exciting Mediterranean species of arum, some with heavily spotted spathes, others evil-smelling, to attract pollinators. Quite a few of them do not flower until the leaves are already withering. They are apt to be on the tender side or to appear to be thriving for a few years, only to give up the ghost, suddenly. Still, well worth a try, for none are dull.

Aruncus

Rosaceae

Aruncus dioicus (2m/6ft) is one of those indestructible plants that one has always known. It was *Spiraea aruncus* when I was young and later *A. sylvestris* or *A. silvester*. Hard to get it right. Furthermore, it is sometimes known as goat's beard, which I find confusing, since I was brought up to assign this name to *Tragopogon pratensis*, alias Jack-go-to-bed-at-noon. To make confusion worse confounded, *Astilbe* and *Aruncus* are superficially so similar, with their bipinnate leaves and plumed panicles of tiny flowers, that it is easy to overlook the botanical inevitability of the former belonging to Saxifragaceae, the latter to Rosaceae.

A. dioicus has an enormous distribution in the northern hemisphere, and prefers damp, partially shaded places, usually in mountainous country. I first met it in the Carpathians of Transylvania (Romania), but was then rather astounded to find it again in British Columbia.

In the garden, it makes a bold, architectural feature, with its creamy panicles rising above a platform of horizontal leaves. These, I will mention in passing, are commonly attacked by the small, gregarious larvae of a sawfly, which make lacy patterns of a few leaves, or parts of leaves – never enough to worry about.

The sexes are on separate plants, males having the whiter, fluffier flowers, but they start turning brown and withering within a week of reaching their best in June or July. The females are greener and remain in good condition as the seed heads ripen. There is a place for both but if you want to be sure of your sex, propagation must be by division, 'easy with a pickaxe', as an American friend put it. Self-sown seedlings are frequent, but reveal their sex only when large enough to flower.

This is the kind of plant that survives neglect by a long succession of uninterested garden owners, remaining comfortably at the back of an old herbaceous border, rife with ground elder, of which it will remain unaware. But it well deserves deliberate use in a damp, wild area, as it might be near a stream and in the company of gunneras and *Campanula latifolia*, also self-sowing.

The clone 'Kneiffii' (1m/3ft or less), has ferny, deeply divided leaves, 'as though eaten to the veins by caterpillars', to quote Beth Chatto, 'but the lacy effect is charming...' I grew this 30 years ago, but allowed it to die out. Thirty years later, it reappeared in exactly the same spot – such is the longevity of its seeds.

I do not know *A. aethusifolius* (30cm/1ft), although it is described as 'widely available' in *The RHS Plant Finder*.

Arundo

POACEAE/GRAMINAE

The giant reed, **Arundo donax** (3.6m/12ft) is the tallest, noblest grass that we can enjoy in southern England. Further north and with lower temperatures, it gives a progressively weaker account of itself. In southern France, you see it grown for shelter in flat areas, along dykes and rivers. It looks hideous, the reason being that old shoots are not cut down. For a clean, smart-looking plant, this must be done, right to the ground, annually, the best time being early winter when the plants are already in disarray. The giant reed does not flower in Britain and this is no loss.

The leaves are glaucous and arranged in two ranks, arching to the horizontal at their tips. It is a domineering plant, in need of placing in a strong context, not necessarily at the back of a planting at all; right at the front and in the middle can also be effective. I find that large-headed hydrangeas make good companions.

The rhizomatous rootstock is only mildly invasive in our climate and propagation is from offsets, taken in spring (colonies should never be disturbed in autumn or winter). The type-plant is generally hardy in Britain, but its delectable variegated form, **A. donax** var. **versicolor** (or 'Variegata') (2m/6ft) is not and its variegation makes it considerably weaker.

It is one of the most beautiful of all variegated plants, with broad, (almost) white stripes either side of a green centre. In some clones, the white is much reduced. These, being more vigorous, make easier propagation material. Buy your plant when you can see it growing and yourself always propagate from the best variegated growths. Plants will survive most winters outside, but much weakened and slow to get going next season. Better to lift with minimum root disturbance, in November, pot up and overwinter under barely frost-free glass. Before you cut back in spring, the old stems may make side-shoots, and these, severed as cuttings, will provide a further (though uncertain) method of propagation. *Versicolor* stands out well in plantings of tender and warm-temperate plants, including dahlias.

Asarum

ARISTOLOCHIACEAE

These are ground-cover plants, some evergreen, some deciduous. They have rounded, cyclamen-shaped leaves, sometimes marbled like cyclamen, but these far eastern kinds are not too easily made happy with us. The American **Asarum caudatum** (30cm/1ft), which is deciduous, was a plant I admired in its homeland, but it has not given me joy in my garden.

34   Streets ahead of the rest is the evergreen **A. europaeum** (30cm/1ft), which has such a shine on its foliage that it reflects any light there is around, even beneath a quite dense canopy of trees. This has a cheering result. It is a good mixer and should not be planted in isolation, but with the fern *Athyrium niponicum* var. *pictum*, for instance. Winter aconites colonise well in its company. The scarlet tuberous-rooted *Begonia* 'Flamboyant' is a nice summer companion.

Asclepias

ASCLEPIADACEAE

Most genera in this family are North American and Linnaeus was a bit hazy when he named **Asclepias syriaca** (1m/3ft). A coarse plant with leaves far too large to balance small flowers, but it is a principal food plant, on the east side of the USA, for the noble Monarch butterfly. The long seed capsules, tapered at each end, are also notable, as are those of other members of Asclepiadaceae. They split longitudinally to release quantities of 'silk', attached to the seeds, and silk weed is one name for these plants; butterfly weed being the commonest name for **A. tuberosa**.

A distinguishing feature in asclepias flowers, which you are sure to notice even if you do not go on to analyse it, is the central column of united stamens, which then divides into five horn-like lobes. *A. tuberosa* (60cm/2ft) is a hardy, clump-forming prairie plant, which flowers in late summer in our climate. It is a splendid perennial if you can make a go of it but our summers are insufficiently hot to please it altogether. The flowers are borne in umbels and are a wonderful shade of rich orange. A splendid contrast to blue flowers, like *Salvia patens* or *S. farinacea*. If seed is fresh, it offers by far the best method of propagation, but it seldom is, not ripening in Britain.

Asperula – see Galium

Asphodeline

ASPHODELACEAE/LILIACEAE

We meet two species, both yellow-flowered. *Asphodeline lutea* (1m/3ft) is spring-flowering, with stiff, thick stems above extremely narrow, grassy leaves. Starry-flowered. I envisaged a row of these like sentinels along the top of a retaining wall, but the site was too dry for them. In fact, in Syria, I once passed a huge bog-ful of them, in bloom, the colour an intriguing shade of apricot.

A. liburnicus (1m/3ft), makes a basal tuft of narrow, evergreen leaves and throws up graceful spikes of yellow stars in July. The unusual feature is that the stars do not open until 4 in the afternoon, closing at night. I call it the tired businessman's plant, there to welcome his return. It looks nice with *Eryngium* × *oliverianum*.

Asphodelus

ASPHODELACEAE/LILIACEAE

White, or whitish stars in this genus. *A. ramosus* (1m/3ft) (syn. *A. cerasiferus*, *A. lusitanicus*) is a flimsy sort of plant which scarcely pulls its weight in a garden context. Nor do any of the others, but they are wholly inoffensive.

Asplenium

ASPLENIACEAE/POLYPODIACEAE

This is the charming tribe of ferns called spleenwort. Into the genus are now included *Ceterach officinarum*, the rusty-back fern, and *Phyllitis scolopendrium*, the hartstongue.

Asplenium ceterach (10cm/4in), the rusty-back, is most often seen 'in the wild', on one section and one side of man-made limestone walls. I suppose my mother must have introduced it to my garden. Anyway, there it is, in the cracks of a sunny retaining wall and it is a fern to enjoy. Simple, pinnate (or rather pinnatifid) fronds heavily coated with brownish scales on the underside. Drought dries the fronds up completely, but they reappear as soon as it rains.

The hartstongue fern, *A. scolopendrium* (60cm/2ft) is a lime-lover, varying a great deal in size according to how rich a soil it grows in. It has colonised along the bottom of our oldest piece of wall and, being evergreen, is a handsome feature in winter, when border perennials growing in front of it have been cut down. The hartstongue has a relatively narrow, undivided, glossy frond and, in its simplicity, is the greatest contrast to other ferns. It fits into many angles and corners of the garden. There are numerous named variants. Those with crested tips tend to unbalance the leaf's natural elegance. The Crispum group has more or less crimped frond margins, the crimping extending to the rachis. This is a handsome attribute.

There are no cultural problems, but it is generally wise to cut away the old fronds, towards the end of March, before this operation damages the newly-emerging crop.

The other species that you are likely to introduce to your garden deliberately, if it is not already there, is **A. trichomenes** (10-15cm/4-6in), the maidenhair spleenwort. On the rotting plaster of some old walls, this tends to plaster itself, starfish-wise, but otherwise makes tufts of growth, especially welcome in the risers of steps. The leaves are simply pinnate, the small, rounded leaflets being separated by a black rachis. This is in strong contrast to **A. viride** (10cm/4in), which you never see in gardens, but is a joy to discover in lime-rich rock fissures in the wild. The whole plant is brightest of bright green throughout.

The wall rue, **A. ruta-muraria**, is common in or on most old walls, though seldom planted. It is often the first true plant to arrive when rendering starts to rot and crumble, but it abhors competition. This makes tufts of tiny, divided fronds and is a most endearing plant.

Astelia

ASTELIACEAE/LILIACEAE

A group of evergreen, sword-leaved plants from the general direction of New Zealand. The best make beautiful foliage features (the flowers are nothing), but their hardiness is not altogether dependable. Still, one plants and hopes and gives them a bit of protection in winter and generally things turn out all right.

Basically, they make rosettes of longish, grooved leaves, grey-green with quite a glittering sheen on them. Largest-leaved is **Astelia chathamica** (1m/3ft), often sold as 'Silver Spear' so as to add a spot of glamour. As good, though smaller, narrower-leaved, is **A. nervosa** (60cm/2ft), and there are similar hybrids with bronze-tinted foliage.

Suddenly a plant may die, which is a great grief and is probably brought on by a soil-borne fungus. This leaves you feeling rather helpless. They are wonderful spot-plants for effect, as John Brookes used one at Denmans, nestling against a large ornamental pot in an area of gravel.

Aster

ASTERACEAE/COMPOSITAE

Most asters are autumn-flowering and are known in Britain as Michaelmas daisies (Michaelmas: 29 September). In America, from where most of them come, they are asters. This name, with us, is often applied to the annual China aster, *Callistephus*, so there can be confusion.

Asters bring the season of perennials to a splendid conclusion, seething with blossom and much visited by bees, butterflies and other insects. But their foliage, especially in the *Aster novae-angliae* and *A. novi-belgii* sections, is dull and heavy in the long run-up to flowering. In a large garden, a border specialising in asters can be afforded, since it can readily be ignored in its dull season. In a small garden, go easy with them unless their foliage is attractive. Even in borders setting out to focus on early autumn colour, other flowers and the inclusion of cream and yellow, could jolly up the aster, which seldom departs far from purples, mauves and white.

Like many composites, asters move successfully from the open ground while in full growth. So, presuming a back-up area in which to grow them during the summer, they can be watered heavily a day or so before being moved into their flowering positions, just as they are coming into bloom. Room will be made for them by annuals or perennials that have passed their peak, which most of them have by early or mid-September. The former will be thrown out, the latter moved back into the spare plot whence the asters came. Each aster clump, together with a large ball of soil, is placed in a roomy hole made ready to receive it and its roots are there douched with a can-ful of water, turned upside-down, the soil being returned to fill the hole just as the water is draining away.

Or, you may prefer to bring your stock on in large (say 5 litre) pots on a standing ground, in which case transferring them to the border will offer even less of a problem, since there will be no root disturbance.

Most of the small-flowered asters have tiny leaves. When these are interestingly coloured, as in the bright green **A. ericoides** 'Esther', or the purplish **A. lateriflorus** 'Horizontalis', they become an asset as foliage plants before ever a flower appears. Then, again, some have such a long flowering season that a permanent border position is assured. Such is *A. × frikartii* 'Mönch' (see below), and clumps of it could be interplanted with small bulbs, such as *Tulipa linifolia*, for early interest. The bulbs would not need to be moved.

Propagation of most asters is by division. Fleshy stolons can be seen, at the end of the growing season, to radiate from the base of the flowering stem that will be cut down. Each cluster (or each stolon, if you need to work up stock quickly) detaches easily from the clump, to make a new plant. This can be done any time from autumn to spring. Spring, however, is safest when it comes to meddling with asters that make only small, basal buds with which to overwinter, notably *A. amellus* and *A. × frikartii*. Cuttings of young shoots when a couple of inches long, in spring, also root easily in a cold frame, making the base of the cutting the point at which it joined the old rootstock.

To take the heavyweight favourites, *A. novi-belgii* and *A. novae-angliae*, first:

A. novi-belgii has a running rootstock and colonises waste places, such as railway sidings. It self-sows and is a pest in gardens. The cultivars, such as the large pinky-mauve 'Fellowship' are showy. They do not cut well, the 'petals' rolling back after a day or two. This class of aster has a number of serious ailments. Powdery mildew makes the foliage unsightly. Verticillium wilt is a soil-borne fungal disease which kills the plant. A typical symptom is when, from ground to tip, one longitudinal half of a branching shoot dies, leaving the other half green, for a while. Then there is a microscopic mite which destroys the inflorescence, leaving only a rosette of leafy bracts where colourful rays and disc should be. If your plant seems to be flowering poorly, this will be the cause. It is equally apparent on the dwarf novi-belgii asters, sometimes referred to *A. dumosus*.

These dwarfs form a popular group, often used as a prim edging to paths or to a border next to mown grass, where overlapping plants are unwelcome. They are generally dull and dumpy, totally lacking character. Exceptionally, 'Rosebud' has some charm of form as well as flower.

Of the tall kinds, 'Climax' (1m/3ft), an old, single-flowered variety, lavender-blue in colour, deserves mention. Although tall, one can usually get away with not supporting it. A well-spaced, widely branching structure composes a shapely pyramid. Many of the cultivars have been reduced in height to 60-100cm/2-3ft in order to avoid staking, but they correspondingly suffer from reduced grace in habit.

There could never be any claim to grace in the stiff and sturdy **A. novae-angliae** Michaelmas Daisies, but they seem to be entirely trouble-free and, once established, are self-supporting, though leggy. Their leaves are rough and hairy (smooth, in most asters). The one that seems to survive in every back garden seen along terraced urban houses from the railway, is the pinkish-purple 'Barr's Pink'. A great improvement came with the clear colouring of 'Harrington's Pink', though its legginess requires a planting in front of it. The arrival of 'Andenken an Alma Potschke' (shortened to 'Alma Potschke'), with its vivid magenta-carmine colouring (not a bit autumnal in mood), caused a sensation.

None of the asters so far mentioned are in full flower for much longer than two weeks. If it seems longer, that is because the moment is prolonged by our intense enjoyment.

The small-flowered September-October asters have won increased popularity of recent years. With many of them, it is deceptive to ascribe a definite species name. *A. cordifolius*, for instance, should have heart-shaped, basal leaves. 'Sweet Lavender' and 'Silver Spray' are two such – light-textured plants making a feathery impression. Of mixed parentage, 'Photograph' (1m/3ft) is good, in pale lavender blue, and long flowering. 'Ochtengloren' (Dawn Glory) (1.2m/4ft) is of Dutch breeding, with starry pink flowers and very free. 'Little Carlow' (1.2m/4ft) is as blue a shade of lavender as you will find in any aster, and that gives it definition.

Under *A. ericoides*, a yellow-and-white haze, with yellow predominating, is created by the prominence of its disc in 'Brimstone' (1m/3ft). The well-named 'Pink Cloud' (a mere 60cm/2ft) is a winner. 'Esther' (60cm/2ft), mentioned for its bright green foliage, is another low yet graceful one, flowering with increasing brio over a long stretch.

One of the staunchest of the old cultivars is *A. lateriflorus* 'Horizontalis' (1m/3ft), with strongly horizontal branching that makes it resemble a bush, before flowering starts, in September. It reaches a peak in mid-October. I have double hedges of this aster, linking topiary 'peacock' specimens where lavender once performed this office. On heavy soil irreparable gaps frequently appear in lavender hedging. The aster is a complete success. The purplish foliage is echoed by prominent purple discs to each daisy, the reflexed rays being whitish. Thousands of these seen together are a sight to wade through, where the hedges flank a path on either side. The plants retain their shape in winter and sparkle when silvered by hoar frost. We cut them down in March. Between the rows, giving interest in late June, are columns of a deep blue form of the bulbous *Iris latifolia* (syn. *I. xiphioides*). In 'Prince', a recent *A. lateriflorus* cultivar, the leaves are a deeper shade of purple. I can see no advantage in this.

Of the typical michaelmas daisy as popularly conceived, last mention shall go to *A. turbinellus* (1.2m/4ft), actually a hybrid offered in two forms, one of which was, without dissent, given the AGM on the trial of *Aster* at Wisley in 1992. On a previous trial, 30 to 40 years earlier, it gained no recognition – such is the change of taste – but my mother and I, seeing and falling for it then, removed a basal cutting of vegetative growth (we enjoyed collaborating in this act of dishonesty), and from that I have grown it ever since. Stems and small leaves are dark, well displaying a long succession of lilac daisies.

The European *A. amellus* has rough leaves and rather large daisies on a lowish plant. The breeders have increased flower size, but too often the result has been a clumsy plant that will not stand up, even though a mere 45cm/1½ft tall.

Nevertheless, 'King George' is a popular and showy lavender-blue clone. My choice would go to 'Veilchenkönigin' – Violet Queen – (45cm/1½ft), of reliably up-standing habit, with moderate-sized flowers of an intense shade of violet. This combines successfully with an interplanting of the bright pink South African bulb, *Nerine bowdenii*. To ensure that the flowering of the two coincides, water the nerines heavily in early September, should it be dry, so as to break their dormancy and bring forward their flowering.

The hybrid between *A. amellus* and the Asiatic *A. thomsonii* produced the hybrid **A. × frikartii**, whose most admired cultivar is 'Mönch' (75cm/2½ft) (named after the Swiss Bernese Oberland mountain). On a plant which, when established, is sufficiently self-supporting, it carries its sizeable lavender daisies in a continuous succession from late July into October. Unfortunately, on heavy soils, it can easily be killed in winter by slugs eating the small, resting shoot buds. Otherwise, there are no problems. On a small scale, old clumps can be divided in spring (not autumn) and cuttings taken then root easily.

48 **A. sedifolius** (*A. acris*) (1m/3ft) is an old border favourite for August-September flowering. Individually, the mauve flowers are spidery and shapeless, but in the mass they form a huge eiderdown of colour, through which I like to thread some strands of bright orange or red nasturtiums, self-seeding from year to year. The aster makes dense clumps of overwintering, green shoots. It needs thorough support, in May, and because this is a nuisance, a dwarf strain, 'Nanus', has been developed, but I have never seen it deserving garden space.

Aster macrophyllus (60cm/2ft), with pale flowers of nondescript colouring, is useful for colonising rather dry, shady spots. But the recently appeared clone 'Twilight' (75cm/2½ft) is a winner, with broad panicles of 4cm/1½in-wide, rich mauve daisies, flowering from July into September.

Finally, latest in flower but too late to succeed in our cool British summers, **A. tartaricus** (2.4m/8ft). It makes a striking October feature in East Coast states, like North Carolina and Georgia, swaying about with large panicles of mauve daisies held aloft on strong stems.

Astilbe

Saxifragaceae

The Far Eastern genus, *Astilbe*, is a three-syllabled word over which most gardeners have few problems, though you do still meet astileebs. These hardy, moisture-loving perennials are in the top flight of second-rate border, bog and open woodland plants, most of them at their peak in July. They were greatly 'improved' by Georg Arends, in Germany, during the first half of the 20th century. While adding to their range of colours, introducing brilliant shades of red, as in 'Koblenz', crimson and magenta, a certain stiffness of habit also crept in.

Although their pinnate foliage is always agreeable and the faded panicle retains its shape without looking seedy, the actual time when the colouring of the flowers is at its peak lasts for a mere fortnight. The violence of some of the brightest and most densely presented colours can be mitigated by a situation beneath trees, always remembering, however, that the astilbes' fibrous root system is highly intolerant of drought, any suggestion of which will lead to a shrivelling of their leaves. They need replanting every three or four years in improved soil, into which plenty of bulky organic matter, such as mushroom compost, has been added.

It is a pity that the practice of forcing pot-grown roots into early flowering has lapsed. They are potted in early autumn, plunged outside until renewed growth becomes evident in early spring, then brought on under heated glass.

Astilbe chinensis (2m/6ft), albeit a fairly weak shade of mauve, makes a pleasing impression in a large-scale setting. The white 'Professor van der Wielen' (1.2m/4ft), with gracefully loose panicles, is one of my favourites, though it is apt to stop flowering if not frequently re-planted. It seeds itself and remains true.

40 Rather later than most, 'Superba' (syn. *A. taquetii* 'Superba') (1.2m/4ft), has splendid foliage, akin to *A. chinensis* (1m/3ft) and long but narrow panicles in brightest mauve, being quite long-lasting. That self-sows agreeably and it can also be interplanted with spring-flowering bulbs. I grow it near to the refined yellow daisies of *Inula hookeri* (1m/3ft). *A. chinensis* itself is less often seen than *A. c.* var. *pumila* (30cm/1ft), which is August-September-flowering, the same bright mauve as the last. Not everyone's colour, but certainly mine.

There is a group of dwarf hybrids with particularly pleasing, crimped foliage under the umbrella title ***A.* × *crispa***, of which 'Perkeo' (30cm/1ft), with pink sprays, is deservedly a favourite. ***A. simplicifolia*** is a parent of good dwarfs, notably 'Sprite' (25cm/10in), which is pink as is 'Inshriach Pink' (25cm/10in), another that has struck me in Scotland, where astilbes thrive so enviably. In my garden, that one faded away and I know that it was my fault. It was crowded out.

One that I find robust is the species **A. rivularis** (2m/6ft), which is a quester, with its rhizomes. The foliage has quality. The inflorescence, in July, is cream-white soon fading to green, though pleasantly. Again, this astilbe has the rather tiresome habit of ceasing to flower when overcrowded, which it soon becomes.

Astilboides

Saxifragaceae

Hived off from *Rodgersia*, **Astilboides tabularis** is a striking foliage plant in moist, partially shaded positions where it will not get burnt up. Happier, therefore, in Scotland than in the south of England.

The round, peltate leaves, scalloped at the margins, may be up to 1m/3ft across on 1.2m/4ft stems. Greenish white flowers add considerably to this height. The colouring of its leaves, when young, is an unusually bright shade of green. This mixes in well with other moisture-lovers and looks different from any other plant we grow.

Astrantia

Apiaceae/Umbelliferae

Astrantias are umbellifers with a difference. The enclosing involucre of bracts is greatly enlarged, forming a ruff, within which is a neat arrangement, like pins in a cushion, of the flower umbel itself. The leaves are palmate. These are moisture-loving plants, especially suitable for woodland, although some kinds do not show up well in shade. They flower from early summer on, their season being markedly prolonged by self-sown seedlings, which mature later than those already established.

Self-sowing is a marked attribute, in this genus. While it is welcome in a woodland free-for-all, it can be a nuisance under border conditions, for the rootstock is remarkably tough (rather as with *Alchemilla mollis*), and soon becomes an effort to extract.

The inflorescence is in muted shades of green, white, pink and red. Having style and lasting well in water, it is a good cut flower, though the smell, in bloom, is somewhat disgusting.

Astrantia major is the principle species and it has been much selected and hybridised. Many clonal names have been given but all too often, these are illicitly used for seedlings, so you want to watch your sources.

For a typical astrantia, but outstandingly strong and bold, I would choose Margery Fish's 'Shaggy' (1m/3ft), which some people have tried to re-name 'Margery Fish'. It has long bracts, white with green tips. 'Sunningdale Variegated' (60cm/2ft) is a form of *A. major* with very brightly cream-variegated foliage in spring, later becoming a vaguely dirty green. Its flowers just about justify their existence.

Red-flowered astrantias are notably less vigorous and their bracts are short, making less impact. Neither are they easily placed so as to show to advantage. The best I have seen so far is 'Ruby Wedding', in which the bracts are lustrous and quite bright. But these astrantias cannot be left alone for long without a falling-off in quality. Frequent division and well-nourished leaf soil, is what they respond to.

The species **A. maxima** (60cm/2ft) is quite large-'flowered' and a surprisingly clear shade of pink. There is a slightly offputting element of coarseness in the foliage. It forms colonies with gradually running rhizomes, and is good beneath a light canopy of thin-textured shrubs. Easily divided.

Athyrium

Woodsiaceae/Polypodiaceae

Athyrium filix-femina (1m/3ft) is the lady fern, one of our commonest and a most graceful species. In general outline like the male fern, the bipinnate fronds are far more finely divided. In damp old gardens, you are sure to find plenty of wild stock. It is deciduous, beginning to look tired by September.

There are a tremendous number of variants, some of which are sure to tempt you. Without knowing, it might be hard to guess the parentage of the tatting fern, *A. f-f.* 'Frizelliae' (30cm/1ft), along the stems of which there are alternating bead-like hemispheres with finely-toothed margins. 'Plumosum Axminster' (60cm/2ft) has very finely divided fronds that contrast well with firm-textured leaves like some epimediums'.

A. f-f. 'Minutissimum' is a lady fern in miniature; good where the scale suggests a cornerpiece on a slightly raised bed.

The Japanese painted fern, **A. niponicum** var. **pictum** (syn. A. *goeringianum* 'Pictum') (30-60cm/1-2ft), with relatively coarse divisions, has purple stems and a grey, almost glaucous, frond. It really needs more moisture than most south-eastern gardens can easily provide, though by no means difficult.

8 The canna 'Tropicanna' or 'Durban', with translucent upright foliage

8

10

◁ **9** Exciting colour contrasts from scarlet *Crocosmia* 'Lucifer', steely blue-stemmed sea holly, *Eryngium* × *oliverianum*, yellow *Coreopsis verticillata* and magenta *Lychnis coronaria*.

10 More July mixed border contrasts, with a pink border phlox in foreground, flattened yellow heads of *Senecio doria* (centre); between them, the lacy green columns of *Helianthus salicifolius*. Two flanking, biennial *Verbascum olympicum* and (centre back) *Clematis* 'Jackmanii Superba', trained up a pole.

11 Mainly foliage. Silver *Plectranthus argentatus*, purple annual perilla and yellow-striped Canna 'Striata', all interwoven by purple-flowered *Verbena bonariensis*, which self-sows. ▷▷

13

12   A telling vertical formed by hollyhocks, *Alcea rosea* seedling.

13   Happy coloniser of damp shade or sun, a superior form of bistort, *Persicaria bistorta* 'Superba'.

14   The dark, ferny-leaved *Dahlia* 'Bishop of Llandaff' with contrasting foliage of *Canna indica* 'Purpurea'
       behind and interweaving *Verbena bonariensis*.

B

Baptisia

PAPILIONACEAE

An American genus having obvious affinities with lupins. Only one species, **Baptisia australis** (1m/3ft) is so far widely grown in gardens. The spikes of indigo blue flowers are borne in early summer at 60cm/2ft, the plant making considerable vegetative growth afterwards. It is a fresh, clean-looking plant, the flowers well spaced, instead of being in whorls, like lupins. Rootstock tough and resenting disturbance. Seed is the obvious method of increase.

I have not seen **B. lactea** (syn. *B. leucantha*) (1m/3ft) as a garden plant but it is handsome in the wild (near Lake Michigan), the inflorescence a sparsely but widely branched candelabrum of white-flowered spikes. It looks promising on Thompson & Morgan's trial ground.

Begonia

BEGONIACEAE

19 Within this amazingly varied and attractive genus, there is far greater scope for experiment than has yet been tested. There are, of course, many seed strains, both of fibrous- and tuberous-rooted kinds, for use in bedding. As a general comment, single-colour strains are more effective than mixtures. And there is greater excitement to be expected from tuberous-rooted kinds – those with single flowers as well as doubles – than from the fibrous-rooted begonias loosely known as Semperflorens. The latter, however, do include strains with bronzed foliage, which can attractively highlight white or pink flowers.

Tuberous-rooted begonias have an advantage in being easily stored, dry, in winter. Grown from seed to flower the same year, a good bit of heat is needed in the early stages, but if you can afford to take two years over raising them, a summer sowing will require no more than sun heat under close conditions. The small tubers that result can be stored dry, in the usual way, and started again in spring, in moist peat and close conditions, using sun heat. They will flower well in this second year.

The hardiness of tuberous-rooted hybrids is seldom tested, but is often equivalent to that of dahlias, the tubers surviving winter outside but returning late into growth. The species best known for its hardiness is the pink-flowered **Begonia grandis** subsp. **evansiana** (45cm/1½ft). It likes semi-shaded conditions (as do the majority of begonias) and well-nourished soil with plenty of moisture. Even so, flowering gets under way quite late in September and is often interrupted by weather chilly enough to cause flower and bud drop.

At this late stage, the plant will make tiny bulbils in its leaf axils, which are a ready means of propagation. It is a good plant under the greenhouse bench, where it will maintain itself for many years. So will the smaller-flowered, soft orange **B. sutherlandii**, whose lax habit suits it for use in containers – it combines well with the foliage of *Helichrysum petiolare* 'Limelight'. This begonia also makes leaf axil bulbils in autumn and may overwinter outside.

Among the greatest strengths of many begonias is their beautifully marked and textured foliage, not to mention the intriguing leaf shape, which is invariably eccentric. Many such species and hybrids can be bedded out for the summer, where they will get light overhead shade. They make exotic foliage features. Among the easiest
17 is **B. scharffii** (syn. *B. haageana*) (60cm/2ft), whose felted leaves and stems are bronzed, while it additionally carries sheaves of blush-white blossom with pink petioles.

Work up stock under glass, until you have a good-sized plant (of whatever it is) and then plant it out in late June, lifting and rehousing in October (or earlier if you catch early frosts). 'Marmaduke', with large leaves handsomely patterned in a mosaic of bronze and lime green, is an excellent, low-growing bedder, once it has accustomed itself to outdoor life. You should also consider begonia species grown principally for their flowers, like the graceful, pink-flowered **B. fuchsioides** (1m/3ft), which makes an admirable display plant for containers.

Belamcanda

Iridaceae

Belamcanda chinensis (60cm/2ft), from the Far East, is reminiscent of a tigridia in miniature. The leaves are iris-like; the flowers last for a day but open over a couple

of high summer months. They are star-shaped with narrow segments, orange but liberally spotted with a deeper colour. It doesn't quite make a show but is nice to have. The
inflated seed capsules split to reveal quite large, shiny black seeds which are irresistible, if
strange to you and seen in someone else's garden. Alas, the temptations of the flesh.

The plant is deciduous but reasonably hardy, requiring a sunny, well-drained position. It self-sows a bit.

Bergenia

Saxifragaceae

16 Seekers after no-trouble ground cover, with landscape architects at the van, fawn
upon bergenias. They have bold, evergreen leaves and can safely be left without attention for years on end. And they really do suppress the weeds. As a low feature to
emphasise the bulge in a border or the corner where it starts, there is nothing to
touch them (unless you start to think, which is a great mistake). They are hardy and
thrive on windswept exposure (just like private and public school English boys were
supposed to do). If their leaves turn the colour of chilblains, in winter, that is one of
their greatest attractions.

'Goodness knows why', wrote John Raven in *A Botanist's Garden*, 'but the insuf-
ferably coarse genus of Bergenia is apparently coming back into favour. If you grow
bergenias for their leaves you can have no appreciation of elegance and if for their
flowers you must be colour-blind'.

While chuckling with appreciation, I must, of course, come immediately to the
bergenia's defence. If every plant we grew was elegant, we should long for the
strength and sinew which such as bergenias provide. And the flowers, although they
can be disagreeably coloured, are often full of vitality. Some, anyway, are white or
palest pink – hardly the stuff of colour-blindness.

Bergenias, known as megaseas when I was young, were the darlings of Gertrude
Jekyll and all her followers to the last syllable of recorded time – or, at any rate, to
the present. They are rhizomatous perennials, the rhizomes soon comprising a dense
and impenetrable network, above which are carried the tufts, or rosettes, of foliage.
The one that I was brought up on – in quantity, and in obeisance to G.J. – was
Bergenia cordifolia 'Purpurea'. This has the leatheriest leaves and, being evergreen,
they become tired and wearisome with time. Furthermore, if leaves of this kind are
damaged – perhaps by vine weevils, perhaps by strong-jawed slugs – the damage remains undisguisable for a very long time. The dense heads of flowers are borne in

April on fleshy, rhubarb-like stalks and are themselves a rather dirty, blue-magenta. I don't mind the colour but can sympathise with anyone who does.

Old colonies (and this applies to a great many bergenias) cease to flower except at the margins, where they have found new soil and hence fresh vitality. The leaves around this fringe will also be larger and healthier-looking. Bergenias have a way of extending the area that they were originally intended to occupy. So, looking across a landscaped garden, they are apt to occupy a disproportionate area with ponderous emphasis.

Like much ground cover, they are greatly improved by quite frequent replanting – but then that undermines the principal object of ground cover, which is to save trouble. When replanting, sever a length of rhizome some 10cm/4in below the crown and reduce the leaves on this (if large and floppy) by half. If you are serious about working up a fair amount of stock, cut lengths of rhizome, as you would cut a swiss roll, into inch-long slices. Dip the open surfaces into a fungicidal powder. Then prick them out, barely covered and top (proximal) side uppermost, into a seed tray of light, potting compost. There are dormant 'eyes' all the way along these naked rhizomes, which will break into growth when given the stimulus of being treated individually. Water and place in a close frame. This can be done at almost any time of the year but late winter is probably best.

Another stalwart, whose popularity dates back to the 19th century, is **B. × schmidtii**. Its leaves are as undistinguished as you could imagine, but its pink flowers are charming and generously borne – very early in mild winters, as early as February. However, the slightest touch of frost browns them. It is particularly popular in the front gardens of Hastings – my nearest seaside town – and probably escapes all but the worst frosts in that maritime climate.

Although bergenias are never difficult to grow, few give of their best in sheltered gardens or on heavy soil. Those whose leaves colour in winter, given full exposure and light soil, are hopeless with me. At Beth Chatto's, however, on her hungry Essex gravel, they are ideally served. Here are some of her successes, as she described them to me. All may be taken to be up to a foot tall, when flowering, their season being March to May.

'Abendglut' (many have been bred in Germany) has smaller, neater leaves than some. It colours well in winter on light soil and should be planted so as to be caught in the beam of your headlights as you drive home. The flowers are 'vivid rose-red' (which, in nursery-speak, usually means magenta). 'Autumn Red' has bright winter colour. The leaves are shaped like a spoon turned upside down. Soft pink flowers. 'Baby Doll': clear rose-pink flowers in quantity. No winter leaf colour. 'Beethoven' is free with well-shaped white flowers that fade pink. 'Bressingham White' is a cleaner white, retained longer. 'Schneekönigin' has large flowers, blush white, apt to be spoilt by frost. 'Silberlicht' starts white, fades pinkish. Nice in bloom, horrid in winter (my comment).

'Eric Smith': best for winter effect. The leaves being held upright, show a polished, bronze-tinted upper surface, and carmine-red undersides, especially effective in low sunlight. 'Eroica' is striking with branching heads of rose-pink flowers held high (60cm/2ft), on rhubarb-red stalks, above the foliage. In 'Morgenrote', the leaves are nothing much but the bright pink flowers are borne twice over, with a generous second crop in August. 'Rosi Klose' is the best, Beth reckons, for flowers (the leaves, unexceptional), these, well presented, being rosy pink with a touch of salmon and flared at the mouth to form an open bell.

Although its flowers stand tall on long stems, 'Sunningdale' was originally selected for its reddish winter leaf colouring, but has since been superseded in this respect. 'Wintermärchen' took my fancy on the nursery stock beds with small, neat, bright green oval leaves, in autumn. Both surfaces are polished. Some turn brilliant scarlet, before dying. Flowers, 'deep rose'. Hm. But never mind.

Bergenias with small, upright leaves of this kind are in a class of their own. They are what I call prick-eared, having none of the heaviness of the majority. Admittedly their foliage is not markedly ground-covering, but the network of rhizomes prevents all but a few weeds from penetrating. One of the most distinguished is **B. purpurascens** (syn. *B. delavayi* and *B. beesiana*), which has similar (long-oval) leaves and habit to the last. They (can) colour well in winter. The prolific flowering, in May, is bright rosy-purple, displayed on long (1m/3ft) stalks.

B. stracheyi, is a small-, neat-leaved variety that I use for early spring bedding, as it is often at its best in late March. Its abundant clusters of pink flowers make a show. They are good in association with mats of mauve or purple aubrieta. 'Alba' is a white-flowered version.

Finally, **B. ciliata**, my favourite by far. It is deciduous (apart from a few, very small leaves at the centre of each rosette), and therefore subject to none of the leatheriness of most of its tribe. Pale pink flowers open early, but are of little importance and anyway get frosted. But the soft leaves, furry on each surface, are huge, where there is good feeding and plenty of moisture, and they catch the dew magically. Partial shade is best for this species, though it doesn't scorch in sun. I also have the form called *ligulata* (which I collected on a shady rock face in Kashmir in 1971), but it is nowhere near so good; partially evergreen and hairy only around the leaf margins. The foliage is of only moderate size.

Berkheya

ASTERACEAE/COMPOSITAE

From South Africa, a substantial yellow daisy, **Berkheya macrocephala** (60cm/2ft), whose distinguishing feature is the prominent ruff of thistly bracts which frames the inflorescence. The leaves are an asset, shining green and somewhat thistly. A sound perennial increased by division.

Bidens

ASTERACEAE/COMPOSITAE

Bidens ferulifolia (30cm/1ft) has of recent years become one of the most popular of all hanging basket and trough plants, but is also an excellent, long-flowering bedder. Spaced 1m/3ft apart, a large bed can quickly be covered by a mixture of one of this (the dominant plant) to two of grey-leaved *Helichrysum petiolare*. It is a variable species and, from seed, both upright and trailing strains are offered. A main attraction in the yellow, coreopsis-like flower is the double curve in each ray. This is absent in some strains.

The species is generally taken to be only half-hardy, but self-sowing is frequent and I have seen it making a permanent feature, in Somerset, in the cracks of a flat, paved area.

B. heterophylla (2m/6ft) is a recently introduced, late-flowering perennial with a running rootstock. Typically, the flowers are of a washed-out yellow and badly shaped, with wide gaps between rays. Breeding and selection could radically improve matters. Hardiness so-so.

Blechnum

BLECHNACEAE/POLYPODIACEAE

The hard ferns are evergreen and insist on acid soil. Fertile and sterile fronds are separate, the former upright and often twice the height of the latter.

Blechnum spicant (60cm/2ft or less), is our only native species but extremely widespread. Grown well, it is a handsome plant, with glossy, pinnate lance leaves. It is suited by moist, woodland conditions.

B. penna-marina (15cm/6in), from the south of New Zealand, is hardy and its small rhizomes run over the surface to form a mat. It can be a delight filling in paving cracks under moist, shady conditions. The young, fertile fronds, in spring, are bronze. Looking its best in summer, it ties in well with the growth cycle and habit of *Cyclamen hederifolium*.

From the south of South America, comes ***B. tabulare*** (syn. *B. chilense*) (60cm/2ft), whose fronds in our climate are nearly all sterile. Simply pinnate with wavy margins to the pinnae. Young fronds are produced throughout the growing season and are coppery, in contrast to the deep, rich green of those that have matured. The hard texture makes it feel very satisfying to grasp a frond and run your hand up and along it. The rhizomatous habit builds into colonies, which can be split and replanted in spring when, also, the old fronds should all be cut down. One of the best ferns for acid soils, I should on the whole recommend a sunny position, which highlights the colour difference between old and young fronds.

Boltonia

ASTERACEAE/COMPOSITAE

Very similar to typical michaelmas daisies, boltonias flower in October. They are always white and the clone of ***Boltonia asteroides*** called 'Snowbank' (1.2m/4ft) is much grown in New England, where rich, orangey-brown Monarch butterflies make a thrilling contrast as they feed.

In this country, *B. asteroides* (2m/6ft or more) is inconveniently tall and needs skilful support. The 1m/3ft var. *latisquama* 'Nana' is more manageable.

Bomarea

ALSTROEMERIACEAE/LILIACEAE

Closely related to Alstroemeria, bomareas differ in being climbing (twining) herbaceous perennials. They have similar fleshy roots and similar clusters of funnel-flowers, often drooping gracefully at the ends of their shoots.

They come from Central and South America, and there are many species that would be worth trying in Britain but have never been available here. The best known, ***Bomarea caldasii***, seems to be pretty hardy. The flowers, speckled inside, are a soft shade of orange-red. If they flower early enough, good seed will be ripened. This should be given the same warm-and-cold treatment as Alstroemeria.

B. *caldasii* is normally cut to the ground by the first autumn frost and is unlikely to flower on its new growth the next year, before the end of July. In Dublin, however, I saw a specimen that had retained its old growth through the previous winter and it was in full flower by the first week in June.

Boykinia

SAXIFRAGACEAE

Ah! *Boykinia*, you exclaim with mild pleasure, as you meet **B. aconitifolia** (60cm/2ft) once again when on a garden visit. It is entirely forgotten in the intervals. You once grew it yourself, in the kind of damp half-shade that it likes. It did all right but got crowded out by neighbours and you only missed it when seeing it somewhere else. A modest, hardy perennial, with monkshood-like leaves and open sprays of small white flowers in July.

Brodiaea – see Triteleia

Brunnera

BORAGINACEAE

Brunnera macrophylla (syn. *Anchusa myosotidiflora*) (60cm/2ft) is a coarse, spring-flowering perennial much used as ground cover in shade. Its sprays of blue, forget-me-not flowers seem fresh on their first appearance. It has large, orbicular leaves which have given rise to several more or less variegated clones, notably 'Dawson's White', better known as 'Variegata'. The leaf is broadly margined in white, which later scorches easily in hot, dry conditions. If roots are damaged, the new plants resulting will have plain green leaves. B. *macrophylla* is a useful plant for the bored gardener.

Bulbinella

ASPHODELACEAE/LILIACEAE

From open grassland in New Zealand (seen with *Aciphylla aurea*), where it grows in handsome drifts, comes **Bulbinella hookeri** (45cm/1½ft). It makes clumps of lanky, linear foliage and strongly upward-thrusting spikes of starry, asphodel-like yellow flowers. It needs moist soil and is a far easier garden plant in Scotland than in the south, where the requisite open position is too apt to dry out, with disastrous consequences.

Buphthalmum

ASTERACEAE/COMPOSITAE

I first met **Buphthalmum salicifolium** (30cm/1ft) in open woodland in Austria, where it was flowering in August. But it has a long season, starting in May, with a succession of rich yellow daisies on wiry, branching stems. One is grateful to it for its extended flowering, but it is a shame that the rays die brown on the plant. It is an easy, clump-forming perennial. (See also *Telekia*).

Bupleurum

APIACEAE/UMBELLIFERAE

A difficult genus to pigeonhole, since it includes biennials, perennials and shrubs. A notable feature, unusual in this family, is the plain, undivided foliage. The involucral bracts are often prominent.

Bupleurum falcatum (60cm/2ft) is a self-sowing biennial that makes a haze of euphorbia green for much of the summer, a colour that contrasts significantly with scarlet, as it might be *Crocosmia* 'Lucifer'. **B. angulosum** (38cm/15in) plays hard to catch but is a splendid tufted perennial when pleased, of upright habit; the bracts a particularly vivid and 'unnatural' shade of green.

In **B. longifolium** (60cm/2ft) the leaves are almost as broad as long. The inflorescence is chocolate-brown. If grown above a bark mulch, this is ideal material for The Invisible Garden.

B. fruticosum (2m/6ft) makes a large and distinguished-looking evergreen shrub, even broader than tall but it responds to cutting back. Glossy, convex leaves make a background to typical umbelliferous flowers, in a light shade of green. Not necessarily hardy, but always growing larger than expected, when suited. Seed will germinate only if sown fresh.

Butomus

BUTOMACEAE

The flowering rush, **Butomus umbellatus** (1m/3ft) is a glamorous native wild flower of dykes and disused canals. With rush-like leaves, it is easily grown in shallow water and flowers in June-July, with umbels of clear pink blossom. Sometimes flowering is shy, in which case the plant is not worth growing.

Calamagrostis

POACEAE/GRAMINAE

Taken year-round, **Calamagrostis × acutiflora** 'Karl Foerster' (2m/6ft) is possibly the most valuable of all hardy ornamental grasses. Of clump-forming habit, it flowers late June to early July, with panicles of soft mauve puffs. The flowering stems are at that time flexible and easily weighted to the ground by rain. Usually, they right themselves when dry again.

The panicles gradually close, stiffen and bleach, remaining in this totally upright, rod-like condition throughout the winter – a fine, sculptural feature. Cut down in March.

33   In 'Overdam' (1.5m/5ft), the narrow leaves are variegated in green and white. This is also worth having.

Calamintha

LAMIACEAE/LABIATAE

Aromatic herbs requiring light soil (they fade out on clay) in an open, baking position. **Calamintha nepeta** subsp. **nepeta** 'Blue Cloud' (23cm/9in) is a blue shade of lavender and excellent for rather late flowering in the right position, making clouds of tiny labiate flowers. This is the same as *C. nepetoides*. The species itself, *C. nepeta*, (taller at 45cm/1½ft) is also good.

Calla

ARACEAE

Americans refer to zantedeschias as calla lilies but the true *Calla* is **C. palustris**. It is a floating aquatic of shallow water and very hardy. My recollection of it in the wild is in south Sweden, in association with voracious, giant spotted mosquitoes. That was in June. Its small white arum flowers are not showily displayed but it is a nice plant all the same and easy.

Caltha

RANUNCULACEAE

Our native kingcup, or marsh marigold, makes clumps of dazzling yellow, in spring, usually at the juncture between water and dry land. The flowers are like a much enlarged buttercup's. This is **C. palustris** (30cm/1ft) and the double version, 'Flore Pleno' (30cm/1ft) has, for garden purposes, even greater flower power, with petals packed into tight rosettes. *C. p.* var. *alba* is an albino version, a sweet thing though thin-textured. Even earlier in flower than the type.

The plant we knew as *C. polypetala* should, we are told, be **C. palustris** var. **palustris** (45cm/1½ft). Its habit is quite different, as it roots at the nodes below each inflorescence. It thus makes colonies extending both on to moist land and into shallow water. The yellow flowers, especially the first of the season, in late March, are extra-large.

Camassia

HYACINTHACEAE/LILIACEAE

A group of western North American bulbs, whose Indian name, quamash, indicates their edibility with its onomatopoeic scrunching sound. (I made that up, but it should be true.) The flowers are star-shaped, borne in spikes well above lank, basal foliage. In colour, they range from white to deep blue (always with a tinge of mauve or purple).

In borders, they are apt to look lanky and to flop around, but are seen at their best (as in the wild) under meadow conditions, flowering from late April and through May (in June, soon after snow melt, in Nevada). Within a species, their depth of colouring varies a good deal, being often a washy shade of blue. But even this colour, when combined with a strong, clump-forming habit, as in **Camassia leichtlinii** 'Electra' (1m/3ft) can look handsome during its brief season (for they are soon out and over). Use, under mixed border conditions, to give early interest in a position that will later be covered by slower-developing perennials such as *Geranium* 'Ann Folkard'. By June, the camassias will have died down. *C. leichtlinii* subsp. *leichtlinii* (1m/3ft) has white flowers and there is an amazing double version of this, albeit incorrigibly top-heavy.

C. cusickii (1m/3ft) is strongly erect and clump-forming under meadow conditions but the clone in most general cultivation fails to set seed, which provides the best way of naturalising a plant such as this. It flowers late April and is a decent shade of pale blue.

Best for naturalising under meadow conditions is the, generally, deep blue **C. quamash** (syn. *C. esculenta*) (45cm/1½ft), which shows up vividly in a green grass setting, rather like a bluebell apart from the star shape. This forms clumps and they can be shy-flowering if the previous year was cool, but generally put on a good show throughout May if you have mixed clones, some flowering early, some late. Seed ripens freely about the end of July and is a good indication of when it is safe to cut the grass in which they grow.

Campanula

CAMPANULACEAE

It would be difficult to be unkind about the bellflowers, which are a particularly graceful lot and with colouring that does not disturb the sensitive. Campanula blue is the colouring by which we often describe other flowers. It is never pure blue but includes some mauve. Purple and grey campanulas are also frequent.

A number of species are biennial, making a rosette of foliage in the first year. I grow several of these, and they often make handsome pot plants: *Campanula formanekiana*, *C. medium* (Canterbury bell) and *C. incurva* (with fat, greyish-blue bells), for instance. **C. pyramidalis**, the chimney bellflower, makes a notable 2m/6ft pot plant, flowering in August, but is then biennial. When it seeds itself into a well-drained spot in the garden, like a retaining wall, plants can last for a number of years. Each bloom, however, withers three days after opening and spoils the overall appearance of the long spike, on which buds open over a several-weeks period. In the house, away from pollinating bees, each bloom lasts for three weeks. This rule applies to the majority of campanulas.

Most campanulas are at their flowering peak in June and early July. Typical of the best is the peach-leaved bellflower, **C. persicifolia** (1m/3ft), which dislikes light, hungry soils but will otherwise thrive anywhere, in sun or in shade, often seeding itself underneath shrubs and hedge bottoms, from which it pokes out its head unexpectedly. It will also colonise the once-flowering shrub roses, for which some gardeners entertain an extraordinary passion, its blue colouring in ideal contrast to their pinks and crimsons. It goes well, in a similar way, with the lactiflora peony hybrids, and it picks well, as peonies do, so both can be arranged together. *C. persicifolia* will also colonise the larger ferns.

The pure white 'Alba' is a match for the typical blue and there are various degrees of doubling to be had in both. 'Telham Beauty', when correctly named, is an outstandingly large blue cultivar, with open saucers rather than the usual bells. Grown from seed, you may get anything but results can be good.

Similar in habit to this species, making mats of evergreen, lanceolate foliage, borne in rosettes, is **C. latiloba** (75cm/2½ft). The flowers are open saucers, rather than bells, and cling closely to the whole spike length, rather than spraying loosely on long pedicels. They are campanula blue but more intense in 'Percy Piper'. 'Hidcote Amethyst' is pinky mauve and that is attractive among the roses at Mottisfont Abbey, Hampshire.

Another principal mainstay of mixed and herbaceous borders is **C. lactiflora** (2m/6ft), which is typically mauve, the flowers making large, domed panicles in July. It self-sows and has welcomely appointed itself among hydrangeas, in my garden. The colour of each seedling will vary slightly. A pale colouring seems to be associated with height, the very light pinkish mauve 'Loddon Anna' (2m/6ft), being one of the tallest. Conversely, 'Prichard's Variety' (1m/3ft) is the richest and most intensely coloured. A revolting little dwarf, 'Pouffe' (30cm/1ft), from which any hint of the grace to which campanulas are heir, has been eliminated, should be reviled.

I have seen this species successfully naturalised in rough turf, in Scotland, but have so far failed to do the same. The roots are thick and long and do not transplant or split well, but cuttings of young shoots are easily rooted in spring, when 7.5cm/3in long, detaching them with a sharp blade, where they spring from the stool.

A number of native species have been adapted as garden plants. *C. latifolia* (1.2m/4ft) is frequent along road verges in the north country. It makes a long raceme of, most often, pale mauve bells, but its intensity of colour is much improved in 'Brantwood', which is almost purple. This is a tough, clump-forming perennial that self-sows liberally, if given the chance, and the seedlings may be of any colour. I cut it all to the ground before the seeds are ripe. It hardly deserves a place to itself, as its flowering is no longer than two weeks, but associates well among shrubs.

The nettle-leaved bellflower, *C. trachelium* (60cm/2ft) is purple; happy in partial shade. It has been improved, 'Bernice' being double and correspondingly weak in the stem. *C. glomerata* (30cm/1ft) is chunky, with dense, almost globular heads of purple bells. Not in the least graceful. Delightful to find in the turf of limy downland. In the garden, it is uncomfortably invasive and, as it chokes itself into starvation almost immediately, flowering becomes sparse. However, 'Superba' is boldly handsome, in its June season, and a rich shade of purple. Split and replant in improved soil immediately after flowering and at frequent intervals.

Best of the natives is *C. rotundifolia* (30cm/1ft), the harebell, or bluebells of Scotland (they call our bluebells wild hyacinths). The basal leaves are rounded, but the cauline foliage is linear. This is a most graceful plant, native of grassland, most often. I am about to try to establish strong plants, raised from seed and grown on in pots, in one of my meadow areas.

C. carpatica (23cm/9in) is a good-tempered, front-of-border, clumpy perennial that has always gone down to slugs, with me. There are quite a number of selected clones and all have upturned saucer-flowers. 'Burghaltii' (38cm/15in) has arresting flowers, being exceptionally long, grey-mauve bells, but they are too heavy for the strength of its stems. Discreet support is not easily given.

I took against *C. punctata*, which is murky and covered in spots. It has an invasive rootstock as has the fairly recently introduced (from Korea) *C. takesimana* (60cm/2ft). That has long, thin, white and mauve bells and would probably be suited to a woodland glade. The ultimate Trojan horse is *C. rapunculoides* (1m/3ft), which beguiles with long, graceful spires of pendent, deep mauve bells. But it has a devilishly invasive rootstock, which gets into everything, "and, apparently, every one of the millions of seeds germinates", to quote Clifford Crook, whose monograph, *Campanulas*, (Country Life 1951) is so thorough as still to be by far the soundest reference work on this genus.

Don't confuse this species with the perfectly harmless biennial rampion, **C. rapunculus** (60cm/2ft), which flowers attractively (like the similar *C. patula*) with wide sprays of small blue bells, but whose main claim to fame is said to be its edible, fleshy roots, in the first year. When I have grown it, no fleshy roots have been forthcoming, and I wonder whether I was supplied with the right thing.

C. poscharskyana is essentially a ground-hugger and, indeed, a good ground-cover plant, if you will but perform the essential office of tidying it up immediately after flowering. This merely entails quickly grabbing all the flowered shoots in huge double-handfuls and tugging. They break away cleanly from the base, leaving a central tuft of leaves, which is all that the plant requires at this stage and from which it may throw a second, lighter crop of flowering shoots, later in the season.

But the habit of *C. poscharskyana* is not solely ground-hugging. Given a vertical surface in its path, like a hedge (to which, if clipped and formal, it will do no good) or a wall, it will climb to 60cm/2ft and make a curtain of blossom. It self-sows and is admirable as a filler in rather dark territory among shrubs. The flowers are starry and, typically, a rather weak shade of pale mauve. But 'Stella' is a more intense campanula blue, a little less aggressive and an altogether desirable clone. Furthermore, it makes an excellent pot plant. Brought into the house as the first buds are opening, in late June, it will last in condition for the best part of a month. **G. garganica** is a similar species, but much smaller. Nice.

The old favourite which we used to know as *C. muralis*, but is now irrevocably **C. portenschlagiana** (15cm/6in), has been much used as an edging to paths, but I like to have it running through the cracks of dry-walling, which is easily organised if you initially plant it on the wall top and allow its creeping habit to have its rein. The numerous bells, in June, are a rich shade of campanula blue. Treatment after flowering is as for *C. poscharskyana*.

Finally, fairy's thimbles, **C. cochleariifolia** (once *C. pusilla*; 7.5cm/3in), which is pale blue, and its albino form, 'Alba'. Although a tiny plant, this runs about and is a great joy in paving cracks where you are not too busy with herbicide.

Canna

CANNACEAE

2, 49 Cannas are making a steady, if uphill, return to popularity (helped by me, I believe) after long eclipse. They were popular in Victorian bedding and thereafter survived as a tropical feature in public gardens bedding schemes. Therein lay their downfall. Used unimaginatively as dot plants and quite unintegrated with their surroundings, they stick out like the proverbial sore thumb. Decried as vulgar by snooty private gardeners of the silver and grey, impeccable taste, school, they languished for many years.

But their flamboyant colours combined with magnificent foliage convey a great charge of excitement which cannot be indefinitely suppressed. So they are back into the world of private gardening, their care being similar to and no more complex than the dahlia's.

I fell irremediably for cannas when I saw generous plantings in the dappled shade of trees and beside a rushing stream – in Nairobi around 1945 or '46. In that setting they didn't look self-conscious but absolutely right. Quite recently, however, I have seen them bedded in huge strips of one variety, along the central reserve of motorways in Georgia, USA, and they looked awful; the more so as a caterpillar had found them out (pests and diseases always follow where monocultures provide them with an easy living) and the foliage was in ribbons. The showier a plant is, the greater tact needs exercising in its uses.

Cannas are also known as Indian Shot. They do not hail from India but from the West Indies; hence the botanical name of the commonest species, **Canna indica**. Shot, because like grape shot, the spherical seeds are hard and black. The range of cannas extends through much of tropical and warm temperate America.

The simple, paddle-shaped leaves are often large and, being held at an upright-oblique angle, lend themselves to translucence at each end of the day. As well as green, they may be purple, green with purple veins and/or margins, or variegated in a range of manifestations.

The flowers have little shape, else they would resemble gladioli, but are bunched like silk handkerchiefs at the crown of tall flowering stems. These stems frequently branch once or twice, with the branches flowering later than the tallest, central raceme, so their season is extended.

The rootstock is rhizomatous, the rhizomes being thick and fleshy enough to carry the plant through its dormant season. That would doubtless be a dry spell, in its native habitats. It is good for cannas to be rested at some stage, in the same way as dahlias. In our climate, hardiness is not to be depended upon. After their top-growth has been frosted, the blackened leaves hanging like garments on a scarecrow, they are cut down, the rhizomes lifted and stored in old potting soil, in a cool but frost-free spot – we have a cellar. To prevent shrivelling, it is wise to visit them once weekly, giving them a thorough watering if the soil has nearly dried out.

In India, a memsahib of the old regime told me that they dug up the cannas and simply made them rest on the soil surface. And to feed them while growing (for cannas are greedy as well as thirsty), 'We gave them horse; pure horse'. Meaning horse dung (in case there should be any misunderstanding).

In our climate, the cannas are brought out of storage when they show signs of being on the move, in spring, and are brought on in a greenhouse, still in their overwintering boxes or pots of old compost, hardened off outside and planted where they will flower, some time in June.

If you want to work up stock of a new variety quickly, keep it growing under heated glass throughout the winter; split off and treat separately all new growths as they appear.

The hard-coated canna seed is said to require special treatment in order to allow water to reach the embryo. This has not been my experience, with seed ripened by my own plants (*C. glauca* is a generous seed producer and comes true). Seed sown under unheated glass in late spring, germinates without difficulty and we also find self-sown seedlings of varying parentage in the area where we regularly grow cannas.

Scarlet or red seems to be the natural colouring of cannas related to *C. indica*. 'Purpurea' (2m/6ft) is one of the most robust, purple-leaved with small red flowers. 'Black Knight' (2m/6ft) has exceptionally dark leaves and rich red flowers. One that has for many years grown in a bed outside glass at Wisley is now being called 'General Eisenhower' (1.5m/5ft), with doubtful authenticity, but a plant is useless for trading without a name. The purple foliage rises in tiers like a sculpture in bronze, eventually crowned by orange-red flowers, which remain in good nick into October. In richest orange, with purple foliage, is 'Wyoming' (2m/6ft).

C. iridiflora (1.5m/5ft) is exceptional, with very large green leaves, edged by the thinnest line of purple. The flowers, rich, pure pink, are borne on an arching inflorescence. 'Louis Cayeux' (1.2m/4ft) is salmon pink and looks well in the company of *Phormium* 'Sundowner' (1.2m/4ft), a New Zealand flax in which the variegation contains broad pink stripes.

One of the first and most prolific cannas that I grew was 'Richard Wallace' (1.2m/4ft), which is pure lemon yellow with bright green leaves.

In a number of cultivars, a particular virtue is made of variegated foliage. One of

14

the best has been known, in this country, as **C. malawiensis** 'Variegata' (2m/6ft), a name never met in the USA, where it is most often known as 'Striata'. The leaves, particularly effective with back-lighting, are boldly striped green and yellow. The stem sheath between nodes is pink and the flowers orange. Arresting, to say the least.

'Durban' (1m/3ft) is striped green and pink – an amazing sight. Its flowers, surprisingly, are orange. 'Strasbourg' is green-and-white-variegated. I have not seen this growing but understand that the white scorches disastrously. Most amazing is 'Cleopatra' (2m/6ft), in which some shoots are purple-leaved with red flowers, some green-leaved with yellow flowers, some green-tinged-purple-leaved with red or yellow or mixed red and yellow flowers. Truly of 'infinite variety', like Cleopatra herself.

Striking as a foliage plant is **C. musifolia** (2.7m/9ft). No one that I know has seen it flower, even when grown on the Côte d'Azur, but it is a magnificent foliage plant, well called banana-leaved – green with purple trimmings. Plant it for back-lighting.

Canna glauca (1.5m/5ft) is unusual. My original plant was wild-collected in Argentina. The foliage is narrow and pointed, markedly glaucous. The rather spidery but most attractive flowers are pale yellow. It grows well emerging from shallow water and overwinters like any water plant, if not subjected to thick ice. This, with reflections, is a beautiful way to see a canna. The species was hybridised at Longwood, Philadelphia, and the offspring are all good water plants (which does not necessarily preclude others from being the same). Thus, 'Erebus' (1m/3ft) is salmon with glaucous leaves; 'Panache' (1.8m/6ft) buff, with red central markings, but this does not have the flowering side-growths of most cannas, and is less free-flowering. 'Ra' (1.8m/6ft) is deep yellow; 'Endeavour' (1.8m/6ft) red and 'Freedom' (1.2m/4ft) soft orange.

In mixed plantings, cannas make a bold contrast to plants with stringy leaves, like grasses – for instance the pampas, *Cortaderia selloana* 'Pumila' (2m/6ft) – or kniphofias. A bold leaf and flower like 'Wyoming' will also pull together small-flowered perennials like the cream plumes of *Artemisia lactiflora* (2m/6ft) or the haze of blue in *Salvia uliginosa* (2m/6ft) or *S. guaranitica* 'Blue Enigma' (2m/6ft).

In a planting for exotic effect, their leaves contrast effectively with pinnate foliage, as in *Rhus × pulvinata* Autumn Lace group (*R. glabra* 'Laciniata'), *Ailanthus altissima*, the tree of heaven – both these having pinnate leaves; or with the glaucous, juvenile foliage of *Eucalyptus gunnii*. These would be stooled quite low, each spring, and would make 2.4m/8ft of growth in one season. Add in dahlias for colourful flowers and grasses like glaucous *Arundo donax* (giant reed grass, 3m/10ft) and white-striped *A. d.* var. *versicolor* (1.2m/4ft), for different leaf shapes.

Cardamine

BRASSICACEAE/CRUCIFERAE

Most of *Dentaria* has been subsumed into this genus, which is that of our native lady's smock or cuckoo flower (a food plant of the Orange Tip butterfly). ***Cardamine pratensis*** (60cm/2ft) makes a spring display in damp meadows or ditches, where it is sometimes so thick as to be quite staggering, with its heads of pale mauve flowers. It looks good with the early goldilocks buttercup, *Ranunculus auricomus*, which also likes damp places.

The double lady's smock, 'Flore Pleno' (30cm/1ft), makes neat rosettes, rather like a miniature stock, and slowly spreads, on damp soil, by suckering. The pinnate leaves are cress-like.

C. raphanifolia (syn. *C. latifolia*) (30cm/1ft) has leaves like watercress and makes strong colonies in damp ditches, flowering in May. The flowers are larger than in *C. pratensis*, and a pinker shade of lilac, but their production can be on the shy side.

Of the *Dentaria* group, ***C. quinquefolia*** (30cm/1ft) is the showiest, with rosy-lilac flowers against bold cut-leaves. It likes leaf soil in a damp, partially shaded border and flowers in April.

Cardiocrinum

LILIACEAE

Understandably removed from *Lilium*, ***Cardiocrinum giganteum*** (2.4m/8ft) is nevertheless a lily of giant proportions but with large shiny, orbicular leaves that look most unlily-like. If you can regularly produce a flowering colony (June-July) of its imposing flower spikes, your reputation in the gardening world is made. The flowers are long white trumpets, purple within, and down-drooping so as to be well presented from below. They last for only a short while but are followed by handsome, upright, sausage-shaped seed capsules.

After this the plant dies, but leaves a legacy of decent-sized bulbils, which take several years to make up to flowering size themselves but provide a quicker means of propagation than seed. The development of flowering-sized bulbs is speeded up by very deep cultivations, before planting out, and the use of cool, leaf soil and garden compost in open woodland or partially shaded conditions. Growing *C. giganteum* well becomes a way of life, occupying a major slice of your gardening hours. All your efforts may easily be thwarted by slugs devouring the young shoots as they re-appear in spring.

Carex

CYPERACEAE

The sedges appear to come somewhere between rushes and reeds. There are said to be over 2,000 species. Many prefer damp or badly drained locations. Our handsom-est native species is the large-growing **Carex pendula** (1m/3ft), which has arching, catkin-like inflorescences. It is well worth including a clump near a pond. Self-sowing could become a problem.

18   **C. elata** 'Aurea' (syn. *C. stricta* 'Bowles's Golden') (60cm/2ft) is a yellow-leaved variant of a dyke-margin native species, found by Bowles in East Anglia. It is a first rate plant either for shallow water at a pond's margin or for a damp border, where it contrasts excellently with the foliage of glaucous hosta or of rodgersias. The blackish inflorescences appear in May, but it is soon after this that the leaf colouring comes into its own and is retained into August. A sunny or, at least, a light position is needed to bring this out.

    C. riparia 'Variegata' (60cm/2ft) is dazzlingly white-striped, some leaves entirely white, and it loves moisture, but is a runner and needs thoughtful placing. **C. muskingumensis** (60cm/2ft), from the Great Lakes region of North America, is happy in any soil, in sun or in partial shade. It is a clumpy plant with bright green fo-liage whose lustre is retained right into fall. The leaves are distinctively arranged in whorls of three. Of its kind, an excellent plant.

    I have yet to be certain whether the New Zealand species I grow is **C. buchananii** or a bronze form of **C. comans**. It makes 45cm/1½ft tufts of narrow leaves whose brown colouring causes some people to say that it looks dead. The healthy sheen on them sufficiently proclaims otherwise. The flowering stems trail at ground level to nearly twice the length of the leaves and self sowing can be over-abundant. Excel-lent in paving cracks.

Carlina

ASTERACEAE/COMPOSITAE

A small group of large-headed, imposing thistles. **Carlina acaulis** and its subspecies *simplex* (30cm/1ft) seem to be interchangeable in cultivation. There is a single, large thistle-head to each stem, the wide, pale disc surrounded by silvery rays, and these by deeply cut, leaf-like bracts. Late summer is their season. The inflorescence closes at night and in damp weather but is admirable for drying. Give a sunny position at a border's margin.

Our native **C. vulgaris** (23cm/9in) is biennial and well worth growing in good soil, where it produces a multiheaded inflorescence, in July. It cannot be relied upon to self-sow. You must collect seed and sow in a pot, pricking out the seedlings.

Catananche

ASTERACEAE/COMPOSITAE

From south-west Europe, **Catananche caerulea** (60cm/2ft) is a reliable perennial, easily raised from seed. The near-naked, branching flowering stems rise from a tuft of grey-green, linear leaves. Papery bracts enclose an inflorescence of lavender blue (or white) ligulate rays. A mildly pleasing but second-rate plant.

Cautleya

ZINGIBERACEAE

Cautleya spicata 'Robusta'(75cm/2½ft) is a handsome plant when well grown, in rich, moist soil. The broad, smooth leaves are like a hedychium's. Loose spikes of deep yellow flowers, supported by reddish-purple sepals, open in summer. The season is not long. This comes from the Himalayas.

Centaurea

ASTERACEAE/COMPOSITAE

Centaurea cyanus is the annual cornflower. None of the perennial species is as clear a blue as this. **C. montana** (60cm/2ft) comes nearest, its flowers twice as big and scented. It makes a sprawling plant, flowering May-June. Cut back after this and it bears a second crop but the foliage may need protecting against powdery mildew. The fleshy roots make new plants if damaged. There are named cultivars in various shades of pink, mauve and white.

31

'Pulchra Major' should probably be known as **Leuzea centauroides** (1m/3ft). A robust plant whose promise exceeds fulfilment. In early summer it makes handsome knob-like flower buds with overlapping bract scales. After that, downhill all the way.

Albeit a coarse plant, **C. macrocephala** (1m/3ft) carries striking, well spaced thistle-heads in bright yellow. The July flowering season is on the short side. **C. glastifolia** (1m/3ft) is like a refined version of this, with smaller, more numerous yellow inflorescences.

C. cineraria, better known as **C. gymnocarpa** (1m/3ft) is a rather tender, soft shrub, seldom living more than two or three years but propagated from soft, autumn cuttings. It is grown entirely for its foliage and is one of the most beautiful of all grey foliage plants, with double-comb leaves. In spring, it has a yen to flower – little purple thistle heads. They should be removed as they appear and the plant (if a good strain) will then settle down to producing foliage only. But it is useless to raise this species from seed, the product being far too inclined to run to flowers. Get a well selected, vegetatively propagated strain.

Centranthus

VALERIANACEAE

Centranthus ruber (60cm/2ft) is the red valerian, not a true native but widely naturalised, especially on stony ground and on chalk cliffs near the sea. Also, if allowed to, in the walls of ruined buildings, but its long, thick roots are outstandingly destructive. It looks beautiful in paving and in dry-stone walling, flowering first in June, with domed panicles in various shades. Red is best and white (**C. r.** 'Albus'). There is a rather nasty pinkish red and a nice, though not widespread, pink, common on the coast of Galloway (south-west Scotland).

Self-sowing is free and seed ripens quickly. Best to cut plants hard back to their woody rootstock, immediately after their first flowering. Young growth will then generally (at least in the south) flower a second time in September.

Cephalaria

DIPSACACEAE

The tree scabious, long known as *Cephalaria tatarica*, should be **C. gigantea** (2.4m/8ft) – a stemmy, self-supporting perennial with pale yellow scabious heads.

Some strains grow freely from seed while others are sterile. Flowering in early summer, this combines attractively with blue or purple delphiniums.

C. alpina (2m/6ft) is shorter and a better mixer, while *C. a.* 'Nana' is shorter still.

Ceratostigma

PLUMBAGINACEAE

These might be described as hardy plumbagos, though none are scandent. *Ceratostigma griffithii* (60cm/2ft) is particularly neat-leaved but, except in the warmest positions, seldom brings off a successful flowering.

C. plumbaginoides (30cm/1ft), hardy and herbaceous, can be very successful ground cover. Cut right back in winter, it should be inter- and overplanted with small spring bulbs. The heads of deep blue flowers, in autumn, are joined at the end of the season by fiery tints in its foliage. Its habit is creeping and it is a most successful feature when established in dry-walling, in time making a curtain of growth.

Best known is *C. willmottianum* (1m/3ft), which is shrubby although, in most winters and in many sites, it may get cut to the ground. That means that it will not start to open its heads of clear blue, rotate flowers until September. Cold weather changes them to a shivery, wan shade, so its season is much curtailed. If it does retain its old wood, as against a warm wall, flowering starts in early July and a great display follows, highlighted by the partnership of red fuchsias.

Chaerophyllum

APIACEAE/UMBELLIFERAE

Chaerophyllum hirsutum 'Roseum' (1m/3ft) is a cow parsley, Queen Anne's lace-style plant but with rosy-mauve flowers. May (to June) is their season and they combine in a rich harmony with the globe heads of *Allium aflatunense* (*A. hollandicum*). In some gardens, both self-sow.

Chasmanthium

POACEAE/GRAMINAE

Chasmanthium latifolium (*Uniola latifolia*) (60cm/2ft plus) is a handsome North

American grass. Its leaves are broadish and its carriage upstanding until the weight of its flower heads arches them over. Flowering in our climate is not till autumn, and although a shady habitat is common in the wild, a sunny position with us will help to promote full flowering before growth ceases.

The widely spaced, diamond-shaped flower spikes are flattened, like a bug before it has had a meal. They are retained well into winter as is the foliage, which turns warm brown. Increased from seed or spring division.

Chelone

SCROPHULARIACEAE

These are extremely hardy, moisture-loving perennials from the east side of America, mostly flowering in late summer. They faintly resemble and are related to *Penstemon*, but the flowers are inflated, which presumably accounts for the name turtle-head.

The most popular species is **Chelone obliqua** (1m/3ft), a self-supporting plant with coarse foliage that shows too prominently beneath short, condensed racemes of puffy flowers in a disagreeable shade between pink and mauve. Colour photographs invariably cut out the mauve element, which is an improvement that has not been transferred to the real-life plant.

Chionochloa

POACEAE/GRAMINAE

From New Zealand a few of us have **Chionochloa conspicua** (2m/6ft), a large, stately grass of tufted habit. Its blossom consists of open, drooping panicles. This is a fine feature near the entrance to the Logan Botanic Gardens, in south-west Scotland. I have lost it twice (once to ants, nesting in the crown). I suspect that it prefers the cooler, damper Scottish climate.

Chionodoxa

HYACINTHACEAE/LILIACEAE

Spring-flowering, scilla-like bulbs. Naming is confused but the one sold as

Chionodoxa luciliae (10cm/4in) has the larger flowers, wide-open blue stars with a white central zone. It will colonise beneath roses, for instance, and self-sow freely. *C. sardensis* (7.5cm/3in) has smaller, more intensely blue flowers without the white zone, though the stamens form a small white eye. Good.

Chrysanthemum

ASTERACEAE/COMPOSITAE

I write of the perennials that we all know as chrysanthemums, although there has been a move to hive them off into *Dendranthema*. They are autumn-flowering daisies and they have a spicy, autumnal smell that belongs to no other flower or plant. It is on this account – their smell – that they belong so distinctly to their season and why all-the-year chrysanths seem so inappropriate, winning the flower arrangers' movement (together with liliums, roses and carnations) a fair degree of opprobrium. Most of us want to forget about chrysanthemums in winter, spring and early summer.

I am not concerned with chrysanthemums for exhibition. As garden flowers, they get going in August. There are exceptions. **Chrysanthemum rubellum** carries sheaves of single, pink daisies in early autumn, from the current year's shoots, but if vegetative growth from the previous year comes through the winter alive, it will flower as early as June.

Stock that you wish to overwinter is generally most safely lifted (and cut back), in late autumn, boxed up and placed in a cold frame or, if you expect severe weather, in a cool greenhouse. The same stools can be split and used again, but better results are obtained by taking cuttings of the soft young shoots, in late winter or early spring, and renewing your stock in this way. Always line out and grow on in new ground. In this way, damage by chrysanthemum leaf eelworm (or nematode, in more accurate American parlance) will be minimised. Some chrysanthemums are so hardy that they are left on the same site for many years.

Time of flowering is critical. If normally so late that the blossom is damaged by frost before it has reached its peak, that variety should be discarded. On the other hand, it is very nice to have a row to pick from in late October and early November. And so, as cut flowers rather than for garden display, it may be worth taking greater risks.

If you are picking branches of chrysanthemums for the house, be sure to remove all the larger leaves, to bash the stem ends and to give a long drink in deep water before including them in an arrangement. I never bother about disbudding, myself, but am happy with the natural spray. It is amazingly invigorating and satisfying, fresh from the garden; nothing better.

The Fanfare F¹ Korean types can give pleasing results, from seed. Sow in April. At the first flowering, heights will be around half those of subsequent years, but you can make a preliminary selection for retention of those that you think worth saving. The shorter kinds are the most manageable.

For *Chrysanthemum uliginosum* see *Leucanthemella serotina*, p. 213. For *Chrysanthemum maximum* see *Leucanthemum* × *superbum*, p. 215.

Cicerbita

ASTERACEAE/COMPOSITAE

Cicerbita (once grown as *Lactuca*) *alpina* (2m/6ft) is a pleasing, if coarse perennial, not unlike *Vernonia* but blue-mauve and much earlier flowering (June-July). It likes some shade and suits the margins of a wild garden.

Cimicifuga

RANUNCULACEAE

The pongy leaves of *Cimicifuga foetida* are said to drive bugs from your bed: hence the Latin name, which we translate as bugbane. I shall not attempt to sort out this thoroughly confused and confusing genus, on which James Compton based his PhD studies. He is convinced that *Cimicifuga* and *Actaea* are one and the same genus.

C. simplex (up to 2m/6ft) gives us some of our best garden perennials. The tangle of roots is close to the surface and vulnerable to drought in the summer, so plenty of humus should be provided and abundant moisture during the growing season. The bipinnate foliage is a handsome feature, providing a platform beneath sparingly branched flower spikes, which rise well above it. Being of a see-through nature, this species is often suitable at a border's margin, perhaps with deep blue aconites, *Aconitum carmichaelii* behind. The conspicuous feature in the white flowers is the stamens, arranged in a dense, bottle-brush-like spike. The scent is sweet and (agreeably) sickly on the air, attracting flies and bluebottles as pollinators. Flowering stems are often dark, which makes a striking contrast. The fruit capsules are ornamental and ripen speedily after flowering.

C. simplex var. *simplex* (2m/6ft) is September-flowering. The Atropurpurea group has purple leaves, but since stock is often raised from seed, the intensity of this feature varies and you need to choose your plants while growing. *C. s.* 'Elstead' (1.5m/5ft) has purplish stems, while 'White Pearl' (1m/3ft), flowers so late, often into November, that its scenic uses in the garden are limited.

Cirsium

ASTERACEAE/COMPOSITAE

Cirsium rivulare 'Atropurpureum' (2m/6ft) is a distinctive perennial, grown with the greatest ease in Scotland, sometimes failing when you had not expected it to, in the south. It is a clumpy thistle (none too easily divided), with basal, only moderately prickly leaves. The thistle flowers are borne, mostly in early summer, above largely naked stems and are coloured rich, reddish purple. It can be increased from root cuttings.

Clematis

RANUNCULACEAE

Many books have been written on this genus (some by me) but most *Clematis* are woody or die back, in winter, to a woody base, so I here include only one species, **C. recta** (1-2m/3-7ft), which is truly herbaceous. Coming from Europe and west Asia, it is an old garden favourite. The pinnate leaves are only weakly clasping. The stems are weak, and if you don't want it flopping all over its neighbours, efficient support is essential. We give it with brushwood, to 2m/6ft, as ours, a purple-leaved form, is vigorous. 'Purpurea' is often raised from seed and a well-coloured form is so handsome in spring (before it needs to be trussed up), that it might as well be grown instead of the green-leaved type-plant.

By the time of flowering, the leaves of 'Purpurea' are dark green. The flowers are white and foam abundantly. They are cruciform and sweet-scented, though not strongly. It makes a good cut flower. Flowering is quite brief. The seed heads are pleasing, but if you choose to shear the plant over just below the inflorescences and immediately after the display, a secondary crop of young leaves and flowers is sometimes a worthwhile bonus.

Codonopsis

CAMPANULACEAE

There are many insignificant species of *Codonopsis*, from a gardener's viewpoint, but others that are very beautiful, though with an irritating preference for the Scottish climate rather than that of southern England. They come from mountainous regions in east Asia. Easily raised from their minute seed, they flower young but can be difficult to retain as garden plants. I find that **C. convolvulacea** and the similar but to-be-preferred **C. forrestii** are best grown in large pots. They are herbaceous climbers and require support to 1m/3ft in the growing season, flowering with campanula-blue saucers in August. *C. forrestii* is interestingly marked in the centre of the flower. They overwinter as fleshy tubers and can be repotted then.

C. clematidea (60cm/2ft) is the best known species and quite easy. No support needed. The 'blue' flowers are bell-shaped and beautifully marked within, if you lift the bell to look. The smell is disagreeable. My favourite is **C. ovata**, which has pale blue bells flared at the mouth. If you live in the south and want to keep it, concentrate on what you are doing. I didn't.

Colchicum

COLCHICACEAE/LILIACEAE

Often described as and mistaken for autumn crocuses, colchicums are not remotely related. An easy distinction is that they have six stamens, whereas in *Crocus* there are three. Pinky-mauve **Colchicum autumnale** is our native species, flowering in autumn without any leaves, but with a background of grass. As its common name, meadow saffron, indicates, it is a plant of pastures. It is poisonous and cattle avoid it but may be in trouble if the foliage is included in hay. Other common names, naked boys and naked ladies, indicate disapproval of its flowering without foliage. This, of course, is only noticeable when it is grown as a border perennial, but the situation can be avoided.

Colchicums have shiny, brown-skinned corms, giving tactile satisfaction. They are dormant from early summer, when the leaves dry up, to late summer or early autumn, when a new growing season is heralded by the corm's flowering. In the Netherlands, corms (often of 'The Giant') are purchased dry and arranged without soil or water in a bowl, there to flower, after which they are discarded. There are spring-flowering colchicums, but they are not of easy cultivation.

With the autumn-flowering kinds, the foliage appears in early spring and is at its lushest in April, broad and shiny and a handsome feature in its own right. It dies off rather conspicuously, in early summer, but can then be cut to the ground. If in a border, you can then interplant your colchicum clumps with something that will cover the bare space in summer and provide a background for the colchicums' flowering, later on. *Helichrysum petiolare* 'Variegatum' provides a good foliage background of suitable vigour for the white chalices of **C. speciosum** 'Album', in September. For a pinky-mauve colchicum, the ground-hugging *Petunia* 'Purple Wave' makes a striking companion.

39

In turf, I have not found colchicums to spread by self-seeding under my conditions, even though some of them do ripen seed. To obtain a meadow display, it is best to increase stock in a cultivated area (and it makes up quickly), thereafter transferring it while dormant. The smaller-flowered kinds probably look the most suitable in grass – *C. autumnale* itself, 'Album', which has small white flowers on strong stalks, **C. agrippinum**, which is checkered like a fritillary, while the double flowers of 'Waterlily' will largely be prevented from toppling over under their own weight, by the supporting grass surround.

Colocasia

Araceae

These are tender aroids from the Far East, with handsome, sometimes very large leaves, for which flower gardeners grow them, though seldom, as yet, in Britain. They die back to a tuber in winter and are then to be found in Chinese food markets. I have not seen them flower.

Colocasia esculenta (1m/3ft) has huge, shovel-shaped leaves, perfectly smooth and liable to drip from the sharp tip, even before dewfall. The leaf venation, seen translucently, is of the greatest delicacy. A wonderful plant for subtropical effect. Popularly known in the USA as elephant's ears.

A colocasia that I have received from US friends has smaller leaves of so deep a purple as to be almost black. It is named 'Black Dragon' and looks well combined with the green-and-white grass foliage of *Arundo donax* var. *versicolor*. It can also be grown in shallow water but must be stored frost-free in winter.

Commelina

COMMELINACEAE

With their lank, linear leaves and triangular flowers, **Commelina tuberosa** Coelestis group (syn. *C. coelestis*) (45cm/1½ft) is clearly a near relation to *Tradescantia* and, like the spider worts, the flowers wilt soon after noon unless the day is dull and chilly. But its great distinguishing feature is the rich, dazzling blue colouring. It can be raised from seed though inferior strains produce unnecessarily small flowers. The fleshy, perennial tubers may be destroyed by frost but can be stored overwinter in the same way as *Salvia patens*. Flowers late summer. The similar **C. dianthifolia** is well spoken of but I have not seen, let alone grown it.

Convallaria

CONVALLARIACEAE/LILIACEAE

Lily-of-the-valley is **Convallaria majalis** (20cm/8in) (*majalis* means flowering in May). It is a native plant of limestone, often in woodland and spreading into large colonies by its rhizomes. Flowering in dense shade is often shy; in sun, prolific, but growth is far dwarfer. The upright leaves are borne in pairs, whether the shoot includes a flowering raceme or not.

The clone usually cultivated has larger flowers than are seen in the wild and they are quite large enough without seeking increased size from 'Fortin's Giant'. Var. *rosea* is dirty pink. 'Variegata' has yellow leaf veins, which is pretty, but large sections of a colony will have plain green leaves while the flowers are as small as the wilding's.

Lily-of-the-valley has a reputation for being temperamental. It is always seeking new territory at a colony's margins and takes in paving cracks, when questing. Its value as a garden plant is limited, although it can look pretty with forget-me-nots nearby. I have read of its scent being transported on the air to an admirer sitting nearby but I have not had this experience. Probably because I pick everything within reach to enjoy near where I sit indoors.

Convolvulus

CONVOLVULACEAE

Convolvulus althaeoides subsp. **tenuissimus** (60cm/2ft climbing) is a charming perennial which either dies fairly quickly or makes a fair bid to get out of control, for it has the kind of running rootstock that we associate with convolvulus. Its finely divided foliage is pale grey while the flowers are a soft and pleasing shade of pink. Excellent for running through paving cracks where nothing could be easily planted, and not really difficult to control if you put your mind to it.

C. sabatius (syn. *C. mauritanicus*) (trailing) is generally treated as a tender perennial to set out for the summer in troughs, ornamental pots and hanging baskets. In a sunny position and on lightish soil, it will often prove hardy for many years, especially if its old stems and foliage are not cut back until the spring. Some strains are hardier than others; in my experience, the dark blue forms are tender.

The flowers are open funnels, diagonally creased in a rather intriguing way. Their lavender colouring is richest on opening in the morning. A freely growing plant will flower pretty continuously throughout the summer. Division on a small scale can be practised in spring, but cuttings of young shoots are the normal method of increase.

C. cneorum (30cm/1ft) is a highly desirable shrub of which you will be proud if it survives a few winters – most easily achieved in rather poor soil and on the edge of a retaining wall in full sun. It is evergreen, with silky grey, spathulate leaves. Flower buds are formed in a terminal cluster, in autumn, and may be killed in winter. If not, the flowers – white with a blush reverse – will make a great display in May. On vigorously growing plants, there is a worthwhile second flowering in the autumn. The plant makes a rounded hummock, wider than high. Increase from cuttings of soft young shoot tips.

Coreopsis

ASTERACEAE/COMPOSITAE

Coreopsis are renowned for their penetrating and clear shades of yellow, arousing terror in those unable to handle this colour. **Coreopsis grandiflora** (60cm/2ft) is a rangy perennial of which the best known cultivar, for many years, was the single 'Badengold'. Although good for cutting, it is an unsatisfactory border plant with a tendency to relapse into a non-flowering condition. There is a similar failing in some of the seed strains, with semi-double flowers, such as 'Early Sunrise' (1m/3ft) and 'Sunray' (45cm/1½ft). From a spring sowing, some plants will flower, some will not. Early sowing helps. Once a plant has flowered freely, it is better discarded. Those plants that have not flowered in their first year, if sufficiently numerous, are worth treating as biennials and keeping for a second.

9   *C. verticillata* (60cm/2ft) is a reliable perennial, making a dense tangle of yellow rhizomes. Its habit is stiffly upright and its finely divided leaves are a great asset. Flowering July–August, the individual daisies are half the size of *C. grandiflora*, but numerous and effective. I prefer this type-plant to the AGM-winning *C. v.* 'Grandiflora', which is coarser. The pale yellow 'Moonbeam' (30cm/1ft) is an attractive colour but generally gives a miserable account of itself, with spidery flowers and a spidery habit. Where summers are hotter, it behaves better. This species likes a heavy, moisture-retentive soil.

The October-flowering **C. tripteris** (2m/6ft or more) has sheaves of small yellow daisies, excellent for picking but of less use as a garden plant.

Coriaria

CORIARIACEAE

A strange little genus, distinct, easily recognised yet seemingly without relations. The simple leaves are arranged, often with elegance, either side of a wand-like stem. Hardiness is questionable and the plant often dies back in winter to a woody base.

Best known is **Coriaria terminalis** var. **xanthocarpa** (60cm/2ft). Of suckering habit, its growth is also wide-spreading. Each shoot has a terminal spray of insignificant flowers, but the five petals enlarge, become deep yellow and berry-like and eventually enclose the actual fruit. They make a worthwhile display if not prematurely eaten by birds. There are other species, like **C. microphylla** (syn. *C. thymifolia*) (1m/3ft), which deserve to be considered as foliage plants.

Cortaderia

POACEAE/GRAMINAE

The largest grasses we can flower are included in this genus. From swampy areas in New Zealand comes **Cortaderia richardii** (3m/10ft) correctly *C. fulvida*. Its early-flowering habit makes it particularly popular (often as a front garden specimen) in Scotland, where it will be flowering by August or earlier. Its panicles lean outwards,

◁ **15** *Sisyrinchium striatum, Geranium sanguineum* var. *striatum* and an early-flowering grass soaring behind.

16 A bergenia taking on purplish tints in winter, and the straps of *Yucca filamentosa* 'Variegata'.

17 The fern *Dryopteris wallichiana* with tender *Begonia scharfii*, which flowers generously.

18 Arum lilies, *Zantedeschia aethiopica*; *Gunnera tinctoria*'s large, indented leaves; grass-like *Carex elata* 'Aurea'. ▷

19

19 Begonias, the dainty white *Impatiens pseudoviola* and a self-sown annual amaranthus (centre).

20 Our native hard fern, *Blechnum spicant*, showing upright fertile fronds surrounded by a collar of sterile ones. ▷

22

◁ 21   The bramble *Rubus cockburnianus* 'Goldenvale' with willow gentian *Gentiana asclepiadea* in August.

22   Naturalised snakeshead fritillaries, *Fritillaria meleagris*, generally purple but with many albinos here.

23   Late June–flowering *Eryngium alpinum*, with tight rosettes of *Geranium pratense* 'Plenum Violaceum'.   ▷

giving them a one-sided appearance. In texture, they are on the thin side. A well-flowered group is handsome at its peak but bad weather makes a terrible mess of it, later on.

The pampas grass, **C. selloana** (variable height to 3.6m/12ft), is South American and there are many variants, some dioecious. Many seedlings have been raised and there is much rubbish about, though it may masquerade under as august a name as 'Sunningdale Silver'. Safest to beg a piece from a colony you have admired. Only in spring and summer should these grasses be disturbed and divided. Old foliage should regularly be strimmed to the ground, in spring. Burning it gives a momentary thrill but leaves a hideous charred mess for weeks afterwards.

Pampas grasses generally flower in autumn, sometimes developing too late in Scotland. They are seen at their best when generously grouped in a landscape setting and reflected in water. In the role of urban front garden dot plants, they have earned a bad name. The glittering sheen on newly opened panicles has remarkable freshness. Even the pink-flowered kinds look good at this stage, from close up, but they melt into their background, at a distance, and they age badly.

'Gold Band' should be called *C. s.* 'Aureolineata' (2.4m/8ft) and it is a good foliage plant, sometimes shy-flowering. 'Pumila' (2m/6ft or more when established,) is relatively small, the upright brushes in dense clusters. They contrast well with late kniphofias (e.g. *Kniphofia rooperi*) and with the scarlet hips of sweetbriar, *Rosa rubiginosa*. Also, in a generous autumn planting, with the blue *Salvia uliginosa* and the yellow sunflower, *Helianthus salicifolius*.

Corydalis

PAPAVERACEAE/FUMARIACEAE

All *Corydalis* have spikes or dense racemes of tubular, asymmetric flowers in spring and early summer. Their airy, pinnate leaves are an asset. They like part-shade; the Far Eastern species want a leafy, woodland soil.

Commonest are two similar European species which colonise dry walls by self-seeding. **C. lutea** is yellow; **C. ochroleuca** pale yellow and white. Both about 23cm/9in tall. Cheerful and undemanding.

The big noise of recent years has been the Far Eastern **C. flexuosa** (23cm/9in), distinguished by several named cultivars of which 'Père David' is one of the choicest. They flower for quite a long period before going to rest. The flowers, which Beth Chatto evocatively likens to shoals of fish, are a mixture of purple and (to me) a rather uncomfortable shade of electric blue. Although easily increased by division, this species is not easily kept going without the frequent attention of re-planting. Overrated but a great seller.

C. cava 'Alba' (*C. bulbosa* 'Alba') (23cm/9in) will self-sow in part shade and makes a most delightful impression in early spring with spikes of well-spaced white flowers. It will mix well with similarly shade-loving and early-flowering perennials. *C. solida* (15cm/6in) tends to be a rather muddy shade of pinky-mauve but has many good variants and it is easy enough with a mildly running habit. That is April-flowering and so is *C. cheilanthifolia* (23cm/9in), which makes clumps of ferny leaves. These frame clustered racemes of fairly pale yellow flowers with a hint of green in them. It self-sows.

I have not grown but like the look of a more robust species, *C. sempervirens* (60cm/2ft), with elegant glaucous bipinnate leaves and small hooded flowers in a mixture of pinky-mauve and yellow. This works well.

Crambe

BRASSICACEAE/CRUCIFERAE

The two widely cultivated species, *Crambe maritima* (60cm/2ft) and *C. cordifolia* (2.4m/8ft), are perennial; others, like *C. tatarica*, are monocarpic.

Seakale, *C. maritima*, is often the first plant above the tide-line to colonise a shingle beach. The crimped young leaves are purple at first, then glaucous. Flowers begin to open in early May, those lying on the beach and receiving radiated heat opening first. They make a dense, honey-scented white cloud. Spherical seed capsules follow, if you have more than one clone, for cross-pollination. In cultivation, however, stock is often increased vegetatively from root cuttings. In that case, it is best to cut plants right down, as soon as flowered. They will renew themselves with fresh foliage. This is often attacked by Large White butterfly larvae and a frequent search is worth making for clusters of pale yellow eggs, before they have hatched. They are usually on the undersides of the leaves, unless these are upright.

37 Even in a wet climate, such as west Scotland's, *C. cordifolia* is easily grown and flowered provided the ground is well drained. Otherwise the roots will die of bacterial rot. Large, orbicular green leaves are surmounted by a huge open structure of small, white, cruciferous flowers, in June, sweetly scented but reminiscent of drains. If seed is set, the developing capsules will keep the inflorescence alive and comely

for a long time and it can be clothed with annual climbers like *Rhodochiton atrosanguineum*.

Crepis

ASTERACEAE/COMPOSITAE

Despite hot competition, **Crepis incana** (23cm/9in) remains a principal delight in the July garden. It makes a multiple, tufted crown of dandelion-like, grey-green leaves. Most of the public remain uninspired and caustic. Not so when the soft, clear pink dandelion-shaped flowers come into bloom. Then the plant becomes everyone's friend. The colour is entirely unexpected.

Good drainage and an open, sunny position but well nourished soil best suits this plant. It can be struck from root cuttings, but a well-established specimen can be pulled to pieces so that each of many rosettes makes an easily rooted stem cutting.

Crinum

AMARYLLIDACEAE

A genus of large bulbs, mostly from warm regions south of the Equator. Many grow in damp places and may be flooded at certain time of the year. This may explain the bulbs' long neck, which brings the crown and leaves above water level.

Crinum × powellii (1m/3ft) and its white-flowered form, 'Album' (1m/3ft) are the hardiest, being reliable border plants in most of Britain. I also grow *C. × powellii* in shallow water at the margin of my natural pond, and it is happy enough, though without increasing much. The flowers are typically a crude shade of pink, long funnels borne in a typical amaryllid umbel. Rather cheaply scented.

The leaves are deciduous, but long and lanky in their season, definitely not an asset but this disadvantage can be overcome by siting a group so that, from where they are seen, the leaves do not show. The flowers rise well above them. Seen from the other side of a lowish fence is ideal. Give them sun. A hard winter will turn the tops of the bulbs to a mush, but they recover surprisingly. The bulbs are always near to the surface but go deep. They multiply freely so that it is a major operation to dig out an established clump without severe damage to some of the units.

C. moorei and its albino form are reasonably hardy in southern gardens and are far larger growing, with larger blooms to match. This is a majestic species and deserves the space it demands if you can spare it.

Crocosmia

1, 48 *Crocosmia* is a growth industry. New seedlings are constantly being produced (easily done) and there is much duplicate naming, so that nomenclature is in a seething mess. We have lost the good old name *Montbretia* entirely, and gone is Aunt Eliza, the friendly corruption of *Antholyza*. These have sunk into the Bob-a-Job category.

Crocosmias make corms, which build up in chains, one link being added year by year. It is last year's new corm which will produce this year's new shoot, but if the chain is broken up, each link is capable of becoming its own independent unit. The young shoot is produced and starts to elongate, albeit underground, quite early, when most plants are apparently becoming dormant. Therefore, work on replanting colonies should be completed in autumn, if possible (it often isn't, of course), because new shoots readily break off during their handling. Another will be produced but it won't be strong enough to flower. In fact, newly planted crocosmia colonies are often shy in their first season (the debutante syndrome).

On the other hand, some of the most vigorous kinds quickly become congested and cease to flower freely for that reason. You should either be frequently busy with crocosmias or else, with the most vigorous, naturalise them, allowing them to get on with their own business and accepting that there will be a fair amount of blindness.

Crocosmias are most obviously related to gladioli, but on a smaller scale. They vastly cheer the midsummer to autumn garden scene, mostly in shades of yellow, apricot, orange and red. They are exciting garden plants with a flavour of the exotic and their sword leaves generally help them.

The commonest kind, with orange flowers and growing like a weed in many waste places (where it is welcome), is **C. × *crocosmiflora***. It is an important parent of many cultivars. An old one among these is the generally weak-growing 'Solfaterre' (45cm/1½ft), whose apricot-orange flowers are set off by bronzed leaves. It harmonises well with a dwarf, bronze zinnia like 'Chippendale' and I like to mix in the silver-grey tangle of *Artemisia alba* 'Canescens'.

The August-September-flowering 'Citronella' (1m/3ft) is a favourite; vigorous (it needs frequent replanting) and with unusually bright green foliage. The flowers are crocus-yellow and it contrasts nicely, in its season, with heaving 'blue' mounds of *Aster sedifolius*. Unfortunately its name is still being tossed around. It might be 'Sulphurea', but any alternatives I mention will quickly be outdated.

'Emily McKenzie' (30cm/1ft) is a quite large-flowered bicolor; 'Jackanapes' (30cm/1ft) is another, but smaller-flowered. Rather weak but nice above a mauve viola like 'Maggie Mott'. 'Star of the East' (1m/3ft) is vigorous and rather late-flowering, apricot-orange; I fancy it with a late blue agapanthus. There are many more cultivars.

C. masoniorum (75cm/2½ft) appeared on the scenes soon after the Second World War. It is a bright, brash, rather difficult shade of orange, with boldly presented flowers, on an arching, horizontal inflorescence. The type-plant is little seen now, there being preferred hybrids. From a batch of seedlings, I raised 'Dixter Flame' (75cm/2½ft), which is rich red.

9, 46 One of the most popular of all crocosmias is Alan Bloom's 'Lucifer' (1.2m/4ft) – immensely vigorous, vivid undiluted red and having handsomely ridged foliage. It does have a rather short (July) season and is apt to fall around if not somehow supported. The seed heads are attractive. If you want a daring combination, allow the magenta-flowered *Lychnis coronaria* to seed itself around a colony. For spring, in among 'Lucifer's' corms, I have the celandine, *Ranunculus ficaria* 'Brazen Hussy'; yellow against bronze foliage.

Having small red flowers, **C. pottsii** is on a par with *C.* × *crocosmiflora*; too invasive and shy-flowering for border use, but holding its own in turf. As does **C. paniculata** (1m/3ft), which is naturalised in many parts of Ireland. Broad, ridged sword leaves, still looking good when brown but before being frosted. The small flowers are deep crimson red. Its naming has gone through *Antholyza paniculata* and *Curtonus paniculatus*.

Montbretia/Crocosmia rosea has been hived off into *Tritonia*, and is now **T. disticha** subsp. **rubrolucens** (30cm/1ft). It flowers rather briefly in June and is a pleasing shade of pink. The corms are surprisingly large. It is invasive, but when I moved it into meadow conditions, it gave up immediately.

Crocus

IRIDACEAE

Crocus species have a wide distribution in Europe and western Asia, but those, in many cases, only approximate to the crocuses we grow in our gardens. These are either hybrids or selections for their showiness, and in many cases they are sterile. Any naturalising we wish to bring about must be done by dividing and replanting our stock.

A background of meadow grass particularly suits the genus. In it, the lank foliage can be 'lost'. Luckily, there are a number of robust crocus, whether hybridised or not, which do self-sow with a will, so we tend to lean heavily on them.

This flower has the joyful quality of opening wide to sunshine and warmth. While mousy and demure for much of the 24 hours in a day, when dark, dull, chilly or raining, the flower, on expanding, more than doubles its size and luminosity. The inside of the petals, or perianth segments, thus revealed is far brighter than the flower's exterior, beautifully marked though that may be, and the central stigma, yellow, orange or red, becomes a feature in its own right. Like tulips, crocuses seem to communicate *joie de vivre*. They are among the most gladdening of flowers.

Also the most maddening, because they so often remain resolutely closed just when you most want them to display themselves. Perhaps four days out of five, in February, and two out of three in October. If you can only be in your garden at weekends you may miss out on their display entirely, and it is no comfort to be told (with an element of *Schadenfreude*) that an hour after you had left on a Monday morning the crocuses had revelled as never before. So it is understandable that some gardeners show a preference for snowdrops over crocuses. The crocus lover can only plead that when they oblige, crocuses are unbeatable.

They divide themselves into two groups: those that flower in autumn and those that flower from January to March – in our gardens, that is. In the wild, the latter may run on into July, thanks to altitude and snow cover.

Many species are difficult in cultivation. If you read 'easy in a sun frame', this means that the corm wants a complete baking, in summer. The sun frame is not a beautiful display unit and most of us will be glad to dispense with it.

Autumn

Autumn-flowering crocuses are all in shades of mauve, purple and white. None easy enough for us to grow are yellow or orange. They are frequently confused with *Colchicum*, which are loosely termed autumn crocuses. Colchicums, with their six stamens, belong to the lily family; crocuses, with three stamens, to that of the iris. Colchicums often have a pink flush in their mauve colouring; crocuses never do. The leaves are entirely different, but as they are often borne a long time after flowering, this may be of no help.

The two best species for naturalising in grass are *C. speciosus* (12.5cm/5in) and *C.*

nudiflorus (12.5cm/5in). Given meadow conditions, the grass will probably have been cut and carried for hay or composting in July or early August. If at all possible, give it another cut just before the season of the colchicums and autumn crocuses, so that they show up to best advantage. Then, a final cut-and-carry in November, or even early December, if the ground is not too sodden, after the autumn-flowerers have finished but in readiness for snowdrops and crocuses from January, on.

C. speciosus, as marketed, has quite a large, but sterile, bloom and it makes the bluest impression of any crocus, thanks to the heavy, dark veining of the segments. These highlight a brilliant scarlet stigma. There is a strong sweet scent (if you lower yourself to savour it), similar to that of some early-flowering tulips. 'Albus' is rather thin-textured to make a really white bloom, but would look good against a dark mat of *Acaena microphylla*. *C. speciosus* makes quite a large colony, in time, and a great display, usually in late September or early October, but timing depends to quite an extent on moisture availability. If the ground is dry, flowering is delayed. The bright green 'grass' of its foliage, stands out in its freshness, in February, before grass itself has greened up much.

Spring is a good time for dividing and spreading this species around, as also **C. nudiflorus**. That flowers a warmer shade of purple and its perianth tube, which acts as a stalk, is stronger than in *C. speciosus*, which generally takes on a reclining, Mme Recamier position, after the first day of flowering.

C. nudiflorus has a stoloniferous corm. Not being plump and easily stored for marketing, it is much less readily available and more expensive. But just as easily grown.

C. kotschyanus (syn. *C. zonatus*), is pale mauve with a yellow base. I suppose it depends on your source, but the clone I bought, years ago, scarcely ever flowers, though it makes a healthy tuft of 'grass'. I much admired its var. *leucopharynx* (white throat), at Beth Chatto's, in late October. It grew in her gravel garden, making clusters of lilac-blue flowers, shading to white at the centre and with white stems. Also **C. medius**, which is an outstandingly rich shade of lilac with bright red stigmata. It was flowering (in the gravel garden) with bright pink *Nerine bowdenii* and light purple *Verbena bonariensis* (hovering above), for company.

C. pulchellus does well and increases, for me, setting good seed. It is light mauve and I have it with the autumn-flowering *Saxifraga fortunei*, with open panicles of lopsided white flowers. They are in a border. The only trouble with crocuses in border company is that you tend to forget where they are, in their off-season. But that is where I grow the November-flowering **C. ochroleucus**. It has small chalices, pure, solid white; yellow at the centre. Its leaves are there with the flowers, as is also the case with **C. serotinus** subsp. **salzmanii**, which has pale mauve flowers and needs a baking to be prolific. If you grew these autumn-leafers in turf, they might suffer from the last mowing.

Winter and Spring

The first winter crocus may, in a mild run-up, be out before the new year. Some time in January is usual, while in the winter that I'm writing 3 February saw the first, which was 'Blue Pearl', a hybrid between *C. biflorus* (always some shade of blue) and *C. chrysanthus*. Many of the crocuses listed under *C. chrysanthus* are hybrids. This species is the shape of an electric light bulb, when closed, opening to a bowl. It often has dark, longitudinal stripes on the outer segments. That is the way 'Snow Bunting' should be, and otherwise cream-white, clumping up well, early flowering and sweetly scented. More frequently, nowadays, some other small white crocus is given this name, and it may be late-flowering, odourless, pure white and without the dark markings. I like to buy some 'Snow Bunting' every autumn to grow in containers, in a cold frame, and have handy to bring indoors for a few hours each day, so as to be able to enjoy their sight and scent at close range.

There are many colours among the cultivars under the *C. chrysanthus* umbrella, and they are usually at their peak in late February (in Sussex). 'Gipsy Girl' is a favourite, with bronze outer striping, otherwise orange-yellow. That is early. 'Cream Beauty' is soft, pale yellow. 'Advance' is amazing, pale buff yellow within but palest blue without. 'Ladykiller' is almost white inside but has a broad purple bar on the outside. The older 'Warley' is similar.

All these, when planted close to one another, interbreed, with thrilling results and you are tempted to pick out your winners for further development, segregation and naming. Don't, is my advice. Leave that to others and get on with your gardening.

C. sieberi 'Violet Queen' is a neat, early-flowering little crocus of rich violet colouring that mixes with the others but the two supremos, in February (besides *C. chrysanthus*) are *C. flavus* subsp. *flavus* and *C. tommasinianus*. Both are fertile and self-sow. They naturalise well together, but do not appear to interbreed.

C. flavus subsp. *flavus* (which we knew more comfortably as *C. aureus*) is small-flowered but of such an intense shade of orange that it is certainly large enough to put its personality across. It is the obvious parent of the ever-popular 'Dutch Yellow' crocus, which you see lined out along the roadside margin of suburban front gardens. Its proper name is *C.* × *luteus* 'Golden Yellow'. It is sterile, but clumps up with a will and is easily divided, after flowering, to spread around. That is early-flowering, on the orange side of yellow and vigorously cheering in the same way as forsythia, but a few weeks earlier.

C. tommasinianus has been appropriately likened to a toothpick, when closed, so pale and slender and unobtrusive. But when the sun beats upon it, there is a transformation scene and it will open almost flat, pale mauve in colouring, but not wishy-washy. However, the 'Whitewell Purple' clone is well worth acquiring. These, by self-seeding, will form vast colonies, and they can, if not overdone, be allowed to spread themselves in flower borders, especially under deciduous shrubs. If it comes to bedding the borders, in summer and autumn, the crocus corms can be trusted to look after themselves, and can be ignored.

C. imperati is like a more solid Tommy, of a richer mauve-purple and with handsome, dark, parallel striping on the outside of its outer segments.

In March we reach flood tide of the Dutch hybrid or polyploid forms of **C. vernus**. They are white, purple or in a range of intermediate shades, some of them stripey. They are sometimes sniffed at for being coarse, but I would say showy, rather, and no harm in that. They clump up and they self-sow and they make a huge mantle of colour which, when naturalised under meadow conditions, is unmatched. Furthermore, they can be mixed into daffodils and narcissi, and will still show up, their successors being quite short at that time.

A bulb planting tool, operated from a standing position, is the one for gaining a random effect, when initiating a crocus colony. It is available, but apt to be expensive. Vary the distance between the plugs taken out, otherwise you will end up with straight rows, however random you thought you were being. The short-cut method of turning back three sides of a flap of turf and setting clumps of corms under that, before replacing the flap, always gives horribly artificial-looking results.

I have seen rose beds underplanted with these crocuses, to stunning effect. Prune the roses as hard as you dare, before the crocuses get going, so as not to be unnecessarily aware of that ugly array of thorny sticks. Crocuses enjoy good living, so they will not object to the heavy manurial treatment generally accorded Hybrid Tea and Floribunda roses. By the time the roses are ready to flower, the crocus foliage will have died away.

But there are better ways of gardening than with beds of roses.

Curtonus – see Crocosmia

Cynara

ASTERACEAE/COMPOSITAE

The cardoons come from Mediterranean regions, their hardiness in Britain always a little questionable but often dependable. They are handsome both in leaf and flower. *Cynara cardunculus* (1.8-2.4m/6-8ft), having often been raised from seed, is variable. The strain I have been growing for fifty years is handsomer than that most often seen, more widely branching and with more divided, grey-green leaves. A wonderful back-of-border plant, first for its foliage in spring, then for its candelabrums of blossom, producing platforms of scented, lavender-blue blossom in August; finally for its winter skeletons, well worth leaving till spring. The only attention needed by these long-lived plants is support of the strongest calibre, given as the inflorescences become heavy.

Good seed is set after hot, dry summers and remains viable in cool storage for at least five years. The ripe capitulum explodes to much more scenic winter effect if filled with viable seed, than if merely soggy and sterile.

There is an excellent strain growing in the Chelsea Physic Garden which comes more or less true from seed. It is dwarfer than normal and more prickly on leaves and flower heads, which is a handsome attribute.

The edible globe artichoke, albeit often segregated as a separate species, **C. scolymus**, is certainly a derivative of *C. cardunculus*, selected for large, spineless heads. It should always be acquired as a named clone, never as seedlings, which are of inferior eating quality. Grown in an ornamental flower border, it lets you down once beheaded for eating, in June, or earlier. Best to cut the stems right down, at that stage, and to hope for a late summer crop of young foliage, as with crambes and rheums.

C. hystrix (1m/3ft), from North Africa, should be *C. baetica* subsp. *maroccana*. It makes a virtue of being incredibly spiny. The leaves are narrow and the plant generally gives an impression of terminal illness.

Cynoglossum

BORAGINACEAE

Literally, hound's tongue, referring to the leaf shape, particularly of our native biennial **Cynoglossum officinale**, which grows around rabbit holes on alkaline soils and near the sea, untouched by rabbits, as is common elder.

C. nervosum (60cm/2ft) is a very hardy perennial, though often short-lived in the south. Excellent in Scotland. Clump-forming, it carries smallish, deep blue flowers May-June. Good on poor soils with snow-in-summer, *Cerastium tomentosum*, and yellow lupins.

Far more arresting is the dazzling, pure blue biennial **C. amabile** (60cm/2ft), which can also be grown as an annual. Best sown in autumn, however, but not very hardy. Lovely with *Leymus arenarius*.

Cyperus

CYPERACEAE

Most of this genus is from the tropics, but galingale, **Cyperus longus** (1.2m/4ft) is a hardy native and looks excellent in a fair-sized pond. A branching inflorescence above grassy leaves is its main feature. The dead foliage provides excellent cover for water birds, and moorhens nest in it in spring.

The umbrella plant, **C. involucratus** (syn. *C. alternifolius*) (60cm/2ft), is generally grown as a house plant but can be plunged into shallow pond water in summer. The foliage must first be gradually accustomed to the much brighter light outdoors.

C. eragrostis (60cm/2ft), better known as **C. vegetus**, is generally hardy and, for its strong shape, a valuable garden plant. Naked scapes are crowned by radiating, leafy bracts and these subtend a central boss of yellowy-green 'flowers' (they hardly appear as such). It self-sows freely but single specimens are more effective than a colony.

Most exciting is the Egyptian papyrus, **C. papyrus** (2m/6ft), which is tender and requires a fairly high winter temperature, but goes like a bomb in temperate summer conditions, planted out in June. It makes great mops of bright green, finely divided leaves, and contrasts well with castor oil (*Ricinus*), cannas and dahlias. Easily raised from seed, young plants are more conveniently accommodated in winter than large old ones.

Cyrtomium

POLYPODIACEAE

The Japanese holly fern, **Cyrtomium falcatum** (60cm/2ft), is a handsome evergreen, traditionally used as a house or conservatory plant. It often self-sows under greenhouse benches. The uncomplicated fronds are pinnate, with substantial, glossy, angularly shaped pinnae. It is often hardy in the garden, but gets away to a rather slow start in spring. So it is more rewarding if potted up and housed, in autumn, returning it to the garden for the summer months.

C. fortunei seems to be of similar hardiness and can be treated in the same way. Its pinnae lack the gloss of *C. falcatum* but it is still a fine species.

D

Dactylorhiza

ORCHIDACEAE

Of all the hardy, terrestrial orchids, those of the genus *Dactylorhiza* are the most likely to succeed as garden plants. And, at last, they are being offered by quite a number of nursery enterprises – a situation which is likely to improve, I think. The point about them is, that their tuberous roots make up quickly, so that clumps can easily be divided to make more. Seed is a possibility with all these orchids, where it is produced, but techniques are tricky. They are, however, being developed.

D. foliosa (60cm/2ft) (syn. *D. maderensis*) has long spikes of very bright, reddish purple flowers. It is a winner, excellent in part shade among lower-growing *Polystichum* ferns. **D. elata** (60cm/2ft) has longer, looser foliage and paler mauve flowers. It is strong and willing. Then there is **D. × grandis**, which I showed to the RHS, thinking it was just a good form – spotted leaves, substantial deep mauve spikes – of our native *D. fuchsii*. It was given an award, subject to naming, and Kew came up with this hybrid. That grows strongly. All three flower in June.

26 **D. fuchsii** itself grows wild in the woods around my home and (helped by my mother and me, when I was young and innocent) it established so enthusiastically in our meadow areas that it seeds itself everywhere. As it does not flower till June, its seeds are not ripe for dispersal till August. We are careful not to cut any of these

areas until we are certain that dispersal has taken place. The seeds are small and light, easily borne on the wind, so we have *D. fuchsii* in paving cracks and in borders that have been left undisturbed for a few years.

Clearly, the fungal microrhiza that it needs for a successful partnership, are ready to hand. Experience has taught me that it is the native orchid species growing wild around us – and no others – which will establish easily in captivity. The others, with us, are the early purples, *Orchis mascula*; the green-winged orchis, *O. morio*; and the twayblade, *Listera ovata*. These sow themselves abundantly, and we have masses of them at Dixter, especially of *O. morio*.

Dactylorhiza fuchsii is very variable; sometimes washy, with small spikes, sometimes bold and showy, with rich mauve spikes. So, if you are buying a plant, it is wise to make enquiries on this point or, ideally, to see the plant in flower that you intend buying.

Dahlia

Asteraceae/Compositae

2   Dahlias epitomise the flamboyance of late summer and early autumn. Faint-hearted gardeners cannot abide the way they flaunt their brilliant, clean colours. How are they to be handled?

How, indeed? Many of those who love them would say: 'grow them in beds by themselves'. That can look good but it is the exhibitor's recommendation, individual blooms, often of great size, being the attraction. Good luck to them, but it is not my way of gardening. It should be possible to assimilate dahlias into the garden's fabric, and indeed it is, that being by far the most appealing way to see them.

Their own foliage is generally mundane – pinnate, like a potato's; rank-smelling when handled, in a way that I personally enjoy but is only occasionally a definite asset. The one variety cited as desirable, by garden snobs – 'the only dahlia we allow' –

14   is 'Bishop of Llandaff' (1.2m/4ft). And it is good – semi-single, pure red and with purple leaves that are almost fern-like in their dissection.

For the most part, their foliage can easily be passed over if they flower abundantly and if they are associated with other kinds of plants whose main strength is their foliage – a grass like the green-and-white *Arundo donax* var. *versicolor*, castor oil (*Ricinus communis*) with palmate leaves in green or purple, cannas grown principally for their foliage, or the strange, pinnate-leaved *Amicia zygomeris*. Dahlias are good, too, for pepping up a haze of michaelmas daisies, or to contrast with the spikes of light blue *Salvia uliginosa* (2m/6ft) or deep blue *S. guaranitica* 'Blue Enigma'.

Dahlias spell excitement and we can do with some of that in our lives. They originate from Central America and were much hybridised in the 19th century. A few species are seen around, mostly grown as curiosities. The giant **Dahlia imperialis** (5m/15ft) is of tree-like proportions, with a woody trunk. The leaves are handsome but it hardly deserves garden space, as flowering, if reached at all, is so late in the autumn and the flowers quite small, though numerous. It is hardy in maritime regions like the Isle of Wight.

D. merckii (2m/6ft) is surprisingly hardy, even in central Scotland. It has a following but I'm not in the queue. Pleasantly pinnate leaves on a tall, rangy plant, the size and numbers of whose flowers give no sense of display. A rather unpleasant mauve in colour, the 'white' form still retains an all too broad hint of dirty mauve. **D. coccinea** (1.2m/4ft), a single red, is nice.

Not being quite hardy, dahlias do present cultural problems. They get through the winter with tubers in which carbohydrates (inulin, not starch) are stored. You can risk leaving them in the ground, and this works best with the seed strains that provide us with dahlias for bedding. They are abundant makers of tubers. I have had one, a single, left undisturbed for ten years, that still regularly puts in an appearance. If you haven't the time or space to store, you can still have dahlias. The danger, especially on heavy soils, is from slugs. And from severe frost, of course.

Don't lift your dahlias until their growth has been frosted. An open autumn will often promote tuber formation right at the end of the season. Some of the most delectable dahlias in other respects, are notoriously poor tuber makers. It is better, in their case, not to store them entirely dry, because the slender apology for tubers that they make will simply shrivel away. We pot or box them up into old potting soil and give them occasional waterings through the winter.

The method of carrying them forward used by professionals and open to any of us, if we will take the trouble, is by producing pot tubers. Reserve stock is grown in pots – deep, 12.5cm/5in pots are ideal – right through the summer, plunged into the ground in a reserve area. Flowering is discouraged by disbudding. In this confined space, the dahlia will make fine tubers, however reluctant it may normally be to do so. The tubers, in their pots, are overwintered under cool, frost-free conditions, as usual. When brought into warmth in late winter or early spring, the sprouts made will provide material for cuttings and your stock for the next season is assured.

The normal procedure, with willing tuber makers, is to sprout them on a bench in a heated greenhouse, for early results. Detach the shoots when no more than

7.5cm/3in long, using a sharp knife to detach them from the tuber at the point of juncture, and root them, either individually or several in a pot, under close conditions. When rooted, pot into a more nourishing compost and harden off for planting out in early June.

If you have no artificial heating, sun heat, as in a close, cold frame, will be perfectly adequate for achieving the same results, but results will be delayed. In fact, there is quite an advantage in having a stock of late-made plants with which to fill gaps left by annuals or biennials, in late July or early August.

Tubers carried on from year to year, will be most people's idea of dahlia-growing. A good cluster of tubers can be split. The growth buds are not made on the tuber itself, but just above it, at the base of last year's stem. You should promote growth from your tubers before attempting to split them. Then you can see what you are doing.

For a bedding display of plants not much more than 60cm/2ft high, raising a seed strain has become increasingly popular, of recent years. This is to treat them as annuals, without worrying about carrying stock forward. Of course, you can do so, and a seed-raised batch will enable you to mark and save the best examples, while discarding the rest.

Mixed seed strains make for a very jolly overall display, seen from a distance, though easily faulted on closer inspection. I have had particular pleasure from a 'Dandy' mixture, this consisting of Collerette dahlias. A single flower has a collar of half-sized, narrow rays, often of a different colour, within the principal circle of broad 'petals'.

In some strains, like 'Burnished Bronze', the leaves are all chocolate coloured. When the flowers are light, in contrast, as in the dwarf, named clone 'Yellow Hammer', the flowers are well highlighted. But if the flowers themselves are on the dark side, the effect is funereal.

Single-colour seed strains are generally the most effective. 'Sunny Yellow' is one such and the dark red, single 'Mignon Rotes Band'. But in some cases the breeders have been too clever by half, so reducing plant size that the richest growing conditions become necessary and even then, a short burst of blossom is followed by little more. The 'Figaro' strains belong here.

If you are raising bedding dahlias from seed, there is no necessity for providing heat artificially. You can sow in May, in a cold frame, potting the seedlings off individually so that they are eventually in 12.5cm/5in pots and ready to burst into flower in early July, when they can be planted out to replace biennials like sweet williams and other early flowerers. That way you will escape the common trap, following an earlier sowing, of having plants that turn yellowish because the weather in May is so much colder than they like.

Among standard, named dahlias, vegetatively propagated, the two main classes are Decorative, having a full flower with flattened rays; Cactus and Semi-Cactus, with rays rolled back so as to make a spiky-looking bloom. A section of Decorative has been hived off into Waterlily, where the bloom is looser than usual, with fewer rays and a more relaxed look. The pale, slightly greeny yellow 'Glorie van Heemstede' is one of the oldest of these. Pompon dahlias, with formal, ball-shaped flowers no more than 5cm/2in across, used to appeal to me strongly. I have gone off them, their general effect on a by no means dwarf plant, being spotty.

The best way to choose dahlias is not from the show bench, where the examples have been disbudded and appear different from the way they are when grown as un-doctored garden flowers, but on the trial ground, as at Wisley, where there is a large dahlia trial every summer. You can ask for suppliers' addresses to be sent you at the end of each season. Many, unfortunately, offer no mail order service. You have to collect. Misnaming is only too frequent. Dahlias come and go, but I shall describe some of those that I regard highly and enjoy or have enjoyed in my own garden.

54 'Claire de Lune' is a Collerette, wherein the collar is the same pure yellow as the single row of 'petals' framing it. A fresh-looking dahlia that goes well with the light purple of *Verbena bonariensis* (1.5m/5ft). Another, most intriguing, Collerette is named 'Chimberazo' (1m/3ft). The 'petals' are deep crimson red with a contrasting pale yellow collar, flecked red. 'Ellen Houston' (75cm/2½ft) is, like 'Yellow Hammer' (see above), a dwarf bedding dahlia with bronze leaves. The blooms are semi-double with a dark disc and deep orange rays. It has a longish span, but late-struck cuttings produce plants that are particularly luminous and free right to the end of the dahlia season (which I always hope will last through October). 'Grenadier' (1m/3ft), with rich red colouring, goes well with it from late-struck cuttings. It is naturally one of the earliest in flower, by the beginning of July. I don't at all mind having dahlias flowering then. Not for me the affected shudders of those who exclaim 'Not dahlias (or hydrangeas) already!', as though a twinge of frostbite was already numbing their extremities on the mere sight of a flower they consider should be relegated to September, at earliest. 'Grenadier' is a small, open-centred decorative with re-flexed rays.

The extremely popular 'David Howard' (1.5m/5ft) deserves every scrap of the praise lavished on it. Above bronze foliage, it carries a prodigal, non-stop succession of rich apricot-orange, smallish decorative blooms that show up brightly from afar. To an extent, dead-heading might be ignored on this variety, so far as looks go, as new blooms and foliage are continuously rising above and concealing what has gone before.

An excellent, long- and free-flowering small cactus dahlia of pure, mid-red colouring, is 'Alva's Doris' (1.2m/4ft) and there is no problem in overwintering its tubers as we have had with a couple of the most dazzling scarlet varieties, 'Geerling's Indian Summer' (1.5m/5ft), a medium-small cactus, and 'Jobi's Scarlet' (1.2m/4ft), another small cactus. 'Witteman's Superba' (1.5m/5ft) is a top-notcher in the red field; rich red – not too dark to show up from a distance – of medium semi-cactus form and size, long retaining a somewhat button-like centre which shows a purple reverse to the small rays composing it. Truly sumptuous. Though technically described as a small decorative, I should give 'Pearl of Heemstede' (1.2m/4ft) waterlily decorative status. Its pink blooms (I don't grow many pink dahlias – it is a difficult colour to get right – have a soothing air and go well with the purple-flowered *Solanum rantonnetii* (a tender shrub, whose height varies according to pruning) and the purple-leaved castor oil, *Ricinus communis* 'Carmencita'.

Near top in my list, if I had to choose an order, would be 'Hillcrest Royal' (1.5m/5ft), a spiky medium cactus of brilliant purple (not quite magenta) colouring. It is wonderful behind the pure red spires of the lobelia 'Queen Victoria' (1m/3ft), but even more so with a good form, having the widest white stripes, of the grass *Arundo donax* var. *versicolor* (1.2-1.5m/4-5ft). Back these up with more good leaves, as it might be the glaucous juvenile foliage of seedling *Eucalyptus gunnii*.

Several viruses affect and weaken dahlias, noticeable from twisted foliage with yellow streaking and stunted growth. The symptoms are most obvious early in the season and may become masked later on, if vigorous growth is promoted by generous feeding (which all dahlias appreciate). Affected plants should be destroyed.

Earwigs are the most tiresome pest. Trapping earwigs is one thing but disposing of them thereafter, is another. When cornered, I prefer a nasty systemic spray. The black (broad) bean aphis must be sprayed, also.

The question of dead-heading is important in dahlias. Partly this is a question of appearance – not so important in the single or semi-double-flowered kinds, which automatically shed petals from faded blooms, but essential with the doubles, which need our help to remove their debris. The other reason is that if the plant is allowed to ripen seed, it will not need to make more flower buds, since its whole object in life will have been fulfilled. For a prolonged display, we need to thwart this tendency.

It is no good just pulling the heads off. The remaining stalks will build up into an unsightly forest. You must cut back, with secateurs or knife and leaving no snags, to a stem branch above which there is another bud developing. Ideally, this should be done every 3 or 4 days. With bedding dahlias, raised from seed, so many dead heads are involved that you may understandably feel 'this is too much'. Reluctantly, I have to acknowledge the existence of a human element.

If you are dead-heading bedding kinds, which are much visited by bees, it is as well to wear gloves, so as not to be stung by a sleepy lurker.

Bedding types should not need to be staked. All the rest do. Serious dahlia growers, by which I mean those whose focus is trained on show-worthy blooms, knock in their hefty posts before planting. Or they may plant, stop the main shoot so that the plant branches and then knock in a stout cane for each resulting shoot.

Most of us will prefer not to be contemplating an array of undisguised canes or posts for a large part of the summer. My preference is to leave staking till it becomes necessary and then to use canes of a suitable stoutness but not projecting far above the plant. Only two ties should be needed – one immediately, the second, later on. Make a clove hitch around the cane, leaving plenty of soft twine at the free end. Loop this around each principal stem as you come to it and finish off close to the cane with a reef knot. If there are several canes, you will take each of them into your circuit, with a clove hitch, as you come to it.

Danaë

RUSCACEAE

Clearly related to the butcher's broom, *Ruscus aculeatus*, the monospecific **Danaë racemosa** (60-120cm/2-4ft) has similar leaf-like stems, called cladodes, but is otherwise much softer textured. It makes sprays of cheerful, yellow-green foliage, for which it is grown, its height varying according to how pleased it is with its siting and treatment. Excellent on limy soils, it also prefers half-shade and a rich, moisture-retaining, leaf soil.

Each spray lasts about two years and there is a great surge of juicy, new shoots (not unlike asparagus) from the base, each spring. Just before these appear is the time to remove old sprays, cutting as low as possible. Younger ones, still in good nick, go excellently with yellow trumpet daffodils in flower arrangements, but I also grow 'February Gold' daffodils in front of my Danaë colony.

The fruit consists of bright orange berries, borne terminally on the sprays, but is produced only shyly, in this country. I wondered if there was some cross-pollination problem and if more than one clone was necessary. So I raised seedlings from the few berries borne. The seed germinated easily and seedlings were planted out near the old plants, but made no difference to berry production. We need hotter summers.

As a foliage plant, I rate this highly.

Darmera

SAXIFRAGACEAE

The Water Saxifrage, **Darmera peltata** (1m/3ft) was known as *Saxifraga peltata*, when I was young, then as *Peltiphyllum peltatum* and next.....? It is one of the best of all hardy waterside plants, coming from the western States of the USA.

It has a thick, rhizomatous rootstock which, in late April, starts to throw up a succession of 38cm/15in flowering stems, well before the leaves appear. The stems are thick, pink and fleshy, covered with soft bristles, and are crowned by a domed inflorescence of pink, starry blossom. This is pretty as an Easter bonnet, but sparingly produced in Scotland where, however, darmera is a superior foliage plant.

The leaves are peltate, like a miniature gunnera, and ground-covering. In autumn, in the south, they just turn brown, but in Scotland they can generally be relied upon to turn crimson, in the same way as does *Rodgersia podophylla* (q.v.).

Delphinium

RANUNCULACEAE

Like aconitums, delphiniums belong to a branch of their family with irregular flowers. The showiest part is composed of sepals, one of which carries a spur, although, when fully doubled, the spur disappears. The petals compose the 'bee' or 'eye'. Leaves are a handsome feature. A group of delphiniums in a mixed border, in April and May, is a feast in itself and an excellent setting for oriental poppies, for instance.

In writing that, it is of the **Delphinium elatum** hybrids that I am thinking, the kind of delphinium that first comes to mind when this flower is mentioned, quintessentially with long spikes of pure blue flowers, perhaps with a black 'bee', perhaps with a white. Delphinium spires have a unique stateliness in the June-July border. Other colours that come naturally to them are almost as welcome as blue:

alternating blue and mauve, mauve itself, pinky mauve (often called pink), purple and white. The 'bee' varies in colour between black and white with a kind of sooty grey somewhere in between. They are matchless cut flowers (until they suddenly shatter, on the third day), for a spacious setting, especially when combined with the globes of pink peonies. However, since the advent of indispensable 'oasis', we now see delphiniums presented upside-down, as against the poles supporting a festive marquee. Such indignity. How would you like to be presented to the public, upside-down? Never be a party to these antics.

In the garden, the modern hybrids with double or semi-double flowers, often have an unfortunate tendency (as also have double roses) to retain their petals (actually sepals) after they have faded.

Modern hybrids grow exceedingly tall, 2.5m/8ft being nothing unusual. They need secure staking but stakes should reach no higher than just below the spike. If the stem is too bloated and puffy for the spike not to hold up without additional support, as is often the case with seedlings, the plant is useless. I prefer not to stake early, leaving this operation long enough for a single tie to suffice for the season. Stakes are not beautiful and, in a border setting, should be visible for as brief a period as possible.

There are shorter strains available, but when a heavy spike is held on a shortish stem, the result is graceless. But a seed strain like 'Magic Fountains', purporting to be dwarf, is actually quite well balanced as well as manageable.

Delphiniums – the elatum types – should be fully perennial, but improvements which they have undergone in other respects have sometimes resulted in a shorter-lived plant. On heavy soils, they are martyred in winter by slugs, which devour their dormant buds. It helps to heap grit over their crowns.

The year's cycle, for a delphinium, starts with early movement, often in February. When this becomes apparent is a good time for shifting plants, should you need to. Autumn is dangerous, when they are dormant. Unless you are very careful (and that is possible, in your own garden), the root ball can lose sizeable chunks of fragile root and the plant will be unable to make good the damage at that season.

At flowering time, powdery mildew may set in, though this is less common or serious under mixed border conditions than where delphiniums are being grown on their own, as the exhibitor prefers. They must be protected with a suitable fungicide. After flowering, the plants will be cut back, leaving some foliage. They will often sprout again from the base and flower a second time, in September. I welcome this bonus but anti-mildew sprays will need to be repeated.

Propagation of named varieties must nearly always be from cuttings (though division, on a small scale, is possible in spring), made with the young shoots in early spring, when they are some 10-15cm/4-6in long. Each cutting is severed, with a sharp blade, from its juncture with the parent stock. Insert in pots in a light and gritty cutting compost, to half the cutting's length. Rooting needs no special apparatus and will succeed in a close, cold frame, in a light but not scorching position. Apply shading if necessary. After hardening off, the young plants can be planted out at the end of May.

When delphiniums are propagated from seed, this needs to be fresh. Sown in February or (in a cold frame) March or April, the seedlings can be potted individually into square modules, 18 to a seed tray, and will be ready for planting out from mid-May. Flowering will start in late July, the height of the plants in this first year being a couple of feet shorter than in the second, when they will flower from mid-June.

Seed strains, in general, are not being rigorously selected. It was different when the Pacific Hybrids were first launched. Nowadays the commercial seed producers tend to spend as little money on selection as they can get away with. Consequently, although it is well worth the fun of growing them from seed, you need to have high standards on what you will retain. More than half the seedlings are likely to need discarding, but something good should remain. You will do better to purchase seed strains purporting to be in a single colour range, rather than complete mixtures, which are a pretty hopeless jumble.

Really, named varieties that have been through the RHS trials should be preferred. Choose them on the trial ground at Wisley, if you have the chance. Being able to see their relative heights is useful, as are their relative times of flowering.

Florists' flowers come and go, quickly. Here, even so, are comments on a few of the cultivars that please me. 'Skyline' (2.5m/8½ft) is light, clear blue and flowers late. 'Shimmer' (only 1.7m/5½ft) is also later than most; semi-double, true blue with a white eye. 'Mighty Atom' (2m/6ft) has a well-furnished, lavender blue spike and looks good, in my border, behind the pale yellow platforms of an achillea.

'Joan Edwards' (2.4m/8ft) is pure, strong blue, white-eyed. 'Blue Nile' (2m/6ft), deep blue with a white eye. 'Cassius' (2m/6ft) is a mixture of blue and mauve with a dirty brown bee, but surprisingly nice. 'Turkish Delight' (1.5m/5ft) has large, pale pinky-mauve flowers. 'Can Can' (2m/6ft) is very double, blue and mauve. 'Tiddles' (1.2-1.2m/4-5ft) is pale blue-mauve and very double. An old, fully double variety, 'Alice Artindale', which has smallish, blue-and-mauve rosettes, is particularly good for cutting when in its prime, to dry, as it can be hung upside-down (in the privacy of a darkened room) and will retain its shape without the florets closing or drooping.

Delphiniums have a wide geographical range and there is quite a choice of species, let alone hybrids. In an inland valley in British Columbia, it stuck in my mind that a grassland area where we set up our tent, had been eaten tight by cattle, except for yellow dandelions and a blue delphinium species, which had been sedulously avoided and were making the only possible floral display.

Delphinium grandiflorum (30cm/1ft), often misnamed *D. chinense*, plus a selling name like 'Blue Butterfly', can be grown as an annual. It has single, intense blue flowers and would be a lovely thing if it would only grow more willingly and make a larger plant. Some plants survive the winter and will be bushier in their second year. This has been crossed with *D. elatum* to give us the Belladonna group, some of which, like 'Lamartine' (blue) and 'Moerheimii' (white), have been named. The white seed strain, 'Casa Blanca', was particularly impressive in its first year on a Wisley trial, but hopeless in its second. Still, worth a try. These Belladonnas have a few flowering side-branches which are as dominant as the leader. They are light-framed, graceful, generally 1m/3ft tall. 'Connecticut Yankees' are a mixed seed strain and similar.

'Pink Sensation', which looks like a Belladonna, is truly pink (though not a great plant) and owes this to two scarlet Californian species, **D. cardinalis** and **D. nudicaule**. These two, plus the yellow-flowered **D. semibarbatum** (syn. *D. zalil*) have been crossed with *D. elatum* and given rise to some most exciting hybrids in a psychedelic colour range, including pure red, orange, pink, cream, yellow and magenta. Alas, they are hopeless in a practical role. Not hardy, not perennial and difficult to propagate true. But we live in hopes.

Deschampsia

POACEAE/GRAMINAE

Tufted hair-grass, **Deschampsia cespitosa** (1-2m/3-6ft), is a native species but with a wide distribution, even to New Zealand and Tasmania. It favours badly drained, clayey soils in sun or in open woodland. The tussock of leaves is undistinguished but the Germans have worked on a range of variations in the colour of the inflorescence, this consisting of open panicles of tiny flowers.

'Goldschleier' (Golden Veil) is one of the best, expanding in June to palest, shimmering green, but maturing to pale, straw-yellow. It stands out well as a single specimen, rising above the plants around it. Reaching a climax in early summer, it ages badly in autumn, but there are plenty of other grasses to take over then.

Dianthus

CARYOPHYLLACEAE

This is the genus of carnations, pinks, sweet williams and many hybrids between them. They all like light, well-drained soil and are notably successful where this is alkaline. Modern hybrid pinks need well nourished soil. In general it may be said that the more perpetual-flowering they are, the oftener they will need renewing. They otherwise become scrawny, woody plants. The life of a dianthus enthusiast is full of tasks.

There has to be a balance between barren and flowering shoots. In middle age, a dianthus like the small, double 'Pike's Pink' (15cm/6in), or the single, white, green-eyed 'Musgrave's Pink' (or 'Charles Musgrave') (23cm/9in), will go into a non-flowering decline, producing only barren shoots. Such as these need renewing every third year. On the other hand – and this is most noticeable in seed strains – a large part of the plant may flower, leaving few non-flowering shoots to carry it into the next year. In such cases, it may be sensible to treat it as a biennial.

Carnations derive from **Dianthus caryophyllus** from southern Europe and North Africa, whose most notable feature was its clove scent. In the course of breeding, and in particular, where the tender, perpetual carnation (of buttonholes and stereotyped floral arrangements) is concerned, the scent has been almost entirely lost but is still to be found in some border carnations, like 'Old Clove Red' and it turns up in the F[1] seed strain, 'Crimson Knight'.

Border carnations have a long tradition as florists' flowers, with strict rules as to what is correct in form and markings. I know nothing about them. From seed, some carnations are annual and often tender. Others, notably 'Floristan' (75cm/2½ft), do not flower until their second year. They make fine bedding plants, in the same way as sweet williams, but should be discarded after their July flowering. They are sweetly scented; most have double flowers. There are some pale yellows, which are odourless, deriving from the only yellow-flowered species, **D. knappii** – a sprawling plant not worth growing for itself. These carnations are not strong in the stem and need discreet support, with brushwood.

Carnation seed germinates at quite low temperatures. Treated as biennials, April sowing in a cold frame will be early enough. Having pricked the seedlings out, they should be lined out for the summer. Their glaucous foliage is handsome through the next winter. Bedding them out in the autumn, it makes a good foil for red tulips, interplanted.

F[1] hybrids, like the Knight series, come very expensive, which is probably why they are not more popular. All dianthus seed is brittle and easily crushed when handled, which is the reason for its often being recommended to mix it with fine sand, prior to sowing. Sometimes it is so mixed in the packet.

The common pink (which may equally be white, leading to some confusion) derives from **D. plumarius** (30cm/1ft), from south-east Europe. Making mats of glaucous foliage, it will live and flower freely in the crevices of old walls, for many years. Its sweet scent (quite different from carnations'), borne on the air, is the essence of early summer. There is nothing to touch it.

There are seed strains of *D. plumarius* which can be grown as bedding plants in the same way as I have described for 'Floristan' carnations, but they have not been sufficiently selected and developed. 'Spring Beauty' (38cm/15in, self-supporting) is one such mixture, and includes a good proportion of doubles. There was a strong emphasis on a poor magenta, with too much of blue in it, but of late this has been greatly improved. 'Highland Hybrids' (38cm/15in) is another seed strain, single-flowered with a dark zone at the flower's centre. All these are well scented.

D. barbatus (45cm/1½ft), the sweet william, with broad, green leaves and dense heads of flowers on stiff stems, is by nature perennial, but is often treated as biennial by growing it so well that every shoot carries flower heads in their second year. Again, treat as 'Floristan' carnations. I interplant with tulips, for spring interest. Flowering of the sweet williams will not be completed much before the end of July, and they need a follow-on from late-sown annuals or bedding plants such as dahlias. If sweet williams take their place in a mixed cottage garden border, they will often survive for years, always flowering partially.

The central and southeast European **D. carthusianorum** (60cm/2ft), of alpine meadows, is closely related, bearing small heads on long stems of bright magenta flowers. I am trying to establish that in my meadow areas, its pungent colour being just what is needed in June-July.

D. barbatus has been crossed with *D. plumarius* to produce green-leaved, sterile 'mules', which flower the summer through but need frequent renewal. I find it best to take cuttings in April, but barren shoots can be used for this purpose any time between spring and autumn. Remove the bottom pairs of leaves with a sharp blade and make a transverse cut just below a node. Pipings are sometimes recommended but are less effective. By this method, you grip the bottom of a sterile shoot in one hand, the top pairs of leaves in the other, and pull them apart. The break is made cleanly just above a node, whereas just below is a lot more effective. Root in a sandy medium in a cold frame but do not keep close for longer than is necessary, where glaucous-leaved dianthus are in question, or they will rot.

Carnations and pinks were crossed to produce the **D. × allwoodii**-type pinks of which the many named varieties are present-day currency, their advantage being repeat-flowering through the summer. The ever-popular (and detestable) 'Doris' is typical. It is double, salmon, with a simpering, toothpaste-advertising smile. Plants need frequent renewal (if your tastes have not changed, but take no notice of me).

There are some splendid modern pinks and the permanent trial run at Wisley is always worth a visit. One I greatly fancied (but not for its non-selling name) is 'Kesteven Kirkstead' (30cm/1ft), with a very clean-looking single, pure white flower and a maroon central zone. 'Haytor White' (30cm/1ft) is a repeat-flowerer that has been a favourite with me for some years: a well-formed, double white – good for a buttonhole and the more so for being scented.

Something more should be said of the old-fashioned, once-flowering *D. plumarius* cultivars, many of them dating back to the last century. A particularly well-scented, double white, and still a name to conjure with is 'Mrs Sinkins' (1868). It is a ragged-looking flower as the calyx invariably splits. 'Sam Barlow' (30cm/1ft), a small, double white, purple at the base of the petals, is one we grew a lot when I was young, and that has the right scent. So does 'Inchmery' (23cm/9in), single pink with overlapping petals (when they don't get displaced).

The laced pinks, like 'Dad's Favourite' (30cm/1ft), are deserved favourites, usually with a blackcurrant-purple margin to each petal. 'Laced Joy' (30cm/1ft) is one that I admired at Sissinghurst, combined with the nodding umbels of *Allium cernuum*.

Some of the modern, seed-raised dianthus, with green foliage, include dazzling, pure scarlet in their colour range, though not always easy to come by from retail sources. The plants sometimes last a second year. 'Queen of Hearts', 'Telstar Scarlet' and 'Princess Scarlet' are names to look out for. They are long-flowering and would go well behind a carpet of blue pimpernel, *Anagallis linifolia* 'Gentian Blue'. To get large plants before they become intent on putting all their energy into making flower buds, sow these dianthus in early autumn, pot them off individually and overwinter them in a cold frame.

There is one dianthus seed strain that I would never want to be without, although it is usually best to treat it as a biennial. That is 'Rainbow Loveliness' (38cm/15in), derived from **D. superbus**, of alpine meadows. The petals are deeply fringed and colours range from cherry red, through mauve and pale pink to white. The extra-sweet scent on the air is transporting on June evenings. Seed will be ripe by late July, just in time for immediate sowing. Pot off the seedlings and plant them out that autumn or in the following spring. If you wait till spring to sow, the plants will be thin and lacking in body.

I have yet to mention our native maiden pink, **D. deltoides** (15cm/6in), magenta with a darker central zone. The plant makes a low mat, suitable for paving cracks and the small flowers are borne over a long period. There is a pleasing white form in which the magenta zone shows up especially well. 'Brilliancy' (15cm/6in) is a larger-flowered derivative and exceedingly showy with its rich magenta colouring. Sow in the autumn before the summer you wish it to flower.

Diascia

SCROPHULARIACEAE

A South African genus of annuals and perennials, closely related to Nemesia. Until the 1980s, nobody took any notice of them. **Diascia barberae** was offered as seed and grown as an annual, but that was it. Suddenly, they were everywhere, and a good deal of hybridisation took place. It is extraordinary how a genus can remain in obscurity, until it is, for some reason, taken up. The most striking in this new wave was **D. rigescens** (45cm/1½ft), which is also one of the tenderest in cultivation. It has long racemes of largeish salmon-pink flowers. Far from remaining rigid, it lolls and is thus well adapted to cultivation in hanging baskets.

While one of the most exciting at a first meeting, it is one that you soon weary of and that goes for a good many diascias. They specialise in salmony shades, though venturing into buff, apricot, a few cleanish pinks and some dirty mauves. Well, 'Lilac Mist' and 'Lilac Belle' (both, with the varieties mentioned below, have an average height of 23cm/9in though often with a wider spread) are actually rather pleasing and I grow them both. 'Red Start' is a good, clear red.

Some diascias are quite persistent and hardy perennials, but they all perform best as young plants. You should constantly be renewing them by taking cuttings (or Irishman's cuttings) of young shoots in the autumn, overwintering them under cold glass and planting them out in spring. They flower and flower, from late May to late autumn, but become dreadfully straggly if just left to get on with it. They should be shorn over, halfway through the season. That rejuvenates them, but it may be hard to make yourself do it, as there are always flowers at the ends of the shoots that need to be shorn.

The deep pink 'Ruby Field', which is a selection of *D. barberae*, is one of the most compact (though still in need of shearing), and it mixes well and on equal terms, in a sink or on a ledge, with the lavender *Verbena tenuisecta*. **D. vigilis** has an upright habit, is light, fairly clear pink and one of the more persistent. I should prefer 'Black-thorn Apricot' to 'Joyce's Choice', if for no better reason than the latter's insupportable name, though its weak shade of apricot is more intense than some. 'Salmon Supreme' is free and compact, but seems to have escaped from the menu of a cheap restaurant.

D. fetcaniensis and **D. integerrima** are two of the best pink and hardiest species. I have grown and enjoyed them both but do not feel orphaned since their demise. Well, there are plenty more, but you don't want too many of this spineless kind of plant, or your garden will be in danger of melting away altogether.

Dicentra

PAPAVERACEAE/FUMARIACEAE

Fleshy perennials, both in stem and root, with dissected, ferny foliage. Most prefer shade and moisture and some, like **D. macrantha** (38cm/15in) far prefer the cool climate of Scotland to the south of England. I have never actually seen this flowering, which it does, briefly, in spring, but its foliage is good.

Deservedly the best known species is **D. spectabilis** (60cm/2ft), flowering in April–May. Pet names include bleeding heart, lady's locket and lady in the bath. The sizeable, locket-shaped flowers dangle on the underside of arching racemes and are bright pink outside, white within. If your clone sets it (some don't), seed is the readiest method of increase and self-sown seedlings frequently occur. The thick clusters of roots have shoot buds at the top, which can be gingerly separated with a knife, in February–March, when growth is about to be resumed. 'Alba' is a fine albino clone with much lighter green leaves and pure white flowers.

Most of the other dicentras leave me cold, though they make popular ground cover under woodland conditions. **D. formosa** (30cm/1ft) is typical in having grubby pinkish-mauve flowers. **D. f. alba** is grubby white. 'Stuart Boothman' (23cm/9in) has delicate, ferny leaves of earthy colouring with a tinge of mauve and similarly coloured flowers. So subtle that, seen against damp soil, the plant is almost invisible.

D. scandens (to 2.4m/8ft) is a herbaceous climber that appears to be reliably hardy. In a good, yellow-flowered strain, hung with little chains of blossom for most of the summer and autumn months, it gives me much quiet pleasure. Mine is sterile but there are seed-setting strains.

Dictamnus

RUTACEAE

Dictamnus albus (syn. *D. fraxinella*) 75cm/2½ft, dittany, is one of the most handsome and distinctive hardy perennials in the repertory. The plant has dark green, thick-textured pinnate foliage, subtending elongated panicles of irregular, white, rather insect-like flowers. Followed by distinctive, highly glandular, winged seed-pods, these and the stems smell strongly, when touched, of lemons, to which the plant is related.

These, while still green, give off essential oils. At the end of a hot, still day, preferably when the sun has moved off them, hold a lighted match to the base of the inflorescence and little spurts of flame will rise, making a gassy noise and emitting a delicious aroma, all the way up each panicle (which remains unmarked). Hence, the other common name, burning bush.

When the seed capsules are ripe, they open explosively, ejecting round, shiny black seeds to some distance. Propagation is from seed, several years passing before a flowering-sized plant is obtained. The fine white roots are fleshy and resent disturbance. A healthy colony should be left undisturbed, unless you are moving home.

Var. ***purpureus*** has pinkish-purple flowers, marked in two shades, and is the one I have seen wild, in open woodland in Hungary. There is a wide European distribution. Dittany is good on chalk; it likes a light but well nourished soil. The white form shows up the better as a garden plant, flowering May-June.

Dierama

IRIDACEAE

A South African genus of evergreen perennials. By far the best known species is ***Dierama pulcherrimum*** (90–120cm/3-4ft), known as wand flower or, more popularly, angels' fishing rods. Its appearance is distinctive and arresting. The dark green, linear leaves are extremely tough. They are borne in multi-tufted crowns and many will be dead and unsightly at winter's end. They must be pulled (not cut) off, by gloved hands.

The unbreakable flowering stems rise to three times the height of the foliage, in July, arching beneath the weight of a series of pendent racemes of bell flowers. These are typically magenta, but there are many variations, through rosy mauve to near white, some of them cloned and named. Each series of bells is subtended by a scarious bract, which catches the light, when back-lit, most attractively and these last well into the seeding stage. Seed is plentifully ripened, but seedlings will not normally flower until their third year. The plants make corms in series, like crocosmias, and can be divided in spring, sulking for a while thereafter.

This is not a plant for the mixed border but rather where it can be seen solo or in groups separate from other plants. It is good in paving cracks, as on the margins of a terrace, but self-seeding will need controlling. Overhanging water looks natural but the pond should be lined as dieramas need good drainage. They suffer in a hard winter but are otherwise undemanding.

D. pulcherrimum has been hybridised with the dwarfer **D. dracomontanum** and there are many variants both in height and colour.

Passing over *Digitalis*, for whose dusky, not to say dirty colourings in the perennial kinds, I can be no protagonist, we reach the far livelier *Doronicum*.

Dimorphotheca — see Osteospermum

Doronicum

ASTERACEAE/COMPOSITAE

Known as leopard's bane, these are spring- and early-summer-flowering perennials from Europe and western Asia, bearing cheerful yellow daisies of some size. They like moisture in spring and some shade obviates bleaching.

Widely naturalised in the north and on the east side of Scotland, is **Doronicum pardalianches** (1m/3ft), of branching habit and running rootstock. More of our woodland gardens should establish this.

'Miss Mason' (60cm/2ft) is a good standard variety that would go well alongside *Pulmonaria* 'Lewis Palmer'. 'Frühlingspracht' ('Spring Beauty') has double flowers and is a mistake, the flowers too heavy for their stems. There is an excellent seed strain no longer listed by D.T. Brown as **D. caucasicum** (correctly *D. orientale*) 'Magnificum'. Sown in spring, it will have made strong flowering plants a year later, with just enough individual variation to look interesting. This is excellent bedded out with tulips.

As doronicums are nothing to look at in the summer, we often lift them after flowering, cut them back and line them out for the summer, but it is important at this stage to keep them well watered until obviously established.

Dracunculus

ARACEAE

Dracunculus vulgaris (75cm/2½ft) is one of many fascinating and wicked looking aroids from the Mediterranean, but this one is hardy and fairly widely grown in Britain. The rootstock is a flattened tuber which, in good, humus-rich soil, quickly makes offsets. Division and replanting of tubers every other year will ensure abundant flowering, a partially shaded position suiting this species best.

The spotted shoots appear in April; narrow, tapering cones which look like snakes' tails disappearing into the ground. The glossy leaves are pedate, that is with leaflets radiating from an arc (as in *Helleborus foetidus*). They make the plant somewhat top-heavy and it is as well to supply light support sometime in June.

The large, typically arum-like flowers, bloom in July and are deep, rich purple, both spathe and spadix. They last for three days and on first opening, emit an appalling stench of rotten meat. This attracts a host of blow-flies which are the pollinators. In days 2 and 3, the smell has gone and it is safe to exhibit some blooms at the village flower show.

After flowering, the plant rapidly withers.

Dryopteris

DRYOPTERIDACEAE/ASPIDIACEAE

One of the commonest of all our native male ferns, alias buckler ferns (on account of the kidney- or buckler-shaped spore protector (indusium) on the backs of the fertile fronds) is the common male fern, ***Dryopteris filix-mas*** (60-90cm/2-3ft). It can be a weed in many gardens, but its self-sown presence is a useful indicator of where a more interesting replacement fern might be planted and thrive. This fern is deciduous, beautifully fresh in spring, rather a dull green in summer but colouring attractively just before withering in early winter. At this point the fronds should be cut as low as possible and they are useful for the protection of doubtfully hardy garden plants.

Make use of the spaces thus revealed between the fern's multiple crowns, to grow early flowering bulbs such as snowdrops and *Scilla bithynica*.

There are many crested forms but one of my favourites is 'Linearis', with very narrow pinnae (the frond's primary sub-divisions). In later summer, the plant's appearance is somewhat sullied by the brown effect caused by release and deposit of its abundant spores.

Another similar native and even commoner in the wetter parts of Britain of the north and west, is the golden-scaled male fern, **D. affinis** (syn. *D. pseudo-mas*, *D. borreri*) (60-90cm/2-3ft). At its best this is a far handsomer species, with much of gold in the young fronds and their wealth of scales. It remains noticeably brighter than *D. filix-mas* well into summer but copes and increases less well in the dry southeast.

The broad buckler fern, **D. dilatata** (syn. *D. austriaca*) is abundant everywhere, especially in shade. The open-textured fronds are particularly wide at the base. Highly recommended.

17 Two foreign species are especially noteworthy. **D. wallichiana** (60-90cm/2-3ft), from the Himalayas, is handsomest of the lot, especially in spring when the very dark, almost black scales are sharply contrasted with bright, lime green fronds. As the fronds uncoil, they have an animal-like energy. The crowns seldom multiply, which means that each, with its circle of fronds, can be admired as an uninterrupted unit. Propagation from spores gives abundance of prodigy, clusters of sporelings usually being sold as single units, but the prudent gardener can readily separate these into discrete plants.

The other popular foreigner, from Japan, is **D. erythrosora** (60cm/2ft), whose young fronds are in various shades between orange-red and warm brown, gradually turning green. This needs more moisture than most and a good bit of shade in the south.

Echinacea

ASTERACEAE/COMPOSITAE

Close relatives of *Rudbeckia*, echinaceas come from the same areas in the USA, chiefly differing, in gardening terms, by their purple, rather than yellow, colouring. The species we grow, in one form or another, is **Echinacea purpurea** (1m/3ft). It is an easily grown, stiffly upright perennial, with hairy stems and leaves, of coarse appearance, crowned with large, well-spaced daisies. The rays are in some shade of rosy purple, sometimes a trifle dingy, yet always distinctive and there are a number of improved, named clones. But it is also easily grown from seed and some pleasing colours can be sorted out from the seedlings. No echinacea has been so far thought worth an AGM, I may say. They do not appeal to the ruling party, with their focus on hellebores, snowdrops, epimediums, pulmonarias, colchicums and the like.

The central disc boss is a prominent feature, made the more so by vivid orange anthers, which are in startling contrast to the rays (I don't know what worshippers at the Colour Wheel have to say about that). In 'White Lustre', the contrast is even sharper, but the rays are a not very clean white.

Echinops

ASTERACEAE/COMPOSITAE

It would be hard to imagine a traditional herbaceous border without its groups of July-flowering globe thistles. The prickly leaves are coarse. The globe heads of tubular blue florets are pleasing, while in bloom, and much visited by insects, but do not last long and the plant's skeleton is of the disintegrating kind – it doesn't make old bones. This is the plant that we have always known as **Echinops ritro** (1.5m/5ft), though it should, perhaps, be called *E. bannaticus*. I long ago decided that it wasn't worth its space.

25

26

27

29 Globes of *Allium cristophii*, spires of *Eremurus × isabellanus* 'Cleopatra', and a backdrop of conifers.

30 *Iris laevigata* doesn't mind swimming, and 'Variegata' has the cleanest variegation of any iris. *Primula pulverulenta* likes moisture but not immersion. Both are June-flowering.

31 A maytime combination of perennial cornflower, *Centaurea montana*, and a *Libertia ixioides* hybrid.

32 Lupins raised from seed the previous year, and *Allium hollandicum* 'Purple Sensation'. After flowering the lupins are discarded; the alliums harvested, and the space replanted with later summer flowerers.

▷ ▷

30

31

Another species that you sometimes meet is the giant **E. sphaerocephalus** (2.4m/8ft), with dirty grey globes of some substance, but this is a coarse monster.

One of the best is **E. ritro** subsp. **ruthenicus**, with elegant leaves that are an asset to the plant and bright blue flowers. It is variable; I am currently growing seedlings on and have hopes. Another good one is **E. strigosus**, of which seed is on offer, but not plants.

These echinops come from dry, rocky areas in countries like Turkey and they tend to suffer, in cultivation, from too rich living. I believe they have a lot of mileage yet to run and that we shall some day be growing well-balanced plants with pale, elegant foliage, the whole not more than 1m/3ft tall. Some of the most promising species are not yet in cultivation.

Elymus – see Leymus

Eomecon

PAPAVERACEAE

One species, **Eomecon chionantha** (30cm/1ft) from China. It is easily grown in half-shade and leaf soil, but is hardly worth the disappointment. The rounded leaves are nice, but the ephemeral white flowers so sparingly produced as to make no sort of display. To flower freely, I think it needs warmer summers than we can provide. At Ayrlies, not far from Auckland in the North Island of New Zealand, I saw it in September, making a real show.

The rootstock is rhizomatous and running, forming a colony. When wounded, a reddish latex is released, rather as in Canadian bloodroot, *Sanguinaria canadensis*.

Epilobium

ONAGRACEAE

The rosebay willowherb, **Epilobium angustifolium** (2m/6ft), spent some time as *Chamaenerion angustifolium*, but is back where it started. One of the plants known as fireweed, it tends to follow fires, forest clearance and land disturbance, being a feature on many roadsides. Its tall racemes of bright carmine flowers are a great sight, in

July, and are echoed in the colouring of the developing seed capsules in the lower part of the raceme. As it has a running rootstock, its colonies often cover a great area.

As may be imagined, this is not a recipe that will appeal to any but the most slovenly gardener. The seeds are so light on the air that this willowherb is sure to make an appearance in your garden, but is easily controlled by herbicide, if too well established to dig out.

But the white variety, *album*, has achieved limited popularity of recent years. In a garden setting, it is hard to accept the weedy habit of such a plant, and once it has truly run to seed, it looks a shambles.

A Canadian once showed me slides he had taken in Yukon, of different variants of this species. There, it does vary in flower colour and patterning, extensively, but we probably don't need further introductions of that kind.

E. dodonaei (45cm/1½ft), which I knew as *E. rosmarinifolium*, is a modest plant, yet with showy pink blossom. The weedy habit is still there, but much less noticeable in a so much lower plant. **E. glabellum** hort. (23cm/9in) which we are told is not that species but probably a hybrid, used to be a star performer at the front of my border. It is generous with open-funnel flowers that are cream-white, produced untiringly through summer and autumn. This means that the plant soon exhausts itself. It does not set viable seed. Propagation is from unflowered shoots coming from the base of the plant. None such are produced on older plants, so stock is easily lost. I lost mine.

Epimedium

BERBERIDACEAE

This, along with *Bongardia*, *Jeffersonia* and *Vancouveria*, is among those interesting members of the berberis family which are herbaceous. Epimediums have a distribution in the wild from Turkey across the whole of Asia. They hybridise freely, thus allowing plenty of scope for confusion in identity. They have been taken up by those who count, in the gardening world, of recent years, so aspiring young plant buffs could well do worse than specialise in this genus, bringing out a monograph before someone else does.

The trouble with many epimediums is that they are not showy. You carefully pluck a bloom between finger and thumb, then hold it, myopically, close to your face, revelling in its design, which is curious, often including petals with long spurs. The leaves are an asset – compound but with discrete leaflets, heart-shaped, generally drawn to a point. They are often beautifully coloured, in spring, with bronze-red areas separated by green veins.

Some are deciduous, some evergreen. By the end of winter, the latter are looking shabby and it is a good plan, at the turn of February – March, to cut all the foliage off, so that the flowers and young foliage which will shortly follow, are seen in a pristine setting. In a large area, where epimediums have been used as ground cover, a colony can quickly be gone over with a strimmer, which avoids the tedium of snip-snip-snipping.

All prefer damp half-shade and a humus-rich root run, but the toughest, **Epimedium pinnatum** (30cm/1ft), will put up gladly with dry shade and not resent limy soil. Alas, as with us, the more obliging and cooperative the plant, the duller its companionship is likely to be. *E. pinnatum* has wan yellow flowers, in spring. It is reliable ground cover.

50 But you might just as well grow its vastly superior but equally amenable subspecies *colchicum*. This has larger flowers, bright yellow (but not the sort of yellow to make you take cover), borne in conspicuous racemes, April-early May. If you get very few flowers, it is because house sparrows are picking the buds off. It will be necessary to stretch some (not a network of) black cotton between bits of stick or cane, three or four inches above the plants. The hint of an unseen trap is enough to deter sparrows.

I would always go for epimediums with conspicuous flowers, avoiding those that are dusky mauve, violet, brownish red or, indeed, so miniscule as to make virtually no display at all. You have to strike the epimedium, to quote Tony Schilling. **E. × rubrum** is a non-starter in my canon, with dull-red flowers totally absorbed by the subtle matching colour in its young leaves.

With its long spurs, clear yellow colouring and distinctively drawn out leaflets, **E. davidii** is not to be resisted. I killed it within a year. I did all right with **E. grandiflorum** 'White Queen' (38cm/15in), for two or three years. It is deciduous and the largeish white flowers are borne well above its young foliage. I wondered why there was a warning note in Elizabeth Strangman's catalogue description. I divided mine, in early spring, and lost the lot.

E. × youngianum 'Niveum' (30cm/1ft) is another showy, white-flowered epimedium, but I have not yet given it the opportunity to be killed by the master.

Eranthis

RANUNCULACEAE

In compiling this personal choice, I am being made aware of failure or ignorance on an uncomfortably large number of occasions. I shall not dwell on the fact that I have yet to establish a healthy colony of winter aconite, **Eranthis hyemalis** (10cm/4in), but so it is. Others can boast of it as a weed.

A European woodland plant, it is usually at its best, in gardens, under a deciduous tree, where there is little or no competition or likelihood of disturbance. A horse chestnut or a lime will suit it well. It is among the first flowers announcing the approach of spring, and at its best in February, when it consorts admirably with the mauve of *Crocus tommasinianus*, both plants making colonies by self-sowing. It also flourishes among colonies of hostas, having completed its growth by the end of April and before the hostas are shading the ground.

Winter aconite tubers each produce a yellow flower, framed by a ruff of green leaves. They are unmistakeable. Seed is ripe by early May and may be gathered then, to be sown fresh, often simply by scattering it over the surface of a promising area in which to establish a new colony. In the first year after sowing, *Eranthis* makes a shiny pair of cotyledons – no more. They are easily mistaken for weed seedlings, at this stage. Their shine is a give-away, being unlike the seed-leaves of any weed I know. The next year, a circular leaf is produced, and the next, the first flower.

Eremurus

ASPHODELACEAE/LILIACEAE

The stately foxtail lilies are of unique appearance, in the early summer garden. Their naked scapes are crowned by a long, thickly set spike of star-shaped blossom. As there are gaps between the spikes, *Eremurus* can be planted in any part of the border, including the front, without danger of blocking the view, but their crown of lank basal leaves is already dying by the time they flower. Some masking of this condition might be a good idea, not forgetting, however, that they like full sun in which to grow. Sharp drainage, too; and they are happy on highly alkaline soils. In some gardens, where there is little competition around them, they self sow freely, the seedlings taking four years or so to reach flowering size.

Eremurus come from Asia, mainly in the area between Turkey and the Himalayas. As they are left untouched by cattle, they are able to form large colonies where much else is grazed near to extinction. In cultivation, where there is the opportunity, they hybridise freely. Some of the best, such as the Shelford Hybrids, have originated in English gardens.

The colour range is not great. **E. himalaicus** (2m/6ft) is white, early-May-flowering; **E. robustus** (2.4m/8ft), flesh pink, flowering late May; **E. bungei** of gardens, which should be called *E. stenophyllus* subsp. *stenophyllus* (1.2m/4ft), June-flowering and petite in habit, deep yellow; the hybrids include soft orange. No visitor to your garden will overlook *Eremurus*, possibly producing the facetious question, 'Do you call that a lupin?'

The plants have thick, fleshy roots which radiate, horizontally, from a central crown, in starfish fashion. They are easily damaged, inadvertantly, but you will be reminded of their presence if you cover their crowns with sharp grit. This both protects them from slugs and from frost damage, if the shoots break prematurely into growth before frost danger is past. In a soft winter, this could be as early as February, with *E. robustus*.

Plants are entirely dormant from the time the leaves die off to September, and this is the period in which to lift, divide and replant congested colonies. The roots are so brittle that agonising breakages will occur, however careful you try to be. Separating the crowns is made easy if the tangle of their interlocking roots is left on the soil surface, for a day, to dry out and shrink a little. Plant just below the surface; you can make a little mound of soil on which to rest the central crown. Include plenty of grit.

As the place occupied by Eremurus is left bare in summer, you need to fill the hiatus some way. Trailing nasturtiums can be suitable, if they will grow in the desired direction. I have also had good results from the perennial mullein, *Verbascum chaixii*, which comes into growth sufficiently late for neither plant to interfere with the other.

Erigeron

ASTERACEAE/COMPOSITAE

Erigerons are the early summer equivalent of michaelmas daisies and, like asters, they come from North America. None are as tall as the majority of asters and they are characterised by several rows of rays, which fill the flower out; also by a wide, flat disc.

Erigeron karvinskianus (syn. *E. mucronatus*) (23cm/9in), from Mexico, is so different from the rest, that one suspects a changeling. It is an amazingly versatile plant, colonising the cracks in paving, dry-walling and other walls with crumbling mortar. Although preferring sun, it will take to shade, also. It is sub-shrubby but, to restore neatness, all growth should be cut back flush with the surface from which it arises, in early spring. It will then start flowering in late May and continue, non-stop, till November. The small daisies open with white rays, which change to pink on ageing, thus promoting a bicolour effect. They are abundant and cheering.

If you have dry walls and paving in which you'd like to see flowers but don't want to be bothered with anything special, this is the plant for you. But if there are precious neighbours, like sempervivums or cushion saxifrages, the erigeron will be apt to smother them. In Cornwall and other mild maritime areas, you will frequently see it naturalised outside any garden. In the colder midlands and north, it is more difficult to establish, but this can be done, choosing a sheltered, sunny site. It may, there, find it more difficult to spread by self-sowing.

The border erigerons mostly have mauve flowers, purple or rosy-mauve. Nearly all those we grow are hybrids, those whose names end in -ity, raised by Alan Bloom. Others are of German extraction, as their names clearly indicate, for instance 'Dunkelste Aller' ('Darkest of All', 45cm/1½ft) – rich, deep purple. 'Foerster's Liebling' (1m/3ft) was understandably his dearest; it is purplish pink. 'Dimity' (23cm/9in), pink, is nice for its low habit, requiring no support. Most of these erigerons are weak-stemmed, and do need twigging. 'Quakeress' (60cm/2ft) was an old favourite, graceful, June-flowering, light mauve, but hopeless without support.

For my money, I would (and do) grow any variant of **E. glaucus** (mat-forming), whether mauve or pinkish-mauve, like 'Elstead Pink'. It has a large, greenish disc. The leaves make evergreen rosettes and if they survive the winter unharmed, flowering is abundant, in May-June. If frosted, you have to cut the plant back to base and it will flower later. It self-sows, sometimes into places, as in a dry wall, where you could never have planted. Colonies are infinitely long-lived and never need other than superficial attention. *E. glaucus* loves the smell of the sea and will be seen in front gardens all around our coasts.

Erodium

Geraniaceae

The storksbills are closely related to cranesbills. If you can tell the difference between a stork and a crane, you are well away. If not, the leaves of cranesbills are palmate, those of storksbills, pinnate or at least pinnately lobed, as in **Erodium** *pelargoniiflorum* (30cm/1ft). Superficially, this looks like a tender pelargonium, but it is hardy, with white flowers for most of the summer. It is suited by damp soil and a bit of shade, and seeds itself around to form a colony. If you get as far as that. It must have considerable appeal, as I have twice had it stolen from my garden.

   E. manescavi (1m/3ft) is a strong-growing plant with bold pinnate foliage and a long succession, June on, of magenta flowers up to 5cm/2in across. As a border plant, it looks a bit weedy and the shade of magenta is on the vicious side. It would look admirable in a meadow setting of grass, where the colour would be ideal, especially in the presence of yellow, but my one attempt to adapt it to rough grass, failed.

Eryngium

APIACEAE/UMBELLIFERAE

The name sea holly, loosely applied to the whole genus, is more precisely applied to the British native, **Eryngium maritimum**. Eryngiums have a wide distribution. Those from America, mostly South America, are evergreen and many are on the borderlines of hardiness in Britain. They are usually propagated from seed. The deciduous kinds, mostly hardy perennials, come from Europe, North Africa and western Asia. They have deep, fleshy roots and are generally propagated from root cuttings. All are summer-flowering. A feature in many eryngiums is the ruff of stiff bracts surrounding a domed inflorescence of quite tiny flowers.

Old World Eryngiums

Some are pretty worthless as garden plants; *E. campestre*, for instance, whose prickly foliage will spoil any picnicking site. The whole plant is green. *E. maritimum* (prostrate), found wild among marram grass on coastal dunes, is quite difficult in cultivation, requiring a very open site, sun and perfect drainage. Not for clay soils. Indeed, many of these Old World eryngiums are apt to get bacterial disease on heavy ground, which rots parts of a colony, though seldom the whole lot.

9   I find this, in particular, with **E. × oliverianum** (60cm/2ft), but it has, nonetheless, been growing in the same patch for as long as I can remember and still gives satisfaction. It has quite large blue heads and is especially notable for the vivid metallic blue colouring and sheen on its stems, when grown in full sun. The variable **E. × zabelii** (60cm/2ft) is similar, though with less blue stems. 'Violetta' is an old cultivar of this hybrid, and of striking violet colouring, but it is a weak grower and subject to bacterial spotting of the foliage.

23   Another large-headed eryngium is the June-flowering *E. alpinum*, which is notable for having quite a series of deeply incised, soft-textured bracts. In some shade of blue, there is a good deal of variation as this species is easily raised from seed.

Eryngiums with small flower heads are less exciting, though they largely make up for size, in numbers. *E. bourgatii* (60cm/2ft) is popular and the cultivar 'Oxford Blue' has an AGM. Having a distribution from Spain to Turkey, it varies a good deal and there are plenty of selections. It is upstanding and the leaves have silvery veins. *E. variifolium* (60cm/2ft) has marbled leaves and narrow, spiky bracts. Worthy but unexciting.

The variable *E. planum* (75cm/2½ft), with small, dark blue heads, has little charisma to my way of thinking – a rather clumsy plant which needs support while looking as though it shouldn't. Plenty of named cultivars, here. *E. × tripartitum* (1m/3ft) has a broad inflorescence of small, blue flower heads. Charming at its best in an open site and probably best allowed to collapse.

E. giganteum (1m/3ft), often known as Miss Willmott's Ghost, is in a class of its own, being monocarpic. If starved, it may take several years to reach flowering size, but if grown without competition, it will flower, seed and die, in its second year. The bracts are silver and broad, though much spikier and narrower in the seed strain from Turkey, called 'Silver Ghost'. The flowering cone is a deep, though modest blue. The inflorescences are quite densely borne and make a striking landscape effect in their July season. They look dreadful as soon as they tarnish and should be cut down or rooted out (a deep tap root that will come out easily only after a thunderstorm).

Colonies, once established, are self-perpetuating from seed but will need thinning and it is difficult to predict exactly where they will be. They can be raised from seed under controlled conditions, but easily become pot-bound and stunted if not planted out betimes.

There is a widespread, though often unidentified, virus affecting this species, easily recognised in the plant's first year by the production of unnaturally narrow leaves. Such plants should be destroyed, as they make miserably stunted flowering plants if allowed to remain.

American Eryngiums

Hardiest, indeed, very hardy, is *E. yuccifolium* (75cm/2½ft) from central USA. I find it easier to please under its natural prairie conditions than in a border. It makes a branching candelabrum of small, pale green inflorescences.

Perhaps the most splendid of the whole genus is *E. proteiflorum* (75cm/2½ft), whose ruff of greeny-white bracts, of unequal lengths, has a span of more than six inches. The central cone is dark sea-green. The terminal inflorescence opens first, but there are four or five to follow, lower down the stem. Basal leaves are linear, with sharp, fairly widely spaced prickles along the margins. Give this species an open situation. You will be proud if you can please it but it often goes down to unspecified ailments.

In **E. agavifolium** (syn. *E. bromeliifolium*) (1.2m/4ft), most of the fairly broad, spine-edged leaves are basal and the flowering stems are perfectly erect, bearing largeish thimble-shaped flower heads, bluish-green in colour. There are no bracts. It is a bold plant but coarse in a rather unpleasant way.

E. eburneum (1.2m/4ft) makes densely clustered basal rosettes of fine, linear leaves. The bractless inflorescences, muted green in colour, are plentiful but quite tiny. They make a charming impression. Inevitably more exciting is the 2m/7ft **E. pandanifolium** (syn. *E. decaisneanum*). It has dense basal rosettes of long scimitar leaves, above which, in late summer, rise the numerously-branched candelabrums, at their best for many weeks in autumn. No bracts, but small, globular inflorescences, generally of a modest dove-mauve colouring. However, at the Chelsea Physic Garden they have a clone which should be separately identified, rather earlier flowering and coloured rich purple. It comes true from seed.

This eryngium deserves a prominent position, not to be hidden in the centre or back of a border. In its native habitat of Uruguay, it grows in very wet places and I have seen it thriving so in southern France. Hardiness is only so-so but an established colony can generally be relied upon to come again from its self-protected centre.

Erysimum

BRASSICACEAE/CRUCIFERAE

This is the genus of the wallflowers, into which the whole of *Cheiranthus* has been included. All are short-lived perennials of doubtful winter-hardiness. In few countries can wallflowers be used for bedding, other than England. Even there, widespread winter losses can occur. In *Erysimum* cultivars that can only be propagated from cuttings, nearly all stock is virus-infected, to the detriment of vigour.

The common wallflower of spring bedding, **E. cheiri** (Cheerianthus cheerii, as it was known in Parks circles), is native to cliffs in south-east Europe, and the flowers are generally yellow. It has naturalised on walls and cliffs through much of western

Europe, north to Scotland and the sweet fragrance received when you stand at the top of a wallflower-colonised cliff is memorable.

There are many colourful seed strains and old plants may, given free drainage, as it might be along a hedge bottom, survive for several years. When virus infected, the colour 'breaks', revealing the yellow under-colouring in streaks. 'Harpur Crewe' is a double yellow form of this species. Cuttings should be taken of soft young shoots, soon after flowering.

Another good bedding plant, though not often used, is **E. linifolium**, treated as a biennial and sown in early July. It makes a low mat and has flowers of a good mauve, in May-June, excellent with the latest tulips, such as the orange 'Dillenburg'. Also, since its own season is long, with the earlier bulbous Dutch irises.

'Bowles's Mauve' (75cm/2½ft) is a bushy cultivar of the same colouring and that has a long season. On very light soils, plants may last up to five years, but this is rare. I lose it after one! Again, propagate from young shoots before they harden.

'Bredon' (1m/3ft) makes a nice bush. The lemon yellow, sweetly scented flowers are well set off by the cluster of dark unopened buds in the centre of the inflorescence. The mat-forming 'Moonlight' is also fragrant but of prostrate habit. There are at least two clones under this name. 'Rufus' is slightly bushy and weak-growing but a lovely shade of warm orange. There are several wallflowers that change colour as the flower ages. **E. mutabile**, endemic to cliffs in Crete, opens yellow and becomes purplish. 'Constant Cheer' is a name that should rightly arouse suspicion – a mawkish yellowy/mauvy/browny mixture.

Several erysimums are quite heavily cream-variegated along the length of their leaves. They are weak growers but very pretty at their best.

Erythronium

L ILIACEAE

These, collectively known as dog's tooth violets, are spring-flowering, bulbous perennials, all but two or three from North America. Their flowers are of the turkscap lily form, nodding, the six perianth segments reflexed. Many of them have beautifully marbled foliage. The overall recipe for making them happy is to grow them in light, leafy soil in part shade. Under mixed border conditions, I find that it is rather too easy to lose them among other plants. They really need an area to themselves – it need not be large – where they can multiply by self-sowing or by vegetative increase of the thin, elongated bulbs. Although division of clumps is, ideally, undertaken as the foliage is dying off, it is more easily organised and remembered immediately after flowering. If you are receiving bulbs by post, deal with them quickly, as they easily shrivel.

I have enjoyed two species in the wild, close to one another in the Olympic Mountains of Washington State, both appearing very soon after snow melt. *Erythronium grandiflorum* (10cm/4in) yellow, is quite tiny; *E. montanum* (15cm/6in) is white and a little larger. Both are pretty impossible in cultivation.

One of the easiest and most rewarding American species, from the Pacific coast, is *E. revolutum* (25cm/10in), which ranges in colour from white to deep pink ('Johnsonii group'). I should prefer a well-defined pink, to white, in this case. The leaves are well marked. This erythronium is probably the best under British conditions for making large colonies by self-sowing, flowering in April.

For a well-defined white erythronium, 'White Beauty' is excellent value, good-tempered but needing to be increased by division. It has two-toned leaves. Nice with yellow *Ranunculus gramineus* and blue *Omphalodes cappadocica*. One of the most popular cultivars is 'Pagoda' (38cm/15in), with plain but shiny, bright green leaves and two or three yellow flowers on a branching stem.

But the one that gives me most excitement, probably because it does so well with me, is the European (Spain to Turkey) *E. dens-canis* (15cm/6in), which I can naturalise in turf under meadow conditions, though it is happiest where the turf is not too dense, near to a hedge or under trees. We try to do a bit of splitting and spreading around, each spring, so as to extend its range, but it does also self-sow a little, even under these competitive conditions.

When its leaves first poke through, mid-March, they have deep chocolate markings. Within a week, the flowers are out but they remain closed, the petals all pointing downwards, until coaxed to open by sunshine. The colour is a quite strong pinky-mauve. This colonises well and synchronises with the little trumpet daffodil, *Narcissus minor*.

Eucomis

HYACINTHACEAE/LILIACEAE

These are quite large South African bulbs of borderline hardiness, though often hardier than they are given credit. However, as the bulbs become completely dormant, in winter, and are among the latest to resume activity in spring, lifting, storing and replanting presents no difficulties and is a safeguard against gardener's nerves. Plant a few inches deep in a sunny position, in good soil.

Bulbs that are left *in situ* from year to year, have the advantage of building into handsome colonies, which always looks better than bulbs that have been planted out at regular intervals, blob, blob, blob.

Eucomis in cultivation are often hybrids and it is difficult to be exact about their parentage, as they are readily raised from seed – taking three or four years to reach flowering size. Some have the handsome adjunct of strongly purple-tinted leaves and, when a batch of seedlings is raised from such as these, you can sort out those with the best-defined colouring (which will later suffuse the inflorescence) at an early age.

These plants have a bold and distinctive presence, in the garden. The naked scape is first crowned by a column of star-shaped flowers; then by a tuft of leaves, or leaf-like bracts, which invariably invite comparison with a pineapple. The flowers open in high, or late summer and their transition to the seeding state is made to seem very gradual, because the perianth persists in a little altered condition, throughout.

The first species to which my attention, as a student, was drawn, was **E. comosa** (45cm/1½ft), then known as *E. punctata*. It is one of the dullest and has a fairly nasty smell. Far superior is the now widely popular (though no one has thought about giving it an AGM) *E. bicolor* (45cm/1½ft but variable). Here, each green petal is margined in purple. This looks extremely handsome as a tub (or large pot) plant, set out in a position for display for the summer, but the bulbs in the tub allowed to increase from year to year. An annual top-dressing should keep them happy for a number of years before re-tubbing becomes necessary (tubs rot and need renewing, in any case). This container would spend its winter in a suitable cellar or shed.

E. bicolor 'Alba' is pale green throughout. But the handsomest pale green species (if it is one) that I have met is **E. pole-evansii** (1m/3ft), of slender, upright habit. For years, at Sissinghurst Castle, it contrasted strikingly in the late summer scene with a pink form of *Lilium speciosum* (which eventually died out, as lilies do). The eucomis has persisted, though its label has been removed – I think because of nervousness over its naming.

I was given a very bold, tall, purple-flowered-and-leaved eucomis by Jamie Compton, some years ago, which I am working on. Some day I shall astonish the world with the wonder of a huge group of it. Just you wait.

Eupatorium

Asteraceae/Compositae

These are flat- or dome-headed composites in which the display is made by the fluffy tubular florets and the stamens. There are no rays. Our native hemp agrimony, **Eupatorium cannabinum** (1.2m/4ft), grows wild by streams and ditches, although also, surprisingly, in the limestone crevices of the Burren, in County Clare on the west coast of Ireland. It has heads of pale mauve flowers and is nice to find at the margin of a natural pond, but the colouring is a bit too wan. In its double-flowered form, 'Flore Pleno', however, the whole inflorescence looks better integrated and purposeful. It is a good border perennial for August-September flowering.

The other eupatoriums we grow are North American, best known to them being Joe Pye-weed which, as a well-known native, they naturally despise. There is as much snobbery in the US as here. This is *E. purpureum* (2.4m/8ft) – a good plant for damp borders but somewhat superseded by *E. p.* subsp. **maculatum** 'Atropurpureum' (2m/6ft), which is a slightly more intense shade of purple. Large plantings of such as this and tall, late kniphofias, late sunflowers and rudbeckias, pampas grass, *Miscanthus*, *Salvia uliginosa* and sweet briar, *Rosa eglanteria*, will create a magnificent scene in autumn, where there is the space, but one seldom sees them.

E. rugosum (1m/3ft) is pleasant in its short August season, with heads of white flowers (turning brown), like an ageratum's. It is hardly worth reserving a space for it, but it has a nice habit of self-sowing in cracks where it makes an unexpected and welcome appearance.

E. capillifolium (1.2m/4ft or more) is a newcomer to my garden. Grown entirely as a tender foliage plant, it has bright green, feathery leaves and this colouring is retained right into October, when it is rare to find such freshness. The flowers develop too late to mature, but I have seen them in the USA and they amount to nothing.

Euphorbia

Euphorbiaceae

'I love all the euphorbias' is a frequently heard claim from fashionable gardeners, for this is a fashionable genus. 'What about the petty spurge?', I unkindly ask, for fashionable gardeners need taking down a peg and **Euphorbia peplus** is just about as miserable a weed as can be imagined. It even suffers from rust. A diseased weed. What could sink lower?

Spurges have come into their own, in the past fifty years, not because the plant hybridisers have been busily improving them – far from it – but for two other principal reasons. Gardeners, to give them credit, are assessing plants in a more enlightened way. They are still dazzled by rhododendrons, magnolias and marigolds, but are now prepared to look at more subtle colouring combined with good structure. Second, and arising from this: those who bring us unfamiliar plants from their native habitats are now on the look-out for such as euphorbias, which previously they largely ignored. And, travel being easier, there are far more of them doing it. So more worthwhile euphorbias will surely reach our gardens yet, and especially those that have been wild-collected from a winter-cold part of their range.

Not that heat and cold are by any means the sole yardstick for hardiness. Our mild winters can be destructive to certain euphorbias as can heavy soil, like my own, which noticeably shortens their life span, even if it does not kill them outright.

Euphorbia is one of those genera that hasn't tuned in to our compartmentalising preference for making a division between shrubs and herbaceous perennials. It is so diverse as to include biennials, annuals and a huge section (someone will surely hive it off, one of these days) of succulents. All exude a milky latex when wounded. By some, this is claimed to cure warts. It did not mine, when I had an outbreak of them. They just decided to go, as they had come, in their own good time. Others – only a small minority, I am glad to say – are allergic to euphorbias, and develop a serious rash through handling them. You can become allergic to almost anything.

Of the shrubby species, by far the most impressive are **E. characias** and its subspecies **wulfenii** (1.2m/4ft). With their columns of dark, evergreen, generally glaucous leaves, they people a garden, often providing much needed structure that would otherwise be lacking. As with many euphorbias, the distribution of this spurge is so wide, in nature, that there is tremendous variation. Many gardeners are growing forms of *E. characias* that are comparatively dull, especially when flowering. The inflorescence can be so near to the colour of its leaves, as scarcely to show up. The dark eye to each flower, which invites a comparison with frog's spawn, when massed, is hardly an asset.

If the plant is assessed purely for foliage, it may still win through, as with *E. c.* 'Portuguese Velvet' (75cm/2½ft), which makes a perfect dome, tightly packed with columns of extra-glaucous, round-ended leaves. Some clones, like 'H. E. Bates' (given to me by the author) turn purple on their shoot tips in winter, but this is often not a well-furnished plant. 'Variegata' (30cm/1ft) is delightful for its generous cream variegation, but so weak in constitution as to require unremitting attention. *E. c.* subsp. *wulfenii* includes some of the best cultivars for the brightness of their domed, lime green inflorescences. Margery Fish's 'Lambrook Gold' is one such; 'John Tomlinson', another.

This species has a long, spring and early summer flowering season. It is heralded (as with other shrubby spurges) in the previous autumn, when shoots that intend to flower bend over at the tips, to form a crook. John Raven likened it to an elephant's trunk in *A Botanist's Garden*. But this straightens as flowering approaches. The smell of this spurge on the air, when flowering, is pungent and musty – not unlike that of deciduous azaleas related to *Rhododendron luteum*.

When flowering is well past and the flowered stems become unsightly, they should be removed, either right to the base or, if there are young shoots being made near the base, back to them. In this way, you rejuvenate your plant, up to a point. But most of the shrubby spurges should be regarded as short-lived and frequently re-newed from cuttings. Detach young shoots with a sharp blade, strip (by pulling off) any leaves from the lower half of the stem and immediately dip into powdery soil, ash or sand to staunch the bleeding. *E. characias* will often self-sow, but this is the way that so much inferior stock is propagated and it should seldom be allowed.

Our native wood spurge, **E. amygdaloides** (1m/3ft) is shrubby, the most popular variant being the purple-leaved 'Rubra'. Not long-lived but it sows itself, generally true to colour. Pretty, in March, when its colouring is at its brightest, among a plant-ing of dwarf 'Tête-à-Tête' daffodils. This species is subject to powdery mildew, which can be a great nuisance and the only effective prevention is with a protective spray.

34   *E. robbiae* is now **E. amygdaloides** var. **robbiae**. It is quite distinct, colonising by suckering. This habit, as well as its tolerance of dry shade, has recommended it for planting as ground cover. Much disappointment has resulted, on account of the spurge dying out, just where it is most required, and travelling outwards from its perimeter to where it is not required, often invading other plants. The dying out is apparently caused by a fungus. It is not invariable. I have an old colony, right at the foot of a line of ash trees, that has been going for more than thirty years and is still a picture of health, making a wonderful display of lime green flowers each April-May. The inflorescence continues presentable till August, but should then be cut out, in-cluding the old foliage, quite low down. This small attention is essential, as your col-ony will otherwise become an eyesore, but it is often neglected.

If grown in sun, the flower heads of *E. a.* var. *robbiae* change to warm coral red, in June-July, which can look most attractive – for instance in a retaining wall, where some of mine have self-seeded. They have also colonised the risers of steps, and that is very welcome, since the steps are wide enough to allow the space at either end. The dark green foliage, albeit a bit sullen, is arranged in comely rosettes, at their best in winter, but it should be mentioned that a really hard winter sets this spurge back seriously. No mildew attacks it.

E. × *martinii* (60cm/2ft) is a first rate hybrid between *E. characias* and *E. amygdaloides*. The inflorescence has a pronounced reddish-brown eye. It makes its main display in spring but is liable to flower at any season, including winter when it is good to pick for the house. The result of such generosity, as so often, is a short life. After three seasons, it is best to replace, even if the old plant hangs on. I like this with bright tulips, in spring.

Tender, but well worth attempting is *E. mellifera* (2.4m/8ft), the honey-scented spurge. You need to find a warm corner for this evergreen shrub, which would be worth growing just for its lush green foliage. The flowers, in spring, are insignificant but waft their delicious fragrance. Unless you want it to seed – and it self-sows freely, if allowed to, the seed being ejected to a considerable distance from the plant – a good deal of pruning out of flowered wood is advisable in the summer, making way for young shoots. Replace at frequent intervals. Young plants are so handsome.

I will continue with more spring flowerers. *E. cyparissias* (30cm/1ft), the cypress spurge, makes a ground-covering colony by suckering, albeit deciduous. On light soil and in sunshine, its foliage flares up in autumn. The lance leaves resemble the juvenile foliage of many conifer seedlings. This is one of the spurges whose lime green flowers sparkle in the sun, thanks to light-catching nectaries. Its scent, again, is of honey. We are often warned against this species as being an invasive weed. People get so neurotic the moment they feel they have lost control. There are places for such plants. One in the sun will suit *E. cyparissias* best. There are a number of named clones, of which 'Fens Ruby', with red-tinted young foliage, is one of the most popular.

E. dulcis (23cm/9in) is a dull thing. It seeds itself freely and the woody rootstock quickly becomes tough to extract. Its big moment is in autumn when its foliage flames. A great improvement, which has quickly become a favourite, is the clone (though it comes pretty true from seed) 'Chameleon', whose foliage is rich purple all through the summer. Subject to mildew, alas.

The first euphorbia to flower in my garden, even as early as February in some years, is *E. rigida* (syn. *E. biglandulosa*) (30cm/1ft), which makes bold columns of evergreen glaucous foliage, some upright, some trailing. The leaves are sharp-pointed and, in winter sunshine, give a feeling of depth, with one leaf casting its shadow against the next. The bracts turn deep coral after flowering, which may not be every year, especially in the north, where it may never flower at all. If this is tender, then heavy soil and excess moisture are the probable reasons. Plant it on a ledge. *E. myrsinites* is similar, better known and hardier, but smaller scale, its shoots always lying on the ground and advancing like a friendly caterpillar. It has a terminal, yellow-green inflorescence in April. Seeds, if you catch them late in June, offer the easiest method of propagation, but the capsules are explosive and your mind may be elsewhere.

E. nicaeensis (38cm/15in) is another with glaucous evergreen foliage. It has a shrubby base, from which its shoots spray to form a dome crowned in May-June by heads of pale yellow-green flowers. It looks nice, as at Sissinghurst, with the purple bells of *Campanula portenschlagiana* in a loose mat around it. Plants need renewing every few years.

I think I like *E. palustris* (60cm/2ft at flowering, up to 2m/6ft later) as much as any, in its spring season. It has a mouth-watering freshness and, like *E. cyparissias*, sparkles, especially in evening sunlight. It has large, soft, pale green inflorescences and loves heavy, moisture-retaining soil. The rootstock is tough and woody, opening out in the centre after many years, and you can plant snowdrops there. Sometimes the foliage colours, before shedding. This species may flop while still flowering, and engulf its neighbours, so discreet support is worth giving. In an open situation, this may not happen.

Although *E. polychroma* (syn. *E. epithymoides*) (1m/3ft) is quite the brightest and nearest to yellow without much green, of all the spurges it does not keep its brightest colour for much more than two weeks in April-May. I like it with red anemones, like *Anemone* × *fulgens* or 'St. Bavo', and with the bright red lily-flowered tulip, 'Dyanito' or the orange, lily-flowered 'Ballerina'. A deep blue rosemary such as 'Benenden Blue' would look well in this context. *E. p.* 'Major' (often called *E. pilosa major*) is similar, flowers a little later and often again in summer. It makes a better-looking plant.

E. griffithii (60cm/2ft at flowering, 1m/3ft later) is exceptional among hardy spurges for its orange to red colouring. But it must have full sunshine to achieve the colour's potential. It is a suckering plant that makes a colony, but not aggressively. 'Fireglow' is bright orange-red with green leaves; 'Dixter' (a seedling that I had from a mixed batch grown by Hilda Davenport-Jones, of Washfield Nursery) is deeper red, its leaves, leaf veins and stems being suffused with purple and red. As the rhizomes in this species are quite widely spaced, you can interplant them with small, early-flowering bulbs, like *Iris histrioides* 'Major' or winter-flowering crocuses.

Turning to the summer flowerers, *E. seguieriana* subsp. *niciciana* (30cm/1ft) is already doing its stuff in late May, and carries on, full blast and on the same inflorescences, into October. Quite how it manages I do not know but the penalty, at least in my strain, is that after three years or so it has flowered itself to death. It ceases to be able to make the green, needle-leaved non-flowering shoots which will carry it forward into the next year. It is easily propagated from cuttings of these, and while still a young and virile plant, abundant propagation material is produced.

There seem to be varying strains of this species in cultivation, which is hardly surprising in view of its wide geographical distribution. Often, they seem to me to be a less bright lime green than mine and to have more leaf, and that may enable them to perennate for longer. I have recently planted this spurge around a dwarf, horizontally spreading *Rhododendron griersonianum* hybrid, 'Arthur Osborn', which carries rich, pure red blossom in June-July. This is in a mixed border context.

Until demoted by the advent of *E. schillingii*, we were all anxious to grow **E. sikkimensis** (1.2m/4ft), whose light yellow-green flowers peak in July-August. But it has a slightly tiresome suckering habit and it is spindly, requiring support, yet this is difficult to provide discreetly. However, it is still supreme in February-March, when the young shoots push through and are the richest shades of red you could dream of.

E. schillingii (1.2m/4ft), if grown well without too much competition from neighbours, flowers solidly from July to September and then on into October from subsidiary side-shoots. It is a good lime green and has a bolder inflorescence than *E. sikkimensis*. Furthermore, it is clump-forming, though still requiring support. Easily raised from cuttings in spring, or (providing more material but with the risk of hybridisation) from seed.

Not distantly related is **E. donii** (1.3m/4½ft), which was first distributed as *E. longifolia*. It flowers from July to October, lime green on a massive, domed plant that stands out from afar. Support is easily and discreetly given, when the stout, clump-forming plant is two thirds grown, with three or four canes and a single piece of string, which should be twisted around each euphorbia stem in between, taking it from cane to cane.

Lastly a biennial species, which will otherwise be omitted from every non-specialist reference book – **E. stricta** (30cm/1ft), which is ideal for sowing itself in paving cracks. The slight dose of starvation given by such a siting ensures the red stem and branch colouring which so well sets off the haze of lime green of the inflorescence, leaves being in almost total abeyance by the time this stage is reached. It flowers all summer. Some call it a weed. They have no soul.

F

Fallopia

POLYGONACEAE

Fallopia is one of the two main genera into which *Polygonum* has been divided, *Persicaria* being the other.

   F. japonica (*Polygonum cuspidatum*) (2.4m/8ft) is the 'terrifying' Japanese knotweed that seems to be a bogey to those who panic easily. It makes annual cane-like growths, clothed in heart-shaped leaves. Panicles of small white flowers appear in late autumn. (*Persicaria polystachya* is often mistaken for this but is much showier in flower, has pointed leaves and does not run as much). In winter, the cigar-brown dead stems are a pleasing landscape feature. Indeed, this is an excellent landscape plant, particularly suitable for motorway planting. However, it does have a deeply running rootstock, and this needs to be appreciated before introducing it to the garden. Roundup will get rid of it if necessary. Panic is uncalled for.

   The variegated form has brilliant pink splashes on the young shoots. It is weaker growing but inclined to revert, so beware. *F. japonica* var. *compacta* (syn. *Polygonum reynoutria*) (60cm/2ft) is a mini-version and deceptively charming, since it runs like a hare.

Farfugium

ASTERACEAE/COMPOSITAE

A beautiful genus of foliage plants, not quite hardy in most of Britain and therefore best treated as bedding plants, lifted and kept under frost-free glass for the winter. The type-plant, **Farfugium japonicum** (syn. *F. tussilagineum*) (30cm/1ft), has foliage rising from a basal rootstock, the leaves orbicular, up to 15cm/6in across, deep green and glossy. In Japan the summers are warm enough to coax it into flower in October – sparsely branching candelabrums of sizeable yellow daisies, like a doronicum that has received lessons in deportment.

   There are two principle variegated cultivars. 'Argenteum' is splashed with white, sometimes in quite large areas. 'Aureomaculatum' is covered with yellow spots of varying intensity, since they become more definite as they mature. Again, that lovely gloss. Some blinkered unfortunates loathe this plant and are rude about it in a cheap, predictable stereotype.

Farfugiums like a moist, organically rich soil and some shade.

Fascicularia

66 An exciting, show-off plant, ***Fascicularia bicolor*** (30cm/1ft) is one of the few bromeliads that can be grown as a hardy perennial through most of Britain. It makes a dome-shaped cushion of spiny-edged, linear foliage, arranged in rosettes. When one of these is ready to flower, in summer or autumn, the centre opens out into a circular pad of flower buds at the bottom of its funnel of foliage, and the surrounding leaves become colourful crimson red bracts. These are in striking contrast to the small, baby-blue flowers themselves, with winking tear-drop nectaries. However, they are fugitive, fading after a couple of days, after which the bracts' own colouring fades. These flowered rosettes should be cut or chopped out, at the end of the season, to make space for those as yet unflowered.

An open position gives rise to the best colouring, while a situation that allows you to see all round the plant, will ensure that in whichever direction an inflorescence is pointing, it will be comfortably visible. I have mine on the floor of our sunk garden, surrounded by paving.

Unflowered rosettes can be (forcibly) detached, pared cleanly at the base and rooted as cuttings.

Ferula

APIACEAE/UMBELLIFERAE

This is the genus of the giant fennels. Although edible, they have little aroma and are not to be confused with the culinary *Foeniculum*.

Ferula are exciting and dramatic plants when found in the wild, between the west Mediterranean and central Asia. Many grow in areas of extremely cold winters and would probably flourish in Britain, but they are hard to introduce. No one of intelligence is around to collect seed at the scorchingly arid season when it is ripe.

Commonest in cultivation is the interestingly variable species, **F. communis** (syn. *F. chiliantha*; 2.4m/8ft) known as giant fennel. While many species are monocarpic – you lose the plant when it has flowered – this species is generally perennial, though it may need to rest for a year or two between flowerings. Established colonies, however, will have several crowns and by dint of feeding, you can generally be assured of some flowering stems every year.

In our climate, growth begins in January. The leaves are enormous, but consist of innumerable, thread-fine divisions, making a wonderful, undulating, mossy platform. In subsp. *glauca*, the leaf is glaucous and even more striking. Growth continues until early June, when the inflorescence develops with startling rapidity. The flowering umbels are yellow. As they fade, the whole plant withers and aestivates, so that it can be planted around with annuals.

Seed is best sown when ripe, in early autumn, though it will remain viable till spring.

A reliably perennial cultivar of *F. tingitana*, named 'Cedric Morris' by Beth Chatto after its donor, is only 1.2m/4ft or so high and has glossy green leaflets, by no means thread-like. It is a good plant.

Festuca

Poaceae/Graminae

Fescues are among the finest and most desirable lawn grasses, but for ornamental purposes, the most popular is **Festuca glauca** (syn. *F. cinerea*, *F. ovina glauca*) (23cm/9in). It makes a hummock of fine blue leaves, the colouring varying considerably in intensity. Seedlings are far too variable and many named cultivars are on offer, 'Blaufuchs' (Blue Fox) being a current favourite.

Small blue hemispherical lumps are not well suited to many gardens, but lend themselves to formal, geometrical ground plans, usually with a bark mulch between clumps and not a weed in sight. They are neat edgers and will not get out of control. They dislike winter sogginess and are not at their best on rich soils, where they will probably benefit from annual replanting from small pieces. At the least, they need shearing over each spring. On the whole, they represent a fairly dismal outlook on what gardening should be about.

Filipendula

ROSACEAE

We have two natives. Dropwort, **Filipendula vulgaris** (45cm/1½ft), grows wild on dry, alkaline grassland and may be naturalised in meadow areas. The lance-shaped leaves are of mossy texture. Creamy panicles of small flowers rise above. The double form, 'Multiplex', is an old cottage garden plant but does not deserve border space, being something of a weed both in appearance and behaviour. The stems are not strong enough to support the panicle and topple over. Its earth-coloured tubers are numerous and hard to extract. It looks nice in paving cracks, where it can do no harm.

Meadowsweet, **F. ulmaria** (1m/3ft), is a plant for damp or boggy places, as are all the other species. Its golden-leaved form, 'Aurea', can look very beautiful if in sufficiently damp soil where it will not scorch. The flowers are nothing. 'Variegata' has a yellow flash in the centre of each leaflet. It readily seeds or reverts to plain green.

F. purpurea (1m/3ft) is bright cerise; excellent if you like this colour and happy to form a colony in semi-wild, meadow conditions. Often confused with **F. palmata**, the latter is usually pink. Beth Chatto speaks highly of the pink-flowered 'Elegantissima', which I have not grown. I do grow **F. rubra** 'Venusta' (or 'Venusta Magnifica') (1.2m/4ft), which is soft pink and runs about happily in a damp meadow area. The very tall **F. camtschatica** (2.4m/8ft in a border) is an excellent June-flowerer, white but with a pink variant.

Foeniculum

APIACEAE/UMBELLIFERAE

Foeniculum vulgare (2m/6ft) is the fennel used in cookery, with a strong aniseed aroma. It grows wild on alkaline soils, especially near the sea. Leaves feathery, flowers greenish yellow. It looks good with *Crocosmia* 'Lucifer'. A great self-sower, it is wise to cut it down before the seed ripens. A new tuft of fresh foliage will be produced before the end of the season. 'Purpureum' has purple foliage, the young leaves resembling mole skins. Second year seedlings of this make pleasing company for late-flowering yellow tulips.

Fragaria

ROSACEAE

The variegated strawberry, however named, is probably of hybrid origin. Its fruit amounts to nothing but, at its best, the white-variegated foliage is quite striking. The plant runs about, rooting at the nodes, like any other strawberry. Unfortunately it readily reverts to plain green.

Francoa

SAXIFRAGACEAE

Francoa comes from Chile and the species are variable. You never know quite what you are getting until it flowers. Commonest and hardiest is **F. sonchifolia** (60cm/2ft). Its hairy leaves are evergreen, stiff and rather succulent. The flowering stems branch into loose spikes of starry, indeterminate pink flowers. Summer. Of quite a rich, reddish-purple colouring is Rogerson's form (45cm/1½ft), though the habit of its dense spikes is stiff. There are often two flushes of bloom. The plants grow without fuss but enjoy good living.

Most graceful is the pure white **F. ramosa** (75cm/2½ft), with pale green leaves (*F. sonchifolia* is often sold as this). It has a gracefully branching inflorescence. It is none too hardy and best treated as a pot plant, as Gergrude Jekyll did, bringing it outside to flower.

Fritillaria

LILIACEAE

Closely allied to *Lilium*, *Fritillaria* have nodding, usually bell-shaped flowers. The colouring is often discreet, even murky. Their north hemisphere distribution is of the widest. Few species are easily grown and much of the genus is for the wildly enthusiastic specialist, who will devote a sun frame to its cultivation in (terracotta plastic) pots. Some are easy garden plants.

22   In England, the native snakeshead fritillary, **Fritillaria meleagris**, is one of these. An inhabitant of water meadows (a few are carefully protected), where drainage is

good for most of the year, it is easily grown under meadow conditions in any garden. Once established, it self-sows and increases. Flowering in April, purple is the usual colouring but there are many shades, leading to white.

The Crown Imperial, *F. imperialis* (1m/3ft), has been a favourite motif in painting and embroidery for several centuries. The colouring is in some shade of orange or yellow. The flowers describe a circle at the top of a stout stem and there is a tuft of linear green bracts above them. Within the bell, there is a tremulous, tear-like nectary at the base of each petal. Flowering is in April; the whole plant emits a strong odour of fox. It is easily grown but sometimes shy-flowering.

F. persica is generally grown in a large and easier version, 'Adiyaman' (75cm/2½ft). The large, glaucous leaves support a raceme of comparatively small, deep purple flowers. Fritillarias are subject to slug damage on heavy soils and I find *F. pallidiflora* (30cm/1ft) easiest (and quite easy at that) as a pot plant, several bulbs to a biggish half-pot making a good show in April. The colouring is pale green. You need a good selection of *F. pyrenaica* (30cm/1ft), with the pale green inside of the bell contrasting with a dark, brownish-purple outside. It must be an easy border plant, as I can succeed with it without trying. *F. acmopetala* (30cm/1ft) is similar, the pale green inner segments contrasting with dark outer ones. In Syria, cropped fields are full of it as the bulbs are too deep to be reached by the plough.

F. verticillata (75cm/2½ft) is an amazing-looking species, with a number of slender stems, linear foliage and smallish, pale green bells, above which there are several tendril-like bracts which can attach the plant to nearby vegetation. It is most elegant.

G

Gaillardia

Large daisies in crocus yellow, bronze, deep bronze red or in zoned mixtures of two of these colours, with the heavier at the base of the rays, all on plants no more than 60cm/2ft tall, would seem to be the basis for a good garden plant. Gaillardias (usually anglicised to gallardia), however, are generally skinny plants, admitting plenty of light to the base and therefore liable to become weed-infested. Like many geums, they have a long flowering season, apt to be dissipated by few blooms at a time.

They like a light soil (chalk is acceptable), but die out pretty quickly when it is heavy or unduly water-retentive. **Gaillardia aristata,** from the west side of the USA, is the parent of all the named perennial cultivars; **G. pulchella** of the annuals, which are not rigidly annual. Here, and as an annual, the one I grow is 'Red Plume'. It is a cracker, with double, bronze-red flowers on a compact, 30cm/1ft plant. It flowers in August-September and at the end of the season, when flowering has ceased, the plant still remains green. I suspect that, if lifted and overwintered under glass, it might prove to be perennial. The cultivars of G. aristata can be rooted from stem cuttings, in autumn, or from root cuttings. I have no personal experience of these methods.

On the whole, I steer clear of gaillardias, but am maybe doing them an injustice.

Galanthus

We all of us need more snowdrops in our gardens – if we like them, that is. I knew a lady, brought up in Scotland, who bewailed the fact that as soon as the snow had melted, up came the snowdrops and it seemed like winter all over again. She was no gardener. Snowdrops are graceful, welcoming, sheer delight and I fail to see how one could have too many of them.

Botanists are of the opinion that **Galanthus nivalis**, the common snowdrop, is not a native, but it takes to woodland life so well, in Britain, especially in Scotland, that it seems to have been there for ever. Animals of most kinds avoid it. Maybe squirrels even spread it around, because woods full of double snowdrops are frequent. These are incapable of setting seed, but some agency besides man must have filled in the gaps. They make a complete carpet.

Clearly, then, if we have trees in our garden, there should be snowdrops beneath them. Beneath deciduous shrubs, too, as it might be a wide-bracketing *Cotoneaster horizontalis*, under the tiered layers of *Cornus alternifolia* 'Argentea', under lilac, and hydrangeas and many more.

Snowdrops have a bit of a struggle in dense turf, as in an open meadow, but where the grass is at all thin, as in the proximity of trees or on the shady side of a hedge, they'll have a fine old time. The single common snowdrop holds its seed-pod at the top of a 15cm/6in stem. This sways over, without bending, when the seeds are ripe, so that they are shed at a distance from the parent bulb. Slowly but surely, a colony's range is extended.

You should look at your garden in February, and note all the bare spots. If these are among plants that are frequently disturbed, like bedding plants or perennials that need splitting and replanting every few years, they will not be suitable for snow-drops. But where plants are left to get on with it for periods of six years or more, then there should be snowdrops among them, so as to make best use of garden space. I have a wettish, shaded border which in summer is full of hostas, rodgersias, *Euphorbia palustris*, *Aralia cachemirica*, but in winter, nothing – except a sheet of 'Atkinsii' (23cm/9in) snowdrops. This is a sterile hybrid, but it increases into fat clumps at amazing speed. Early in bloom, each flower is elongated, like a teardrop, and it grows in huge bunches. It is an excellent variety for starting new colonies any-where, if you can be bothered to make the initial plantings. After that, you just wait and watch.

Another place where I have 'Atkinsii', and its height gives it an advantage, is among plants of the 'Early Purple' hellebore (*Helleborus orientalis* subsp. *abchasicus* Early Purple group), which starts flowering at Christmas but continues for at least a couple of months. Its dark colouring needs highlighting, and the snowdrop does that.

Among deciduous ferns that have been cut back, is ideal, and even among ever-green ferns, like the polystichums, if you cut them back in the new year, in time for snowdrops not to be inhibited. Among colchicums is good, too. The leaves of these push through in February, but there is space between clumps and I have 'S. Arnott' (20cm/8in) among mine. This is a chubby snowdrop, with markedly incurved outer segments. It has a long season because its buds open in succession, not all within a few days. It makes up quickly, but may become so congested as to kill itself through starvation, so when you see a possibility of this danger, split and spread it.

I may say that from specialist sources, snowdrops can be discouragingly expensive to buy. Even when they are quick increasers, like this, you may be asked £4.50 per bulb.

In front of a hedge, where there is often a gap between it and a lawn or path, is good for snowdrops, though you must consider whether the hedge's overall bulk may be in danger of spreading forward rather quickly. Another nice place for them is at the top of a retaining wall. Use a self-seeder, and in time you may find snowdrops growing in the cracks of the wall face.

Besides the common snowdrop, the one I have found most obliging in respect both of clumping up and of self-sowing is **G. ikariae** (10cm/4in) Latifolius group (syn. *G. platyphyllus*). It has shiny green leaves, curving outwards at the tips, and the flowers are elongated with what I can only call a come-hither look. It has a late season which not infrequently extends into April, the main snowdrop month in the south being February.

Collecting snowdrops is quite a mania with galanthophiles, whose ability to bore can only be compared with that of hellebore bores. In a colony of self-sowing snowdrops, there is bound to be a good deal of variation between seedlings. These galanthospotters will light upon one or more that they feel are *really* different and *really* special, so they are singled out and given the wife's or their own name, and so the game goes on. Which can be rather offputting and leads to the opposite view (expressed by a friend): 'I think I like my snowdrops straight'.

I am not a deliberate collector, by any means, but somehow find myself with quite a large number of different kinds of snowdrop – either impulse-buys or given me by generous friends or acquaintances. It is nice to think of them through the plant they gave. Norman Hadden, for instance, long since deceased but once a famous gardener in Porlock, gave me mini-snowdrop, 'Tiny' (10cm/4in). I grow it beneath the branches of a bay laurel and it is tremendously prolific; late-flowering, too.

I bought 'Colesbourne' (30cm/1ft), a note tells me, from Washfield Nursery, Hawkhurst, Kent, in February 1982, and we keep spreading it around but it is rarely offered. A real giant, this, with broad, somewhat glaucous leaves and inner segments which are entirely green apart from a thin white rim.

Beth Chatto gave me **G. caucasicus** (23cm/9in), with grey leaves well below the well-formed flowers. I can detect no scent (for once I can write with examples at my side; all gardening-book writers are at it in February), but should mention before I forget that the honey scent from a bunch of common snowdrops brought indoors is a major attraction. 'S. Arnott' is well scented, too. The white buds of G. *caucasicus* point upwards for a while, before they droop, reminding Beth, as she wrote to me, of a congregation of penguins. She it also was who gave me its winter-flowering var. *hiemalis*. This and the autumn-flowering **G. corcyrensis** are far superior to the long known autumn-flowering form of **G. reginae-olgae**, which has a miserable little flower and undistinguished foliage, which appears later. One should never resent bulbs that flower in autumn on the grounds that they are out of season and 'we don't want to see them yet'. It is perfectly natural for many bulbs to start their growing season by flowering, as you also find with many crocuses, sternbergias, nerines and amaryllis.

Galax

DIAPENSIACEAE.

60 A plant for rather superior gardens of the rhododendron type, **Galax urceolata** (45cm/1½ft) comes from eastern North America and makes evergreen ground cover on acid soil. The fair-sized, leathery leaves are kidney-shaped and shiny. That is sometimes about as much as you see of the plant, which tends to be shy-flowering but becomes twice itself when it does oblige, in early summer, with spires of white blossom, held well above the foliage. G. *aphylla* is the more familiar name.

Galega

PAPILIONACEAE/LEGUMINOSAE

Goat's rue. The common species, having a number of named clones and including *Galega × hartlandii*, is **G. officinalis** (1.5m/5ft). It is one of those tough old stalwarts that you expect to see, infested with bindweed, in a neglected herbaceous border. Its stems are weak and it needs support. Other than that, and a position in the sun, the plant needs no attention, though its tough roots can be divided if necessary.

The pinnate leaves support shortish spikes of pea flowers, white, mauve (typically) or bicoloured mauve-and-white ('His Majesty' is a good selection). The flowering period, of three or four weeks, is centred on July. Then, nothing. I like to see goat's rue at its best – in *your* border.

Grown well, **G. orientalis** (1m/3ft) has greater quality in its appearance. The spikes are longer and held upright, not obliquely. And the colour is a quite intense shade of lavender-blue. The plant has a running rootstock, which can be a nuisance, but it is quite easily lost, too (I lost it). The flowering season is early summer. Graham Thomas says it looks fine behind pyrethrums, and I can believe this. In any long-season border, such plants are a bit of an encumbrance once they have flowered. Pyrethrums can be moved out and replaced with something else for the remainder of the summer. Legumes, however, do not like being disturbed. So this is, perhaps, most satisfactory in a large garden, where there is space for a border devoted to early-flowering perennials, as at Crathes Castle, in Scotland, where I first enjoyed it.

Galium

RUBIACEAE

This genus, with its small white or yellow tubular flowers, opening into four, cruciform limbs, now includes sweet woodruff, **Galium odoratum** (23cm/9in), formerly *Asperula odorata*. This seems sensible, as its whorls or ruffs of leaves, together with their green, leaf-like stipules, are very like the bedstraws'.

Woodruff is a native, usually of woodland on alkaline soils. Its roots are rhizomatous, making a colony, and it is a nice, spring-flowering plant to have weaving among other, fairly static perennials, or over the roots of shrubs with naked lower regions.

The intense green of its foliage in spring, makes an appropriate background for terminal clusters of dead-white flowers – tiny, but highly noticeable. At this stage, they should be picked, dried quickly in sunshine, and allowed to steep in hock – a German practice, particularly on May Day, which makes a pleasant and refreshing drink. Dried, woodruff gives out a long-lasting smell of freshly mown grass.

Of the bedstraws, an ideal component for dry turf treated as a meadow area in your garden is lady's bedstraw, **Galium verum** (60cm/2ft). It has a running rootstock, which is just what is needed for such a situation. Its long, columnar panicles of densely packed, bright yellow flowers make perfect companions in dry turf for harebells, *Campanula rotundifolia*. Both are at their peak in July-August, so the hay cut would want to be delayed into September.

Galtonia

Hyacinthaceae/Liliaceae

Cape hyacinth. A small South African group with rather large bulbs, July-August-flowering. Best known and easiest to manage is **G. candicans** (75cm/2½ft), once known as *Hyacinthus candicans*. Bought bulbs are often virus-infected, so it may be safest to raise your own from seed, which will take two to three years. Seed is freely ripened and plenty of self-sowns will turn up.

Above a naked scape, there is a loose raceme of waxy white bells. Very striking, but not always easily placed. Bulbs need full sunshine, and will deteriorate if cabined in by neighbouring plants. Self-sowns therefore often flourish best at a border's margin. This has the disadvantage of the plant's gaunt and sleazy appearance after flowering. It is effective grouped behind hardy fuchsias, notably *Fuchsia magellanica* 'Versicolor', which, if cut to the ground every winter, will be of just the right height as a foreground to the galtonia at its flowering.

G. princeps (45cm/1½ft) is shorter, stockier, with a dense raceme of green flowers having rather pointed limbs. The leaves stand upright, close against the scape. I like it but would prefer a good eucomis. Of recent years, there has been added **G. viridiflora** (60cm/2ft), with a loose raceme of elegant green bells. The inflorescence is fine but the leaves are tousled and this species is slightly less hardy than the others.

Gaura

Onagraceae

Beware of harbouring too many plants in your garden of which the adjectives graceful and charming perpetually spring to your besotted lips. **Gaura lindheimeri** (1m/3ft) will be one of these. Hailing from the south-eastern USA, it is tolerant of drought and profits from as much sunshine and heat as you can provide. Apt to be denied these in Britain, its season of flowering starts fairly late but is at its intensest in August and September; a hazy, amorphous plant covered with spikes of airy, white blossom, given a blush by pink buds, pink also creeping into the fading blooms.

Grow something near to this that will give muscle to the scene; a kniphofia, perhaps, or a late-flowering agapanthus like the deep blue Loch Hope.

This species is most easily raised from (home-saved) seed. Sown in spring, it is generally a spindly plant in its first year, bushing out in its second and third, after which it is done for. Quicker off the mark are cuttings rooted in early autumn and well established in a cold frame before planting out the next spring. The recent clone 'Siskiyou Pink' makes a change from white.

The leaves congenitally show a curious purplish spotting, which causes needless anxiety to gardeners who were not expecting it.

Gazania

Asteraceae/Compositae

Gazania is, perhaps, supreme among the numerous sun-loving genera of South African daisies, for giving us a tingling sensation (comparable with that from good poetry or good music) when we see them revelling in blazing heat. Most of them are vivid in colouring – those that attempt to be pink or purple generally looking muddy. The base of their rays is often fascinatingly marked and patterned, creating circular zones in which a most unlikely, metallic shade of green sometimes features, for instance in 'Dorothy' (15cm/6in).

This said and given our climate, gazanias are moody in dull weather, remaining closed, or half closed or even merely one quarter closed, to depressing effect. They are as sensitive to weather moods as crocuses.

They lend themselves to propagation both from seed and from cuttings, both methods being equally popular, though the work on seed strains has been strongest, of recent years. A mixed seed strain is almost invariably disappointing, though those having a bias to silver-grey leaves start with an advantage. These mixtures will generally include a few winners, so the obvious solution, for the gardener, is to pick these out in the first year, propagate them from cuttings for the future, discarding the rest.

Seed strains of a fairly uniform colouring fare better. I liked the re-naming of the 'Daydream Bronze' strain, grown one year at Wisley, by Ray Waite (then head of the Glass department) as 'Suntanned Student'. Some of these strains produce enormous plants, 38cm/15in high. The size of bloom is commensurate but the plant is clumsy. Some of the most beautiful gazanias are ground-hugging, decked with flowers like sparklers.

Years ago, there was an on-going trial of gazanias at Wisley, run in the alpine department by Ken Aslet. Clones were named after members of staff and students. Thus we still have 'Dorothy', 'Christopher', 'Bridget', 'George' and others. I fear that 'Flash', the nickname of a particularly slow-moving student, has gone.

Gazania cuttings, made from unflowered shoots severed from the parent just where they join the branch system, can be taken quite late in the autumn (the plants themselves will stand several degrees of frost), but their main enemy in the winter is botrytis, a fungus which envelops them like a fur coat. Regular protective sprayings against this are necessary.

In our coastal resorts, gazanias will often survive many winters without protection. Occasionally inland, also.

Gentiana

GENTIANACEAE

The only alpine gentian that I have grown successfully for any length of time is the European **Gentiana acaulis** (10cm/4in). It makes a mat and I had it lining the paths in front of lavender hedging. Between the two, I once grew double pomponette daisies (*Bellis perennis*), and that was particularly successful, as a contrast to the gentians' rich blue funnels. Some people find this species shy-flowering. I never did, but it becomes shy if not fairly frequently divided and replanted. In the end, I got tired of doing this.

G. lutea (1m/3ft) is a stalwart perennial, the stoutest member of its genus. The deeply veined, orbicular leaves are a feature, rather as in *Veratrum*. They are somewhat glaucous. Whorls of yellow flowers open in June. Seed is freely produced and self-sowns occur.

You find this species plentifully in alpine meadows. It is poisonous to cattle, which avoid it, but it may then be an ingredient in hay (as may *Colchicum*), which could be serious. The fleshy roots are used for distilling a liqueur, Enzian; just about the most revolting drink I have ever been offered.

In alpine woods, you plentifully find the willow gentian, **G. asclepiadea** (60cm/2ft), whose chains of upward-facing funnels, causing the stems to arch under their weight, are at their best in August. These are blue; the white form is not worth growing.

Except that it is not keen on lime, this gentian is not particular. You might naturally choose to grow it in a partially shaded site, but it is quite as likely to sow itself in full sunshine. It looks well with the clubs of orange berries of *Arum italicum* (23cm/9in). Also with the pale yellow shuttlecocks and maple-like leaves of *Kirengeshoma palmata* (1m/3ft).

The roots of this gentian are very tough and, if possible, it should never be moved. Grown next to a lawn, its seedlings will often be found in the turf, before

21

this is given its first cut in spring. If you want a more controlled propagation, sow in autumn, barely covering the seed, and leave the container exposed to frost.

Geranium

GERANIACEAE

In the last forty years, geraniums, alias cranesbills (a name which overcomes confusion with the tender *Pelargonium* pot and bedding plants; they will always be known as geraniums) have assumed a vastly increased importance in our gardens.

A few general observations: in the wild, geraniums cover the whole of the northern hemisphere and some of the southern. Most are hardy in Britain. A large number are more or less evergreen, but not much to look at in the winter. Apart from the short-lived rosette-formers, geraniums have little plant structure. But many have the inestimably welcome habit of weaving. They insinuate their questing shoots into the fabric of their neighbours, thereby creating a tapestry effect, which is the essence of the best gardening, though it has to be under (invisible) control, otherwise something is going to suffer, probably be killed.

Between them, they flower from March to late October. Individually, some flower for a mere two weeks, while others, the weavers, may flower non-stop for five months. If their habit has become untidy, mid-season, they should be cut back, sometimes to the ground. Never plant a lot of cranesbills of different kinds close together. Although their palmate leaves are handsome, the plants themselves are too amorphous. Some, however, make excellent ground cover, while others will provide an extra dimension beneath or among shrubs, especially roses.

King of the tribe and of boldest structure is **Geranium maderense** (1.2m/4ft). It makes a rosette of deeply cut, fleshy-stalked leaves and develops a surprisingly massive trunk, some 45cm/1½ft high, easily distinguishing it from *G. palmatum,* with which it is often confused. The leaf stalks on *G. maderense* bend back but remain stiff as they die, supporting the trunk as guy ropes do a tent. If you remove them, you will have to support the plant artificially.

This is excellent just as a foliage plant, but everyone will want to enjoy the flowers, which make a magnificent display. They start opening in March and continue, in succession, into June. Meantime the leaves die and generally the whole plant, unless it makes side-shoots from the trunk (best detached and rooted as cuttings). Seeds are ripened and, when ripe, discharged to quite a distance, seedlings appearing the next year. The seeds are hardier than the plant, which generally needs to be overwintered under frost-free glass. Right on our south and west coasts, however, *G. maderense* is hardy and will form a colony, with plenty of unflowered seedlings around the mature, flowering specimens, hiding the latter's gawkiness.

If grown in a pot or other container, *G. maderense* may remain unflowered for many years, lacking sufficient nutrients to bring it to a head. You should either plant it into the ground, in a large container, or feed it heavily in a smaller container, re-membering that most of its new growth is made between autumn and spring, so this is when the feeding will be needed.

G. palmatum (1m/3ft) is hardier and will survive most winters in a sheltered, sunny position, maintaining itself by self-sowing. Its flowering is similar to G. *maderense*, but less dramatic. **G. rubescens** (1m/3ft) seems to be near these two, but is very hardy and definitely biennial – freely self-sowing. Its rosettes of cut-leaves are handsome through the winter, as are its red petioles. Flowering from late April to June, it is excellent for contributing a cottage garden effect, with columbines, Brompton stocks, *Anthericum liliago*, and an early-flowering *Gladiolus* such as the cherry-red 'Robinetta'.

The biennial weed, herb robert – **G. robertianum** – if not overcrowded, makes handsome overwintering rosettes of red-stalked cut-leaves, carrying its pink flowers from April to June. I leave it where not in the way. It has a number of colour forms, of which I grow 'Album', whose petals are white, but the calyx, pedicels and peti-oles, as well as the leaf veins, are bronzy purple. There is also a true, somewhat di-minutive albino, with light green leaves and no bronze. Peter Yeo calls this 'Cygnus'. Try to keep these variants in different parts of the garden.

One of my favourite, early-flowering species, at its best right through May, is **G. albanum.** It makes a ground-hugging mat, though its stems quest to quite a distance from the centre of the plant. It sows itself, mildly. The rounded flowers are bright mauve-pink, making a great display, when the sun has opened them. After flower-ing, the plant disappears completely until the autumn, so it ties in well with a late-starting perennial, like *Hedychium densiflorum* or the giant reed grass, *Arundo donax*.

Another species that aestivates, making all its growth in winter and completing its growing season by flowering in April–May, is **G. malviflorum** (often called G. *atlanticum*) (30cm/1ft). It carries quite large clusters of significant flowers, blue-purple in a well-selected strain. This is tuberous-rooted and easily becomes over-crowded, which causes it to cease flowering. Perhaps not worth the effort of pleas-ing it.

G. erianthum (38cm/15in) is hardly a trail-blazer, but nice to stumble on when it opens its tight clusters of pale blue dishes, in May. It makes a compact, totally deciduous plant. **G. *cinereum*** var. ***subcaulescens*** (15cm/6in) makes a cluster of up-right rhizomes (which can be detached and treated as separate cuttings) on which the leaves are partially evergreen. Being a small plant, it is apt to get lost under border conditions, but would be suited to a ledge (or rock bank), perhaps in the company of the pale yellow *Erysimum* 'Moonlight'. Plant several of the cranesbills together, for dazzling effect, in their May-June season. The dark-centred flowers are the most brilliant shade of rich magenta – fit to make you gasp. 'Ballerina' is more mat-forming and longer-flowering. Entirely polite in colouring, too, with purple striations and centre, highlighted by a pale mauve background. Charming, charm-ing, charming (discreet yawn).

An easy, self-sowing species for partial shade is the North American **G. *maculatum*** (38cm/15in), which has a fairly short, May season and looks good in front of the parsley-like *Chaerophyllum hirsutum* 'Roseum', both of them the same shade of lilac-mauve. The cranesbill has deeply jagged leaves which colour well in autumn, as do those of many other species.

Now to May-June-flowering **G. *macrorrhizum*** (23cm/9in), which is more or less evergreen, with leaves which colour highly when they decide they've had enough. They are sticky and smell strongly of oil of geraniums. This is one of the most im-portant and obliging ground-cover plants, making a dense mat of weed-suppressing rhizomes. However, if you should think of replanting it in improved soil, after a number of years, you will be richly rewarded with lush young growth and plenty of out-of-season, as well as seasonal, blossom. This will thrive in sun or in shade and, if you have a large area to cover, it will be made the more interesting for having adja-cent zones of differently coloured clones.

The species itself being variable in colour and sometimes a rather dirty, pinky-mauve, it is better to plant one or more of the selected clones. 'Album' has white petals but gives a pale pink impression overall, thanks to its coloured stamens, calyx and stalks. 'Ingwersen's Variety' is pink throughout; 'Bevan's Variety', the most deeply coloured, is unashamed magenta. It looks well with the pale yellow racemes, rising behind it, of *Thermopsis villosa*, while in front you could have Margery Fish's *Polemonium* 'Lambrook Mauve'.

There is an excellent hybrid between *G. macrorrhizum* and *G. dalmaticum*, a delib-erate cross made in the Cambridge Botanic Garden called **G. × *cantabrigiense*,** though the same cross has also occurred in the wild ('Biokovo'). The Cambridge hybrid (30cm/1ft) has shiny leaves and is bright pink. Alan Bremner, who has been crossing shrubby potentillas and cranesbills in his windy garden outside Kirkwall, Orkney, for a number of years, has given us the white *G. × c.* 'St. Ola' (the area on

Mainland, Orkney, where he lives), which is a cross between *G. macrorrhizum* 'Album' and *G. dalmaticum* 'Album'.

G. dalmaticum (7.5cm/3in) itself is a dense, mat-forming plant with glossy foliage. Its rhizomatous habit allows it to spread, slowly, and it is excellent planted at the top of a retaining wall, along whose cracks it can gradually creep. May-June flowering.

53 May starts the long season of **G. endressii** (30cm/1ft) which, after many years, I have decided I prefer to any of its cultivars or hybrids (perhaps I shall regret that claim). It is a quite compact, not straggling, plant. Even so, it may look tired halfway along its season and, if slashed flush with the soil, will cheerfully return with a refreshed autumn crop – nice with blue-veined *Crocus speciosus* running through and around it. If you grow *Cyclamen hederifolium* nearby, the late summer slash will be obligatory, otherwise the cyclamen's flowers will be overlaid. A situation in partial shade best suits the slightly abrasive mauve-pink colouring of *G. endressii*.

'Wargrave Pink' (rambling) looks mighty like a hybrid, but is still classified as a cultivar of *G. endressii*. I am not over-fond of its salmon-pink colouring, but that is a personal matter. It threads harmlessly among the stems of *Hydrangea serrata* 'Bluebird'.

G. versicolor (38cm/15in), which I first knew as *G. striatum* (both names were given it by Linnaeus), is a rather horrid, weedy-looking thing with whitish petals, veined purple. However, crossed with *G. endressii* we have *G.* × *oxonianum*, with many named cultivars. The only one I know and grow is 'A.T. Johnson' (rambling), and the original clone of that is thought to be no longer extant. The plant we grow under this name is an extremely vigorous, loose mat-former, often used to fill a gap where inspiration fails to think of something better. The flowers are well described as silvery pink and look well at the start of their season, but the whole plant becomes unbearably sprawling, eclipsing any unfortunate neighbours. It can and should be cut back, mid-season, but seldom is. It is a good indicator of a poorly thought-out garden, but perfectly acceptable in some rough spot fighting it out with grass, tree and herbaceous lupins, even ponticum rhododendrons.

The softly furry-leaved **G. traversii** (23cm/9in) comes from the Chatham Islands, and is not too hardy. It died on me, in a hard winter. It is clump-forming and the pale pink flowers are beautifully rounded. The hairs around its leaf margins give a silvery impression. Surprisingly, it readily crosses with European *G. endressii*, the group name for the hybrids being **G.** × **riversleaianum**. The unkind juxtaposition of four vowels in the middle of this name invites either elision or a hiccup.

There are two winners under this name. 'Mavis Simpson' (of variable height) bears sheaves of smallish, clear pink flowers for many months, and is one of the finest clamberers and interweavers, without being in any way aggressive. 'Russell Prichard' (vagrant) fairly closely resembles its *G. traversii* parent in respect of foliage. And it is none too long-lived, needing to be renewed by rooting cuttings from the evergreen shoots, backed up by rhizomatous stems; this being easily managed in a cold frame in winter. It is a splendid plant, coming into bloom in late May and continuing un-abated, without need of cutting back, to late October. Best sited, I think, near the margin of a border that has a roomy width of paving alongside, over which the cranesbill will spread a pool of light magenta, the flowers quite large. It will also spread back and up into any neighbouring plants a little higher than itself. This and *G. cinereum* var. *subcaulescens* reveal different levels of magenta at its finest. However, we have not yet reached *G. psilostemon*.

G. himalayense (1m/3ft) is an old, June-flowering favourite, which used to be known as *G. grandiflorum*. The substantial flowers are deep lavender blue. The whole plant is softly hairy. It is an excellent filler under stiff, gawky-stemmed roses. Flowering lasts a couple of weeks, after which it is best to slash the whole plant down to the ground. It is quickly re-clothed with fresh foliage, which will remain in condition till the end of the season, though with little chance of more flowers. The clone 'Gravetye' (30cm/1ft), formerly known as *G. grandiflorum* var. *alpinum* is a lower growing, freely spreading plant with large flowers shaded reddish purple to-wards the centre. It, also, has a short season.

The double-flowered clone, *G. h.* 'Plenum' (23cm/9in) is a low, scrambling plant which spreads more quickly than its parent. The flowers are a pinkish shade of mauve-purple – not a very reassuring colour. They are produced over a longish season.

G. ibericum is, horticulturally, similar to *G. himalayense*, but inferior, with a less full flower. I am now in deep waters and must confess to being unacquainted with the differences between its subspecies *ibericum*, and *jubatum*, with *G. platyphyllum* and with the hybrid between these, *G. × magnificum*.

'Johnson's Blue' (*G. himalayense* × *G. pratense*) (30cm/1ft) gives the bluest impres-sion of any cranesbill, flowering abundantly but briefly, in June. It has deeply incised leaves. As they were subject to rust disease in my garden, I got rid of it. 'Brookside' (*G. pratense* × *G. clarkei*), of which I know nothing else, is said to be similar in ap-pearance but with a long flowering season.

We are edging closer to *G. pratense* with the nearly related **G. clarkei**, which is a somewhat aggressively rhizomatous, mat-forming plant requiring frequent division and re-planting if it is not to subside into a non-flowering condition. Typically purple ('Kashmir Purple'), I grow the white form, 'Kashmir White' (38cm/15in). The flowers, somewhat cupped, are beautifully formed, white with dark veining. At its best, this is a great plant, but flowers briefly in May. I tried transferring it to meadow conditions, unsuccessfully.

The two large, herbaceous species that are native to Britain are *G. pratense* and *G. sylvaticum*. Their habitats complement each other, the former commonest in England, north to Derbyshire, the latter concentrated in northern England and Scotland – especially the east side and north to the Caledonian canal.

Where abundant, you see **G. sylvaticum** (60cm/2ft) everywhere in its Scottish haunts, in June, under trees, in lush, boggy places and on mountain slopes. Of clumpy, upright habit, its mauve, white-eyed flowers seldom seem quite sufficiently significant to deserve garden space. However, there are improved varieties which do, notably 'Mayflower' and the more intensely blue 'Amy Doncaster'.

The meadow cranesbill, **G. pratense** (1m/3ft), looks wonderful in the wild, flowering in June-July. In fact it is one of the last meadow flowers to bloom, before you begin to wonder how soon it will be safe to cut. In the wild it is generally seen, often along roadside verges, on limy soils. With its sizeable, light blue flowers, it makes a great show. It is easily raised from seed, which is the way my mother originally introduced it to our meadow areas. It does not insist on alkalinity and self-sows. When the grass is cut, meadow cranesbill is the first plant to bounce back with new leaves and it sometimes flowers a second time.

G. p. f. albiflorum breeds true from seed but, grown near to the blue prototype, sometimes turns up with the odd blue petal among the white. 'Mrs Kendall Clark', said to be wrongly named, but everyone knows what they mean by it, flowers early, May-June, and fairly briefly, again coming true from seed. The petals are striped pale blue against pale grey.

There are two double forms, well deserving border space. 'Plenum Caeruleum' is the earlier in flower, loosely double and the same colour as typical *pratense*. It looks great planted next to the light yellow, many-flowered *Hemerocallis* 'Corky'. 'Plenum Violaceum' is purple, the flowers making tight rosettes. Both need support. They may also need spraying against powdery mildew.

Of similar habit is **G. phaeum** (1m/3ft), with small, rotate flowers and protruding stamens. There are ever so many cultivars, but the most popular is close to black – a miserable thing that does not show up at all, especially when grown in the shade of semi-woodland surroundings, which it commonly is. The white 'Album' is slightly more significant, but still undeserving of garden space.

Another native species well deserving of garden space, when in a selected strain, is the bloody cranesbill (blue blood, evidently), **G. sanguineum** (23cm/9in), whose colouring is usually some shade of magenta. This normally occurs on limy soils, and more often near the sea than inland. It is spectacular, in June, on the limestone pavement of the Burren, in Co. Clare, west Ireland, where it vies for the showiest display with the cream-coloured burnet rose, *Rosa pimpinellifolia*.

It is flowering in my border before the end of May and is worth cutting right down, in July, often producing a second crop among rejuvenated foliage. I also have the well-named clone 'Shepherd's Warning', which is vivid carmine pink. 'Album' (30cm/1ft) is taller and of a looser habit. The flowers are pure white but the petals are narrow and thin-textured. Disappointing. *G. s.* var. *striatum* (23cm/9in), long known as *lancastriense*, is very pale pink with deeper striations. Pretty.

15

A *G. sanguineum* × *G. procurrens* cross made by Alan Bremner gives us 'Dilys' (rambling), which I have lately acquired. I think it outstanding. Of low and spreading habit with small leaves, its flowers are bright pinky-mauve (according to me) or reddish purple/magenta-purple (according to two catalogues), produced from midsummer to November.

37

G. psilostemon (*G. armenum*) (1m/3ft) is on a large scale. At its peak in June, running into July, its flowers are magenta-purple with a black eye. Very striking but the colouring is not to everyone's taste, hence the popularity of an emasculated version, 'Bressingham Flair', in which the sting has been taken out of the magenta. Shame on the breeder!

G. procurrens is an important parent of valuable hybrids, but is itself a redoubtable species, becoming a ferocious weed should you mistakenly plant it in the wrong place, where it can oust its neighbours, far and wide. It has a rambling habit and puts out a thick tap root from every node as it rambles. If you try to dig this out but break it, the piece left behind will make a new plant. Roundup should be resorted to. That said, if planted where it can be given its head, it is a beautiful late-flowering, purple species. It seems to associate well, as I have seen it in Scotland, with May-flowering columbines, *Aquilegia vulgaris*.

This was crossed with *G. psilostemon* to give us 'Ann Folkard' (to 1m/3ft but rambling), which is bright purple (not quite magenta) with a dark eye, smaller-flowered than *G. psilostemon*, though larger than *G. procurrens*. Its jagged young leaves are invariably yellow-green and this is not a symptom of ill health. Its rambling habit can be turned to good use, first raising it with the help of brushwood or elsehow, up to 1m/3ft or so and then encouraging it to spread horizontally, so that by the height of the growing season it covers a considerable area. But at the end, it returns to a compact, central crown. So you can plant it around with early-flowering bulbs, like

Dutch irises or tall camassias. These will be dormant by the time the cranesbill's new growth has enveloped their positions. Flowering is from late May to late autumn. Cuttings, if you wish to propagate, must be taken of young shoots early, preferably in March. Late cuttings will root but not overwinter.

'Anne Thomson', a result of the same cross, is said to be more compact, 60cm/2ft high by 1m/3ft across, and without long, scrambling stems. I do not know it. 'Salome' (rambling) is another *G. procurrens* hybrid (with *G. lambertii*), violet-centred, this colouring continued in veining through the paler, outer petal area. I can vouch for it being good and a welcome member of the rambling, integrating fraternity.

Another such is **G. wallichianum**, best known in the strain called 'Buxton's Variety' or, better-sounding but incorrect, 'Buxton's Blue'. It is almost invariably propagated from seed (tedious to collect, as it ripens over a period of six weeks), from which it comes pretty true, but there must be some variation. At its best, 'Buxton's Variety' is blue (or near blue), with a large, white central zone and dark anthers that show up well against this. When it starts flowering, in early July, the colouring is usually a rather nasty mauve, which seems to be linked with hot weather, as it becomes bluer as autumn sets in and flowering continues till late October.

Dying back to a central crown, I like to make use of the vacated space with early spring bulbs, such as crocuses, or the pink, May-flowering *Allium unifolium* (*A. murrayanum*). There are other good clones of *G. wallichianum*. I have one with less of white but very distinct purple veins, radiating from the flower's centre. I also have a clone called 'Syabru'. It is terribly lower class to pronounce this Sherpa name incorrectly, which you will, unless in the know, but I can never remember how that should be. It is magenta-purple, strong-growing and long-flowering. *G. wallichianum* has clearly repaid selection. When I saw it in the wild, in Kashmir, it was an unpleasing shade of pinky-mauve.

I have grown the purple, late-flowering **G. wlassovianum** (30cm/1ft), for many years, but would not recommend it, apart from reliably bright, autumn leaf colouring. The purple flowers are insignificant.

Out on a limb: the tiny, ground-hugging New Zealander, **G. sessiliflorum** subsp. **novae-zelandiae** 'Nigrescens'. Nice to meet in paving cracks, its neat, little rounded leaves are near to black, the even more minute flowers being white. It seeds around.

Geum

ROSACEAE

Most Rosaceae are shrubs and even the herbaceous types have a woody rootstock that makes them quite tough to handle. Of our two native species, **Geum urbanum**, Herb Bennet, with insignificant yellow flowers, is a tiresome weed, first because its woodiness makes it quite hard work to extract, when seedlings are past first youth, and second because hired help will never weed it out, since it makes an important-looking plant. So, in the end, you'll have to do it yourself, whether you have help, hired or unhired, or not.

Where this grows in the wild together with Water Avens, **G. rivale** (45cm/1½ft), our other native species, as I have seen it in Northumberland, there are some interesting hybrids. Water Avens always has nodding flowers. In the wild, they are usually of an indeterminate pinkish colouring, but there are good forms and hybrids in cultivation, blooming in May–June; for instance 'Leonard's Variety' (30cm/1ft), sad pink, and 'Georgenberg' (30cm/1ft), deep, soft yellow; also Beth Chatto's 'Lemon Drops' (38cm/15in) and 'Coppertone' (23cm/9in) – if only more namers of plants would give them descriptive titles like these.

G. montanum (15cm/6in), which I have enjoyed as one of the few and first flowers in bloom in the Carpathians dividing Slovakia from Poland, the soil acid, is showy and bright yellow. Its tousled seed heads, with elongated awns, are similar to those of pulsatillas. This is another parent of good hybrids, including my favourite 'Borisii' (30cm/1ft), which makes a compact plant with deep orange flowers, going well at the edge of a border with a violet-flowered colour form of *Viola cornuta*.

The long-flowering, double cultivars, 'Lady Stratheden' (60cm/2ft) – apricot, and 'Mrs Bradshaw' (60cm/2ft) – red, are old favourites. Although excellent in May, at the start of their season they have a tendency to become sloppy and stringy, later on. These derive from the Chilean species, *G. chiloense*. Odd that geums should be so far-flung.

Gillenia

ROSACEAE

From the eastern USA comes the hardy **Gillenia trifoliata** (1m/3ft), a woody-based perennial with trifoliate leaves that sometimes colour nicely in fall. For a rather brief period in June, it is a flutter of hovering white blossom. No one could fail to be delighted.

If housed in by neighbours it is weakened, yet one would choose to mask its long season as a passenger. Propagation is from seed, which does not ripen till October and whose collection is easily forgotten. Make a diary jotting. Sow immediately and allow frost to vernalise. It will germinate in the following spring.

Gladiolus

The all-too-common practice of using the plural gladioli for the singular as well, should be stamped upon at every opportunity. A gladioli is anathema (as is a cacti, a genera etc.).

It is *de rigueur*, in well-bred circles, to sneer at the size and clumsiness of the florists' flower, but this should not altogether blind us to its dignity and splendour when used in a great spread, like a peacock's train, as a cut flower. Pretty horrible, though, when laid horizontally in a flower arrangement and worse still, upside down, as the ubiquitous 'oasis' makes possible.

Gladioli come in a fantastic range of colours and colour combinations. The cultivation of the tender kinds has been made much more difficult, especially in hot dry summers, since the introduction of gladiolus thrips, minute insects which feed between the basal folds of foliage and in the developing inflorescence, so that the flower buds are already withered before they open. There was a horrific example of this damage in the double herbaceous borders at Wisley, one summer, where gladioli had been extensively used to plug dull areas left by early-flowering perennials. Instead of removing the plants when the damage became apparent, they were left for all to abhor.

Gladioli do not, in any case, lend themselves well to this kind of use. Each plant needs to be staked, which looks self-conscious when there is no foreground planting (as there should be) to mask the stake. Also, regular and frequent dead-heading is necessary, but is seldom performed. Miss Jekyll used gladioli in her borders, but in narrow slivers, rather than rounded groups. In this way their faults could be largely disguised. In any case the largest-flowered cultivars of her day were small and light by comparison with those obtaining now. We have one medium-sized, mauve-flowered gladiolus which has been in my garden since the 1930s. It is perfectly hardy, receives no attention but never fails to perform well. In general, the hardiness of large-flowered gladioli is not to be trusted.

The Butterfly types are more light-weight. In them, the uppermost petal is hooded and there is heavy blotching in the centre of the flower of a different colour from the rest.

I have seen one clever way of using gladioli as ornamental, growing plants (as against their being grown in rows in a picking plot), among *Paeonia lactiflora* hybrids – the June-flowering kinds. These become dull from July on, but the gladiolus season peaks in July and August. Both flowers were supported by discreet netting, held horizontally. Admittedly this makes weeding difficult, especially where goose grass (cleavers) has got a hold. Gardeners have to learn to crawl on their bellies and not to feel this posture undignified.

The species **Gladiolus callianthus** 'Murielae' (60cm/2ft), still often listed as *Acidanthera bicolor*, is tender but lends itself to pot culture, which brings forward its rather late flowering time, often no earlier than September. This can be turned out of its 15-18cm/6-7in pots (several corms in each pot), to plug gaps in your important border(s), at the key moment. There is no such thing as a cheat, in gardening. This gladiolus is strikingly coloured white with a purple, central zone and it is heavily fragrant. Self-supporting, too.

The gladiolus which most endears itself to me is the prolific **G. communis** subsp. **byzantinus** (1m/3ft), long known as *G. byzantinus* and a Mediterranean species, as is the similar *G. italicum* (syn. *G. segetum*) (1m/3ft), being weeds of cultivation, their corms finding their way sufficiently deep to avoid the plough-share. In its widely cultivated form, *G. communis* subsp. *byzantinus* is brilliant, dashing magenta, flowering late May to mid-June. It tucks into many border positions where it will not get in the way after flowering, for example up against a group of border phloxes, which will later cover its position. The plant supplied under this name in the trade is often quite a wan shade of pink.

Another use of it I fancy is in a meadow community, where it holds its own well, though it seldom sets seed and cannot therefore spread itself. But its colouring looks splendid with red clover and contrasting with the many yellows of that season: buttercups, and hawk-bits and -beards and the like.

There are other early summer-flowering gladioli of graceful form. Of those classified as Nanus, my favourite is 'Nymph' (38cm/15in), which is blush white, but with lipstick-stained kissing marks on the lower segments. 'The Bride' (1m/3ft) is suitably white and clumps up well. 'Robinetta' (1m/3ft) is cherry red and somehow spreads around when other border ingredients are being moved, so that there is one area where it comprises a motif, together with the not dissimilarly coloured, biennial *Geranium rubescens*.

7   Finally, the exquisite **G. tristis** (1m/3ft), which starts flowering in April and is fresh creamy green. Its flower spikes appear to emerge from the side of a leaf, the leaves being long and thin and already on the scene in early autumn. This species, far from sad in its appearance, is powerfully night-scented, so you should grow some in pots, to bring indoors while in flower. Cut blooms quickly lose their power to smell.

G. *tristis* is none too hardy, though it seeds itself around. I have one self-appointed in the middle of a hummock of *Rhodanthemum* (*Chrysanthemum*, *Leucanthemum*) *hosmariense*, whose white daisies against silver-grey foliage coincide with the gladiolus' flowering. It would be unthinkable to organise such a pairing deliberately.

A number of gladioli do grow in the winter, which makes them vulnerable to severe frosts, but they should be planted in autumn, even so, and then left to get on with it. The standard, florists' gladioli are generally planted between March and May, the date helping to provide a spread of flowering times. They are lifted in October and stored in a cool, frost- and rodent-free spot.

Glaucidium

GLAUCIDIACEAE

Glaucidium palmatum (30cm/1ft) is a one-off plant which botanists cannot place to their satisfaction. Coming from north Japan, it is a woodlander, liking cool, leafy soil and shelter. Conditions in Scottish gardens suit it more easily than the south of England, where you have to concentrate to keep it going (I didn't). It carries frail and fleeting poppy-like flowers in early summer, mauve, though there is a rare white form, var. *leucanthum*, which I bought from a well-known Scottish nursery, but it turned out mauve. I should have lost it in due course anyway. The palmate leaves are fresh and handsome.

Glaucium

PAPAVERACEAE

The yellow horned-poppy that grows wild on shingly beaches around our coasts is **Glaucium flavum** (1m/3ft). It is nice to find somewhere for this in the garden. Even better, however, and very similar apart from its flower colour, is **G. flavum** f.

flavum(1m/3ft). It might be described as a triennial, not being much use after its third summer, which is its second year of flowering.

Grown from seed, the foliage is a feast in itself, highly glaucous and with wavy margins. The flowers are burnt orange. For spring effect, we interplant a group with small tulips like *Tulipa linifolia* (10cm/4in).

Glyceria

POACEAE/GRAMINAE

Glyceria maxima, reed-grass, is a widespread and abundant native of shallow and less shallow water; a tiresome weed that you are likely to inherit in any 'natural' pond. It spreads rapidly by running rhizomes. However, *G. m.* var. *variegata* (60cm/2ft), besides being rather (only rather) less aggressive, is beautiful; well worth having, so long as you make a point, each spring, of reducing the circumference of your colony.

It is boldly variegated with white striping; pink, on its first appearance in spring. You can also use it as a terrestrial plant in a border, but in that case it is wise to lift and re-plant, annually. Besides controlling its colonial instincts this also gets you the handsomest foliage, if you improve the soil at the same time. This is a more effective variegated grass than gardener's garters, or ribbon grass, *Phalaris arundinacea* 'Picta' (1m/3ft).

Grindelia

ASTERACEAE/COMPOSITAE

The name *Grindelia* sounds like one of the Ugly Sisters, as an American observed to me. This is an American genus of yellow-flowered daisies, of which I grow two species.

G. chiloensis (75cm/2½ft), from the island of Chiloe, off the west coast of Chile, is a sprawling evergreen shrub with columns of wavy-edged lance leaves. Its flower heads are borne singly on long stems, in July. They are imposing and make a great show when the plant is suited (it loves a chalk soil). It should have a fully exposed, open situation and looks well drooping over the edge of a retaining wall.

The flower buds are framed by an involucre of green bracts, in the centre of which there is a gummy, white, protective mucus, characteristic of *Grindelia* and especially noticeable in this species. There are several rows of bright yellow rays framing a sizeable disc. July is its high season and it needs dead-heading, including the flowering stems. Propagation is from cuttings of vegetative shoots, but they are slow to root.

G. robusta (60cm/2ft) would presumably come from cuttings of soft young shoots, taken in spring (I have not propagated it myself), this being a more truly herbaceous perennial. It is smaller in its parts, the even brighter yellow daisies about half the size. But it is a stayer, in bloom for three months, well into autumn. You come to appreciate it more as the season advances.

Gunnera

GUNNERACEAE/HALORAGIDACEAE

If I had a trickle or an ooze in my garden, I should grow the elegant, ground-covering but deciduous **Gunnera magellanica** (12.5cm/5in), a small, creeping species with recognisably gunnera-like leaves on a small scale. It retains a fresh appearance all through the summer.

Best known for its largest of all leaves on any (relatively) hardy plant, is the waterside **G. manicata** (2m/6ft) from southern Brazil. This slowly spreads into a colony, by means of thick, overground rhizomes, the terminal bud of which is covered with protective scales in winter. Nevertheless, it is advisable to bend back the old leaves, once frosted, to protect the crowns. Renewed growth often appears as early as February in a mild winter, and is almost invariably frosted. But this gunnera has a well stocked quiver of embryonic leaves, which continue to unfold right into July. It is not until this month that *G. manicata* is fully fledged.

This means that a good deal of light reaches under the developing leaves in spring and early summer, allowing you to colonise the area with wood anemones, Lent lilies, snakeshead fritillaries, dog's-tooth-violets and suitable terrestrial orchids – whose growing season will have been completed before darkness descends. The compound flower heads in the gunnera are especially conspicuous in May, being of a dull reddish colouring and of phallic outline. They have a primitive attraction, but are frowned on in some circles, their removal being recommended in order to increase the size of the leaves – quite large enough without that, one would have thought. In a partially shaded site, they may be 2m/6ft across, their petioles being armed with prickles – an adjunct found in no rhubarb, with which this plant is compared by the wilfully ignorant. ('What d'you call that? Rhubarb?' followed by a guffaw, only too predictably.)

Gunnera manicata is a noble landscape plant. Though generally grown as a water-side marginal, it will thrive in any damp position. One plant might be the solution to the cry for a no-trouble, small front garden. Propagation is from seed or division. Even after a severe winter, when the main growth buds have been killed, some small young shoots will generally be produced from the underside of the old rhizome.

18   **G. tinctoria** (*G. chilensis*) (2m/6ft) is frequently confused with the last. Though generally a somewhat smaller plant, there's not much in it, when growing conditions are favourable. The inflorescence, however, is slenderer and remains upright, not flopping to the ground, as the season progresses. And the leaves are more deeply indented at the margins, making a frilly impression. It comes freely from seed and has in this way become naturalised on the sea cliffs of north-west Ireland.

Gymnocarpium

DRYOPTERIDACEAE

The oak fern, **Gymnocarpium dryopteris** (23cm/9in) grows wild on acid soils. Black-stemmed, deciduous leaves are produced singly, but make a ground-covering sward. The fronds are twice divided into three parts. They are brilliant fresh green when young and this freshness is long retained, as new fronds unfurl over an extended period. Effectively used at Sissinghurst Castle as a filler between paving and a yew hedge bottom. Try not to allow neighbouring plants to self-sow into and spoil an oak fern colony.

Gypsophila

CARYOPHYLLACEAE

Known in the USA, repulsively, as baby's breath, gypsophilas are among the most amorphous of garden plants. The double-flowered kinds should be preferred to the single, as their blooms, while adding flower power, are so neat and unassertive as, surely, to be inoffensive to the most hard-bitten of single-flower devotees.

G. paniculata (1m/3ft) is the single, white-flowered old favourite, but it has long been (or should have been) superseded by the double white cultivar, 'Bristol Fairy'. Of similar habit is the double, pale pink 'Flamingo'. All flower in June-July and are deep-rooted perennials, happiest on light soils. As the plants bulk out rather late, they need the allowance of sufficient space from their nearest neighbours, so as not to be crowded out (which they invariably have been, to date, in my garden).

'Rosenschleier', commonly known as 'Rosy Veil' (30cm/1ft) has double, pale pink flowers over a long summer period, at a low level, and forms an excellent group at the border's margin, whereas single specimens of the others will sufficiently make their point.

Hacquetia

APIACEAE/UMBELLIFERAE

This endearing little oddity is unlike any umbellifer you have seen. I write of **Hacquetia epipactis** (10cm/4in), each cluster of whose tiny yellow flowers, in spring, is surrounded by a ruff of green bracts – in this being reminiscent of the winter aconite (*Eranthis*). It also has shining green leaves and makes a clump, suitable for moist leaf soil in shady places. It is a calcicole from central and eastern Europe. Among taller plants, it is apt to get smothered.

Hakonechloa

POACEAE/GRAMINAE

The ornamental grass, **Hakonechloa macra** 'Aureola' (30cm/1ft) becomes and remains attractive for about as long as you could imagine any deciduous perennial to be. Its young shoots are brilliant yellow, on first appearing in April. They settle down to a green-and-yellow variegation, which does not become dim but gradually changes to beige, in autumn, when it flowers – not obtrusively, but none the less, pleasingly. It continues contributing warmly to the scene until the New Year, when you might consider cutting it down.

This species very slowly makes a clumpy mat, which may be divided in spring or summer, but divisions take a good year to settle down. To give it added height, I allow *Spartina pectinata* 'Aureomarginata' (1m/3ft) to colonise through it. The spartina has narrow yellow stripes in its broader, green leaves. It is more aggressive than its partner, so, from time to time, I put it in its place by wrenching out all its shoots, at some time during the growing season.

H. macra 'Alboaurea', with white as well as yellow stripes, is also popular, but I have not felt the need for it. *H. macra* (1m/3ft) is the taller, plain-leaved species, and a graceful plant of arching habit.

Hedychium

ZINGIBERACEAE

Closely related to the edible ginger plant, hedychiums are often called ginger lilies. They also have a close affinity with cannas, although the botanists separate them into different families. To the gardener, the similarity is obvious – the broad smooth leaves and the tousled, yet glamorous petals. Each flower has one, prominent and often colourful, fertile stamen.

Hedychiums come from central and south-east Asia. They are herbaceous perennials with thick rhizomes. These can be divided into sections (which are obvious, one for each growing season) and treated separately. Dormancy is broken by placing them in damp peat under warm conditions – a snug cold frame, kept close and receiving sunshine, will suffice, in summer. When shoots and roots become apparent, the pieces can be potted individually into potting compost.

As garden plants, hardiness is the chief concern. Till recently, this was thought to be considerably less than has turned out to be the case. Several of the best can be grown and flowered as hardy plants, given sheltered conditions anywhere in the south of England. Rich soil and plenty of water during the growing season meet their requirements.

Dormancy lasts for half the year and during this period, hedychiums should not be disturbed. Rotting will set in where surfaces have been damaged. New growth does not appear till late May or even later (in this, they resemble eucomis). Then is the time to split and replant, if necessary.

The leaves of hedychiums are conspicuously borne in two opposite ranks. Several are good foliage plants. The flowers are often heavily scented, but only at night and early in the morning.

The first ginger lily that I acquired, from Hilda Davenport-Jones in the 1960s, was **Hedychium spicatum acuminatum** (60cm/2ft), which is one of the hardiest. It never fails to flower, in August–September; cream-white with orange trimmings. Rather boring, actually. The flowers, as in all hedychiums, are very short-lived; the spikes are short, so there are not many flowers and the leaves get shabby.

Equally hardy, **H. densiflorum** (1m/3ft) is far superior, spreading into a dense colony, over which I grow *Geranium albanum*, for the early part of the season, before the hedychium appears. The geranium is mat-forming, covered with mauve-pink flowers through May, after which its foliage dies off while the ginger takes over. This has fresh foliage and the dense spikes of mildly pleasing, biscuit-coloured flowers open in succession, August to September.

44 Far more conspicuous is the clone 'Assam Orange' (1m/3ft), introduced by Kingdon Ward, the flowers being a light shade of salmon-orange, September to October, often followed by chains of orange, berry-like fruits. Sown fresh, these are easily germinated but the offspring are nearly always the pale biscuit colour, probably because I grow the two clones near one another. I find it hard to get any scent from either of them, perhaps through decaying imagination in old age, since they are reputedly fragrant. (You don't have to believe all you read.)

Far superior to either of these, having a comparatively massive inflorescence, is the clone collected by Tony Schilling near Kathmandu in 1965, and named 'Stephen' (1m/3ft), after his son. It is very pale, yet luminous, yellow, with orange highlights provided by the stamens. This really is heavily fragrant.

The other notable Schilling introduction (proudly displayed in the hot-coloured
43 cottage garden at Sissinghurst Castle) is **H. coccineum** 'Tara' (1.5m/5ft), named after his daughter. It is showy, with conspicuous spikes of orange-red flowers. No scent; you do not expect it in flowers of this colouring. Hardiness is most satisfactory, but a lateish flowering season would put it beyond the reach of open-air Scottish gardens.

The freshness of its green foliage is one of the chief assets in **H. forrestii** (1m/3ft), though it has white, scented flowers, late in the season. It seems reasonably hardy, but gets off to a quicker start if overwintered and started into growth under glass, bedding it out after that.

H. greenii (75cm/2½ft) is definitely tender, but I always bed it out for its dark green, glossy foliage, which is bronze on the underside. In the garden, it is apt to make a viviparous bulbil at the tip of each shoot, instead of flowers, but these, under glass, are red – pleasing but not world-shaking.

The showiest hedychium in general cultivation, because of the breadth of its inflorescence and the size of its flowers, is **H. gardnerianum** (1m/3ft). The petals are yellow, highlighting red stamens. Except in maritime climates like Cornwall, it is not hardy, being generally treated as a pot plant. Its night fragrance is almost too powerful indoors, except in a large hall. It is quite feasible to bring the plants on, under glass, and then, when flower buds become apparent, to plunge the pot contents into a border. Flowering can be at any time from late summer to November.

In the North Island of New Zealand, this introduced species has become a serious invader of open woodland and of woodland margins, where its aggressive progress ousts the native flora. It was also reported in the RHS Journal, 1960 as being a great scourge in the Azores. It is amazing, the fortitude with which we can endure the misfortunes of others.

Hedysarum

PAPILIONACEAE/LEGUMINOSAE

Although of slightly weedy habit, **Hedysarum coronarium** (1m/3ft) is an engaging, albeit short-lived perennial. It comes from southern Europe and has sometimes been used as a fodder crop, rather after the style of our own sainfoin, *Onobrychis viciifolia*. Raised from seed, it must be grown well to earn its place as a garden plant and will be at its best in its second year. Of branching habit, each branch terminated by a dense spike of red pea flowers. The leaves are pinnate.

Helenium

ASTERACEAE/COMPOSITAE

Sneezeweeds are stalwarts of the old herbaceous border, hailing from North America. I saw **Helenium autumnale**, wild, on the banks of a sluggish river near Chicago. They have a preference for damp soils.

Heleniums quickly build into clumps, which need fairly frequent division. Their foliage is dull, but favoured by slugs. Being much hybridised, it is easiest to refer to them by their cultivar names, many of which are German. In height, they range from 60cm to over 2m (2-7ft) and any above 1m/3ft will need support, as the inflorescence branches in its upper parts and the weight of the daisies is considerable. They are easily recognised by the prominent boss (not a cone), which is the disc, yellow or brown in colour, and by the down-drooping angle of the rays, which makes some anthropomorphic gardeners think they look depressed and hence depressing. July to September is their flowering season. The flowers are yellow, brown or bronze, or some combination of these colours.

The early-flowerers have the chance to produce a second crop, and this is notable in the best of the lot, 'Moerheim Beauty' (1m/3ft). Its colour is warm bronze, fading to brown and it combines well, at the same height, with the purple spikes of *Salvia* × *superba*. After this flush, you should dead-head. From each inflorescence, remove the central cluster of flower heads with the stalks below them, entirely. On the outer stalks, it will be seen that there are small, embryo buds. Cut back to these and they will supply the second crop of blossom in August-September (at the same time as the salvia's second flowering).

The rays of 'Moerheim Beauty' are not regular and do not form the neat ruff of more modern cultivars, but none of them have the same capacity for putting on a double act. The tall heleniums take up a lot of space for their three weeks or less of flowering, in the autumn, and they are entirely without interest during the summer.

Helianthus

ASTERACEAE/COMPOSITAE

There is considerable development in seed strains of annual sunflowers, but the perennials have long lingered on the fringes of popularity, being sneered at by the good-taste brigade as being chiefly responsible for the yellow-daisy fever that many gardens subside into, in late summer and autumn.

Neglected gardens do still harbour montbretias (now crocosmias), Japanese anemones and yellow sunflowers, as long survivors. These last include Jerusalem artichokes, **Helianthus tuberosus** (2.4m/8ft), which may still be useful as a shelter belt or temporary screen in summer. But it should not be forgotten that artichokes cast a lot of shade on lower plants growing near them.

The naming of perennial sunflowers is extremely confusing, with many synonyms and hybrids. One of the principal runners, with invasive, tuberous rhizomes (often red-skinned), is *H.* × *laetiflorus* (up to 2.7m/9ft), (laetus means pleasing), which also enjoys the synonyms *H. scaberrimus* and *H. rigidus*. There was an enormous group under the last name at Wisley, when I visited in October, in their double herbaceous borders, standing out in isolation and unintegrated with any companion plantings. It could look comfortable, in an informal setting, with purple *Vernonia crinita* and one of the vigorous, late-flowering persicarias, such as *Persicaria polystachya*. But there are better sunflowers than this, which has moderate-sized flowers with a dark disc and about two rows of yellow rays.

Of the dark-centred, bright yellow kinds, 'Monarch' (2m/6ft) is a splendid example, with flowers 15cm/6in across or even larger, if you indulge in a little disbudding of side-shoots. Very striking, even if not supported, which it really needs. Stock can die out and is best re-planted annually, in spring.

'Loddon Gold' is double; I have no personal experience of it. But 'Capenoch Star' (1.2m/4ft) is a favourite; self-supporting, clump-forming, with bright yellow daisies in which the central, tubular florets enlarge, as the flower matures, to form an anemone-centre. That flowers from July on. Split and re-plant every other year.

'Lemon Queen' (2m/6ft) is delightful for its soft yellow colouring, the flowers quite small but numerous, once they have got going. A bit disappointing at the start, in September, it gathers momentum. Needs support.

All these sunflowers originate in North America and *H. angustifolius* needs the extra summer heat that most east coast states expect, to get it flowering in October. At that time, I was bowled over by long hedges of it, flowering around a North Carolina property and besieged by Monarch butterflies.

10, 56 That cannot make the grade in Britain, but a star performer, mostly on account of its foliage, is *H. salicifolius* (up to 2.7m/9ft), known in Miss Jekyll's day as *H. orgyalis*. The willowy, drooping leaves are densely arrayed to form long columns of foliage, reminiscent of some luxuriant lily or of the Egyptian papyrus. The stems may collapse under their own weight, but quickly right themselves at a slight distance from base, and are generally not worth staking.

This perennial makes an excellent green break feature in a flowery border. Late in September, it unexpectedly decides to flower itself, in an open panicle of small daisies – nice to pick for a big arrangement. In winter, the old stems remain interesting, taking on the greyish tones of oxidised lead. The rootstock runs; not seriously, but replanting every few years is a good plan.

Helictotrichon

POACEAE/GRAMINAE

H. sempervirens (syn. *Avena candida*) (30cm/1ft) is a hummocky grass, making a dome of stiff, glaucous foliage. Young plants are the most comely. The plant's winter aspect is dismal, but a degree of spring cleaning can be exercised, by running your (gloved) hands repeatedly through each hummock, thereby extracting a large amount of dead foliage.

As a solo feature above a flat area, as it might be, paving, *H. sempervirens* looks its best, especially when it rises to flower, at 1.2m/4ft, in early summer, swaying gracefully in light airs. Unless you have an exceptional plan in mind, resist planting in coveys, the flowers on one plant entangling with the neighbours'.

Plants can be pulled apart for rejuvenation, in spring, and you will enjoy a certain amount of self-sowing.

Heliopsis

ASTERACEAE/COMPOSITAE

The plant we used to call *Heliopsis scabra* is now designated, just to make life simpler, **H. helianthoides** var. **scabra**. There are a number of cultivars, some with a single row of rays, others, semi-double. Of the last, 'Incomparabilis' was the one I grew in the 1950s but I think 'Goldgefieder' ('Golden Plume') (1m/3ft) is more striking, though not strong-growing enough to have survived conditions in my border.

However, heliopsis are too good to be passed over. They are sunflower-like, generally 1m/3ft tall, definitely requiring support. They are July-August-flowering and nearly always the same intense shade of crocus-yellow – a really strong, vital colour, which I have time for, though Phillips & Rix describe it unkindly as 'brash orange-yellow'. The gardener/reader must decide.

Helleborus

RANUNCULACEAE

Hellebores are an addiction, like *Galanthus*, *Euphorbia*, *Epimedium* and several other fashionable genera. Their particular appeal is in flowering at a time when there is not much else about. A few practised devotees have, with painstaking breeding programmes, vastly improved them as garden plants in recent years.

The flower habitually has five showy sepals, which are, however, generally referred to as petals. The true petals have been converted into funnel-shaped nectaries. When these become enlarged and petal-like, we get a range of 'double' flowers.

Helleborus niger, the Christmas rose, is the most symbolic species in the genus, though seldom in flower by Christmas. There is a premium on long-stemmed strains, as the naturally short kinds are apt to get spattered with winter mud, unless protected by a cloche or a horizontally fixed, overhead pane of glass. This is the only hellebore that stands reliably in water without drooping. Because of this defect, if it is one, and because the majority of hellebores hang their heads so that it is difficult to examine their markings without physically lifting each bloom, they are frequently brought indoors on very short stems and floated in a shallow bowl. Rather a horrid practice, on the whole.

The most popular group is **H. × hybridus**, commonly referred to as the Orientalis hybrids. It includes a number of species in its ancestry. They are also called Lenten roses, flowering in the main from late January to early April. They are herbaceous and cover a range of colours from white, through green and greenish yellow, pink, purple and so dark a colour as to be near black, sometimes with a steely hint of blue. The numerous pale anthers show up well against such a dark background, but the flowers themselves are not easily highlighted in a garden setting. Many hellebore enthusiasts, however, are more interested in the individual flower than in its setting.

Many of the Orientalis hybrids show up well and combine nicely with an early yellow daffodil like 'February Gold'. or with a background of female *Aucuba japonica*, whose showy red berries are newly ripened and fresh in February. If the turf is not too dense, as it might be close to a tree, these hellebores will flourish in a meadow setting.

The highly variable **H. torquatus** is mixed into the parentage of Orientalis hellebores. In the wild, it is usually some shade of green, but some very deep near-black strains have been selected and some of the best doubles owe their doubleness to this species. It might be thought a travesty to double such a flower, which is already perfect in its own way, with just five petals and the central nectaries and stamens, but some of the recent doubles are really beautiful flowers in their own right, and of quite a size.

H. orientalis subsp. **guttatus** is horticultural terminology, but refers to Orientalis-type hellebores with heavy spotting, usually purple, in the central petal area, and this is a feature that breeders sometimes take into account.

Of the semi-shrubby species, the two best known are **H. argutifolius** (syn. *H. corsicus*) and *H. foetidus*, which is a British native. Both are splendid evergreen foliage plants. In *H. argutifolius* the leaves are sea green, trifoliate and margined with mock prickles, while the bright green flowers are assembled into domed heads reminiscent of a hortensia hydrangea's. **H. foetidus** comes second to none as a foliage plant, with rich, dark green, deeply divided leaves foming loose rosettes through the summer and autumn. The bell-shaped green flowers start opening in January and develop a purple rim at the mouth. This coloration is emphasised in the strain called 'Wester Flisk', in which the stems and petioles are also reddish, but an open, not shaded, position is needed for this colouring to develop.

These two hellebores tend (at least in my garden) to be fairly short-lived, but they self-sow freely. A good place for the stinking hellebore, *H. foetidus*, is at the foot of deciduous shrubs, where it will show up strongly once the shrub's leaves have been shed.

Similar to *H. argutifolius*, but smaller and less hardy is **H. lividus**. Crossed with *H. argutifolius*, it gives rise to **H. × sternii**, a nice-looking plant, often with well patterned leaves. An even better cross is between *H. argutifolius* and *H. niger*, the hybrids being known as **H. × nigercors**. Good foliage and a succession of large white, slightly green-tinted flowers.

Many hellebore species and hybrids on sale are described as such-and-such a strain. This is because propagation by division of colonies is so slow and seedlings are the obvious alternative. If rigorously practised, this hybridising and selecting will constantly be upgrading the quality of any given strain, but if the breeder is lax and unselective, the strain will be downgraded. It is therefore important to go to a good source, when buying stock. Hellebores are easily raised from seed, which should be sown fresh, leaving the containers where cold weather can reach them. Germination will then often be around Christmas time. Unless deliberate selection of parents has been practised, unselected seedlings are unlikely to be an improvement on the parents. As with all popular genera, there are too many named clones or strains about. Still, we must have our bit of fun without having too many do's and don'ts imposed on us.

Hellebores will thrive in sun or in shade, so long as the moisture is there. They like an organically rich soil and can be topdressed with loads of mushroom compost, this being alkaline in reaction. Most hellebore species come from lime-rich soils. They are deep-rooted and resent disturbance. When this is necessary, spring, just as growth is being renewed, is the best time.

Young growth in spring can be plagued by aphids. These must be dealt with. The most serious disease is black spot, caused by the hellebore's own special fungus, *Coniothyrium hellebori*. It will be most prevalent where there is a large collection, and it is worst in wet winters. The blackened areas often show as concentric rings on the tougher leaves of a species like *H. argutifolius*. Leaves, stems and inflorescences are attacked and the entire plant may be killed. Protective fungicides when frequently applied between autumn and spring will stop the disease's entry into healthy tissue. But is life too short? That depends on you.

With herbaceous hellebores, notably the Orientalis hybrids, it is sound practice to remove all the old foliage, whether dead or not, in early winter. This often carries disease and anyway the plant, when flowering, generally looks better without it. You want to remove the leaf stalk as well as the blade, so the job is best completed before young flowering stems become prominent, otherwise your carelessness will cause wishful regrets.

Hemerocallis

HEMEROCALLIDACEAE/LILIACEAE

Day lilies, as they are affectionately known, come early into the gardener's life. There is something affecting about the ephemeral nature of a flower that lasts only from morning to night. So much so, that we instinctively touch them with our fingers, out of sympathy. If we can also catch their scent, so much the more moving.

Although a clumsy word, hemerocallis enters our vocabulary almost as easily as delphinium. But I knew one nursery which abbreviated to hems (not quite as repulsive as eucs, for eucalyptus, which I met in Scotland), and there are probably many more. The genus hails from the far east and, in the wild, this is a modest-looking flower. The breeding work that has gone on in recent years, largely in America, has beefed day lilies up to prize fighter status. Hundreds are given new clonal names each year and any nursery in the USA that specialises in day lilies will stock no less that 1000 cultivars, often between 2000 and 3000. This is not only bewildering, but silly. There seems to be no stopping it. Only hostas are in a worse case.

The natural colour of most day lilies is yellow, and it is from them that we can expect the delicious, fresh day lily scent – notably from *H. flava*, now renamed **H. lilioasphodelus** (75cm/2½ft). This unpretentious species, introduced in the sixteenth century, is still popular. It flowers abundantly in early June. Any yellow-flowered hybrid is quite likely to have inherited fragrance. The running rootstock of *H. lilioasphodelus* can be a slight nuisance in a highly organised border, but an asset in semi-wild conditions, where it could interweave with the common yellow Peruvian lily, *Alstroemeria aurea* (*A. aurantiaca*), whose season takes over from the day lily's.

Of similar antiquity in cultivation is **H.** × **fulva** (1m/3ft), a strapping triploid with tawny-coloured flowers and no scent. It naturalises easily in quite rough places and is a common sight in India, by the roadside. No doubt it was planted in the first instance, because it cannot set seed, but once there it spreads by rhizomes to form a colony. The day before the blooms open, the flower buds are habitually gathered to eat raw or stir-fried, and they are even more scrunchy in the double-flowered variety, 'Flore Pleno', alias 'Kwanso'. A friend who at one time gardened in Hong Kong, could for a long while not make out why his day lilies seemed always on the point of flowering, but never flowered. His Chinese cook was responsible. I can recommend the flavour, which resembles that of green figs.

Until recently, day lilies have been remarkably free of pests and diseases – almost the ideal no-trouble garden plant, in fact; hardy and, in many cases, seldom requiring division and re-planting. However, there is a hemerocallis gall midge, fairly new to this country. It has reached my garden and is a nuisance. There is only one generation of this midge each year, but it lays its eggs on the young flower bud, inside which the larvae live and feed so that the bud becomes swollen but fails to develop naturally and never flowers. The midge pupates in the soil nearby, so once you have it, you are unlikely to get rid of it. As soon as we notice the trouble, we spray our hemerocallis with a systemic insecticide, repeating the treatment ten days or a couple of weeks later. You can tell whether this will be necessary by cutting a swollen bud open. Small though they are, the larvae can be seen wriggling, if they are there and alive.

The foliage of hemerocallis is both an asset and a liability. Some are very early into leaf and the young shoots of *H.* × *fulva* are a particularly fresh yellow-green. This also has a variegated form, 'Kwanso Variegata', in which one longitudinal half of the leaf is purest white. This can look wonderful, but the plant is weakly and needs generous feeding. Additionally, it has a strong tendency to revert to making plain green shoots, which would soon overwhelm the whole plant if not promptly removed. I did not remove mine and soon lost my stock.

Hemerocallis lend themselves ideally to interplanting with narcissus. The latter can be a liability in a border, as their lank leaves die off so obtrusively, after flowering. Among day lilies, however, the latter's own strap leaves will quickly obscure the daffodils' unsightliness.

Unfortunately, day lilies themselves become a pretty sordid spectacle, once flowering is past. With an early flowerer, like *H. lilioasphodelus* itself, the moribund condition has already set in by early July and I often cut the whole colony down then. It has time to regenerate with fresh young foliage and sometimes even flowers again, a little, in autumn, but I have to admit that the next year's performance is somewhat weakened. The answer, I fear, is not to plant your garden up with too many hemerocallis.

Now, as to what to look out for and what to avoid when choosing day lilies. There is nowadays a wide range of colours available. Don't be carried away by a single bloom seen out of context. Many of the colours, especially in the pink and salmon range, are basically muddy and won't pull their weight. Dark, coppery reds can be exciting, but need to be appreciated at close range and in sunshine. Yellows stand out best. So-called white cultivars are always cream, not pure white.

While being dazzled by large blooms, remember that small-flowered hemerocallis are the most prolific. Furthermore, their individual flowers tend to die off discreetly, whereas large-flowered kinds really need dead-heading every morning, to prevent the colony from becoming slovenly. Quite a number of modern monsters become costive in their production of flowering stems, quite early in the life of the clump. They will need frequent division.

As with so many 'improved' plants, enlarged flowers are often matched by an increase in leaf size and coarseness. Watch out for this. Then again, the naked flowering stem should present its blooms well above the foliage, this being the graceful effect that gives the flowers style. The dwarf 'Stella d'Oro' (30cm/1ft) is extremely popular, on account of its extended season and the fact of its being small, but it is a disappointing plant, the flowers appearing among and even below the leaves.

The RHS held a trial of hemerocallis at Wisley, over a period of several years. As one of those judging it for the Award of Garden Merit, I made critical notes. Day lilies come and go and there will be further trials in the future. Nor did this trial lay any claim to being comprehensive; one hundred or so of cultivars were as many as space would allow. For what they are worth, I give some of my personal assessments. Some cultivars are quite old and were included for comparison with today's products. If sources are a problem (and not all, even those holding the AGM, feature in *The RHS Plant Finder*), contact the RHS at Wisley.

'Missenden' (75cm/2½ft) dates back; a bold bronze. A student, working near to a patch of it in the gardens, commented that it was 'good to eat'. They do learn something at Wisley. 'Amersham' (1m/3ft) is another well-tried oldie, reddish, prolific and a good garden plant. 'Frans Hals' (1m/3ft) is very free-flowering. The three outer segments ('petals') are dusky orange; the inner three, bronze with a yellow central stripe. These colours and shades harmonise and are an exception to my theory that bicolours are ineffective at a distance, as the contrasting colours become blurred and cancel each other out.

Among other red AGM winners: 'Chief Sarcoxie' (1m/3ft) is free-flowering, but too dark for effect; 'Berlin Red' (1m/3ft), strikingly rich bronze; 'Berlin Red Velvet' (75cm/2½ft) is intense at close range in sunlight; 'Royal Mountie' (1m/3ft), large, rich bronze-red; 'Red Precious' (75cm/2½ft), strong bronze; 'Apple Tart' (75cm/2½ft), intense and powerful, bright copper-bronze (not everyone's idea of an apple tart, inside or out). This goes on well into August, while most hemerocallis peak in July.

Pinks are seldom clean enough for my liking, but 'Stoke Poges' (75cm/2½ft) is good of its kind, while 'Fairy Tale Pink' (75cm/2½ft) is a nice colour and size and not too coarse.

'Burning Daylight' (60cm/2ft) is intense orange-yellow but with flowers set too close to its foliage. 'Colour Me Mellow' (1m/3ft), apricot, I had to mark up as strong, if obvious, but it was horribly coarse, as suggested by the name.

A group of three first-rate AGM winners all have it in common that their flowers are small and abundant. 'Golden Chimes' (75cm/2½ft) is light orange with bronze on the outside of the outer segments. It has not the length of season of 'Corky' (75cm/2½ft), which is otherwise similar but yellow. This goes well with the double blue meadow cranesbill, *Geranium pratense* 'Plenum Caeruleum'. 'Lemon Bells' (1m/3ft) is like 'Corky', but a little larger and taller. Its dead flowers are the same colour as its buds – a welcome exercise in camouflage.

We come to yellow day lilies, which are at the heart of this genus. 'Green Flutter' (60cm/2ft) is luminous yellow, shading greenish at the centre. Dark anthers stand out attractively. Although not favoured by the public, I rather like 'Gay Music' (1m/3ft) a free-flowering, semi-double, warm yellow day lily. 'Nova' (75cm/2½ft) has the advantage of being very late, right at the end of August. A big, lemon yellow bloom, but on too short a stem. 'Berlin Lemon' (1m/3ft) is large-flowered, bright greeny-yellow. Excellent. From the USA, 'Tetrina's Daughter' (1.2m/4ft) is pale yellow, scented, very free, tall and elegant.

The deservedly popular 'Marion Vaughn' (1m/3ft) is clear lemon yellow with a somewhat jutting undercarriage, medium-large, long flowering, into August. It goes well, in my border, with *Phlox paniculata*, the tall, mauve prototype.

An outsider, of which I am fond, is **H. altissima**, which carries fragile, yellow blooms at 2m/6ft, so let us hope that it can hang on to its appropriate name. It has a long, July-August, season and is night-flowering, the scent being most apparent at the end of a dewy night.

Hesperis

BRASSICACEAE/CRUCIFERAE

Sweet rocket, ***Hesperis matronalis*** (1-1.2m/3-4ft), from southern Europe and western Asia, is widely naturalised; especially (in Britain) in northern Scotland and Orkney, where, in rough grass, roadside verges and abandoned croft sites, it makes a conspicuous feature in June. The flowers are mauve or white (var. *albiflora*), resembling *Lunaria annua*, but very sweetly scented on the air at night.

The plant is a short-lived perennial, which can be allowed, in informal woodland areas, to colonise by self-sowing. I grow var. *albiflora* for late spring to early summer bedding, discarding and replacing the old plants in late June. Seed is available as a distinct colour strain and should be sown in spring, the seedlings lined out for the summer and bedded where they will flower in autumn.

Double white sweet rocket, 'Alba Plena' (60cm/2ft) is a choice plant propagated from cuttings. The flowers are neat rosettes. It was riddled with virus diseases, making it weak and difficult to grow, but micropropagation has enabled stock to be cleaned up, to spectacular effect. The process will need repeating, as the viruses are easily transmitted.

Heuchera

SAXIFRAGACEAE

Patches of ***Heuchera sanguinea*** have inhabited old gardens since before any of us can remember. Gnarled and woody (in the same way as unattended-to bergenias can become), they pass unnoticed from year to year, throwing up a few sprays of red flowers in early summer, but showing little zest for living. But, more recently, they have received a great deal of attention and there are many cultivars.

All come from North America and are hardy. They have attractive foliage, basically heart-shaped but variously lobed and often strongly patterned. It is the calyx which contributes the main colour and substance in the flowers. These tend to be bell-shaped, often facing outwards, rather than downwards, on open panicles.

For the successful cultivation of heucheras, you need to appreciate that they hate heavy stodgy soil; this must be light and open-textured with the help of abundant bulky organic matter. And heucheras need replanting every other year, if they are not to get woody, with reduced leaf size and general exuberance. They are excellent in partial shade, but shade should not be overdone. A position under a north wall could be made ideal (it must not dry out); or in open woodland.

I have never taken *Heuchera* seriously, but I like to see well-grown colonies (a rare experience). They should be much more used in the woodland areas at Wisley, among camellias and rhododendrons, where there are still huge areas between the shrubs where bare ground is the easy substitute for thought.

At Longwood, Pennsylvania, I was impressed, in late September (though it starts flowering much earlier) by **H. villosa** (60cm/2ft), used as ground cover beneath trees, with pleasingly fresh foliage above which hovers a mass of tiny greenish-white blossom. Some are excellent for picking, like the upstanding 'Greenfinch' (75cm/2½ft), with panicles of pale green bells above naked scapes. The leaves are well patterned.

H. micrantha var. **diversifolia** 'Palace Purple' (1m/3ft) caused a great stir on its first appearance and is much planted now, though often adulterated through being raised from seed ('Palace Putsch' might then be more appropriate). The leaves are large, drawn to sharp points, shiny as though lacquered and (when true) a deep, rich bronze-purple. Its insistent personality can become tiring, being in good condition throughout the summer and carrying a mass of tiny white flowers followed by bronze seed pods. How ungrateful can one be? The heuchera trial at Wisley has high-lighted many new stars, both for flowers and for foliage.

× Heucherella

Saxifragaceae

The cross made by Alan Bloom of *Tiarella* with *Heuchera* gave us × **Heucherella** 'Bridget Bloom' (45cm/1½ft). This is a seething mass of tiny, airy pink bells in May and I used to grow it effectively with the first flush of *Viola cornuta* 'Alba'. It is really for a late-spring to early-summer border. Replant every other year at least.

Hieraceum

Asteraceae/Compositae

These are the infinitely variable yet similar hawkweeds, the most desirable of which have been given the separate genus *Pilosella* (q.v.). Of the remainder, **Hieraceum lanatum** (30cm/1ft) and **H. villosum** (30cm/1ft) are of rock garden status with broad, pleasingly woolly grey leaves and a branching inflorescence of the usual, but not to be despised, yellow daisies, these consisting entirely of rays (ligules), as in dandelions. **H. maculatum** (30cm/1ft) has chocolate-spotted leaves. They do self-sow freely but scarcely alarmingly.

Hosta

HOSTACEAE/LILIACEAE

Although their flowers are a supporting asset, the great strength in hostas (once known as funkias) is in the foliage. It is plain, bold and light-reflecting, which is a major asset in a plant that is so often grown under trees. Hostas light up dark places.

They are amazingly hardy and, while having a strong preference for partial shade and moisture, are tolerant of whatever cultural conditions you may throw at them. If you want best results, you will, of course, treat them with consideration, incorporating plenty of bulky, moisture-retaining organic matter into the soil where they will grow.

Because of their easy-going nature, Americans have a fixation on hostas, and it is there (as with day lilies) that most of the breeding work on thousands of registered cultivars has taken place. It should be mentioned, however, that prolonged hot weather does not suit them and that they do not flourish in Los Angeles, for example. But they gladly accept the winter cold of a central state like Minnesota, where a nurseryman in perennials told me that one third of all his sales were of hostas. And this arose entirely from demand, not from any preference of his own.

A mania for one plant will lead to mindless monoculture. Yet, as is always the case, the provision of contrasts will greatly enhance the impact and effectiveness of your favourite. The dissect fronds of ferns offer an ideal complement to hosta foliage, and ferns enjoy the same cultural conditions. Astilbes also, for the same reasons; astelias (if they will survive your winters), with their sword leaves and the maple-like foliage, contrasted with dark stems, of *Kirengeshoma palmata*. Hellebores like *Helleborus argutifolius* and *H. foetidus*, with their strong forms and leathery textures, make an excellent contrast.

The colouring of hosta leaves takes in various rich greens; waxy, glaucous hues; yellow-greens, often verging on yellow and especially luminous under trees; as well as a range of yellow and white variegations. The breeders have played on the possibilities of a range of combinations and the differences are often so slight as to debase the currency, so to speak. Hostas suffer from virus diseases and it may happen that you can no longer satisfactorily grow varieties that you once found easy. If the variegation in a hosta leaf is caused by viral infection, the plant should be destroyed, not cherished.

Propagation is still, largely, by division of crowns, though micropropagation offers a much quicker method of working up stocks. Particularly where variegated cultivars are concerned, the results are often unstable. There are, for instance, a number of versions extant of *Hosta sieboldiana* 'Frances Williams'.

Physical division of a large old clump is a considerable undertaking. It is only necessary to retain one bud on each division, but to reduce a colony to this fraction is quite demanding. It is really more satisfactory to divide quite young clumps at frequent intervals.

Most gardeners imagine that once a hosta has been planted, their responsibilities are at an end for the remainder of their gardening lives. Tolerance of neglect is not the same as enjoying it. If you will re-plant your hostas every five years or so in improved soil, their performance will be notably improved, although they'll take a year to settle down after the re-planting.

Damage by slugs and snails is the bane of hosta growing, since the inroads made, often quite early in the season, remain as a hideous reproach for the rest of the summer. My observation is that these troubles are not nearly as serious in the USA as in Britain. Their hostas, in September, are a lot more presentable than ours. The nematode which attacks slugs will give protection for six weeks or so, and that may be enough, but it does not tackle snails. There are metaldehyde slug and snail pellets, but they are lethal to many animals, including dogs, and as they are sweet-tasting, they are a dangerous attraction. Sometimes I wonder if, for this reason, hostas are really worthwhile. Because of their harder winters, slug populations are less of a problem in much of the USA than in Britain.

One effective way of side-stepping this trouble is by growing them in pots, tubs or other large containers. They display their foliage magnificently, like that. If allowed to become pot-bound, their strong roots may, like agapanthus, break the container.

I will take a very few examples of the different kinds of hosta. For its mauve funnel flowers, **H. rectifolia** 'Tall Boy' (1.2m/4ft) is showy and reliable. **H. ventricosa** (75cm/2½ft) has its off-years, but the lavender flowers, in July, are slightly closed at the mouth and the curved stamens are a bonus. Its seed pods are quite pleasing, too. The yellow-variegated 'Aureomarginata', in the Ventricosa group, flowers similarly. **H. lancifolia** (38cm/15in) has very shiny green, overlapping lance leaves and flowers abundantly quite late, August-September, with lavender funnels. It formed a theme in part of one American garden I visited, where the accompanying cast iron chairs and table were painted a matching shade of mauve. I happened to be wearing my mauve shirt at the time, and felt rather pleased with myself.

33 *Fuchsia* 'Riccartonii' leading
up to yellow *Microceris
ringens* and a purple *Phlox
paniculata*. The grass,
Calamagrostis × *acutiflora*
'Overdam', contributes
over a long season.

34 A quiet combination –
light-reflecting *Asarum
europaeum* and *Euphorbia
amygdaloides* var. *robbiae*.

35 Two shade-lovers in
winter: *Cyclamen
hederifolium* (which flowers
in autumn) and a
wavy-margined hartstongue
fern, *Asplenium scolopendrium*
Crispum group.

36 A happy accident, both
self-sown: an *Alstroemeria
ligtu* hybrid and the
campion, *Lychnis coronaria*.

37 If you enjoy a clash,
magenta *Geranium
psilostemon*, the crimson
oriental poppy 'Goliath' and
a giant buttercup,
Ranunculus acris 'Stevenii'.
White *Crambe cordifolia* is
coming out behind them.

34

35

38   *Houttuynia cordata* 'Chameleon' surrounded by water soldier, *Stratiotes aloides.*

39   *Petunia* 'Purple Wave' surrounding clumps of colchicum,

40   A colour harmony with *Astilbe chinensis* var. *taquetii* 'Superba', *Phlox maculata* 'Princess Sturdza'.

41   A well presented grass for a prominent postion: *Molinia caerulea* subsp. *arundinacea* 'Windspiel'.   ▷

41

Grey- or glaucous-leaved hostas, with waxy foliage include **H. sieboldiana** 'Elegans' (60cm/2ft), with large, rounded, deeply channelled leaves of puckered texture. There are cross-ripples, reminiscent of a sandy beach at low tide. The foliage in this group of hostas sometimes (not always) turns, briefly, to clear yellow, in autumn, before collapsing. The flowers, squashed into a too-dense spike on too-short stems, are an artistic mistake.

The grey 'Krossa Regal' (60cm/2ft) is sometimes my favourite of the moment, because of the presentation of its foliage, which stands upright, with an elegant twist that reveals both surfaces. If this becomes overcrowded, it spoils itself.

I grow 'Buckshaw Blue' in front of the purplish foliage of *Rodgersia pinnata* 'Superba' – an idea picked up from Graham Thomas's writing. They look fine, early in the season, but then, in addition to the usual snail damage, the hosta's leaves take on a tired appearance by July, which is too early for my liking. 'Halcyon' (38cm/15in) is one of the bluest, with smallish lance leaves. Its wan mauve flowers are inoffensive.

The yellow bias in some hostas' foliage, sometimes slight, sometimes so pronounced as to be near to eliminating green, is always fresh and becomes increasingly welcome as summer advances, when much foliage has become heavy. **H. plantaginea** var. **grandiflora** (now var. **japonica**) (60cm/2ft), which Gertrude Jekyll grew, has largely been supplanted by 'Royal Standard' (60cm/2ft), which flowers earlier and more reliably, but should still be coaxed along by a fairly sunny position. The leaves are lime green, the flowers white and strongly night-scented. Those who say the scent is faint have tried it at the wrong time of day. Early morning is good.

'Sum and Substance' (1m/3ft) is startlingly muscular – so much so that even the snails are deterred. With the largest leaves of any hosta, they are deeply ribbed, glossy, golden- or greenish-yellow. You might think coarse. If so, it is the kind of coarseness that I can appreciate. With smaller leaves, I liked 'Sun Power' (60cm/2ft) in a planting at Stourton House (next to Stourhead) with 'Halcyon' (noted above), the lacecap *Hydrangea serrata* 'Bluebird' (1m/3ft), and the fresh purple, green-edged leaves of a *Berberis thunbergii* 'Golden Ring' that was regularly cut back for smartest foliage effect.

'Zounds' becomes ever more chartreuse as the season progresses, while 'Midas Touch', with fairly large, yellow-green heart-leaves, is markedly corrugated over the entire surface.

There are many more and, as we move on to the variegated kinds, **H. fortunei** var. **albopicta** f. **aurea** (30cm/1ft) could be said to have a foot in both camps, its brightest, butter-yellow colouring in spring having faded to wan green by June. In var. **albopicta** (1m/3ft) itself, the leaves, which are on the small side, are crowded into numerous shoots held in upright bunches, in shades of yellow with green creeping in increasingly till all is green by midsummer. Good in an open woodland setting with white bluebells.

H. undulata var. **undulata** (30cm/1ft) was one of my favourites till it went down to virus diseases and it was always slow to pick up after splitting and re-planting, but only needed this occasionally. Its variegation remains fresh into autumn, being spread unequally over the whole leaf, which is attractively twisted as a consequence. Mauve funnel-flowers rise considerably above the leaves. *H. u.* var. *univittata* (1m/3ft) has the white variegation concentrated in the centre of the leaf.

There are many hostas with marginal, white variegation. **H. crispula** (60cm/2ft), in which the margin is quite broad though of variable width, used to be my favourite, till it went down to viruses. It is best in shade, as the white area scorches and becomes transparent in sun. 'Thomas Hogg', now **H. undulata** var. **albomarginata** (75cm/2½ft), is vigorous and easy but rather dull, the marginal line too narrow for effect. 'Francee' (1m/3ft) has a clean, smart white marginal variegation that retains its freshness into September.

I will conclude with the show-off 'Frances Williams' (75cm/2½ft), which has large, corrugated glaucous leaves of the sieboldiana type, broadly margined in yellow. Very soon, the yellow becomes tainted with brown patches and by July the entire colony habitually looks a wreck. Quite a bit of shade will mitigate this, but why bother?

Hottonia

PRIMULACEAE

The water violet, **Hottonia palustris**, should really be called water primula, since the candelabras of pale mauve blossom which rise a foot above the water's surface in May-June, closely resemble those of *Primula malacoides*. It has a wide distribution in Europe, including Britain, and Siberia.

This submerged aquatic is one of the pleasantest for use in the necessary role of underwater oxygenator, to keep pond water clear and prevent the supremacy of disagreeable algae, such as blanket weed, especially obtrusive in early summer. *H. palustris* has bright green, lacy foliage, arranged in rosettes. Gathered together, they form underwater clouds, which are especially noticeable in winter and against which sun-bathing goldfish are sharply defined in earliest spring.

If the water violet flowers well, it is a spectacle, but colonies that have become congested cease flowering. Indeed, the entire colony may disappear without explanation, though it is very sensitive to herbicides. Unlike *Stratiotes*, it co-exists happily with high populations of fish. Even so, some gardeners find it hard to establish. I think it best to plant, late summer, in marginal mud that will later be covered by water.

Houttuynia

SAURURACEAE

One species, **Houttuynia cordata** (30cm/1ft), a creeping, deciduous perennial, susceptible to spring frost damage, but soon recovering. The heart-shaped leaves smell strongly of oranges when bruised, and are edible, but there is a double-take on this smell, which leaves an unpleasant final impression. The small, club-like flower spikes are subtended, at the base by a few white bracts. In 'Flore Pleno', the bracts are more numerous, all along the spike, but smaller.

38 Most popular, these days, is the clone 'Chameleon'. Given full sunshine, its colouring is bright pinky-red (nearest the leaf margin), cream and green. In shade it is dimmer and loses the red. Under mixed-border conditions, especially when moist, this invasive plant is hard to control unless contained. Its slender white rhizomes travel far and deep. Containment is a good idea, which can be practised in shallow water, near to the margin of a pool, where it will make a striking feature right through summer till the first frost.

Humulus

CANNABACEAE

The brewer's hop, native or naturalised in Europe, is **Humulus lupulus** (3m/10ft or more), a climbing, deciduous perennial, and dioecious. Male plants have no great beauty but are useful as pollinators for females, plumping out their fruiting cones with seeds. In their heavy, pale green, aromatic clusters, these are a handsome early autumn feature.

However, the golden hop, *H. l.* 'Aureus', although generally male, has the great asset of conspicuous yellow-green colouring in its compound palmate leaves. Grow over an artificial support, round which its shoots can twine, or over a strong-framed shrub. It contrasts well, both for colour and leaf shape, with a forward planting of glaucous hostas, but the hop will overlay the hostas, if not prevented.

Hyacinthoides

HYACINTHACEAE/LILIACEAE

The bluebells have been shunted from *Scilla* to *Endymion* and now to clumsy *Hyacinthoides*. Our native bluebell, **H. non-scripta**, grows in woodland, in the south, and even if the trees are eliminated it will continue in full daylight, unabashed, if not disturbed. In Scotland, it is generally seen in the open, but often where bracken will later take over.

If you have a woodland garden, a sheet of bluebells will be a great asset, their scent being more pronounced when massed. But you should also introduce them to meadow areas, wherever the ground is damp; and there may, even here, be trees or shrubs near which to colonise them. The blue of bluebells is pretty hopeless to render in photography, as there is an element of mauve in it which becomes accentuated rather disgustingly. The pure white albino will occur as a small fraction in most wild colonies. At Ramster, on the borders of West Sussex and Surrey, whites predominate, to unusual and telling effect.

I do not recommend introducing bluebells to your flower borders. Their foliage dies conspicuously, they seed freely and the bulbs find their way to such a low level as to be hard to dig out.

The Spanish bluebell, **H. hispanica** (1m/3ft) is more commonly offered and grown, especially in urban front gardens, where it makes a horrible mess after flowering. But it is a good plant in its way, larger, bolder and generally of a paler shade of blue. It also has pink- and white-flowered forms, the latter delightful, in half-shade, interlocked with Bowles's golden grass, *Milium effusum* 'Aureum'.

There is a particularly large, bold and clump-forming cultivar of Spanish bluebell, itself light blue in colour, called 'Chevithorn'. It has the great advantage, when used in borders, of being almost sterile and of *not* self-sowing. With fertile colonies that you do not wish to self-sow, you should, after flowering and before the seeds have ripened, clasp a number of stalks at a time between both hands, and tug. They will sever cleanly and easily from the bulbs.

Hyacinthus

HYACINTHACEAE/LILIACEAE

The sweet-scented florists' hyacinths all derive from ***Hyacinthus orientalis***, native of Asia Minor and countries next to it. The white Roman hyacinths, with light stems and making clumps of small bulbs, come nearest to the wild type. They also occur in pink and blue cultivars, such as the pale blue 'Borah' (23cm/9in), which I have had in my garden since 1956.

Indeed, most hyacinths, even though they may start life in pots or bowls, are extremely good garden plants. However I may be intending to grow them, I always choose the smallest sized bulb available in the desired cultivar. Large bulbs have been overfed, and produce clumsy, often fasciated flower spikes. A spell under ordinary garden conditions works wonders in fining them down. In time, with a willing variety like 'Ostara' (mid-blue), you will get a dense colony of spikes, all of them small.

The danger, when growing them permanently outside, is that you will forget where they are, in their dormant season, and unwittingly destroy them. They combine nicely with other April features and they prolong the hyacinth season, outdoor plants taking over from those you grew inside.

61 Try growing them beneath a specimen of *Spiraea japonica* 'Goldflame', whose young foliage is at its brightest in April. I like the effect of a soft pink hyacinth in this context, but you may prefer blue. Then, with the clumpy spring-flowering pea, *Lathyrus vernus*, in its normal, purple version, the pale yellow, late-flowering 'City of Haarlem' is a happy choice. And I like an early white hyacinth with the miniature trumpet daffodil, *Narcissus minor*. The outdoor hyacinths are nice for picking, too, and combining in a posy with other spring flowers.

Their bulbs have the advantage of being unattractive to mice, but we do regularly have badgers digging among ours.

The price of hyacinths of comparable size and kind varies greatly according to source. You will need to go to the expensive firms for unusual cultivars, but in other cases, where you just want a quantity of good but smaller bulbs in a popular variety, they will be available at one third of the price from a wholesale firm (without an expensively illustrated catalogue), that also welcomes retail business.

Hylomecon

PAPAVERACEAE

From the Far East comes a hardy, spring-flowering poppy, **Hylomecon japonica** (30cm/1ft). A clump-forming perennial, it bears rich yellow flowers above a well-furnished, leafy platform. May is its season and it likes a moisture-retaining, leaf soil in partial shade. In summer, it goes to rest. An easy plant, which I grow badly.

I

Impatiens

BALSAMINACEAE

The popular Busy Lizzie of windowsills is generally known in gardening circles as *Impatiens*, which happens to be its correct name. Although treated as an annual it is actually a tender perennial and in frost-free gardens is frequently used as permanent bedding. It is especially valuable in part shade, which also cools down the amazing range of colours found in any seed mixture. In theory, these clash appallingly but in fact they are a triumphant success, orange and red vying with magenta, pink and purple, not to mention white. The solvent is the plants' dark foliage, which is as the night sky to a galaxy of stars.

Breeders have, unfortunately, reduced the size of most impatiens seed strains to dense blobs of colour wherein little foliage is any longer apparent, but looser, more naturally growing mixtures can be found and they improve as the season advances and the plants loosen up. The parentage of these commercial seed strains is so mixed that no latinised name can be given to them.

The genuinely annual impatiens need not detain us but there are other perennials, of which **I. tinctoria** (1.2m/4ft) is the most notable in gardens wishing to create a tropical effect. Above coarsely unattractive lanceolate leaves, it bears a branching inflorescence of surprisingly large white flowers, purple at the centre. They are swooningly night-scented. Often the display is at its peak in autumn, when the first hint of night frost destroys all top growth. Summer flowering can be obtained if capsid bugs are not a problem or are a problem that you have under control. They imbibe the sap from the tips of growing shoots and destroy their incipient flower buds. The roots are tuberous and can be treated like a dahlia's. Sometimes they survive the winter if left *in situ*.

A charming species to bed out for the summer is the low, ground-hugging *I. pseudoviola*, which is well named as its little blush-white flowers do resemble a violet's. It never stops flowering. Easily raised from cuttings but 100% frost-tender.

19

Incarvillea

Bignoniaceae

An exotic-looking genus, none too hardy. All from central-east Asia. *Incarvillea arguta* can make a large bushy plant, covered with pink, penstemon-like flowers in early summer, but seldom like that in Britain. The long, thin seed capsules are notable. Needs a hot position and the best drainage.

I. delavayi (60cm/2ft) is the easiest species and excellent in Scotland. A clumpy perennial, its largeish basal leaves are pinnate, with broad segments. Trumpet flowers are borne, in early summer, in a cluster at the top of a naked scape. They open wide at the mouth and are showy, but of an unfortunate shade of crude pink with a good deal of blue in it.

I. mairei (15cm/6in) is much shorter in the stem but with, if anything, larger flowers, their trumpets open at the mouth and often of a good shade of clear pink. 'Bees Pink' is one such that I grew for a number of years, but it probably went down to bad drainage and slugs. The roots are fleshy. Easily raised from seed, the seedlings flowering in their second year.

Inula

Asteraceae/Compositae

A genus of very hardy perennials having yellow daisies. Most splendid is *Inula magnifica* (2m/6ft), though there are inferior strains around. Large, 6in daisies with finely spun rays which quiver in the wind. A widely branching candelabrum, flowering in July. The winter skeletons are quite good. Makes handsome clumps in a meadow area, but some mulching in winter is advisable.

I. helenium (2m/6ft), is a pale shadow of the last, with quite insignificant daisies, but grown because it is the herb elecampane. *I. hookeri* (1m/3ft) is a winner. The rays are twisted into a spiral, in the bud, which opens with very finely spun rays. Much visited by butterflies. The rootstock runs, but is easily checked with a spade around the perimeter.

I. barbata (30cm/1ft) has sizeable flowers but on quite a short plant. Colonises a little.

Ipheion

ALLIACEAE/LILIACEAE

This genus of bulbs, from Uruguay and Argentina, would surely have been included within *Allium*, but for the fact of its flowers being borne singly and not in umbels. The foliage is typically onion-scented.

Ipheion uniflorum (15cm/6in) has at various times been included in *Brodiaea, Milla* and *Triteleia*, so it is clearly a botanists' headache.

Its lank, strap leaves appear in autumn and the first flowers may be blooming as early as January, though the main flush comes in April-May. The broad-segmented flowers are like prosperous stars, and appear to be white, until you see the white clone, 'Album', when you realise that they are tinted blue. Various more or less blue-tinted forms have appeared, through the years, the deeper their colouring, as in 'Froyle Mill', the weaker their constitution. 'Wisley Blue' is a good compromise, but really the charm is as strong whether blue is dominant or not.

The bulbs increase with a will and make sheets of blossom. I have never seen it grown to better effect than among the carmine shoot spears of *Paeonia lactiflora* hybrids. In summer, ipheions become completely dormant.

'Rolf Fiedler' is a particularly showy clone or hybrid, bluish and with very broad segments, composing a rounded flower. It is not hardy. Pot-grown, the bulbs quickly become overcrowded and hence blind, so it is really wise to re-pot annually, rather thickly in a pan, grading the bulbs for this purpose.

Iris

IRIDACEAE

I shall try to be brisk about *Iris*. As soon as you delve into the ramifications of the genus, you become horribly aware of your ignorance. Irises are incomparably lovely, only pipped at the post by orchids, maybe. The place to see them is in the wild, where they look better than anywhere else, so that it seems futile to try and make them happy under garden conditions (I am not referring to the man-made beauties, of course.) In the wild, whether in the Syrian desert, in the mountains of east Turkey or in the snowmelt of Sierra Nevada, where I had to wade leg-deep to get a closer look at *I. missouriensis* – wherever it may be, they never fail to fascinate in their specialised habitats.

In the garden, they are not necessarily that easy to accommodate among mixed plantings. Their flowering season is largely in early summer, but it is over in two or three weeks and then what? The plants cannot generally be moved out of the way; nor can they be ignored, as they often look quite drab during the rest of the growing season. If they have rhizomes, they may need to be baked in order to flower well the next year, so masking their presence in any way is counterproductive.

Many of the bulbous kinds can be lifted and stored, however, or, since deciduous, they are easily masked in situ, the main point being to remember where they are.

Bulbous irises

The earliest in flower are the dwarfest, which is practical, in view of the weather prevailing. In a mild winter, **Iris histrioides** 'Major' (7.5cm/3in) will be flowering in early January; blue with a yellow flash on the falls. It can best be enjoyed in a pan, grown cold but protected from the weather. However, it is tough and a colony increases with me, interplanted among the rhizomes of *Euphorbia griffithii*, then totally dormant.

The closely related **I. winogradowii** is pale yellow, flowering in February. Best grown hard but in a pan. When repotting in early summer, plenty of spawn (tiny bulbils) can be collected wherewith to grow on new stock. The leaves develop after flowering. I prefer this species to the cheaper and more popular **I. danfordiae**, which has a chunkier flower of a stronger yellow. The original flowering bulb disintegrates after flowering and the bulbils take time to grow on and flower again.

I. reticulata (15cm/6in) flowers late February to March, indigo-purple and graceful though upright, forming prolific clumps over a period. This is really far better in the garden than pan-grown. Under the latter conditions, blindness shows up in some of the bulbs, whereas when clumped up in the garden, this would pass unnoticed. Associates well with a hardy geranium such as 'Mavis Simpson', 'Syabru', 'Dilys' or 'Salome', which make voluminous growth in summer but die back to a central core in autumn, leaving space around them. There are many named hybrid cultivars.

'Katharine Hodgkin' (12.5cm/5in) is a vigorous and easy hybrid, classed as a Reticulata but probably with *I. winogradowii* blood. The flowers are speckled and streaked all over, yellow, grey, off white, in a somewhat reptilian manner. February to March.

In April I look forward to pots or half-pots (some depth is needed) of **I. bucharica**, an iris with permanent fleshy roots that is set back by disturbance. The leaves are outstandingly shiny, the yellow-and-white flowers several to a stem and opening in succession. **I. orchioides** is similar. **I. magnifica** (30cm/1ft) is rather taller and larger-flowered; usually, though not necessarily, a weak shade of mauve. These can all be grown as permanencies in a sunny, well-drained border at the foot of a wall.

The so-called Dutch irises are said to derive from **I. xiphium**. 30-60cm/1-2ft tall, they are excellent florists' flowers, flowering late May through June, but treatment of the bulbs allows them to be flowered at almost any season. The flowers are borne singly or in pairs. Young foliage appears already in the autumn. Get them into a position where they are undisturbed, and they will make clumps that last for half a century (so far). Nice bright colours and others that are subtle. Some of the more modern cultivars like 'Professor Blaauw' (deep blue) and 'Purple Sensation' have a wider flower than normal, with longer, horizontal falls. Spanish iris come in an interesting colour range, always in a mixture, slightly later flowering and less vigorous.

The English can lay no proprietorial claims on so-called English iris (45cm/1½ft), derived from **I. latifolia** (syn. *I. xiphioides*). The colour range is limited – deep 'blue', mauve and white. The falls are wide and long, the standards reduced. Unfortunately these are nowadays often only available in mixture. I have a purple strain which I do not allow to self-sow, as the seedlings do not come true. The bulbs show through in January but are the last of all the bulbous types to flower, in late June. Stock builds up quickly and the surplus is good for naturalising in a meadow. Flowers showing mottling are virus-infected and the bulbs will not last long.

Bearded irises

This is the most popular group and has received the greatest attention from breeders, not always to the flower's advantage. Bearded irises have thick rhizomes, which like to be on the soil's surface and to receive a good baking. They are extremely tough and can be sent dry over long distances and over long periods without being actually killed. In the garden, colonies become over-congested quite quickly, over three years or so, and will need dividing and replanting in improved soil. The earlier in the season that this is done, the fuller the recovery that will be made in the year of division. If you know that your irises are going to flower little or not at all, replant them in April; otherwise, as soon as they have flowered. Early action provides the chance of freer flowering in the next year.

Freedom of flowering varies from year to year for other reasons. In some years, all the irises are bursting with buds and flowers, probably thanks to a ripening summer the previous year. In other years, flowering as between varieties is patchy, some good some poor. It is worth visiting a publicly shared iris garden, at this time, and making a note of the free-flowering types for your own use. In Scotland and other parts where summer heat is only moderate, bearded irises may, with a few exceptions, not be much good at all.

The plants tend to look pretty sordid, later in the summer, and they readily gather weeds among the rhizomes. Best not to get carried away (though I admit that is joyless advice).

Bearded irises vary in stature from very tall – 1.2m/4ft – to only a few inches. They are classified accordingly. The tall kinds need individual staking of the stems, which are rarely wind-firm. Hence the development of the popular intermediates, but their chunkiness is somewhat graceless. The current vogue in breeding circles seems to be for ruffled segments and for falls that stand horizontally. This seems a pity. As the withered blooms spoil the presentation of those that are in prime condition, they really need dead-heading daily.

Moisture-loving irises

Our native yellow flag, *I. pseudacorus* (1.2m/4ft), has a wide distribution in the Old World and is also naturalised in much of North America. Its bright yellow colouring cheers many a bog in June, in the Isle of Lewis, of the Outer Hebrides, for instance, where it quickly follows on the similarly coloured kingcups, *Caltha palustris*. *I. p.* var. *bastardii* is a pleasing variant, pale yellow with thin, dark veining. 'Variegata', is brilliantly yellow-variegated on the young shoots in spring, but this is lost in summer.

I. versicolor (1m/3ft), from the eastern USA and Canada, is also naturalised elsewhere in shallow water or boggy areas similar to those favoured by *I. pseudacorus*, but can be grown as a border perennial. Purple with white and a little yellow at the centre-base. The last two are both subject to a plague of dark brown sawfly larvae, which strips their leaves. Under pond conditions it is difficulty to do anything about this as sprays are liable to damage pond life.

I. × robusta 'Gerald Darby' (1m/3ft) is purplish-blue with distinctive purple stems and a graceful flowering habit. The foliage turns attractive yellowish shades in late autumn. That is excellent in shallow water.

I. laevigata (60cm/2ft), from Japan, has large, spreading falls and is a beautiful, fresh shade of bright blue. It is usually grown under water. It often flowers a second time in October. The pure white 'Alba' is also good, while 'Variegata' has the cleanest white variegation of any iris and also flowers well (blue).

I. ensata (1.2m/4ft), also from Japan, has been greatly developed by hybridisers both there and in the USA, giving us the Kaempferi hybrids. They like a lot of moisture in their growing season but decent drainage in winter. In most, the rounded falls or outer segments are much enlarged, while the standards or inner segments are reduced, though in some cases the latter are of almost equal valency to the former and, being all in the same plane, give the appearance of a rotate bloom, even semi-double. Purple, mauve and white are the principal colourings, or mauve with purple veining. 'Rose Queen' is old-fashioned, with smaller, pinkish-mauve flowers, the falls drooping, the standards tiny.

The typical *I. sibirica* (1m/3ft), as we have grown it in gardens for many, many years, is an upright, many-stemmed, clump-forming plant with masses of grassy leaves surrounding the flowering stems. The flowers are a bluish shade of purple, small but numerous. In a border I like it combined in its season with scarlet oriental poppies, but it is a tiresome border plant later on, when the leaves splay outwards, tending to overlay neighbouring plants. However, it is excellent naturalised in damp places and can cope with rough grass.

The related *I. chrysographes* likes similar conditions, though it is rather less robust. The most popular variety is simply known as black form. Its flowers are astonishingly dark. *I. forrestii* (1m/3ft) comes in here; a quiet shade of yellow, its flowers well presented and numerous.

Spurias

Most of the hybrids connected with *I. spuria* are tall, sometimes 2m/6ft or even more but self-supporting and they have an air of great solidity, which makes them very striking in their season, though a bit of a liability after it. They like rich, moisture-retaining soil. and not to be frequently divided. Blue, yellow, apricot and buff is their principal colour range.

I. orientalis (long known as *I. ochroleuca*) (1.2m/4ft), white with a yellow flash, is typical. *I. monnieri* is clear, strong yellow, but there are many interesting shades.

Unguicularis

The Algerian iris, *I. **unguicularis*** (30cm/1ft), was long known as *I. stylosa*, on account of the apparent stem, which you pick, being actually the flower's style, the ovary being at ground level. Its great popularity is on account of its habit of flowering in any mild spell from autumn to spring. The silky-textured mauve flowers seem too fragile to stand the weather of that season, but flower buds about to open can be picked to unfurl indoors, and will last for two or three days.

The foliage is extremely untidy, but on the whole it is best to do nothing much about that; rather to site the plants where they are convenient for picking, but out of obtrusive view in the summer. They need a baking position but not too poor soil. Division and re-planting should be rare, as the plants take a year or more to settle down again. Spring has traditionally been the season for this operation, but autumn may possibly be better, as that is the time when this species becomes active again, after semi-aestivation. When gathering buds for the house, always pick, never pull them. The buds occur in pairs, low down and out of sight, one developing before the other. If you pull, both buds will break off together and the later one will never develop.

There are several good cultivars. 'Walter Butt' is pale mauve, early-flowering. 'Mary Barnard' is seldom in bloom before the new year; a rich, deep shade. The albino 'Alba' is rather thin-textured, usually fairly late-flowering.

Closely related is *I. **lazica*** (30cm/1ft) of an open-centred, slightly spreading habit, with small, purplish flowers in spring. I threw it out.

A few others

In *I. **japonica*** (45cm/1½ft), the fans of evergreen leaves stand on their supporting rhizomes well above ground level (this is an even more prominent feature in *I. **wattii***, a rather tender species). The pale mauve flowers are borne, in spring, in sprays, rather like some orchids. Beautiful at its best and there is a good variegated form, but prone to disfiguring slug damage. Good in shade.

*I. **graminea*** (30cm/1ft) is just about as insignificant an iris as you are likely to find, with small, purplish flowers buried among its leaves. But they have a delicious, fruity scent, for which we grow this undemanding plant.

*I. **foetidissima*** is the stinking iris (the leaves smell a bit if crushed), native to woodland on alkaline soils. The flowers are nothing to seek out but the fruits split open in autumn to reveal sheaves of bright orange, long-lasting seeds. Tuck it away under a shady wall or hedge bottom.

On the western side of the USA grow **I. douglasiana** (30cm/1ft) and **I. innominata** (15cm/6in), both shade-lovers, the latter having given rise to the more interesting colour forms, especially apricot. Lots of flowers, all together, in May, on a low, evergreen plant. These are calcifuge.

From Japan, we have the May-flowering, sun-loving roof iris, **I. tectorum** (30cm/1ft), but Japanese summers are wet and steamy and it does like moisture at that season. Not a difficult garden plant with quite bold, blue flowers. There is also a fine white form, 'Alba'.

Ixia

Iridaceae

South African corms. Rather tender in Britain but well worth growing in a sunny position where drainage is good. As growth is made through winter, frosting of the foliage, then, is the chief danger. The flowers are generally borne in spikes and the weight of blossom arches them to a height of 30cm/1ft or so. Flowering is in early summer and the flowers are sensitive to light and warmth, remaining closed when conditions do not suit them. They open to bowl or star shapes.

Bought as mixtures, they can be disappointing, with little colour range, but this can include white, yellow, orange, pink, carmine and, in **Ixia viridiflora**, vivid, al-most metallic green. There are a number of named clones. If ixias like you, their numbers will build up over the years. In Victoria, Australia, they make a fine, self-perpetuating ingredient under meadow conditions or in roadside verges.

J

Jaborosa

SOLANACEAE

Jaborosa integrifolia (15cm/6in) is not showy, but still a strangely compelling plant. It comes from the central south of South America and is clearly related to *Nicotiana*, but very low-growing. It has a running, rhizomatous habit. The leaves appear singly from ground level and are dark green, elliptical, rather leathery. The flowers, also, are borne singly, white, a long tube opening at the mouth into a star with rather narrow petals. It is powerfully and agreeably (albeit immorally) night-scented.

K

Kirengeshoma

HYDRANGEACEAE

A Japanese genus of woodland plants. Best is ***Kirengeshoma palmata*** (60cm/2ft) (*K. koreana* is similar but with a flower shape of less distinction.). It likes a leafy soil (is unhappy given high alkalinity), plenty of moisture and partial shade. Its stems are near to black; the broadly ovate leaves margined with sharp points and rather maple-like. Flowering is in late summer and autumn, with open sprays of soft yellow, shuttlecock-shaped, yet slightly asymmetrical flowers, with a more prominent lower lip.

There is nothing like it. A good contrast is made with an adjacent planting of an arum bearing clubs of scarlet berries.

Knautia

DIPSACACEAE

To all practical intents a scabious, **Knautia macedonica** (60cm/2ft) has a popular appeal which I find it hard to justify. The small scabious flower heads are very dark red, not showing up at any distance. They are borne over a long season, but the plant is extremely vulnerable to powdery mildew.

Kniphofia

ASPHODELACEAE/LILIACEAE

Named after Professor Johann Hieronymus Kniphof (1704-63), of Erfurt, Kniphofia as generally pronounced in English-speaking countries is incomprehensible in every other language. Knip is one syllable, hof another; we should not really run the p and the h together as we do. The antiquated synonym *Tritoma* is still used in a few old-fashioned catalogues.

This genus of South and Central African evergreen perennials, with sturdy spikes of red, orange, yellow, green or white, tubular flowers, is one of the most powerful for summer and autumn border use. Winter hardiness can be a question. In Britain, most of us can succeed with most of those that are likely to come our way.

In the wild, kniphofias usually grow in wet, even boggy, places. I recollect, in 1946, while travelling by train from Kenya to Uganda, seeing a whole marsh of, possibly, **K. thomsonii** var. **snowdenii**, in bloom. But in latitudes with marked winters, good drainage at that season is important.

The larger kniphofias need a good deal of space, for their long, lanky foliage, which maddens the orderly gardener. Does, or does one not shorten them, when tidying the borders in autumn? I recommend leaving them alone and not tidying the borders until spring. By then, new leaves will be sprouting from the centre of each cluster. Carefully steadying and preserving these, you can peel away the old leaves, one by one. By the end of this operation, your colonies will be looking unbelievably spruce. You can then give them a good surface mulch and a dressing of fertiliser. Splitting and replanting is rarely necessary, but it is easily performed (always in spring), each rosette comprising a new and separate plant.

In the case of the woody-stemmed **K. caulescens**, I find that frequent division of its crowns, every second year, gives rise to the handsomest foliage, which is the main point of this species. Pieces can be cleanly severed from the stock, the leaves shortened back by half (old leaves being peeled off) and replanted with some woody stem for anchor but no roots at all. Again, in spring.

Kniphofias have a long and varied season of flowering. Some, the least distinguished, will be in bloom by early May. Among the handsomest are the majority of autumn-flowerers, October being an excellent month. But, within the same species, you'll often get outliers, so to speak – out-of-season spikes, either early or late.

They hybridise readily and are easily raised from seed, so there are a great many named varieties about, with the raisers showing a strong inclination to see their geese as swans. There is also much overlap in naming. A flush of bloom from a showy cultivar – and there are few showier perennials – may easily bowl you over, but consider that some get their flowering done all in a matter of two weeks, with nothing to follow, while others spread their flowering season so that, without ever being unduly sparse, they may be making a good display for a couple of months.

Red-hot-poker is the commonest popular name, but is loosely and deceptively applied to the entire genus, whose members are frequently a long way from red. In many, the colour changes markedly from the bud to the open, tubular, flower.

Among the most overpoweringly red-hot (there is a masochistic pleasure in being overpowered, on occasion), is the August-September-flowering **K. uvaria** 'Nobilis' (2.4m/8ft). It is everyone's idea of what this flower should be, and then a good bit more. The flowering stems are massively crowned by thick spikes of orange-red flowers. The tubular shape of these, incidentally, attracts nectar-feeding birds – the most grotesque and unlikely of these, in Britain, being the house sparrow. This kniphofia looks well in front of the long, lavender spikes of *Buddleia* 'Lochinch' and next to the creamy plumes of *Artemisia lactiflora*.

K. linearifolia (1.2m/4ft), which has a wide distribution, is very variable. In the clone that I have from Kew, where it grows next to the Palm House, the leaves are an outstandingly fresh green, so that one need not resent its not flowering till October – bold spikes of soft orange, becoming yellow. This is also known as **K. uvaria maxima**. 'Samuel's Sensation' (1.2m/4ft) is one of the most striking of the red pokers, with dark stems and not inconveniently tall.

Tall kniphofias tend to get knocked sideways by wind. Clearly, a flower with a long, naked scape of this sort does not lend itself to staking, but the stems right themselves, in their upper reaches, so that the overall effect, with spikes at varying levels, is not at all bad, especially at a distance.

45 'Lord Roberts' (1.5m/5ft) has long, elegant red spikes, with just a hint of pink in them and the same colour in buds and flowers. Autumn-flowering. *K. rooperi* (1.2m/4ft), with orange buds, opening yellow, has squashed-up-looking spikes, almost as broad as long. It goes well with the creamy plumes of newly opened pampas grass, *Cortaderia selloana* 'Pumila' (2m/6ft).

Of unusual appearance is *K. thomsonii* var. *snowdenii* (1.2m/4ft). The coral-coloured flowers have slightly bent tubes and their spacing on the spike is wide.

Small kniphofias should suit small gardens. In fact, I think they look best in large groups, especially Beth Chatto's 'Little Maid' (60cm/2ft). From mid-August for two months, it makes a prodigious number of flower spikes, pale green in bud, cream to white when open. Brimstone (60cm/2ft) is well named, October flowering. *K. galpanii, K. macowanii* and *K. nelsonii* are all synonyms for *K. triangularis* subsp. *triangularis* (60cm/2ft), but many different hybrids are sold under one or other of these names. The leaves should be fine, the flower colour, coral to orange. This is September-October-flowering.

K. northiae is most unusual, making a low, broad-leaved single rosette of leaves. I am not fond of it. *K. caulescens* is a lot better, though extremely variable. Some clones flower in June (60cm/2ft) and ripen good seed. Others flower in September (soft orange to pale yellow) and do not seed. One immense clone that I had from Dublin, is June-flowering. Most make a number of young, leafy rosettes, after flowering, from which they can be propagated, but the Irish clone divides into only two. It has ripened seed, so I have hopes.

This species makes a fine feature on a border promontory (a change from bergenias and lamb's lugs). There is a great apron of it, projecting over gravel, at Crathes Castle, near Aberdeen, Scotland. If not frequently divided, it stops flowering. Leaf tips tend to die off prematurely – my one slight grouse.

L

Lamium

This is the genus of the dead-nettles (dead, because they look like stinging nettles but don't). In the canon of the elite, among hardy plantsmen, they come pretty low and I have to admit to not being very well up in them myself.

Lamium purpureum is one of the commonest annual weeds in my garden, probably in yours, but it has its moments of looking as though it should be saved. Seedlings that have overwintered have leaves of a rich purple and the deep pinkish purple flowers show up well with this background.

L. maculatum, a ground-cover perennial, introduced from Europe in forms having a white blotch in the centre of the leaf, has been considerably worked on by selection. Typically, it has a wealth of pinkish-purple blossom in spring. Of the many cultivars, 'Beacon Silver' is grown for its small, whitened leaves – highly prone to mildew. 'Chequers', correctly named, has a white stripe down the centre of each leaf.

'White Nancy', with considerably whitened leaves and pure white flowers, I grow with *Pulmonaria* 'Sissinghurst White' in rather deep shade beneath *Osmanthus delavayi*, and they show up well. 'Aureum' has bright yellow leaves in spring with a paler stripe down the centre. The pinky-mauve flowers are in startling contrast. It is rather weak growing and 'burns' in bright sunlight but I have seen it looking good. I have an effective salmon-coloured flower form whose name I have lost.

Our native, woodland archangel is **L. galeobdolon** (38cm/15in), though it spent a spell as *Galeobdolon luteum*. The yellow flowers are arranged in whorls along a vertical spike and it is a handsome feature where coppicing has been recent. This spreads by overground stolons, a habit abundantly shared by the preferred ground-cover cultivar, 'Florentinum'. This is such an aggressive plant that it roots itself into all its neighbours and is difficult to get rid of. Furthermore, unless cut to the ground, annually in winter, it clutters itself with the hoops of old stolons. However, there are places for such a plant and, provided it does receive its yearly cut, it is handsome, first with flowers, in spring, and then its silver-variegated foliage. 'Hermann's Pride' is a clone with a pattern of variegation in which the veins are dark against a silvered background. The leaves' outline is toothed and comes to sharp points. With me, it has been a disappointment.

Lapeirousia – see Anomatheca

Lathraea

SCROPHULARIACEAE

The only true parasite in this work, **Lathraea clandestina** (7.5cm/3in) makes brilliant patches of purple, almost like an analine dye, for several spring months. From a distance you might mistake it for Dutch crocuses (*Crocus vernus* cultivars). It come from west Europe and seems pretty well hardy in England. There are magnificent displays of it beneath the willows along the Backs at Cambridge. The flowers are borne in tight clusters and are hooded, two-lipped like a labiate. There are no leaves, the plant feeding entirely on the roots of its host.

L. clandestina has a wide range of hosts, but shows a preference for willows and poplars. Where I have the silver willow, *Salix alba* var. *sericea*, pollarded, in my main mixed border, this toothwort is established to provide early interest at ground level before the foliage of other plants can mask it (in this I have been *partially* successful).

If you know of a colony having a friendly owner, ask for a lump of lathraea roots (any season) and plant them near to the roots of the chosen host. You may even get flowers the next year. It can also be propagated from seed, scattered in the right place, but this takes far longer to establish and may be unsuccessful, in which case you'll have lost a few years, waiting.

Lathyrus

PAPILIONACEAE/LEGUMINOSAE

Of the annuals in this genus, the sweet pea is by far the best known. It is therefore irritating, I find, to hear one or other of the perennials referred to as everlasting *sweet* peas, seeing that their flowers have no scent at all.

In spring, however, we first encounter **Lathyrus vernus** (30cm/1ft), a clumpy, non-climbing perennial with bright purple flowers. I like it in front of a fairly severely pruned bush of *Lonicera nitida* 'Baggesen's Gold'. It is easily propagated from seed, if you remember to catch it at the right moment. From seed, you will sometimes get plants of the milk-and-roses, pink-and-white form called 'Alboroseus', which makes a change.

Come June, we are into the herbaceous climbers. ***L. grandiflorus*** (2m/6ft) is the true everlasting pea. It has a running rootstock, which can be a problem in mixed company. We dig out what we can and pull out the young shoots when they appear in the middle of some other plant, rooting them as soft cuttings, for sale. The flowers are quite large, for a perennial species, and vivid magenta of the best quality. It can look splendid climbing through a dark-leaved *Cotinus*, such as 'Royal Purple'.

L. tuberosus (60cm/2ft) enlivens the roadsides in Hungary and other European countries. It runs around and perennates with tubers. The fairly small flowers, borne in racemes, are bright carmine. It might be a nuisance in a border but when I tried to establish it in my meadow, it was unable to cope with the turf.

I suppose ***L. latifolius*** (3m/10ft) is the best all-purpose species, clump-forming and not invasive. It is an excellent herbaceous climber, with quite long, showy racemes of moderate-sized flowers over a long season. The colour varies from a fairly aggressive magenta, with rather too much of blue in it, through a pleasingly soft pink to pure white. The last is, perhaps, the best, combining particularly well on wall or fence with one of the yellow, bell-flowered clematis such as 'Bill Mackenzie'. This is often named 'White Pearl', but as cuttings of young shoots, taken in early spring, are a tedious and limited method of propagation, it is usually offered as seedlings or seed. That may give rise to plenty of pink seedlings as well as white, so you just have to select.

L. rotundifolius (2.4m/8ft) is smaller-flowered and its colour varies, being sometimes on the blue side of red, but in the most desirable form (and it is usually raised from seed), it is pure brick red and very lovely.

Lord Anson's Pea, ***L. nervosus*** (1m/3ft), is made a great fuss of, though a coarse plant and easily lost (I'm not sure why). The spikelets of fair-sized flowers are an unexpectedly bright blue, in June-July, but it is a mouldy-looking plant and extremely prone to mildew. Try it once but don't bother a second time.

Leucanthemella

ASTERACEAE/COMPOSITAE

Leucanthemella serotina (2m/6ft) has been tossed around among the botanists. Known to Gertrude Jekyll, who grew it in her michaelmas daisy border, as *Pyrethrum* *uliginosum*, it was next *Chrysanthemum uliginosum* (the specific epithet helpfully indicates its preference for boggy ground) and is now *Leucanthemella serotina*, and *serotina* does correctly indicate that it flowers late, that is, in October.

The plant, which spreads by short, white rhizomes, has heavily toothed leaves, but is visually no great shakes in the long run-up to its flowering. Its fair-sized, white daisies have a green disc. They are born on stems which branch fairly high up.

Because of its height, this plant is likely to need support under border conditions. However, this height can be materially reduced by pinching out the tips of the shoots when 60cm/2ft tall. Also by regular lifting and replanting of the crowns, each spring.

It may be too much of a passenger, in most herbaceous or mixed borders, even in large gardens, but it has its place; for instance in a fairly coarse, large-scale planting near to water, with such as *Eupatorium purpureum* and zebra grasses – *Miscanthus sinensis* 'Zebrinus' and 'Strictus'. It is such a nice, fresh-looking plant in its season, that one would like to have it somewhere. A michaelmas daisy border, together with boltonias and Japanese anemones, would also be ideal.

Leucanthemum

ASTERACEAE/COMPOSITAE

Leucanthemum vulgare (45cm/1½ft), once *Chrysanthemum leucanthemum*, is the moon daisy or ox-eyed daisy. It is a beautiful component in meadow turf, best introduced by raising plants from seed; then, when they are strong, after being lined out to grow on, transferring them to meadow turf. You can scatter seed, if you have enough of it, but this is a hit-and-miss method. Moon daisies have a strange habit of disappearing from areas where they were once abundant, and I have arrived at no explanation for this.

There are other ways to enjoy them in the garden. They colonise the paving cracks on our sitting-out terrace, making a wonderfully generous display from late May for three or four weeks. The way their daisies turn to face the sun is especially noticeable here. We also have them in and on top of dry walling.

Best management is, immediately after flowering, to seize all the stems together on a plant, low down, and to tug, so that they break off near the base (from which they will soon make new leaf growth). While doing this, you are particularly aware of the plant's dog's-turd smell – but no harm done. The plants will remain discreetly in abeyance till the next spring.

The perennial we knew as *Chrysanthemum maximum*, is now said not to be a species, but a hybrid between a Pyrenean and a Portuguese species, and it is exiled from *Chrysanthemum*, becoming **Leucanthemum × superbum**. This is the shasta daisy, but it was only recently that I realised it had no connection with the Shasta mountain, tribe or area of North California.

Shasta daisies are blank, staring white, while their foliage is darkest green. The combination can be rather overpowering. One mitigation will be to grow single-flowered cultivars, with a yellow disc. The flowers of 'Everest' (1m/3ft) are large and handsome, though often disfigured by the capsid bugs which feed on the inflorescence. If you don't know what a capsid looks like, you may be sure of seeing them sunbathing and feeding on the discs and rays of your shasta daisies. They are green and quickly disappear on the approach of a shadow. 'Phyllis Smith' (1m/3ft) has each ray deeply divided down the centre, giving a lacy (or ragged) effect.

'Double' shastas, have enlarged, off-white tubular florets, so that the centre as well as the rest of the flower is white. This made them especially popular for use in funeral wreaths, when white wreaths were popular, the preferred variety being 'Esther Read' (60cm/2ft). This is a very long-flowering variety of some merit, but it will die out fairly readily if not regularly replanted each spring. That is the case with many long-flowering perennials, which tend not to provide themselves with enough non-flowering, overwintering shoots.

Shastas daisies, in any case, though most are long-lived perennials when entirely neglected (they can be a good feature in rough grass), perform far more glamorously if replanted, one or two crowns in each position and in improved soil, every spring. The taller kinds may need support.

The white flowers can be changed to yellow if enclosed with fumes of ammonia. Blue and pink dyes have also been frequently resorted to for the benefit of the florists' trade in cut blooms.

Leucojum

AMARYLLIDACEAE/LILIACEAE

These are the snowflakes, in contrast to snowdrops. All are of European origin. First on the scene is **Leucojum vernum** (23cm/9in), the spring snowflake. Its white bells are quite sizeable and usually have a green spot at the tip of each segment, though this is yellowish (and rather dirty), in var. *carpathicum*. The best variety to grow is *vagneri*, which generally has two flowers to a stem; the others, frequently, only one.

The spring snowflake is generally at its best in March, in England. It does not like to naturalise in meadow turf but prefers a partially shaded position among deciduous shrubs. Slugs feed voraciously upon it. Some gardeners find this an easy species. I can grow it but without being proud of the results. It looks well in the company of *Scilla bifolia* and I also have the greeny-yellow young foliage of *Valeriana phu* 'Aurea' in the same planting.

Summer snowflake is something of a misnomer for **L. aestivum** (45cm/1½ft). In the strain most widely grown, I have had the first blooms as early as January and a colony is generally at its best from late March to mid-April. The leaves are dark green and show through in November. 'Gravetye Giant' should certainly be the preferred clone, being stronger and more upstanding than any of the others and with larger bells. These are gathered in terminal umbels, some four or five in each, opening in succession. There is a green dot at the tip of each segment.

Culturally, these snowflakes are most obliging. In habit, they make clumps like daffodils and can be naturalised in the same way, perfectly happy in dense turf. They are used to growing near to water, often in waterlogged soil and, I am told, even in shallow water. I have not yet succeeded in establishing them in my pond; the bulbs have always floated away. I feel sure that a large clump, established in summer when the water has receded, would succeed. A good siting is among the stools of dogwood, *Cornus alba*, kept regularly pruned. *L. aestivum* is a native, sometimes called the Loddon lily, on account of its growing along that river, a tributary of the Thames.

The only other snowflake that most of us are likely to grow as a garden plant is **L. autumnale** (23cm/9in), which is rather tiny for my sort of gardening, but I am fond of it. The leaves are lank and thread-fine; the flowers, several to an umbel, small, but delightful to discover amid the gaudy panoply of the August garden. They are white and open over a long season. Seed will be ripened, if you start with more than one clone, and self-sowing will be quite normal.

Leymus

POACEAE/GRAMINAE

Blue lyme grass grows wild on sandy dunes and dykes, near to the sea. The best colony I have seen was in Orkney. The foot-long flower spikes, like a giant couch or even wheat, are very handsome and dry well. They may rise to nearly 2m/6ft but

49 *Leymus arenarius* as a foliage plant, cut to the ground annually, as I do, is not much more than 60cm/2ft. Removing all the old growth means that everything thereafter is new and fresh and glistening blue, but you get no flowers with this treatment.

It is a flat-leaved grass and a great border feature. Some purple orach, *Atriplex hortensis*, seeds itself behind mine and the combination is satisfying.

Lyme grass is one of those terrifying runners whose far-reaching rhizomes can be hard to extract where they have invaded neighbouring plants. In a tight corner one can always resort to Roundup, thank goodness. We have not had to. Fergus under-takes, annually, to dig up the whole clump, when we are 'doing' the border, and follows each sucker (with a few exceptions, which I later gleefully point out to him) to its growing tip. That takes him the best part of an hour. Then we return the core of the plant to its allotted position.

At one time I thought to thwart the thug by growing it in an old galvanised iron wash tub, sunk into the ground, but the grass was so inhibited as only to give half of its natural beauty. I had to relent, for this is not a plant to be without.

Liatris

Asteraceae/Compositae

These are prairie and savanna (prairie with scattered trees) plants from the USA, fairly late-flowering and sometimes short-lived, as is the case with **Liatris pycnostachya** (1.5m/5ft), which is my favourite. The flowers consist of tubular flo-rets gathered in clusters along a spike. In this species, above stems that are liberally clothed in linear leaves, the spike is up to 45cm/1½ft long, the colour, bright bluish magenta. I have seen as many as five tortoiseshell butterflies supping simultaneously on one spike. A feature in liatris is that the spikes open – and die – from the top, downwards. **L. spicata** (60cm/2ft) is a shorter, sturdier plant with much shorter spikes. 'Kobold' is magenta and 'Alba' white. They are reliably perennial, with tu-berous rhizomes which can be divided.

I have failed, with the above two species, to establish them in my 'prairie'. Having raised them from wild-collected seed and lined the seedlings out for a season, we transferred them to meadow conditions, but they only survived for a couple of years thereafter.

Libertia

IRIDACEAE

A genus of evergreen perennials with tough strap-leaves and white, seemingly triangular, flowers. Although there are six perianth segments, three of them are much more prominent than the other three, thus giving the triangular effect, as in *Tradescantia*. Libertias come from both New Zealand and South America.

L. formosa (1m/3ft), from Chile, is the easiest species. It has clusters of small, white flowers all along stiff stems and makes a great show in May. It self-sows freely and from the performance of one seedling on the north side of my house, seems to be as happy in shade as sun. After about three years, the plants get cluttered up with their own, unsightly, dead leaves, which won't be pulled out, as you can with *Dierama pulcherrimum*. They make a great dormitory for snails. Most of us, at some stage, have resorted to shearing them over. They respond happily to this treatment and grow through the shorn leaf stumps, but these continue to look unsightly and a plant is never the same again. The only solution, I feel, is to throw old plants out as soon as they begin to look shabby, and to let young seedlings take over.

31 I have never grown *L. grandiflora* (1m/3ft), from New Zealand, but it appears very similar – a little less stiff and stodgy, perhaps. I grew *L. ixioides* (1m/3ft) for a number of years but the colony died out in a hard winter. I didn't mind too much but am much enamoured of a libertia that came to me from Helen Dillon's garden, in Dublin, and which appears to be a *L. ixioides* hybrid (1m/3ft). Its very dark green foliage admirably sets off the white flowers, which are carried in elegant sprays. It does not set seed but can be divided, best done immediately after its June flowering. You could divide in spring, but at the expense of that year's flowers.

L. ixioides is a New Zealander and so is *L. peregrinans* (45cm/1½ft), but this is essentially a foliage plant. The plant spreads by thin rhizomes to make a colony and the fans of leaves are separated one from another. The leaves are perfectly stiff and upright with a prominent orange-brown midrib, the rest of the blade being a few tones dimmer. In all, this is a striking species which catches the public's attention at any time of the year, though it is at its brightest in cold weather. The clone 'Gold Leaf' is supposed to be brighter, but neither Fergus nor I can see any difference.

The flowers of *L. peregrinans* appear in early summer at a lower level than the leaves. They do not make a great impression but are sometimes produced freely enough to earn a pat.

Ligularia

Asteraceae/Compositae

Ligularia, like *Senecio*, has been the plaything of the botanists, taking species out, putting others in. What a game.

Most important loss to know about is **Ligularia tussilaginea**, which becomes *Farfugium japonicum*.

Most ligularias are coarse, moisture-loving perennials, best suited to the wild, or bog garden. All have large, lush leaves and yellow or pale orange daisy flowers. **L. przewalskii** (1.5m/5ft) has beautiful, deeply cut leaves, which droop and look pathetic as soon as the sun touches them. In July, it carries spikes of spidery yellow flowers. Because of its leaves, I prefer it to 'The Rocket' (2m/6ft), whose rounded leaves are little more than toothed, but it is otherwise a bigger, bolder version, its dark stems highlighting the flowers.

L. dentata (syn. *L. clivorum*) 'Desdemona' (1.2m/4ft) has the edge in popularity over 'Othello' – well, look at the way he behaved. Here, the leaves are orbicular, somewhat reniform, and they are reddish purple on their undersides – all over, in fact, when young and I recommend planting a tall, deep red tulip, like 'Halcro' or 'Redshine', among the crowns of 'Desdemona' for spring effect. The July-flowering of 'Desdemona' is what I call crocus yellow – a pale shade of orange. Slugs are the great problem, with large-, smooth-leaved ligularias. They make such a visible mess of them, quite early on, as to be a disgrace to you for many months thereafter.

Other coarse species and hybrids that I have grown are **L. veitchiana** (2m/6ft), **L. wilsonii** (2m/6ft) and **L. × hessei** (2m/6ft). The last has columns of yellow daisies which I planted behind the shocking mauve panicles of *Astilbe* 'Superba', siting orange **L. dentata** 'Desdemona' in front. That was rather strong meat even for me.

Lilium

Liliaceae

There must be many like me who, as a child, was transported by the drama of the first bud in a head of *Lilium auratum* bursting open, exposing its red-spotted interior and the rufous anthers, and unleashing its powerful fragrance (none too subtle, but who cared?).

The rest of one's life is a love affair with lilies, but, as is the way with such affairs, constantly fraught with frustration and disappointment. It has been said, with a wry element of truth, that the bond between turkeys and lilies is that their sole ambition in life is to die. There are a few genuinely persistent lilies, like *L. martagon* and *L. pyrenaicum*, but even they are under threat.

Since they are so obtruding, I will consider the obstacles to successful lily-growing, first, and get that over. There are the breeders: Dr Christopher North was a shining example of the kind of lily breeder we need. Working on an exposed site, overlooking Dundee, on the east side of Scotland, all the results of his work had to be able to stand up to the strong winds of an open-field site, with need of no support. Too often, lilies have been given the Award of Merit, simply on the basis of their cut blooms and with no consideration of the strength of stem supporting them. Furthermore, much bulb production has gone forward abroad, under highly artificial conditions, quite unlike those that will be experienced in the consumer's garden.

Then there are the marketers, who are mainly bulb merchants. Lily bulbs do not reach them, like hyacinths, tulips and narcissi, early enough in the autumn to be marketed at the same time. So they are sent out separately, from December, when planting conditions are at their worst, the bulb's basal roots have at least partially shrivelled and it is too dormant to be able to cope with adverse conditions.

Ideally, lily bulbs should be lifted and re-planted soon after flowering and while the foliage is still green. Then they can immediately settle into their new positions and make new roots before the soil grows cold and winter arrives. Clearly, this is no recipe for large-scale commercial transactions, but it would make a great difference to the outcome if the bulbs could at least be dispatched, and planted, in early autumn. Bulbs that are allowed to lie exposed on sales counters, where they are submitted to drying and to widely fluctuating changes in temperature, will suffer worst of all. The ideal we should aim for is home-grown bulbs that are already attuned to our climate, or something worse, and which are procurable in the best condition for being quickly established. This is most likely to be realised from small, non-specialist nurseries.

Now for the troubles that lilies meet when in our gardens:

REPLANT DISEASE. If you decide to lift, split and re-plant a healthy colony of lilies on the same site, it will probably fail the second time, unless a vast bulk of soil is replaced before re-planting. So long as a colony remains healthy and free-flowering, leave it alone, even if it seems overcrowded. You can surface-mulch it, to keep it happy.

BOTRYTIS − Grey Mould fungus. Lilies have their own species of botrytis, which will attack and rot their foliage (and stems) in dank or wet weather, long before the leaves have stopped supplying the bulb and roots with nutrients. It is on this account that you so often see flowering colonies of Madonna lilies, *L. candidum*, whose stems are clothed only with dead foliage. Timely spraying with protective fungicides will prevent this.

BULB AND ROOT ROTTING. Lilies can cope with a lot of water at the root when they are growing strongly prior to flowering, but not afterwards, nor in the early stages of renewed growth. If you can control the amount of rain or irrigation they receive, do so. If not, mitigate its effects by planting the bulbs on sharp grit (obtainable from builders' merchants) and by dropping more grit over the top of the bulb. This will also deter

SLUGS. The small, black slugs which live underground and may make their homes between lily scales, are your chief problem. Liquid slug-killer may also be resorted to.

APHIDS. Greenfly will usually attack the upper parts of the plant when they are soft and lush and buds are being formed. Whatever means your principles allow you to adopt to counter aphids, make sure that it acts quickly. You cannot afford to wait for populations of ladybirds and hoverfly larvae to build up, in response to the food available to them. The lilies will have been crippled in the meantime.

LILY BEETLE. This recently-arrived pest, whose epicentre started in Surrey and which has steadily been increasing its radius of activity from there, is making it difficult to grow lilies as garden plants, at all (it is no problem where they are grown in pots). The beetle is easily seen, being bright red. Both the adults and the colonies of slimy larvae eat the foliage of lilies and fritillaries and they are about from April to August, with a succession of generations. Going out each sunny morning to catch the adults and squash them between your fingers is time-consuming and only partially effective, especially if you have self-sown lilies, like *L. martagon*, some of which you are likely to miss. Furthermore, at the approach of a shadow the beetles will drop to the ground, somehow making themselves impossible to see. A spray regime may work, where all lilies are gathered into discrete colonies, but is pretty impossible under mixed-border conditions and where the lilies are naturalised, which is the way one most enjoys seeing them.

VIRUS DISEASES. Lilies are vulnerable, some species more than others, to a complex of virus diseases, causing a mosaic pattern of yellow streaking on foliage, which, like the flower buds, becomes distorted. There is no cure. The affected plants must be destroyed. All too often, you are buying infected bulbs from the merchant. If he is selling growing bulbs, this will be plain to see.

Some lilies, like *L. lancifolium* (syn. *L. tigrinum*) are resistant to the effects of viruses, but are nevertheless a source of infection (aphids being the vectors) of clean stock belonging to susceptible lilies. *L. formosanum* is highly and visibly susceptible. Stock grown from seed is initially virus-free but is all too likely to contract infection within a couple of years. A ready source of infection is broken tulips, which will be only slightly weakened themselves, and are visually very attractive.

Madonna lilies, *L. candidum* are highly susceptible. The reason for cottage garden colonies persisting for many years is probably that there are no other lilies, nor tulips, growing near them. As soon as the gardener owner becomes a lily (or tulip) enthusiast, trouble moves in. If you never become a specialist, most of these concerns will pass you by.

It seems a shame to have expended a thousand words on its troubles, at the start of a piece on this most beautiful flower, but it is a reflection on the importance of the problems. They are much reduced in Scotland, where lilies grow particularly well; aphids and virus diseases are scarce and lily beetles have not yet arrived. The cool climatic conditions suit many lilies and they can there be grown in full sunshine. For most of us, the majority will do best with their heads in sun but their roots kept cool, as among shrubs.

Plenty of organic matter in the soil, such as leaf mould, pleases lilies greatly. **L. candidum** (1m/3ft) is something of an exception. It loves to be baked in a sunny position, with the bulbs planted only just below the soil surface. Chalk soils suit it ideally. The loose spikes of open-funnel flowers, with an early July season in England, are amazingly sweetly scented on the air. Dormancy is brief and overwintering basal leaves appear in early autumn. Most bulb firms cater for this lily and for the nearly related *L. × testaceum* (1m/3ft) by dispatching them with narcissi and the like, from September.

L. × testaceum is expensive but easily grown, with turkscap flowers that are downward-facing with recurved petal tips, soft apricot in colour with orange-red anthers and a sweet scent. I have not found **L. monadelphum** (syn. *L. szovitsianum*) (1m/3ft) exacting, either, though it goes down to viruses. This has downward-hanging, open bells, slightly recurved at the tips, and bright yellow. The smell would generally be accounted rank and disagreeable, as with the next three species.

Perhaps because its native habitats are not far away, **L. martagon** (1m/3ft), the original turkscap lily, is easily grown and naturalised throughout Britain. It even seeds into my paving cracks and comes up from the bottom of yew hedges. The colour is muddy purple. More glamorous is var. *cattaniae*, which is quite a rich shade of purple and has a high surface gloss. Better still is the albino, var. *album,* which is pure white, with yellow anthers that show up brilliantly. This is a lily to light up a shady place, in its June season.

L. hansonii (1m/3ft) is a close relation – the whorled leaves are a handsome arrangement. It flowers in June; a rather boring shade of orange-yellow. It successfully crosses with *L. martagon*, the hybrids being known collectively as **L.** × **marhan**. Not much to get you excited, there.

L. pyrenaicum is so easily grown as to be sneered at by lily snobs, who are a numerous class, I may say. With masses of grassy foliage up its stems, the flowers themselves are small, greenish-yellow, heavily spotted turkscaps, with orange anthers. This makes huge clumps in the outlying and neglected parts of old gardens in the north of England and Scotland, surviving neglect when all else has perished that would give any clue that a garden had existed. I have not seen evidence of its self-sowing, however. Its var. **rubrum** is rich orange-red. These flower in June. I rate them well.

Sometimes known as Mid-Century Hybrids, there is a class of robust, June-July-flowering lilies, coarse, willing and showy. Their flower may face down, horizontally or upwards, in which case they are open-funnel-shaped, like a wine glass. Best known is the ubiquitous 'Enchantment' (1m/3ft), whose colouring is sometimes aptly described as nasturtium red. It is most easily digested when grown in shade. I once saw it combined, in shade, with pink *Alstroemeria ligtu* hybrids and, when I had got over the shock, had to admit that this worked pretty well. No less compromising, but in yellow, is 'Connecticut King'.

The American species are calcifuge and not too easily grown, in many cases. No trouble with **L. pardalinum** (1m/3ft), however. Above whorled leaves it carries heavily spotted orange-red turkscaps, shading paler towards the base of the petals. Not many flowers to a stem and the majority of shoots are often blind. For this lily makes a colony, its rhizomatous bulbs spreading horizontally. A great improvement is var. *giganteum* (2m/6ft), which flowers abundantly, to brilliant effect in July.

The Bellingham Hybrids are a fine race from American species, with whorled leaves and generally orange turkscap flowers. 'Shuksan' (2m/6ft) is one that has made a great impression in the Savill Gardens at Windsor Great Park. Somehow one gets the impression that they are not for the likes of us.

Derived from Asiatic species comes a race of scented trumpet lilies. They definitely have the turkey syndrome. The 'African Queen' selection are a variable, seedling strain, in warm shades of apricot. They are cheap on the market but often blind, even in their first year, and rife with viruses.

Lilium regale (1m/3ft) is an old, heavily scented favourite, especially happy on chalk soils. The white trumpet is pinkish on the outside, flowering in July. It is easily propagated from seed. In one garden, on light alkaline soil that evidently suited it, the seeds were drilled in the open, as one might radishes. The seedlings would flower for the first time, two years later.

Another Far Eastern species that is easily raised from seed is **L. henryi** (2m/6ft), a tall, July-August-flowering lily that persists well in the garden and is tolerant of lime. The strong apricot-coloured turkscap flowers are of fair size.

The golden-rayed lily of Japan, **L. auratum** (1.5m/5ft), has the largest blooms of all, so open a trumpet as to be almost a saucer. Var. *platyphyllum*, with broader leaves, is more easily grown and persistent. That flowers in August and is only a little earlier than **L. speciosum**, always grown in one or other of its named clones. It can be white, but is usually in some very agreeable shade of pink, such as 'Grand Commander'. It has large, turkscap flowers, spotted and with a syrup-sweet scent. One of my favourites, but I don't keep it for long. The best I ever saw were 2m/6ft high and in tubs, at Nymans (Sussex), but they died out. There are many glamorous (or vulgar) hybrids between this species and *L. auratum*.

I don't know the parentage of 'Casa Blanca' (1.2m/4ft), but it looks and smells like a white Auratum, is cheap and satisfactory as a pot plant.

With an extended season but often flowering in late September, is the elegant Trumpet Lily, **L. formosanum** (1.2m/4ft), which can actually be grown from seed to flower in one year, though not attaining its full height till the second. The outside of the long, narrow trumpet is purplish, the inside white and it wafts a delicious scent at night. Excellent in pots. There are dwarf strains of this – 60cm/2ft at most – to wit 'Little Snow Elf' and var. *pricei*. They may be the same and are anyway grown from seed. They are pretty hardy and persist in some gardens.

There are many delightful *Lilium* species which it will be well worth attempting in the garden, should your conditions generally suit the genus. These have qualities of refinement which the hybrids do not attempt to match.

I have referred, tangentially, to lilies in pots, but this is the way I grow most of mine, since my slug-infested, heavy clay garden soil is inimical to most of them. Furthermore, you have greater control over lilies that are in pots and lily beetle will not be a problem since the pot soil, in which they would have to hibernate, is changed. Slugs are easily controlled, too, and so is water. We stand the pots in a cold frame,

42 An aggressively spreading bulb, *Ornithogalum umbellatum* (Star of Bethlehem) sited to peer through the trailing branches of Japanese maple *Acer palmatum* var. *dissectum* Atropurpureum Group.

43 A surprisingly hardy member of the ginger family, *Hedychium coccineum* 'Tara', flowering in early autumn. ▷

44 Hardier still is *Hedychium densiflorum* 'Assam Orange'. ▷▷

45 This red-hot-poker, *Kniphofia rooperi*, has a strange individuality of shape. Mainly October-flowering. ▷▷▷

46   *Sanguisorba tenuifolia* 'Alba' with annual poppy, *Papaver commutatum*, and *Crocosmia* 'Lucifer' behind.

47   The Darwin hybrid tulip 'Red Matador', fascinatingly marked in lurid green and yellow at the centre.

48   *Hydrangea arboreum* 'Annabelle' behind, *Aster sedifolius* centre, crocosmias and *Allium cristophii*, front.

49   Blue lyme grass, *Leymus arenarius*, *Salvia coccinea* 'Lady in Red', cannas, *Viburnum opulus* 'Compactum'   ▷

from the time they are re-potted, in February, removing the lights only when enough growth has been made to reach the glass. After flowering, when lilies can easily rot from drowning, the pots, standing outside, can be turned on their sides during wet weather. In winter, they are stored in a cold shed, watering them very occasionally to prevent the bulbs and roots from completely drying out and shrivelling.

A soil-based compost, such as John Innes Potting No. 2, is best, having reserves of nutrients with trace elements. Since it is heavy, the pots are more stable at the time the lilies are tall, and by the same token, clay pots, rather than plastic, besides looking nicer, are heavier and more stable. Of course, if they do blow over, they may break.

Re-potting, and dividing your bulbs, can be exciting and satisfying, if they have long, healthy basal roots. Many lilies, especially those most suited to pot culture, have annual stem roots, as well as well as perennial basal roots. The stem roots arise from the base of the young stem, just above the bulb. In re-potting, you clean them all away, as they will be dead by then, though small bulbs have sometimes been made in the stem roots, above the main bulbs. These, too, should be removed. They can be treated separately, if you need them.

The depth at which to plant lily bulbs is a question on which I differ from most authorities. They say that with the stem-rooters, the top of the bulb should be at least 10cm/4in below the soil surface. I would say, only just below is deep enough. The stem roots don't have to be told which way to travel. They will find their way down into the soil, even if they started above it. In the garden, the main reason for deep planting would be to keep the bulbs from baking, but in any case most species and hybrids will be grown among plants which will shade the soil around them. The likely disadvantage of deep planting is that the bulbs are closer to inimical sub-soil – unless you are blessed with a naturally very deep soil. The top-soil is easily conditioned to suit them and that is where the bulbs should be.

Pot-grown bulbs are better not kept indoors for more than a couple of days at a time, as the light intensity is so low and you want the bulbs to remain in good health, unless you are treating them as annuals (which is always a possibility). I like to stand them outside my porch, where they are a welcome as one enters. There, too, you can easily see and remove the petals which have faded, without their making a mess.

Limonium

PLUMBAGINACEAE

The entire genus is known as sea lavender and it has specialised habitats wherein the soil or mud is rich in salt. To see a salt marsh covered with several acres of lavender-coloured *Limonium*, in bloom, is an unusual and moving experience. Generally, limoniums are to be found near the sea.

Some species, especially those from the Canaries, make good greenhouse pot plants, but by far the most important hardy garden plant is **L. platyphyllum** (60cm/2ft), better known as **L. latifolium** (from south-east Europe and southern Russia). From a woody rootstock arise coarse, orbicular, wavy-edged leaves. The whole plant smells of carrion, on the air. Borne on naked scapes, the flowers are distributed in broad, elegant sprays, excellent for cutting but not as everlastings. It is the soft corolla which has the lavender colouring, in August-September. Unfortunately, nowadays, in many gardens this species has become seriously prone to powdery mildew. If you spray anything else against this, you may successfully include your L. platyphyllum. It is propagated from root cuttings, taken in winter. In the garden, the plant likes a sunny position; it never needs disturbing.

The 'annuals', which are so popular as everlastings, are really perennials treated as annuals, because generally tender (except in maritime gardens). The plants may be saved by lifting and potting them in autumn, and overwintering under fairly frost-free glass. In this way their flowering season, normally on the late side but continuing without interruption until the first frosts, is usefully extended, starting in early July. The less coarse kinds make excellent bedding plants. They derive from two Mediterranean species, **L. sinuatum** (75cm/2½ft) and the yellow **L. bonduellii** (60cm/2ft). In these, it is the papery calyx which provides the colour; the soft corolla is white and ephemeral. Known everywhere as statice, the final e should be spoken as a separate syllable – but rarely is.

Linaria

SCROPHULARIACEAE

The most obvious difference between antirrhinums and toadflaxes is that the latter have a spur at the back of the corolla.

The common toadflax, **Linaria vulgare** can be a tiresome weed, in gardens, on account of its freely running rootstock. Even so, its spikes of yellow snapdragon flowers, with an orange lower lip, can display themselves well in dry-walling. Better still in a hungry shingle garden, as in the late Derek Jarman's, Dungeness, Kent.

L. dalmatica (75cm/2½ft) is a clump-forming plant, though it runs a little, and its long spikes of yellow flowers make a bold impression. That, too, will display itself best in a gravel garden, rather than under mixed border conditions.

L. purpurea (1m/3ft) has numerous small flowers over a long period, seeding itself freely. The right plant for a disorganised gardener. The typical purple form is usually replaced by white or pink ('Canon Went').

Linum

LINACEAE

The tender blue of flax, **Linum perenne** (60cm/2ft), and the fact of its petals shattering at midday if the sun is blazing, are assets which touch the human heart. These are ideal plants for light, gravelly or chalky soils. They hate clay and anyway tend to be short-lived plants, but self-sow, if they like you. **L. narbonense** (60cm/2ft) is a more intense shade of blue and its cultivar, 'Heavenly Blue' has the AGM, though whether it is generally true to name seems highly doubtful.

Two sub-shrubby species, **L. arboreum** (30cm/1ft) and **L. flavum** (30cm/1ft) ('Compactum' is the favoured cultivar) have brilliant, pure yellow flowers, when the sun opens them, in early summer. They are a gladdening sight. Again short-lived, but easily raised from soft cuttings.

Liriope

CONVALLARIACEAE/LILIACEAE

Close to *Ophiopogon*, this genus likewise comes from Japan and the Far East. When you meet it in the USA, you realise what a huge range of cultivars (including several variegated) there are and how luxuriantly they can grow, how freely they can bloom. They need warmer summers than we can provide.

Liriope muscari (30cm/1ft) is the principal species from which most of the variants have been obtained. It is an easy and generally free-flowering plant, with evergreen strap-leaves. The flower spikes, which have a long autumn season, are not much taller than the leaves. The flowers, being closed at the mouth, look like beads, along most of the length of the spike. They are coloured indigo-blue and are apt to bleach in strong sunlight. So, although liriopes like overall warmth, a half shaded position may produce the best results. 'Majestic' is a larger, more important-looking clone, but it rarely flowers in Britain as it should.

The old foliage of *L. muscari* becomes tatty after a couple of seasons. I sometimes shear the whole colony back to the ground in spring, which rejuvenates it, but possibly reduces the amount of subsequent flower. 'Variegata', with a long, cream stripe on each leaf, is an attractive foliage plant. It deserves rich feeding to make it grow.

Lobelia

CAMPANULACEAE

Horticulturally, one can divide lobelias into two main groups: those, from South Africa (and Australia), making small, tender, bushy or trailing plants, used for bedding and hanging baskets; and those, from America, making tall, herbaceous perennials with comparatively large flowers. The latter have been greatly developed, of recent years, to the advantage of all gardeners, though some are less hardy than others.

The first article I ever had published by the gardening press, in 1952, was on the cardinal flower, **Lobelia cardinalis** (1m/3ft), although in retrospect I think it was probably, with its reddish-purple stems and leaves, 'Queen Victoria' (1m/3ft), though none of us knew any better then.

L. cardinalis comes from boggy areas and streamsides in North America. It has spidery red flowers, green leaves, and the stems branch a bit. It dies down in winter, but perennates with a rosette of small leaves made at the base of each stem. This is a common atribute in all these North American lobelias and their derivatives. 'Queen Victoria' is one of the most popular and showy lobelias, with intense, pure red flowers. The stems are generally unbranched. To make a show, close planting is advisable, or else plant out clumps having a number of shoots.

It is seldom advisable to leave plants in the garden over winter; better to lift in autumn and bed them into a cold frame. In the spring, you can see whether the clumps are dying out in the centre, which they frequently do (often with the help of slugs), and need dividing, treating each surviving rosette separately; or whether they can be planted out as intact clumps. They like rich, well watered soil and are of a colour with endless uses in the late summer and early autumn garden. They usually need one stake and a tie, for each clump. As they can be moved with ease from the open ground at any time during the summer, even when they have already started flowering, it may often be convenient to line them out until they are about to perform, and then to move them into a border where some early-flowerer is finished and needs removing from the scene. These remarks apply to most of the modern hybrids.

Some of these are seedling strains, though they can be propagated vegetatively. The other species that has been used for breeding, introducing pink and purple shades in the progeny, is the ultra-hardy **L. siphilitica** (60cm/2ft), a native of the eastern USA. Its flowers are quite close to pure blue but the ratio of luxuriant, oval green leaves to flowers is rather too high. Hybrids between this and *L. cardinalis* are collectively known as **L. × gerardii**. One of the oldest of these is 'Vedrariensis' (1.5m/5ft), which needs support. It is pretty hardy and can be left out to overwinter. It also self-sows. The colour is a rather dead shade of purple. It can be pepped up in its August-September with bright yellow rudbeckias. 'Tania' (1m/3ft) seems to have the same parentage. It is a much brighter shade of reddish purple but cannot safely be left out.

L. × speciosa is another hybrid strain which, like the above two cultivars, includes *L. fulgens* in its parentage. You can buy seed of these hybrids and select your own favourites from the progeny. Seed is exceedingly small and should be sown, without covering it, at 68° F (20° C) in February. There are named clones of this parentage, such as 'Pink Flamingo' and 'Russian Princess' (sometimes wrongly sold as a purple clone), both pink-flowered; 'Dark Crusader', which is too dark a red to be an effective garden plant unless placed with extreme cunning; and 'Cherry Ripe', which is a brighter cherry red.

There are now some excellent seed strains, those within a single colour band giving more satisfactory results than mixtures. In the 'Compliment' series, 'Compliment Scarlet' (1m/3ft) is green-leaved with scarlet flowers. With other members of this series, it can safely be left out over winter. The F^1 'Fan' series, in my opinion, includes the best garden plants of any, to date. Although they have a tall, central spike, they branch so freely as to make a bush of blossom, creating a fine display from August to October. 'Fan Deep Red' (60cm/2ft) was my favourite in the RHS trial; although fairly deep, it was bright and showed up well. In practice, 'Fan Scarlet' has turned out to be even more effective. Others, pretty well as good, are 'Fan Orchid Rose' (a good pink) and 'Fan Cinnabar Rose' (deeper pink). Members of this series should be lifted in the autumn.

Of other American species, **L. laxiflora** var. **angustifolia** (1m/3ft) has been unprotected in my garden for many years. The leaves are linear, the flowers tubular, coral without, yellow within. But it produces very few flowering racemes. Once, after a frost-free winter, all its summer growth was retained, and it flowered all over, in early summer. Otherwise in dribs and drabs, any time in summer or autumn. **L. tupa** (1.2m/4ft or more), from Chile, can be a splendid plant when a large bush of it is covered with hooded, brick-red flowers above broad, bold foliage. More often, a dismal flop and it easily dies on you. It dislikes being wet or subjected to much frost, in winter, but needs a lot of moisture when growing. Some strains of this species, which is often grown from seed, appear to be more satisfactory than others.

Lunaria

BRASSICACEAE/CRUCIFERAE

The perennial honesty, **Lunaria rediviva** (1m/3ft), is a European native of woodland and is good in part shade with us. It makes a well-balanced, self-supporting clump and its pale mauve, sweetly scented blossom peaks in May. The pods are a more elongated elipse than in the better known biennial, *L. annua*. That has no scent.

Lupinus

PAPILIONACEAE/LEGUMINOSAE

32 Spelt lupin in Britain, lupine in America, this is a genus of herbs and soft-wooded shrubs (some annuals, also), mainly from North America. If you visit the Pacific coastal states in June, you see lupins everywhere, even breaking through the tarmac of road margins. On Hurricane Ridge (5230ft), on the Olympic Peninsula of Washington State, a silky silver-leaved lupin species (possibly **Lupinus subalpinus**, though *L. lyallii* and *L. lepidus lobbii* were other names bandied around) is one of the first plants to show itself, together with the yellow turkscaps of *Erythronium grandiflorum*, as the snow melts, soon bursting into blue-flowered blossom.

Down on the shingly sea shore at the north end of this peninsula (looking out to Vancouver Island), the tree lupin, **Lupinus arboreus**, colonises, though you also see this even more spectacularly as an adapted alien in dried-up river beds in the South Island of New Zealand.

The most familiar, herbaceous lupins of our gardens, are mainly derived from **L. polyphyllus**, introduced from West North America in 1827, and most of the breeding work that has made lupins such showy garden plants has been achieved in the 20th century. George Russell, working in York in the 1930s, gave his name to the most famous strain, crossing *L. polyphyllus* with *L. arboreus* and with one or more annual species, from which derives the Russell Lupins' reputation for being short-lived. Inroads by a complex of virus diseases seems as likely a cause.

Most of us are little bothered by these, since we raise our lupins from seed and the seedlings start with a clean bill of health. There are such good seed strains, nowadays, that few amateur gardeners – or professionals either, come to that – bother to increase their lupins vegetatively. Being deep-rooted, they do not divide well, but this is possible. It is better, and easy, to take cuttings of young shoots in early spring. Lupins are early on the move and already showing young growth in February. Hence, they should always be established in their flowering sites by the previous autumn.

A trial, at Wisley, of lupin cultivars, raised vegetatively, clearly demonstrated that good though the seed strains are, selected clones are a whole lot better. Today's specialists in their production are Woodfield Brothers, a Midlands nursery. Their red cultivar, 'Troop the Colour', is outstanding.

The colour range in herbaceous lupins includes white, cream, yellow, orange, red, pink, 'blue' (never true blue) and purple. If allowed to self sow indefinitely, they revert to shades of 'blue' and pink and they are adept at forming roadside colonies in sandy, acidic wasteland. From north to south, you can admire these all over Britain, in early summer, but they are a considerable tourist attraction in New Zealand's South Island, where their increase is encouraged by the deliberate sowing of sophisticated Russell-type seed strains and postcards feature these at the expense of New Zealand's fascinating, though less showy, native flora. As one such tourist, I was agog with admiration, myself.

The modern lupin has such a dense inflorescence as to appear an undifferentiated mass of blossom, though the individual flowers are often bicoloured, the keel (or flag) of the flower's lower half being a completely different colour from the standard and wings. Instead of growing a total mix, I prefer to go for colour-segregated seed strains and to mix two of these. Thus, one year, in the Band of Nobles series, I grew separately 'Governor' (blue shades with a white flag) and 'The Pages' (carmine pink shades); then combined them in equal numbers when bedding out. Another year, it was 'Chandelier' (yellow shades) and 'Chatelaine' (pink, with white flag). A third combination was 'My Castle' (brick red) and 'Noblemaiden' (creamy white).

Variety is the spice of life and it may have been gathered that I do not hold on to my lupin plants after they have flowered, but treat them as biennial bedding plants. After flowering, lupins look pretty much of a wreck, from late June on, even though dead-headed. They have little further blossom to contribute and their foliage goes down to mildew. If thrown out, at the turn of June-July, they can be replaced with anything you fancy in terms of summer and autumn bedding. The replacement plants, if grown from seed, are often not sown till May, so as to be at just the right stage for taking over when their space is vacant.

Lupins are calcifuge and should seldom be attempted on soils of high alkalinity, though the symptoms of chlorosis, with yellowing leaves, do not usually show up in the young seedling but a few weeks later. An acid, sandy soil suits them best, though they are perfectly tolerant of clay if well drained. Most grow to a height of 1.2m/4ft. Their flowering starts in late May and it is always a question whether the weather, by then, may be sufficiently quiet to obviate the tiresome chore of providing adequate support in time before their hypothetical destruction by high winds. I take the risk, but if flowering lupins are blown sideways, their spikes develop an upward curve within a very few hours, and cannot be staked upright again, with the curve turned horizontal. That looks terrible. There are somewhat dwarfened seed strains which are worth attempting on windy sites: the Minarette group, Lulu and the Gallery series (available in separate colours).

The sweet scent of these herbaceous lupins is somewhat peppery. In the tree lupin, *L. arboreus*, it is much sweeter. Tree lupins are generally pale yellow (best), sometimes white and occasionally pale, skimmed-milk-blue. They are nearly always grown from seed and, from a spring sowing, will already be decent-sized shrubs when flowering in May-June the next year. They will reach their peak the year after, perhaps 1.2m/4ft high by 1.5m/5ft across. Their foliage is a bright, fresh evergreen and an enlivening element in the winter. For quick cover to a dry bank, tree lupins, as also brooms and cistuses, are ideal. Although excellent seaside plants, it is ironic that in most gardens they can be expected to break up in their third season. It is sensible to give in to this and to allow replacement by self-sown young stock.

The flower spikes, in tree lupins, are shortish but make a strong impression, because of the series of discrete horizontal whorls that compose the vertical spike. You notice this also in herbaceous *L. polyphyllus*-type lupins that have not been too highly bred.

The bane of lupin growers, of recent years, has been the lupin aphis, imported, like the lupin itself, from North America. It is a large, wax-coated species that can easily kill the plant(s) infested if quick action with a systemic insecticide is not taken. A repeat spraying is generally necessary, a week or so later. This is likely to be in May but infestations, especially of tree lupins, are liable to recur later in the season and must be watched out for.

Lupins, like wisteria and with a similarly evocative scent, are a herald to early summer. They may be a bit of a nuisance to accommodate, but they deserve the effort. A good stand of lupins can be guaranteed to arouse a buzz of delight – from me as much as from the bees.

Luzula

JUNCACEAE

The woodrush, **Luzula sylvatica**, has a yellow-leaved cultivar, 'Aurea' (30cm/1ft), which makes tufts of rather broad straps of a bright and cheering yellow that is freshest in the early part of the year, although, in fact, evergreen. From April, when it flowers nondescriptly, it becomes tired-looking. You don't want to be noticing it through the summer, but a few random clumps, not too far into a border, contrast admirably with the flowers of a light blue pulmonaria. Part-shade and plenty of moisture at the root will keep it looking happy for the longest period.

L. *s.* 'Marginata' has thinly white-margined leaves and makes dense ground cover in shade. Therefore useful, if not stimulating.

L. nivea (60cm/2ft) is grown for its delightful sprays of white flower clusters, at their best in June. Again, for damp half-shade.

Lychnis

CAROPHYLLACEAE

The genus *Lychnis* includes some species of particularly brilliant orange, scarlet, magenta and pink colouring. The sheer vitality of these contributes a wonderful buzz to the summer garden. But it is a testimony to the weak nerves of many of our more affluent gardeners that the breeders have busied themselves selecting more muted and soothing shades within these genera, wherewith to placate the timid. I won't say have nothing to do with them – some have their place – but on no account allow them to oust the genuine article from your gardening. Your blinkered, straitjacketed life would be the poorer.

The German catchfly is a British native, by the skin of its teeth, but the form in cultivation is a much showier plant. This is **Lychnis viscaria** (30cm/1ft); it makes a dense dome of green foliage and explodes into magenta blossom at the turn of May-June – for a not very long season. The double 'Splendens Plena' is even more impressive.

L. flos-jovis (30cm/1ft) flowers at much the same time, continuing to the end of June. Its low leaf cushion is grey (very depressed-looking in winter). Ramrod-straight stems are crowned with a platform of bright pink flowers – bright but kindly. It looks great in contrast to a patch of pure blue *Cynoglossum amabile* (q.v.).

This lychnis is not long-lived but easily and quickly raised from seed, producing strong flowering plants in the second year.

9, 36   From here it is a natural progression to **L. coronaria** (*Agrostemma coronaria*) (75cm/2½ft), which starts flowering towards the end of June and continues at full strength for five weeks or so. It is a short-lived but freely self-seeding perennial which makes a basal, overwintering rosette of grey-felted, rabbit's-ears leaves. Its flowering stems and calyxes are grey, too, and a foil to the blazing magenta, rotate flowers. Plants will probably do a second season but are greatly weakened after that, and best replaced by self-sown seedlings, which are easily moved, if necessary, to where they are required.

The plant is stiff and widely branched and can be made to do duty for brushwood, if sited in front of the grass, *Stipa calamagrostis*, which has a tendency to flop. This lychnis is adept at presenting you with many unlooked-for plant and colour combinations. For instance by seeding itself in front of a group of pure red *Crocosmia* 'Lucifer' (great fun), or, more acceptably, near to and among the blue stems and flower heads of *Eryngium × oliverianum*, which needs a lively partner.

It has many colour variants. 'Abbotswood Rose' is a sterile hybrid, now classified under **L. × walkeri**. It is a strong, deep shade of pink and must be propagated from cuttings. The Alba group is pure white, good in its way and just the ticket in grey-and-white gardening. That can be raised from seed if not tampered with by lascivious adulterers. The Occulata group, likewise, remains true if segregated. The flowers open white but develop a pink eye. I shouldn't bother but it has its devotees.

L. chalcedonica (1m/3ft) is the purest scarlet imaginable, the flowers, which have a deep notch in each petal, gathered into domed heads some 7.5cm/3in across. The stems, rough and thickly clothed in ovate leaves, are stiff but top-heavy after rain, swaying over from the base. Support with a couple of short, stout pieces of cane to each group, taking a length of string around each stem and including the canes on the way. The double 'Flore Pleno' is good, too, but 'Albiflora' is a weak white and the dirty pink 'Rosea' even worse. The true scarlet will go with most border plants, if not bright pink (but deep magenta makes a good contrast); especially pleasing, in July, with the purple spikes of *Salvia × superba*. The one drawback to this lychnis is a rather short flowering season, with little or no repeat when dead-headed.

As strong a colour but at a low, front-of-border level, is **L. × arkwrightii** (30cm/1ft) 'Vesuvius', invariably raised from seed. What the difference is between this hybrid and **L. × haageana**, I am stumped to say, both being offered as seed strains, but avoid the mixtures on offer, as they include some nasty indeterminate shades. Pure scarlet is the one to seize upon. Plants are short-lived. It is not too easy to get fat specimens. I would sow in late summer (not so early as to have the young plants flowering the first year) and bring the young plants on in pots, planting in their flowering sites in autumn. Flowering is in June–July. *Petunia integrifolia*, with its magenta flowers (not an aggressive magenta) makes a good associate and its rambling habit will mask the lychnis when that is running to seed.

Our native ragged robin, **L. flos-cuculi** (60cm/2ft), is not to be ignored, though perhaps not quite deserving of border space. It is a bright and pleasing shade of pink – the white var. *albiflora* good too, and coming true from seed – and best enjoys boggy meadow conditions.

Lysichiton

Araceae

Two species of aroid, with typical club-like spadix framed by a boat-shaped spathe. Both are hardy and enjoy boggy, waterside conditions. They flower in spring, a little before the leaves, which gradually take over.

Lysichiton americanus is the larger growing, coming from coastal regions of the Pacific North-west of America, as far north as Alaska. Sometimes dubbed skunk cabbage, the flowers smell, but not worryingly. They are yellow, the spathe about 15cm/6in long, and can make a great display in the April garden, but I have never made a great success of it. The broad, glossy leaves, up to 1.2m/4ft long, are a strong feature in the summer. Seed is freely produced; self-sowing can be a nuisance in favoured gardens.

The Japanese **L. camtschatcensis** is smaller with pure white spathes (10cm/4in). The two species, grown together, often hybridise, producing plants of intermediate vigour and with cream-coloured flowers. All lysichitons can be increased by division.

Lysimachia

Primulaceae

We can dive straight into this genus with our native creeping jenny, **Lysimachia nummularia**, a jolly little plant with upturned, cup-shaped yellow flowers. It is a prostrate overground runner and, like all lysimachias, likes damp places. It quickly colonised a bomb crater that was excavated on our marsh during the last war. It flowers in June–July. In gardens it is usually represented by its yellow-green-leaved form, 'Aurea'. In a mixed border, this is quite an aggressive plant, engulfing smaller neighbours. The foliage is brightest in sunshine, but bakes brown after flowering. Some shade, but not so much as to eliminate all the yellowness, is best. I still like it in a border, but replanting in improved soil, while reducing its territory, is necessary every other year.

Yellow loosestrife, **L. vulgaris** (1m/3ft), is a native of dykes and sleepy, disused canal arms, emerging from shallow water. It carries open panicles of yellow blossom in July and is always a pleasure to come across, although outshone for garden use by the blasts of bright yellow produced by **L. punctata** (1m/3ft), which has a larger flower, densely set on a columnar spike. A whole colony makes an impressive display in July. In a border, its circumference needs reducing every year, as it spreads, albeit not alarmingly. In shallow water at the margins of a pond, not many miles from my Sussex home, it makes a handsome landscape feature, but I have failed to establish it under water in my own pond. It seems to flourish, but is no longer there at winter's end.

L. ciliata (75cm/2½ft), from North America, spreads quickly by rhizomes just below the soil surface, each one terminated, in the first year, by a ground-hugging rosette of overwintering leaves. This makes the new shoot in the next spring. The saucer-shaped flowers are quite a pale shade of yellow, on open panicles. The purple-leaved cultivar, 'Firecracker' is such an improvement for highlighting the flowers, that I see no point in growing the green-leaved type-plant. I am using this purple foliage, in spring bedding, as a background to the flowers of late yellow tulips. As these fade, the loosestrife takes over.

Most invasive of the species I am describing (but there is still a place for such plants, so long as we know what to expect) is **L. clethroides** (1m/3ft), from China and Japan. Its spikes of small white star-flowers perform a double bend, like a shepherd's or bishop's crook. I try to like this unusual plant, but fail. Its leaves are so uninteresting and the white is impure.

Another unusual species that attracts plantsmen and was introduced from the eastern Mediterranean as long ago as 1820, but is seldom grown, is **L. atropurpurea** (60cm/2ft). It has a lax habit and the stems are clothed with metallic, rather fleshy leaves. The dusky purple flowers are in dense, branching spikes – not a bit showy, but they dry nicely when the capsules are ripe. The cultivar name under which my plant came was 'Geronimo'.

It appears not to run and **L. ephemerum** (1.2m/4ft) is a clump-former – from south-west Europe. Of very upright habit, the leaves vary in colour, but on the best plants are glaucous. The white star-flowers are spread along open spikes. This likes it damp. Something – I never discovered what; capsids, maybe – aborted nearly all the flower buds on my plants, so I gave up trying, but it is a good plant. John Treasure, at Burford House, grew it in the shallow water of one of his streams, and it stood up proudly.

Lythrum

LYTHRACEAE

The purple loosestrife, **Lythrum salicaria** (1.2m/4ft) is a hearty native of boggy areas, river- and stream-sides, flowering in late summer. Its spires of magenta flowers greatly enliven the scene and, in its native habitats, it is well-behaved, its spread being checked by other natives in a balanced community. When, somehow, introduced to the USA, it escaped from wherever it started and, deprived of its natural checks, has taken over large tracts as an aggressive weed. When such an event becomes news, officials are expected to do something about it, so no kind of loosestrife, even if a sterile hybrid, is allowed to be sold or grown in gardens there – a classic example of shutting the stable door when the horse has bolted.

In Europe, this, with its many cultivars, may be considered a showy summer perennial – 'Feuerkerze' ('Firecandle') is the only lythrum with an AGM – but there is a certain coarseness about their foliage which always gives me the feeling that they have strayed from the servants' quarters. This is not at all the case with the central European and west Asiatic species, **L. virgatum** (1m/3ft). 'Rose Queen', for instance, has an airy buoyancy, almost entirely concealing its foliage with an abundance of blossom. Maybe 'Rosy Gem', which has more sales outlets, is even better, but I do not know it.

Strange that *Lysimachia* and *Lythrum*, which are entirely unrelated genera and occupy a diametrically opposed colour range, should both be called loosestrife, both prefer boggy soil and both, in most alphabetical lists, come next to each other.

M

Macleaya

PAPAVERACEAE

Once known as *Bocconia*, the genus *Macleaya* is still sorting itself out. The plant we knew as *M. cordata* was really *M. microcarpa*, Alan Bloom told us, and there it remains. His true *M. cordata* now turns out to be a hybrid, *M.* × *kewensis* (no doubt this discovery was made at Kew).

M. microcarpa (2.4m/8ft) is a beautiful but, I found, in the days before Roundup, rather terrifying perennial, which spreads, by its running rootstock, with lightning rapidity on my heavy, well nourished soil. It took me three years to get the better of it. Now, at Fergus Garrett's request, we have planted it again, for this is undoubtedly a handsome perennial. This time we shall be ready for it.

A soft, juicy plant, its glaucous, scalloped leaves are entirely individual. They are crowned, in July, by a fluffy, paniculate inflorescence consisting largely of stamens, the overall colour being beige. But this is greatly improved to rich coral in 'Coral Plume'. It is easy to buy the wrong clone under this name, so watch out.

The plant we should be calling **M.** × **kewensis**, which received the AGM as *M. cordata* (if I interpret correctly), has a whitish inflorescence and is less vigorous, to 2m/6ft. It features in the white garden at Sissinghurst Castle.

Malva

MALVACEAE

The common mallow, **Malva sylvestris,** is a frequent weed in gardens, which hired labour or unpaid friends, wishing to help with the weeding, will always leave untouched, because, with its mound of dark green, rounded leaves, it looks important. It is a great let-down in flower but has good variants, notably 'Primley Blue'. This makes a large, rambling, sub-shrubby plant of varying height – up to 2m/6ft if against a wall, but 60cm/2ft in the open and with a much wider spread. The near-blue, open-funnel flowers are very pale but with dark veins. Beautiful at its best but susceptible to hollyhock rust disease, which entirely cripples it. If you know what to expect, you can apply a protective spray ahead of trouble and repeat it during the growing season. May to July-flowering.

M. s. subsp. *mauritanica* (2m/6ft) is a tall, gangling, sub-shrubby plant with little branching. Its leaves have longish petioles which hold the blade well clear of the stem, but the flowers are thickly clustered close to and along a considerable length of this; the usual mallow shape but rich blackcurrant purple. It is short-lived and apt to look raggedy, but sometimes distinctly exciting. Easily raised from seed to flower in one year.

M. alcea var. *fastigiata* (2m/6ft) is a true perennial with a woody base. Its mallow-pink flowers are borne for a long while at midsummer and can look rather nice, in a weedy way. It sows itself like a weed, too.

The musk mallow, *M. moschata* (1m/3ft), has deeply indented, rounded leaves and the flowers are a good shade of pink. Deservedly more popular is *M. m.* f. *alba* (60cm/2ft) with white flowers, fading pinkish, borne over a long summer period. It self-sows rather freely and has a tough rootstock to extract.

Malvastrum

MALVACEAE

The South American *Malvastrum lateritium* (15cm/6in) is a hardy, prostrate plant, with a timid inclination to sucker and make a patch. Its typical mallow flowers, about 4cm/1½in across, are salmon with a deeper central blotch. They are produced, in small quantities, over a long, summer season. However, in a border situation they are almost concealed by the plant's own foliage.

If planted against a warm wall, this species retains its old growth over winter and, climbing (with a little support) to 60-90cm/2-3ft, flowers abundantly and conspicuously, in early summer.

Matteuccia

WOODSIACEAE/POLYPODIACEAE

58 The shuttlecock fern, or ostrich feather fern, *Matteuccia struthiopteris* (*Struthiopteris germanica*) (1m/3ft) is very hardy and has a huge, circumpolar distribution. Barren and fertile fronds are separate. The bipinnate sterile fronds, which are deciduous, form an attractive funnel-shaped circle at the end of each stolon – for this is a stoloniferous fern, capable of making huge colonies. It is bright green and wonderfully fresh, in spring. In the south, it has a strong tendency, unless very moist and wholly protected from strong sunshine, to scorch at midsummer and to look rather pathetic from then on.

In cooler, moister climates, like Scotland, it continues to be a handsome feature into autumn. There, its progress will almost certainly need curtailing if something more varied than a monoculture is wanted. The stiff, pinnate fertile fronds appear around midsummer, half the length of the sterile and forming a circle within them.

Meconopsis

PAPAVERACEAE

Meconopsis includes all those fantastic blue poppies of which we southern gardeners are so envious when we visit Scottish gardens in May and June. Envy is stupid, as well as disagreable. There are a great many plants succeeding with us that are a hopeless failure in Scotland. One excellent reason for visiting those parts in spring (for the petiolarid primulas) early summer and autumn (for the heathers and gentians) is to enjoy those plants which are happiest in their cool climate, where the air is moist even if the rainfall is low.

All these meconopsis (apart from the Welsh poppy) come from the Himalayas. All areas, there, to those who have not visited, seem the same (or they do to me), so I need not specify locations. Many meconopsis are monocarpic – they invariably die after flowering and seeding. These need not concern us. There are others which tend to die after flowering, given the conditions they find here, particularly in the south, but in cooler Scotland, they may be sound perennials, merely requiring to be divided and replanted, in spring or autumn, every third year or so.

Such is the legendary blue poppy, **M. betonicifolia** (syn. *M. baileyi*) (1m/3ft). Its flowers face outwards, more or less, looking at you, with four blue petals and a central cushion of yellow anthers. The pure white var. *alba* is just as beautiful. **M. grandis** (1.2m/4ft) is a larger-growing, larger-flowered plant, slightly earlier-flowering (May), more reliably perennial and easily divided. These two species so readily hybridise that it is hard to tell which are hybrids – all grouped under **M. × sheldonii** – and which the species.

The huge-flowered 'Branklyn' (1.2m/4ft), for instance, if it can still be truly identified, takes after the *M. grandis* parent. There is a touch of purple in its blue colouring, most often. I find it a coarse thing, though undoubtedly showy. Some of the pure blue clones are uncomfortably vivid, like certain blue hydrangeas on acid soil. Their colouring is natural but gives the feeling of not being so. Some of your best garden plants will be found under the umbrella of *M.* × *sheldonii*.

M. quintuplinervia (30cm/1ft) is a gem – easy in Scotland in cool, leaf soil (which they all like), with high, broken tree shade. It makes a mat of small leaves and bears, in June, one bloom from the end of each shoot; this on a naked stalk which arches over at the top, so that the flower hangs like a lampshade. It is a delicate shade of mauve and, when newly opened, crowded with white anthers. Such elegance. Because it flowers in the same way, it might be compared with the exquisite **M. punicea,** whose soft red flowers become luminous if touched by sunlight. This species is all too liable to die out after flowering, but by no means always. You have to be prepared for such an eventuality with regular sowings of seed.

The pure, pale yellow-flowered meconopsis are highly desirable. **M. chelidoniifolia** (1m/3ft) has a spraying habit. Its scalloped leaves are reminiscent of the greater celandine's. The smallish flowers, opening in July, are borne on terminal sprays. The plant produces axillary bulbils, from which it can be propagated. **M. villosa** (1m/3ft) has larger leaves and (yellow) flowers, at midsummer, without the spraying habit.

The Welsh poppy, **M. cambrica** (60cm/2ft), a native of Wales and the south-west, preferring cool, shady places, is in most of our gardens, though it prefers acid soils. Typically yellow, the soft orange variant can hold its own in the company of yellow. This self-sows freely and can be a nuisance, but I love its first flush of bloom in May, and it associates well with later-flowering shrubs, particularly hydrangeas. There are double-flowered forms, usually orange.

Megacarpaea

BRASSICACEAE/CRUCIFERAE

A genus of seven or eight Asiatic species, **Megacarpaea polyandra**, from Kashmir and Nepal, is the only one that I have seen or heard of in Britain; my cousin grew it at Keillour, in Scotland. It is a plant that appeals to the imagination. From a basal rosette of pinnate leaves, it eventually, after nine years or so, throws up one huge, branching panicle, to 2m/6ft, clothed with many spikelets of small, scented cream-white cruciform flowers at midsummer. Then it rests again, for another spell of nine years (seven would be so much luckier). If I could get hold of some seed, I would grow it gladly, no matter what my age (79, on the present count).

Melianthus

MELIANTHACEAE

The South African **Melianthus major** (1.2m/4ft) is really a shrub, but best treated as a herbaceous perennial. It is as beautiful a foliage plant as you can have in your garden and, once established, it will last for decades in the same position, though it is always a wise precaution to cover its crown with fern fronds in winter.

The glaucous leaves (which smell, when bruised, of peanut butter), each about a foot long, are pinnate, the pinnae heavily toothed. Thus, in autumn and early winter, when sunlight is low for most of the day, the leaves cast serrated shadows, one against another, giving a strong three-dimensional effect. Each plant will throw up several stems from the base, but aim for a group effect if you have the space. It looks well with pink japanese anemones nearby, or with purple-leaved cannas.

At its best from July on, a few degrees of frost will be tolerated and the plant is generally in good shape till December. After an exceptionally mild winter (or quite normally on our coasts) its growth will survive the winter, but it is still best to cut everything right down, in the spring. As a shrub, it becomes leggy and clumsy. If not cut down, it will flower in May, the tubular flowers, in a short spike, being chocolate. They are curious, not beautiful. Once seen, best forgotten.

Propagation is most easily from seed, but is also easy, on a small scale, from cuttings of the young shoots made from below ground level, in spring. **M. minor** is not worth it and anyway hard to propagate.

Melissa

LAMIACEAE/LABIATAE

The herb balm, **Melissa officinalis** (75cm/2½ft) is a clumpy, non-invasive plant. Its shiny, broadly ovate leaves have toothed margins. It has a pungent odour, akin to *Monarda*. The flowers are mingy and it is best to cut the plant down before it seeds, which it does, too freely. 'Aurea' is variegated in green and yellow and looks nice in the spring, but its seedlings come plain-leaved.

'All Gold', however, is just that, retaining its colour throughout the summer, though scorching if not given some protection from drought combined with blazing sunshine. When it seeds itself, the progeny come gold like the parent.

Menyanthes

MENYANTHACEAE

A monospecific genus with a circumpolar distribution in bogs or still, shallow water. ***Menyanthes trifoliata*** (38cm/15in), called bogbean or buckbean, is a beautiful aquatic whose smooth, trifoliate leaves and flowering spikes stand well clear of the water. It sends out horizontal shoots, like rafts, across the water's surface.

Flowering season depends on where it is growing, but starts in early May in southern England. Blush pink buds open to white stars, the petals heavily fringed.

Mertensia

BORAGINACEAE

The Virginia cowslip (who gave it that name?), ***Mertensia pulmonarioides*** (30cm/1ft), better known as **M. virginica**, is one of spring's freshest and most delightful surprises. It appears quite suddenly, unrolling its quiverful of pale blue (there is a touch of mauve, as in most Boraginaceae), tubular flowers above smoothly glaucous leaves. It looks succulent and edible. The plants have fleshy roots. They may die out if not replanted from time to time, liking part shade and a damp, leafy soil. In summer, they aestivate, and you must remember where they are. Self-sown seedlings appear freely around the parents and are unmistakeable with their pairs of glaucous, ace-of-spades-shaped cotyledons. They offer the easiest means of propagation.

The late John Treasure used to grow **M. echioides** (30cm/1ft) most successfully as ground cover in his Burford House garden (Shropshire). It has racemes of dark blue flowers. I never saw it anywhere else.

Microseris

ASTERACEAE/COMPOSITAE

A very welcome newcomer to my garden, ***Microseris ringens*** (30cm/1ft) features in none of my reference books and the RHS Floral Committee A don't want anything

33

to do with it. It is a yellow daisy, you see. I saw it in Beth Chatto's garden; she let me have a piece and, besides division, I find that it comes easily from seed.

A hardy perennial, its large, obovate leaves spring from basal tufts. Flowering starts in June and continues non-stop well into October. The daisies are all ligulate rays (like a dandelion), small but numerous and borne in sprays from a common stem. A sharper, more acidic yellow than the dandelion and bright. For contrast, I grow a rich purple border phlox behind my group.

Milium

POACEAE/GRAMINAE

Milium effusum (45cm/1½ft before flowering) would have remained a totally unnoticed native woodland grass had not Ernest Bowles spotted a golden-leaved variant, 'Aureum'. Happiest in part-shade, it is a cheering feature in the spring garden, even in winter, if the weather is kind. It combines with blue spring flowers especially well: bluebells, forget-me-nots, *Brunnera macrophylla*.

Individual plants are short-lived but self-sowing is sufficient to keep a colony going, and the seedlings come true to colour.

Mimulus

SCROPHULARIACEAE

The monkey flower, **Mimulus guttatus** (75cm/2½ft), was an import from North America, but has so adapted itself to our streamsides as to seem a native. The yellow flowers are speckled with small red dots. **M. aurantiacus** (75cm/2½ft), better known as **M. luteus**, came from Chile and has large red blotches (so vulgar, my dear) on its lip, against a yellow background.

More to my taste as a garden plant is **M. cardinalis** (1m/3ft), with rather narrow, two-lipped flowers in a soft, brownish shade of red. It comes readily from seed, self-sowing, and there is quite a variation in colouring, embracing quiet orange and pinkish red. All these are for moist areas by a stream or in boggy ground.

Of the small kinds, I used to fancy **M. cupreus** 'Whitecroft Scarlet' (10cm/4in), which is a good colour, but it's the sort of plant that you lose, in this competitive world.

Miscanthus

POACEAE/GRAMINAE

This Far Eastern genus of rather tall perennial grasses, has come up in the world since Miss Jekyll wrote of it as *Eulalia*.

Miscanthus can be grown for their foliage or for their flowers or for both. In the British climate, many are ready to flower only as our growing season comes to an end, so it is an incomplete affair. However, Ernst Pagels, a north German nursery-man and breeder of perennials, with a climate comparable to our own, set out with notable success to breed races which could be relied upon to flower reasonably early. Where summers are hotter than ours, even though winters may be colder, as in many parts of the USA, the majority of *Miscanthus* flower without difficulty. In some of the southern States, **M. sinensis**, the commonest species, is quite a weed, self-sowing incontinently.

4   There are now so many cultivars of *M. sinensis*, that it is difficult to tell them apart. The zebra grass that Miss Jekyll grew as *Eulalia*, was probably 'Zebrinus' (2m/6ft), whose foliage is lax on an upright plant, the leaves cross-banded with patches of yellow. These show up better as the leaves mature. It is not quite so hardy as my preferred 'Strictus'(2m/6ft), which is similarly cross-banded but more pronouncedly. The leaves are quite stiff, pointing obliquely upwards and the plant makes a strong impression. Both flower rather too late, in England, to be noteworthy in this respect.

The same comment applies to 'Gracillimus' (1.5m/5ft), which has narrow leaves with a thin, pale midrib. 'Variegatus', striped in green and white, is in a class of its own as a foliage plant. It deserves to stand, as a single clump, above its surrounding fellows, there to proclaim its grace with arching foliage and a landscape presence which shows up from afar.

As good as any of the easily flowered clones of *M. sinensis*, is one of Pagel's earliest productions, 'Silberfeder' (2m/6ft) – 'Silver Feather'. It starts to flower in late August, being light purple then. The inflorescence, as with all these miscanthus, is composed of a cluster of permanent-wave strands, like a cat-o'-nine-tails whip. The colour bleaches as the stems die but the shape, if your plants are not too much exposed to fierce winds, continues to be a beautiful garden or landscape feature till midwinter or even later. Miscanthus do have a big leaf moult in the new year, however, which could be a nuisance. 'Yakushima Dwarf' (1m/3ft) flowers early and freely and could be useful in a small garden, though it is on the dumpy side – looking better the other side of Christmas, however.

'Malepartus' (2m/6ft) has received considerable acclaim, flowering very deep purple in the early stages. It is uncommonly stiff and undeserving of high praise, I believe. But there are so many more.

M. floridulus grows to 3.6m/12ft in a season and is like a foliar fountain, queening it above its fellows. No flowers to speak of. This and *M. sacchariflorus* are greatly confused, the names often interchangeable.

All miscanthus are clump-forming and do not run unduly. But colonies fall off in quality after five or six years. They deserve to be dug up (a strong young man's job) and replanted in improved soil, but will sulk for the first year afterwards.

Molinia

POACEAE/GRAMINAE

Huge stretches of upland hillside and bog in Scotland are covered with moor grass, also known as deer grass, and this is the constituent which gives the hills in autumn their wonderful, orange-brown glow. Typical moor grass is **Molinia caerulea** subp. **caerulea**. In gardens this is most often met in its cultivar 'Variegata' (45cm/1½ft). It makes a dense, hummocky, non-aggressive clump of cream-and-green-striped foliage, really coming into its own when it flowers in autumn. The whole plant then changes to pale gold. A group makes a good corner or promontory feature in a mixed border, but in winter there is nothing. The whole plant suddenly disintegrates, late November, the stems breaking off cleanly at the base. This is the characteristic of all molinias.

'Moorhexe' (moor witch) (1m/3ft) has stiff, absolutely upright flowering stems and makes a nice vertical feature above a flat surface, as it might be paving.

M. caerulea subsp. *arundinacea* (syn. *M. altissima*) (2m/6ft) represents a tall group of moor grass, of which I find 'Transparent' the most satisfying over a long period. Its inflorescences begin to rise above the foliage in late June and keep on developing till tall and feathery, but never blocking the view, so that a single specimen on a border bulge, rising above lower features, will have a great presence. 'Windspiel' is another, similar cultivar that I grow, but in too confined a situation. It really needs to be in the open, so I am moving that.

Heavy, acid, water-retentive soils suit the moor grasses best, but they should be happy on base-rich soils provided they retain moisture. They should only be moved in spring or early summer and take a long time to settle down, after disturbance. Move large chunks rather than small.

41

Don't forget, they are not grasses for winter effect. July to November is their sufficiently long season.

Monarda

Lamiaceae/Labiatae

Bee balm is the name most usually heard in America, for this genus, which comes from there; Oswego tea is another. In Britain, we most often call it bergamot or monarda. The numerous cultivars are of such mixed parentage as seldom to be ascribed to any particular species.

There are some beautiful cultivars available, in shades of red, purple, mauve, pink and white. All are hardy. All have a characteristic, strong lemony aroma. The hooded flowers are densely arranged in two or three whorls, towards the top of 1m/3ft stems.

Rich, moisture-retaining and deeply cultivated soil suits monardas best. They overwinter as a dense network of stolons carrying rosettes of small leaves. These are apt to kill themselves out by overcrowding, so in spring it is a good idea to surface-mulch with old potting soil, just as the young shoots are lengthening.

Powdery mildew is the bee balm's scourge, these days; it never used to be seen. Protective sprays need to be applied in good time before its appearance. Another drawback is replant disease. Don't replant unless you must. If a colony becomes so weakened that this becomes imperative, move the colony to a fresh site. Under most border conditions, monardas need support.

Moving it to a fresh site was just what I did not want to have to do with 'Cambridge Scarlet', which occupied a key position in my principal mixed border, at its best in July. The colour is not scarlet, but a good, strong shade of red. My other favourite was 'Beauty of Cobham', which has pink flowers, though the overall impression is mauve, because the supporting bracts are purple.

Overall, I find monardas too pernickety, these days, but in a new garden I would say, 'give them a run'.

Morina

Morinaceae/Dipsaceae

The only well-known species in cultivation is **_Morina longifolia_** (60cm/2ft). This is a clumpy plant with dark, evergreen, foot-long leaves having prickly margins – not very prickly. They have a pleasant citrous odour, but only when bruised. Borne in whorls, June-July, the two-lipped flowers are very pale pink on opening, becoming deep pink on ageing – so, an overall bicolour effect.

This is a hardy species but is said not to be long-lived. That is not necessarily the case. It does not split well but is easily raised from seed. Good in Scotland, as well as England. It comes from Kashmir, as does **M. coulteriana** (1m/3ft), with pale yellow flowers. I have always wanted to own this, since seeing it there, but no stock is available and I am not sure why. Perhaps it does not move as a plant and no one with an eye for such things has been on the spot to collect seed at the right time? Most plants from high altitudes in Kashmir adapt well to our climate, so the absence of *M. coulteriana* from our garden repertory is tantalising.

Musa

MUSACEAE

No better plant for achieving a tropical effect in your garden, than with the 'hardy' Japanese banana, **Musa basjoo** (2.7m/9ft). We are not talking about bananas as a crop – I buy from Sainsbury's myself – but as a foliage plant, having leaves 1.2m/4ft or more long. A sheltered situation is necessary, otherwise the leaves get torn to shreds (as seen on banana plantations) and look unhappy.

M. basjoo needs rich soil and plenty of moisture when growing. To preserve its trunk for the next year, thus increasing the plant's overall height, wrap it up in November, in a thick padding of fern fronds. These can be left till late May, the signal for removal being the appearance of a new (if tentative) banana leaf from the top of the apparatus.

Thereafter, new leaves of increasing size will be made for the next four months. When the weather is really hot, the frequency with which each new leaf appears will be increased to one every ten days or even less. Quite an excitement, as they are nothing if not voluptuous. Plant them around with other exotica, like cannas and castor oil (*Ricinus*).

The ground around the plant should also have a fern or other thick mulch, in winter. The great advantage of this species is that it is rhizomatous; if you lose the main trunk, you'll be in business again with surrounding offsets. These are made from quite deep down. If you want to increase your stock (who wouldn't?), it is safest to dig the whole plant out, in late spring, and to sever the offsets, each with some

63

root attached, from the main stem. Establish them under glass, for a month or six weeks, before planting out (or selling, or giving to valued friends).

The other commonest species in cultivation for ornament is **M. ensete**, now *Ensete ventricosum*. This is easily and quickly raised from seed, which is available, but the plant is tender and must be housed under heated glass in winter. It is of indefinite growth and will become inconveniently tall for handling after a few years, but can be renewed from seed. It does not make offsets, nor break from low down, if the stem is cut back.

Muscari

H YACINTHACEAE / L ILIACEAE

There are so many species and cultivars of *Muscari* that they provide a field day for the specialist, who thrives on the minutiae of differentiating detail and is given a feeling of vast superiority by the fact that, to the uninitiated, they all look more or less the same. 'A grape hyacinth is a grape hyacinth is a grape hyacinth', as Gertrude Stein might have said.

I am not head over heels in love with them. One of my abiding impressions is of a mass of lank foliage, all through the winter – I think that may be **M. armeniacum** (30cm/1ft). It flowers in April – they all do. and the blue flowers resemble an inverted bunch of grapes. They are nice to include in bunches of mixed spring flowers, and you should pull, rather than pluck, the stems, thereby getting quite a bit of extra length. You may read a lot about the sweet scent of various species, including this one, but it has never wafted my way.

M. armeniacum contrasts well with dandelion flowers and if you can get it to naturalise in rough grass, that is a good idea. Ours are in a ribbon underneath a dripping, gutterless roof. They do not in the least object. Their bulbs are brought to the surface, because the drip washes the soil away, but that only needs replacing – with old potting soil – every few years.

The clone called 'Blue Spike', is showier. To quote Martyn Rix, 'Each flower has become a miniature inflorescence, giving a monstrous effect'. Well, I'm glad to know what has happened, but the effect is pretty good, especially with double red daisies growing nearby.

In **M. botryoides** (23cm/9in), the leaves are only half the length of the flower stems and they don't flop – a great improvement. Nearly all *Muscari* species give rise to albinos. 'Album', here, is just about the best – very pure and clumping up well.

You can have fun working out what best to plant it near – but do plant it near to something; don't just waste it among a desert of plants that are contributing nothing, at that season.

M. azureum (10cm/4in) is the plant that for years we knew as *Hyacinthus azureum*, though it always looked like a grape hyacinth, except that its mouth is wide open. A most obliging and easy plant.

M. comosum 'Plumosum' (23cm/9in) really is extraordinary – just a haze of mauve threads, rather like a feather duster. **M. latifolium** is unusual in having only one leaf to a bulb – a broad leaf, rather like a tulip species. The flower spike is lightish blue on top, deep indigo in the main, lower section.

Myosotidium

BORAGINACEAE

A garden of snob plants would have to include the Chatham Islands forget-me-not, **Myosotidium hortensia** (syn. *M. nobile*) (30cm/1ft), which is just sufficiently difficult in cultivation without being nearly as difficult as its exotic appearance would lead you to believe. The nearer to the sea that it grows, the easier it is. It will not stand heavy frost.

The leaves are large, orbicular and fleshy. The branching inflorescence of substantial forget-me-not flowers, in late spring, is substantial, too, soon sagging to ground level and often largely concealed by the foliage. At its best, it must be wonderful, but it is more often (except to the besotted) a disappointment. It is a true aristocrat.

Myosotis

BORAGINACEAE

The bedding forget-me-not is biennial, but the water forget-me-not, **Myosotis scorpioides** (syn. *M. palustris*) (23cm/9in) is perennial. It is light blue with a yellow eye and its main flowering is not till June. It likes moisture and seems to be particularly successful in New England. It has a long season. 'Mermaid' is the cultivar most offered here. It self-sows and appears to come true from seed.

Myrrhis

APIACEAE/UMBELLIFERAE

The familiar herb, **Myrrhis odorata** (1m/3ft), is a favourite in herb gardens and is best restricted to that area. It is a deep-, thick-rooted perennial that self-seeds incontinently if not cut down before its seeds are ripe. The whole plant is strongly aromatic, smelling of myrrh (it is said). The foliage is abundant – large leaves, finely divided, certainly handsome. The white flowers, in late spring and early summer, do not amount to much.

This plant is widely naturalised in the north of England, south and central Scotland, being generally associated with habitations, where its uses were culinary; or along roadsides.

Narcissus

AMARYLLIDACEAE

There is no technical difference between narcissi and a daffodil, but in common parlance daffodils are yellow, generally with a trumpet, while narcissi are white, with a small cup.

Daffodils introduce spring in its fullest vigour. There is a great forward thrust in their habit and growth, which reflects the rapidly changing scene around us. No one would want to dispense with daffodils, yet by the time they are nearing the end of their season, there is quite a sigh of relief. 'Too much yellow', is a general complaint. But they have many shades of yellow and if you bear no grudge against yellow as a colour, then the too-muchness can be analysed. They are often bred to be overlarge and blowsy, and are planted too densely and without relief. It is as though the planter wished to show off and to demonstrate that he or she had the money to cover every square inch of the piece of land to be planted up with a blanket of the largest, finest daffodils available.

These are much larger, now, than they were early in the 20th century. Orchards underplanted with daffodils, then, contain more graceful varieties (long since gone from commerce) than similar areas planted in the past thirty years. If you know your cultivars, you can date a planting by the presence of those that were fashionable for naturalising at a certain time.

Naturalised daffodils are extremely persistent and, once established, their replacement is rarely contemplated. One great advantage of planting them in turf, is that the grass sward will grow up and conceal the daffodils' otherwise obnoxiously dying foliage, at just the right moment. It is best to think of daffodils as just one constituent in a varied and prolonged tapestry display of plants suited to meadow conditions, rather than the be-all and end-all of a turf area that you are all the time longing to mow as early as you can without spoiling next year's display, keeping the grass almost as a lawn from the end of May until the New Year.

One of the most nastily contrived-looking practices is to confine daffodils to rings around trees, so that the grass in between can be mown continuously, even before the mower dares to mow over the daffodils themselves. How early is it safe to do this? is a frequent question. You should not go by a date but by the state of the daffodils' foliage, waiting until this is brown and withered. Mid-June would be safe in most areas.

Daffodils are best planted with the help of a long-shafted, bulb-planting tool that can be quickly operated from a standing position. Such tools have become quite rare and they tend to be expensive, but are the only acceptable way, since they allow you to site each bulb separately and precisely. It is a kind of random precision.

I make 50 or 100 holes at a time, spacing them at unequal distances, thickest in the centre of a group with quite wide spacing towards its margins. Have a barrow of old potting soil handy. Break off the top of the plug that is now lying on the surface and push it, upside down, into the bottom of the hole. Then place the bulb and fill in with good soil. There should be about 5cm/2in between the top of the bulb and the soil surface.

Leave wide spaces between groups of bulbs, into which other plants can be naturalised. If you are planting cultivars, it is quite a good plan to alternate yellow-flowered kinds with white, but you may have your own ideas on this. One point I would insist on. Each group should be of only one variety. This looks far more telling than the planting of a mixture, even though the purchase of mixtures may be temptingly cheap. They are whatever the merchant has left over and have no rhyme nor reason about their choice. As well as looking confused, mixtures have the further disadvantage of flowering at different times, those flowering late being seen among the brown, faded blooms of those that were early.

In many contexts, and especially in a meadow, the modern cultivars are so muscular as to look gross and overbearing, especially at close quarters. You should try to foresee this (by reading me), as there's not much redress once a decision has been acted upon.

Confine yourself, in that case, to wildings or to quite small-flowered hybrids. If they are of a kind that will self-sow, as many do, that is a great advantage. Among the best for this purpose is our own native Lent lily, ***Narcissus pseudonarcissus*** (23cm/9in), a yellow, trumpet daffodil. ('Princeps' (38cm/15in), much planted early in the century, is a polyploid version.) This flowers in March. The tiny trumpet species, ***N. asturiensis*** (5cm/2in) is often out as early as January and naturalises happily in short turf. It is followed, in February-March, by ***N. minor*** (10cm/4in). I recommend allowing this to clump up, quickly, in a border, and then transferring the bulbs, when they have just flowered, to a fine-turf meadow, where they will increase, but more slowly.

N. bulbocodium (10cm/4in), the hoop-petticoat daffodil, has very small segments but a much inflated, lampshade-like corona. I like this best in a pale, citrous yellow form, such as var. *citrinus*. There is an ancient colony in the alpine meadow at Wisley. The flowering season is much longer than usual.

Of ***N. cyclamineus*** (7.5cm/3in), there are notable drifts in the Savill Gardens, Windsor Great Park. Coloured citrous yellow, the perianth is reflexed, back to the stalk (peduncle) and the long corona is a prolongation of the same axis.

So far, I have written only of narcissi naturalised in turf, and before leaving this treatment, I will put in a plea for refraining from planting them in roadside verges in the countryside, where their size and sophistication seem wholly out of place and introduce the tainted breath of creeping suburbia.

Daffodils are, of course, much planted in cultivated ground under border conditions. As they go over, the garden often takes on a senile air, from which it may never recover. Some garden owners resort to the practice of tying the leaves of each clump in a knot, to get them out of the way and to show the world that there is someone around who is taking care. But it looks terrible, while also depriving each leaf of about half the light it should receive to help it build up next year's bulb.

I believe that long-, obtrusive-leaved daffodils should be kept out of borders altogether. If required for picking, grow them in discreet retirement near the vegetables. If they have shortish or narrow leaves, which will scarcely be noticed while dying

off, there is a place for them. I grow the late jonquil, 'Tittle Tattle' (45cm/1½ft), between clumps of hemerocallis. The latter's strap-shaped leaves soon overtake the
jonquil's, when that has flowered. It has a neat, pure yellow flower with a small cup
and is scented.

A narrow, rush-leaved miniature, 'Hawera' (15cm/6in), which is a hybrid be-
tween **N. triandrus** and **N. jonquilla**, is easily fitted in. Fairly late, it has a small cluster of downward-facing, yellow flowers, the perianth reflexed, and it clumps up
well, not minding turf conditions. However, I like to use it as a companion for the
low, mat-forming *Veronica peduncularis* 'Georgia Blue', with deep, mauve-blue flowers at the same season.

A daffodil like the small, February-March-flowering 'Tête-à-Tête' (15cm/6in),
can be fitted in almost anywhere – among late-starting *Eryngium × oliverianum*, perhaps. It is a small, yellow trumpet of no refinement, but irresistibly cheerful. All
stock is well known to be virus-infected, but it is so vigoroous, notwithstanding,
that the defect is readily overlooked.

I also grow 'February Gold' (38cm/15in), 'March Sunshine' (38cm/15in), and
'Dove Wings' (38cm/15in), white, with a cream cup, in my borders, because they
are early and soon concealed by their neighbours in luxuriant mixed-border
plantings. These are *cyclamineus* hybrids, having a prominent corona and segments
that are characteristically recurved.

Trumpet daffodils have, unfortunately, been greatly coarsened by breeding for
size. The blame is often laid undiscriminatingly on a quite old cultivar, 'King Alfred'
(1m/3ft) which we had from my grandmother, around 1930, after she had finished
with a bowl of growing bulbs. It is early-flowering and quite a favourite with me;
deep yellow, shading to green at the base of the perianth, whose segments have a
twist on them. However, it is often not truly named. When you come to a cultivar
like 'Golden Harvest' (45cm/1½ft), with a trumpet like a drainpipe, frilled at the ori-
fice, you are in trouble. But there is a most beautiful, not very vigorous, white trumpet, 'Cantatrice' (30cm/1ft), of enviable elegance for this flower type, with a narrow
trumpet and segments which overlap at the base but are drawn to fine points.

The large-cupped narcissi lend themselves to coarsening, but may have a rich orange corona. The early-flowering, one-time commercial favourite, 'Fortune'
(38cm/15in), deep yellow with an orange cup, is still widely on offer.

I have to say that displays of these narcissi in competitive classes at a daffodil show,
make depressing viewing. Seen in specimen vases, usually one, sometimes three to a
vase, always looking at you full-face, it needs great concentration if your eyes are not
to glaze.

'Aflame' (30cm/1ft) is classified as small-cupped, but it seems pretty large, to me, though flattened and crimped; a wonderfully bright shade of red, highlighted by a white perianth. The snag, here, as in many others, is that the cup bleaches badly after a couple of days' exposure to sunshine. When picked, this does not happen.

Split Coronas are an interesting group. In these the corona is divided into six segments, like the perianth, and the former lies flat against the latter. The colours are often contrasting. This seems like a quite different flower from the narcissi we are conditioned to. It can be coarse or it can be beautiful, but you need to shed preconceived prejudices; otherwise, like many another, you will simply be repelled.

Double daffodils may seem like an unwelcome aberration, but when the doubling is loose yet even, they have their own poise.

I have yet to see a clumsy *triandrus* hybrid. There are several blooms to each stem and, typically, they nod, facing down. 'Thalia' (38cm/15in) is deservedly one of the most popular. The flowers are pure white, with narrow, pointed segments, and are borne with exceptional abundance. 'Liberty Bells' (38cm/15in), is easily picked out in a crowd, the flowers a cool shade of yellow. The bell is very slightly, yet noticeably, closed at the mouth.

Scent, in narcissi, means a great deal to us and its quality varies surprisingly. **N. tazetta** (38cm/15in) is bunch headed, with up to seven blooms to each bunch. It is the parent of one of the most popular groups. Its distribution is wide and it varies greatly over its geographical range, but is usually none of the hardiest. My own clone has very dark green leaves and is white, with a small, pale yellow cup. The season is long, starting in February in most years. Its scent, characteristic of the group, is sweet but with a slightly acrid pungence, if you inhale too enthusiastically. The forcing cultivars, 'Soleil d'Or' and 'Cragford' are typical. The double 'Cheerfulness' (38cm/15in) and its sport, 'Yellow Cheerfulness' are doubled in the centre, the stamens converted into 'petals'.

The Jonquilla group, always yellow, have a strong, friendly fragrance. It is worth growing **N. jonquilla** (23cm/9in) itself, an intensely deep yellow. The narrow leaves are tightly folded, longitudinally, so as to appear rush-like. Jonquillas are apt to carry two or three blooms to a head, but only if the bulb is large and strong. If you naturalise 'Trevithian' (45cm/1½ft), for instance, most of the flowers will be solitary. It doesn't matter. This is a graceful, long-stemmed jonquil, of typical yellow colouring and 'Quail' (38cm/15in) is similar, though a little shorter. I also grow 'Pipit' (30cm/1ft) – pale yellow with a paler cup, and 'Suzy' (30cm/1ft), which is a stronger yellow with a small, orange cup, lateish flowering and free. I have mentioned 'Tittle Tattle'. It is a rewarding group.

Finally, and most sweetly scented on the air, the group Poeticus, which has given us the pheasant's eyes, having a very small cup with a thin red rim. 'Actaea' (38cm/15in) flowers quite early, but seems to me to have an unbalanced bloom. Almost the latest is the poet's narcissus. **N. poeticus** var. **recurvus** (45cm/1½ft), which flowers in May. It makes big clumps but quite frequently goes in for a non-flowering year. Still, one must have it.

Last of all is its double form, 'Plenus' – loosely doubled so that the red rim is still visible, in the interior. This produces half a crop of buds which never develop, but wither. I find it a weak grower, but it is widespread and healthy in Scotland. For reasons whose explanation I have not discovered, you see it everywhere, often along a roadside, and especially in Orkney, where it is still flowering in June.

Nectaroscordum

ALLIACEAE/LILIACEAE

N. siculum (*Allium siculum*) (1m/3ft) is so close to Allium, that one wonders why it has been allotted a genus of its own. Its bulbs smell as strongly of onion as any onion you are likely to meet.

Its distribution covers the whole north side of the Mediterranean, but it has been subdivided into subsp. *siculum*, in the western half of its range and subsp. *bulgaricum* in the eastern half. With more of creamy green in its colouring, the latter shows up the better in a garden setting. *Siculum* has more of chestnut in it. It has sturdy scapes crowned by clusters of bells in May. As the flowers go over, the pedicels straighten to a vertical position. The seed heads are supposed to be an asset. I find them irritating.

In fact, this is a plant that does not want to stand forth and be counted, but is the better for being absorbed among other plants of roughly its own height. I like it with *Astilbe* 'Superba' (syn. *A. chinensis* var. *taquetii*). It is an easy bulb, with no fads, but will help to earn you a reputation for good taste, if that has not been irremediably ruined by a liking for cannas and dahlias.

Nemesia

SCROPHULARIACEAE

Nemesias as perennials are a recent acquisition to the gardening world and considerable breeding developments are in progress. The plants have much in common with *Diascia* in habit and performance though there is little overlap in colouring. Most of these perennial nemesias are mauve, sometimes verging on blue, and there are some good whites. In all cases the eye of the flower is white or cream. A number are sweetly scented, which comes as a surprise.

Two of the operative parents of these hybrids are **Nemesia caerulea** and **N. denticulata**. Height is around 30cm/1ft or a little more but some, like the white 'Innocence' and 'Snowstorm', make quite wide-spreading (to 60cm/2ft) bushes. So does the mauve *N. denticulata* 'Confetti', which flowers with great freedom. The flowering season, from early summer on, continues for several months but, as with diascias, growth is liable to become straggling and it is usually advisable to shear the plants back to 7.5cm/3in sometime in July. Some set seed but those that do not are the more inclined to flower uninterruptedly.

Hardiness is not to be depended upon. Plants will sometimes survive the winter but young plants raised afresh from cuttings will give the best results.

Nepeta

Lamiaceae/Labiatae

The catmints are mostly aromatic herbs for sunny positions on light, preferably alkaline soils. The type plant, **Nepeta cataria**, has little visual merit but is the strongest-smelling species and a great attraction to cats.

The most popular catmint, much overused as an edger, is **N. × faasenii** (45cm/1½ft) at one time known as *N. mussinii*, which is one of its parents and is now to be known as **N. racemosa**. Of *N. × faasenii* (as *N. mussinii*) Miss Jekyll wrote that it was 'a plant that can hardly be overpraised'. Flowering for three weeks in June, it makes mounds of open-textured racemes, coloured mauve (nurseryman's blue). Pretty when fresh but in quantity it needs more solid relief, as with an interplanting of bulbous Dutch or Spanish irises. If the central racemes are, on fading, removed just below their base, leaving the rest of the stem, this will flower on side-shoots in August.

'Six Hills Giant' (1m/3ft) is a much more vigorous version and can get laid by heavy rain. *N. racemosa* 'Walker's Low' (1m/3ft) is a distinct improvement on, though similar to (and a little earlier-flowering than) ordinary catmint. It has long, darker 'blue' racemes and dark stems.

The slightly earlier-flowering **N. sibirica** 'Souvenir d'André Chaudron'

(45cm/1½ft) has a somewhat running rootstock and larger, showy flowers. It is slightly coarse and outstandingly pungent-smelling. Easily raised from seed, the unsubstantiated name of **N. transcaucasica** is current for an upright, 90cm/3ft species, having a longish June-July season. Of lavender colouring, it can make quite a bold impression.

N. nervosa (30cm/1ft) can also be raised from seed (or cuttings). An upright, clumpy plant, it carries short, dense racemes in a rich shade of lavender, flowering early summer. Good at the front of a border but in need of fairly frequent replanting.

Quite unlike the rest, **N. govaniana** (1m/3ft) likes moist soil and part shade, carrying open sprays of pale yellow flowers on a non-aromatic plant. Flowers July-August. It can be on the coarse side but then disarms by being charmingly effective. This self-sows, the current year's seedlings providing late flowers.

Nerine

AMARYLLIDACEAE

Nerines are closely related to *Crinum* and to *Amaryllis*, but with umbels of smaller funnel flowers, the petals often reflexed and wavy-margined. They come from South Africa and few are hardy. But much hybridisation of the tender kinds has been done by a few enthusiasts, who display their products pot-grown and kept under cool greenhouse conditions. I have never seen them given a context or associated with other autumn-flowering or with foliage plants. At the time of flowering, they have no foliage themselves; this develops in the winter, which is one reason for their lack of hardiness in cool-temperate climates.

Their bulbs benefit from being congested in their pots, but will need feeding when growing strongly. They become dormant in summer. Best known of these is the Guernsey lily, **Nerine sarniensis** (30cm/1ft), carrying umbels of warm red flowers.

In the garden, best value is obtained from **N. bowdenii** (45cm/1½ft), whose flowers are a brilliant and uncompromising shade of pink, not at all autumnal in mood. They go well with *Aster amellus* 'Violet Queen'. The onset of flowering is affected by soil moisture, and may occur at any time from mid-September. It can be hastened, in dry seasons and situations, by watering the as yet dormant bulbs. Foliage, where summers are hot, dies off naturally at that season, but may remain and look tired and unappetising, into flowering time. It is worth removing this before danger of also simultaneously, albeit accidentally, removing young flowering stems. Late August should be right.

This nerine prefers to have its bulbs at the soil surface. It is remarkably tough and obliging, flowering well through Scotland and even in shaded places, if need be.

N. undulata (syn. *N. crispa*) has flowers half the size and in a soft shade of pink. It is almost as hardy but ineffective unless you can get a good patch of it going. Very charming, then.

N. flexuosa 'Alba', with soft, bright green foliage (highly vulnerable to slug damage), is distinctly less hardy, but can be excellent when well placed near to a sunny wall. It is a true albino with pure white flowers.

Nuphar

NYMPHAEACEAE

The yellow waterlily, **Nuphar lutea** is a native; vigorous, spreading and capable of growing in and coping with quite fast-moving streams. The smallish, bowl-shaped flowers are a deep shade of yellow, pleasing when young but on the whole hardly deserving of garden space.

Where you do see it as a garden plant, it has almost certainly been included out of ignorance, first of its excessive and exclusive vigour and second of its relatively dull appearance.

Nymphaea

NYMPHAEACEA

Waterlilies are among the most easily recognised of all flowers. Their size, many petals and unusual presentation ensure that they cannot be overlooked. I go along with Chris Baines's dictum that 'a garden without water is like a theatre without a stage', but even if every garden had a pool, it would generally offer space for only one waterlily. And the temptation to overcrowd must be resisted from the outset.

Waterlily pads, as we call their leaves, play an important role in shading the water and thereby preventing the serious development of unsightly algal growth (blanket weed), but they themselves need full sunlight and the plants will flower most freely in an open situation. Overcrowding, however, will result in a bunching up of the foliage, which then rises above the water and prevents the flowers from being seen.

Another point to remember, obvious when remarked upon but often ignored, is that the main reason for having a pond is to enjoy the water's surface, whether it is being ruffled by air currents, playing in various directions, or whether it is still and reflective, when the occasional breaking of its surface by dipping swallows or rising fish, will also remind us of the teeming life generated by a pond.

Aim to cover no more than a quarter of the water's surface with waterlilies at the height of the growing season. As they vary in vigour considerably, according to variety, you can choose accordingly. The more vigorous the nymphaea, the deeper the water into which it can be established. On the other hand, if you grow the plant in a container – special baskets are available – this restriction to its spread will in itself reduce its vigour, as also its flower size, allowing some of the naturally strong varieties to be grown healthily under comparatively cramped conditions. But in that case, frequent re-basketing will be necessary and more generous feeding.

Feeding can be done with a fertiliser like John Innes Base, wetting it in a bucket before dropping tennis-ball-sized handfuls over the surface of the waterlilies' rhizomes and roots. Only feed when the plants are strongly active. This, also, is the best time for planting or dividing them; that is, between May and August in the northern hemisphere. If planting into the bottom of a 'natural' pond, with a mud bottom, you can tie the root to a brick, so that it is anchored and will not float away before it has had the chance to anchor itself with further roots.

If the plant you acquire is small and weak, give it its best chance by containerising it, first, and gradually lowering the container so that the depth of water above the waterlily's crown is adjusted to correlate with the speed at which its leaf stalks elongate and bring the pads to the surface. Never grow nymphaeas in moving water (nuphars are better at coping with this) and never where they will be splashed all day by a fountain. Their leaves should be dry for most of the time. A few daily hours of fountain splash can be tolerated – just long enough to see your guests on to and off the premises, should you feel the need to show off in this particular way.

A popular meal-time table decoration is nymphaea blooms in a bowl of water, but they will close, as evening approaches. The next morning, they will open again, so lunch-time is more easily coped with than dinner. You can keep the bloom open by dropping paraffin wax into the base of the petals, before they start to close, but this requires practice. Nymphaeas are quite often sweetly scented; picking them gives most of us one of our otherwise rare opportunities for putting this to the test.

Choosing the right waterlily for you, deserves thought. Their finest breeder was the Frenchman, Marliac-Latour, whose breeding techniques for hybridising were kept a close secret. Many of those we now grow arose in his nursery between 1880 and 1920.

However, if you live in a moated castle, any colourful waterlily may seem too sophisticated. In that case, our native **Nymphaea alba** will choose itself. You see it wild in Scottish lochans, as also in Ireland, in July. The flowers are pure white; the growth not coarse. It will grow, if required to, in 2m/6ft of water.

Most of the cultivated white and yellow waterlilies are vigorous – too vigorous for ponds (in contrast to lakes). 'Gladstoniana' is one of the finest whites. Most of the yellow kinds have purple streaks on their foliage, derived from their **N. mexicana** parent. The best for general lake purposes is 'Marliacea Chromatella'. 'Colonel A.J. Welch' is shy flowering. 'Texas Dawn' is free, however, and its blooms present themselves several inches above the water's surface, which is flattering. Before acquiring it, I admired it on a number of occasions in the 'canal' at Wisley, where the waterlily collection is at last labelled (take no notice of the keep off the grass notices, which distance you from the labels). It is a fact, however, that birds like to perch and defecate on pond labels, making them illegible.

Red is the most popular colour, in nymphaeas. In deep water, Marliac's 'Escarboucle' is still by far the finest, its deep crimson blooms remaining open all day in most weathers, and right into October, when the others have long since packed it in. It should be mentioned that many varieties are not fully open till 11 in the morning and are already closing by 3 in the afternoon.

A nice bright pink is the star-shaped 'Rose Arey', with pointed petals. In 'Rose Magnolia', they are rounded, and that is a pleasing shape. 'Marliacea Carnea' suggests a brighter colour than its wan pink. I threw it out. The bowl-shaped 'James Brydon' is distinctive – of a bright mauve-pink. Very free when in season but that season is 'only' two months long. (In most perennials, this would be considered a long time.) 'Seignouretii' has smallish, yellow-pink blooms, held 23cm/9in above the water.

There are two well-known mini-nymphaeas, which can be grown in a bowl or tub, where there is no space for a pool. **N. tetragona**, usually listed as 'Pygmaea Alba', is white. **N. × helviola** ('Pygmaea Helviola') is yellow.

So far, there is only one nursery offering tender nymphaeas for public sale, in Britain, but in the USA there are many. There, however cold the winters, their summers are (or tend to be) much hotter than ours and these tender cultivars can be treated as annuals. They flower well into October.

The attraction is that the blooms are always held well above the water. Also, besides yellow and pink, they include 'blue' (tinged with mauve) shades, which makes an exciting contrast to any of the hardy kinds. I have tried two of these, 'Blue Beauty' and 'Pamela', but am not supplied till early July, so the season is short. They are not cheap and I have yet to find the secret of overwintering them reliably.

We grow our tender variety in the same pond as the hardies, but in its own container, supplying extra warmth with a small immersion heater, such as is used in aquariums. Of course, one has to lay on an electricity supply. One winter, we left the heater on throughout, and the nymphaea survived, but was still so slow off the mark that it only opened one bloom before the next winter set in. We shall keep on experimenting and feel confident that a way will be found.

There is one extremely tedious pest of waterlilies, the waterlily beetle. Both the adults and the larvae (small, black, slug-like things) feed on waterlily foliage, making terrible inroads on it, which is both unsightly and debilitating. Any chemical sprays are apt to do damage to pond life. As the beetle lives most of its time on the leaves' upper surface, fish cannot reach them. I have no solution. On my tropical nymphaea (the beetles' most preferred variety), I squash them between finger and thumb. You can even learn to recognise the patches of eggs, and squash them prior to hatching.

Oenothera

Onagraceae

Botanists (and hence, also, gardeners by way of spin-off) have had many problems in the naming of *Oenothera* species. Known in common parlance as evening primroses, the general public will have an image of yellow-flowered biennials whose scented flowers open in the evening and wither in the heat of the forenoon. **O. stricta** (60cm/2ft) (it has a nice primrose yellow form, 'Sulphurea') and **O. glaziouana** (2m/6ft) (syn. *O. lamarckiana*, *O. erythrosepala*) are typical. They self-sow and are widely naturalised on dunes, although, like most of the genus, their original homeland is North America.

Of the perennials, the day-flowering **O. tetragona** has been subsumed into **O.**

fruticosa and the best-regarded cultivar here is 'Fireworks', correctly 'Fyrverkeri' (60cm/2ft), of upright habit and with glaringly yellow flowers in clusters. A stalwart though hardly a charmer.

The prostrate, mat-forming **O. macrocarpa** (syn. *O. missouriensis*) has large yellow bowl-shaped blooms that last all day. Good on a ledge. **O. acaulis** (*O. taraxicifolia*) (15cm/6in), is night-flowering, white fading pink. It doesn't contribute much. **O. speciosa** (1m/3ft) is pale pink. Its running rootstock contributes to a weedy habit, though it is none too hardy. There are improved cultivars of which 'Siskiyou' is one. The highly glamorous (though invasive) kinds that you admire in California are not much use in the British climate, but worth trying even so.

Omphalodes

BORAGINACEAE

The perennial species are shade-loving. **Omphalodes verna** (60cm/2ft) comes under the category of useful. Sprays of little blue flowers in spring. **O. cappadocica** (23cm/9in) is on an altogether higher plane – clump-forming (it can be pulled apart in summer) and with a long, spring flowering season. More intensely deep blue than forget-me-nots in the best clone, 'Cherry Ingram'. It will tolerate quite deep shade, as beneath double red camellias, whose fallen petals make a striking framework. It also contrasts well, in a more open situation, with the yellow flowers and glaucous foliage of *Ranunculus gramineus*. With its petal margins in palest blue, 'Starry Eyes' has won all hearts – and lost some of them again.

Onoclea

WOODSIACEAE/POLYPODIACEAE

Onoclea sensibilis (1m/3ft) is a widely distributed North American fern of wet meadows, where its spreading habit makes it something of a weed. It is deciduous and one of the freshest of all ferns in spring. A network of superficial rhizomes produces long-stalked fronds, singly; pinnate, with quite broad, wavy-margined pinnae. They are bright green, when young, and look well with bluebells. Never a serious nuisance in British cultivation. Hardy, but the fronds die off at the first hint of autumn frost, hence its being named sensitive fern.

Ophiopogon

CONVALLARIACEAE/LILIACEAE

Ophiopogon japonicus (10cm/4in) has narrow strap leaves and is much used as ground cover in its native Japan. Small white flowers in August. **O. planiscapus** is best known in the clone 'Nigrescens' (15cm/6in), with strap-leaves near to black. Good interwoven with the creeping New Zealand fern, *Blechnum penna-marina*, or with the yellow-leaved *Lamium maculatum* 'Aureum'. Sometimes linked with snowdrops, but this effect is ephemeral.

Origanum

LAMIACEAE/LABIATAE

Our native marjoram is **Origanum vulgare** (60cm/2ft), of upright habit with dense heads of small purple flowers. It is nearly always seen on limy soils. The sweet aroma is powerful and it is used in cooking (not by me). The variety 'Aureum', golden marjoram, makes a loose mat and looks freshest in spring. The shoots sometimes make rosettes of foliage at their tips, but this is not predictable. It can scorch in summer, in hot, dry positions.

O. laevigatum (60cm/2ft), is a good late-summer-flowering border perennial, with somewhat glaucous leaves. It has more flower power in 'Hopleys' and 'Herrenhausen'.

There are many species of fascinating interest to alpine gardeners, mostly from Turkey. But they need watching and cannot be left to their own devices, being liable to disappear. 'Kent Beauty' (10cm/4in) is a reasonably hardy hybrid between Greek and Turkish species, its rosy mauve bracts overlapping to make cones like a hop fruit.

Ornithogalum

HYACINTHACEAE/LILIACEAE

Best known in this genus of bulbs is the Star of Bethlehem (or one of them), **Ornithogalum umbellatum** (23cm/9in). In cultivated soil it can become something of a weed but is ideal for meadow grassland, where its umbels of greenish-white flowers show up when the sun opens them wide, in spring.

42

O. nutans (23cm/9in) is a charming species, with racemes of nodding green stars, paler at the margins. It does not show up well in grass but is good at the bottom of a hedge or around the base of a tree trunk.

There are a number of species with grass-fine leaves and whitish stars at a low level. You forget about their presence until, after nearly a year's interval, there they suddenly are. But the occasion must be sunny.

Orontium

ARACEAE

The golden club, **Orontium aquaticum**, is a spring-flowering aroid from eastern North America, to grow in fairly shallow water. Its young foliage floats, but the snaky flowering stems rise a little above and consist of a spadix (no spathe), which is yellow at the tip and white beneath. Many of these together make a good and un-usual show. The plant is quite deep-rooted but sows itself readily, always in the water, never on the bank.

Osmunda

OSMUNDACEAE/POLYPODIACEAE

The royal ferns are the most majestic of the hardy kinds. All like acid soil conditions. The only British native is **O. regalis** (1-2.4m/3-8ft), which used to be widely dis-tributed but has, through collecting and drainage, been segregated to somewhat out-lying and less populated areas, though I know of a good colony in an unfrequented railway cutting in Tunbridge Wells.

In boggy spots in Ireland, there are huge old colonies which grow very tall. The bipinnate fronds are brightest green, in late spring, and take on fine rufous tints in autumn. The soil needs to be deep and organic. By the side of streams or ponds is good but the crowns do not like to be submerged. When happy, they self-sow freely.

It is notable of royal ferns that the fertile parts are either on separate fronds or on separate areas of otherwise sterile, leafy fronds. **O. claytoniana** is known as the inter-rupted fern, because there is a fertile area located between sterile pinnae, all on the same frond. Which looks odd and a little dirty once the spores have been released.

This is easy in cultivation and so is **O. cinnamomea** (the fertile fronds turn cinnamon-coloured when ripe). It comes from North America. Indeed, all three of the osmundas mentioned may be found in the same woodland location, in parts of the USA, though their overall distribution is amazingly wide. *O. cinnamomea* is very pale with a covering of silky hairs, when the fronds are young.

Osteospermum

Asteraceae/Compositae

The whole genus has now been transferred from *Dimorphotheca* (meaning two-shaped seeds, which they have) to *Osteospermum* (meaning bone-seed; compare human bone-head). This is one of the joyful band of South African, sun-responsive daisies. Some are mat-forming; others distinctly shrubby; all are evergreen. They tend to be tender, though much depends on where you live and a few are outstandingly hardy and long-lived. All are easily propagated from soft tip cuttings of non-flowering shoots, which can be taken at any time of the year, but most usually in autumn as a precaution against winter losses, the rooted cuttings being housed under cold, or cool glass.

Osteospermums prefer light soil and a position in full sunshine. If they bring their old growth safely through the winter, they will flower prodigiously the next late spring. Sudden death, at any season, is all too frequent, generally on account of the soil-borne verticillium wilt disease. This is particularly troublesome on composites. The pathogen may live for up to twelve years in the soil, I am told. (I'm not sure how you prove this). Fumigation of the soil with Dazomet seems to be the best remedy, but this gas-releasing chemical is not available to the general public, and is anyway difficult to apply in a garden of mixed contents. Formaldehyde applied as a drench is another possibility, but it isn't selective and will kill all plant organisms.

A great deal of public interest has been shown in osteospermums, of recent years, together with a lot of breeding work, which in itself leads to further confusion in naming and identity, aggravated as usual by the systematic botanists realising that something they should stick their noses into is going on.

This led to the RHS conducting a huge *Osteospermum* trial at Wisley, not long ago, covering two seasons so as to include a winter, in which hardiness could be, to some extent, tested (it was a mild winter). The number of trial inspections necessary sorely tried the patience of the judges, some of whom might excusably have wished never to see an osteospermum again, by the end of it. This necessity arose from the fact of the genus having, potentially, such a long flowering season, lasting from April to October, in the open.

Which is not to say that the plants all flowered for that length of time. By no means. Many are affected by day (actually, by night) length, flowering freely during the short days, which project their legacy from winter into late spring; but going into a vegetative, non-flowering state in summer. This would be disastrous in a plant that one hoped to use for bedding, and it had to be taken into account when recommending the Award of Garden Merit. Some varieties flower quite well through summer.

The gardeners who come off best are those, generally close to the sea, who are rarely visited by serious frosts. Their osteospermums will then be large perennial plants that will be set to flower abundantly in May. If you cannot bed out – and then only young plants – till April or May, your stock may remain in an obstinately leafy state from June to September, just when you most need its wholehearted cooperation.

One of the old favourites, then known as *Dimorphotheca barberae,* now **Osteospermum jucundum** (30cm/1ft), is a variable species, but pretty tough and hardy in the best forms. It is a strong mauve-pink, sometimes with a yellow disc, sometimes blue. It makes a large, edge-breaking mat and is at its best in May, if its shoots survived the winter. Even if they didn't, and it has to be cut back and made to start again, it will flower well from July on. Having the same habit, but seemingly altogether hardy, even in our coldest counties, is the sprawling 'Lady Leitrim' (30cm/1ft) (pronounced Leetrum, an Irish friend tells me). Its colouring is a rather dirty shade of white.

Much more compact, and a purer shade of white is the long-flowering 'Weetwood' (23cm/9in). It is reasonably hardy and I would put it in the top class together with 'Stardust' (30cm/1ft) and *O. jucundum* 'Blackthorn Seedling' (30cm/1ft). The former is bright pink, making a cushion of notably upright habit in its flowering, which is of the free-est (though capsids rather spoiled mine until I discovered the trouble). The latter is dark pink, neat and free.

An old favourite which we knew as *O. ecklonis prostratum* has been recycled as **O. caulescens** (meaning prostrate). It is white, blue on the reverse and with a blue disc. Very cheerful when full of bloom in May and reasonably free-flowering after that. Half-heartedly hardy, but suitable for tub culture. With the free drainage that provides, its hardiness is increased.

Of the shrubby kinds, 'Whirligig (45cm/1½ft) is blue and white, each ray pinched to form a waist. 'Pink Whirls' is a pink sport of this. These are tender, fairly free-flowering though apt to peter out by late August. This is a variable attribute, however. When it does well, 'Buttermilk' (1m/3ft) is charming, a tender shade of yellow. Not in the least hardy, it yet likes an open, non-competitive position, during the summer. The blue-and-white-flowered 'Silver Sparkler' (1m/3ft) is so called for its white-variegated foliage; the whole plant airy.

Although it won no award, I fancied 'Giles Gilbey' (45cm/1½ft), which makes a bushy plant, pink-flowered, lime green along the centre of each leaf. Tender.

I think you should try osteospermums in different parts of your garden, to decide where they are happiest (*O. jucundum* is quite happy in part shade, I find). And you must hope that wilt disease does not come your way.

Ostrowskia

Campanulaceae

Ostrowskia magnifica (1.2m/4ft) is a noble member of the campanula tribe, from stony hillsides in central Asia, but none too easy in cultivation. It is easiest raised from seed, which is not easily obtained. The roots are fleshy, so perfect drainage is required and a sunny, but not starved, position, without much winter rain. But it is very hardy. The leaves are sparsely arranged in whorls along the stems and the bell-flowers are few but large (10cm/4in across) and pale grey.

Ourisia

Scrophulariaceae

One of the most delightful genera for Scottish gardens in early summer. Rhizomatous, mat-forming plants for peaty soil in open woodland conditions.

Ourisia macrophylla (30cm/1ft) carries whorls of shining white flowers above a mat of scalloped leaves and is the handsomest species. It comes from New Zealand, where plenty more ourisia species can easily be recognised but are insignificant as to flower size.

O. coccinea (23cm/9in) is from Chile and has more funnel-shaped flowers, intense, pure red. Beautiful when freely flowering but usually rather shy. The man-made hybrid between these two is called 'Loch Ewe' (23cm/9in) and takes after *O. coccinea* as to habit and general appearance, but is bright pink and can flower very freely. I find this vulgar, which is ungrateful.

P

Pachyphragma

BRASSICACEAE/CRUCIFERAE

Among the many cruciferous, spring-flowering perennials, **Pachyphragma macrophyllum** (30cm/1ft) comes from damp woodland in north-east Turkey and is excellent for bringing early spring light and freshness to shady areas in our gardens. The large, orbicular leaves are only half-grown when the dense, pure white, domed panicles of blossom come out in late March and April. The rootstock runs a bit so that colonies make pools of light that gleam from a distance. In summer, the plant is pretty dull but does an efficient ground-cover job.

Paeonia

PAEONIACEAE

With their large, glamorously coloured blooms and a central boss of conspicuous stamens in the single-flowered kinds, peonies add to their attractions with their hardiness. They are among the most popular of all perennial plants. Most of the work in their development initially took place in France and England – but now in the United States, from where newer introductions have yet to reach us.

Well, peonies have faults as well as virtues. Especially in a damp climate like ours, the popular Lactiflora hybrids are often cripplingly subject to peony botrytis, which needs a regular spraying programme, if you are seriously into growing a range of them. If not, as is evidenced in small gardens where, maybe, only one peony is grown, but that a huge specimen, botrytis may never be experienced. In any case, it may be pointed out that some rose enthusiasts willingly bear the yoke of fortnightly sprayings from early spring to autumn, so why not peonies?

As regards growing them as garden flowers myself, my main objection is to the space they occupy for a very short flowering season. I like to have them for picking, as they are wonderful for large, cut flower arrangements, but to keep them out of my borders. This is not altogether fair, so I will state the opposite case, with the hybrids of *Paeonia lactiflora* in my focus.

In early spring, they push through with brilliant carmine shoots, themselves an asset if you choose to make use of it. I like to see them with spring bulbs colonised between the peony groups – for each plant builds into a group, over the years, so they need wide spacing at the outset, of 75-90cm/2½-3ft. If they remain in good health and are not invaded by perennial weeds (always a danger with ground-keepers), a colony could remain undisturbed for 25 years. The sort of bulbs I have in mind are the white or pale blue stars of *Ipheion uniflorum* or the spikes of blue or pink hyacinths, which themselves make clumps under garden conditions, and cease to be lumpy.

Come June, the peonies are in season and this is to some extent prolonged by a branching habit, the side-buds opening later than the principal. In July and August, the area can again be enlivened by interplantings of gladioli. These will need support, but then so will all the double and some of the single peonies, so a horizontal, open-mesh net, with vertical supports, can do duty for both.

You can also grow clematis of the later flowering kinds, among peonies, so long as the latter do not have to bear much of the former's weight. *Clematis flammula*, with a foaming mass of small, scented white blossom, is most suitable. Some of its weight could be taken by brushwood but some growth could be unsupported, appearing coyly into view here and there, particularly at the colony's margins. In September, the majority of these peonies, if their foliage is still in good health, will change to brilliant shades of crimson.

This is the best time to move peonies, if you need to. They have rhizomatous roots, which at planting should be only just below the soil surface. Coming from north China and Siberia, they are extremely hardy. They should be dressed, through the years, with surface mulches of bulky, organic manure, preferably weed-free. A point to remember is that next year's new growth bud (already clearly visible just at the soil's surface, in autumn) is firmly attached to the base of the tough stem of each dying leaf. This must be cut off – as low as possible without damaging the bud. If you try to break it off and tug, the break will come below the new bud. You'll have lost it.

Unless very heavy-headed, sufficient support will be provided to each clump by three stout canes (no higher than the plants) and a tie going round them. The tie could take in the stems of some, or all, of the budded peonies, as it progresses from cane to cane. If you need to pick double peonies for an arrangement, do so just as the bud is expanding into a bloom. If you wait till it is fully expanded, it may get full of rainwater and be hard to dry out, leading to premature rotting in your arrangement.

The scent of Lactiflora peonies is sharp-and-sweet – an agreeable and stimulating mix. In some of the species – *P. officinalis* and *P. mlokosewitschii* come to mind – it is rank, so that they are scarcely fitted for domestic flower arrangements. In a church or marquee, with a great bulk of moving air around them, this wouldn't matter.

P. lactiflora (once *P. albiflora*) is most closely represented, among the cultivars, by the single, white 'Whitleyi Major' (1m/3ft), which is very prolific, with plenty of side-shoots, but may need support (which many of the singles do not). The yellow stamens show up against white.

So they flatteringly do against deep crimson, the colour of 'Lord Kitchener' (75cm/2½ft). This was a name to conjure with in Edwardian times, when many of the peonies that we still grow were created. So was 'Sarah Bernhardt' (1m/3ft), still one of the most popular double pink peonies around – splendid, when cut, with blue or purple delphiniums. 'Festiva Maxima' (1m/3ft) is an intriguing old cultivar, because its white doubleness is spiced by flecks of crimson, near to the centre. 'Bowl of Beauty' (75cm/2½ft) is still one of the most grown of the class of peony called Imperial, where the stamens are converted to a more substantial dome of narrow, petal-like staminodes – cream, in this case – with an outer frame of normal petals in the same or a different colour – deep pink, here.

I visited a well kept peony nursery in Otago, in the South Island of New Zealand, one December. Their rainfall is fairly low – 62cm/25in – and the air dry, which suits the peonies, though a strict protective spraying regime with fungicides still needs to be practised. All the peonies were of American origin – from Illinois, and they were an impressive collection. Some have reached us, some not. 'Alice Harding' (60cm/2ft) has British outlets, being double lemon yellow; its flowers nod. 'Coral Sunset' changes colour from coral to cream as it ages. Not available.

A branching inflorescence is fairly unusual in peonies, but is also found in **P. emodi** (1m/3ft), which I grew for many years. With fresh green, deeply cut leaves, the pure white, single flowers have a boss of yellow stamens. That really does look like a poached egg.

P. veitchii (60cm/2ft) also branches. It does particularly well at Cluny House (open to the public) in Perthshire. Peonies do outstandingly well in Scotland, where you hear them called peeny-roses. At Cluny House, *P. veitchii* (June-flowering) sows itself liberally and you can see quite a range within its magenta colouring, some far more intense and effective than others. The leaves are a great asset.

The second most popular group of peonies derives from **P. officinalis**

(75cm/2½ft), by far the most grown being the double, crimson-red 'Rubra Plena'. But in Scotland more than elsewhere, its other cultivars are widely grown. A coarse plant, one flower per stem, showy but unsubtle. It is really tough.

Peonies, being slow to propagate, are sometimes fairly rare despite being easy to grow. ***P. peregrina*** (60cm/2ft) has pure red flowers, even verging towards orange. It has the unusual property of suckering – mildly. 'Otto Froebel' is the AGM clone of this, also known as 'Sunshine'.

One of the most admired species, because of its soft, yet definite yellow colouring and the lilt of its rounded foliage, is ***P. mlokosewitschii*** (60cm/2ft). To quote myself: 'It flowers for about five days in early May, and is at its ravishing best for about four hours in the middle of this period'. That is why I do not include it in my borders. It is easy to grow but crosses easily with other peonies flowering at the same time. As most of those are carmine, the results are anaemic pinky-yellow hybrids.

P. mlokosewitschii seeds freely – the seeds black with a hint of blue, the aborted seeds bright carmine. If sown as soon as ripe, they will germinate the next spring (allow frost to reach them). If not sown for a few weeks, they will demonstrate epicotyl dormancy, sending down a root in the first spring but no leaf till the second. Flowering may not be for five years, so you must not expect a bargain price that will give no reward to the grower.

Don't be fobbed off with ***P. wittmanniana*** (75cm/2½ft), which is comparable but a washed-out yellow and a coarsish plant. ***P. obovata*** var. ***alba*** (45cm/1½ft), however, is just about the most beautiful peony on earth. Its young leaves, lobed in seductive curves, are purple at first and retain much of this colour in contrast to the single, white bloom, which has a circle of yellow anthers about a reddish-purple centre. At a later stage, its ripe seeds are bright blue.

P. tenuifolia (30cm/1ft) is a charmer, with crimson flowers and yellow stamens, but supported with finely divided, lanceolate leaflets. 'Smouthii' (1m/3ft) is similar, though with less fine divisions. ***P. cambessedesii*** (1m/3ft) is more remarkable for its leaves, which are rich purple on their undersides when young, than for its flowers, which are of a not very distinguished magenta. It flushes early and the young shoots may get frosted.

That is a principal danger with the Moutan 'tree' peonies (shrubs, actually), derived from the Chinese ***P. suffruticosa*** (up to 1.5m/5ft). (This is just as subject to botrytis, as any.) Their pink young shoots, after a mild winter, are already prominent and showing flower buds, in March, and are easily slaughtered by late frost. For this reason, it is recommended to plant them on the north side of a wall, where they will get shelter and not be lured by sunshine into unwise precocity.

Many of the cultivars have Japanese names and selling stock is imported from Japan, being grafted on the roots of herbaceous peonies. The graft should be planted a little below soil surface level, so that it makes its own roots. Double-flowered forms are so heavy-headed that they have to be supported, individually, but this nearly always looks a fright. Single and semi-double cultivars are a better investment. They come in the usual peony colour range.

Those that are yellow are hybrids between *P. suffruticosa* and *P. delavayi* var. *lutea*, the group name being **P. × lemoinei**. The double yellow 'Souvenir de Maxime Cornu' and 'Chromatella' have exciting large yellow blooms, but are unpractical as garden plants. The almost single 'L'Espérance', however, is really good.

Turning to the other principal shrubby species, **P. delavayi** (2m/6ft) is a scraggy shrub, like other tree peonies, but nice to have, even so, seeding itself around freely; with me, in dry-walling, thus creating an unusual feature. The young leaves are suffused with reddish colouring and the smallish flowers are rich maroon red. Its dead leaves, in autumn, cling to the shrub throughout the winter, which is unsightly; they need to be snipped off.

When this crosses with the yellow-flowered *P. d.* var. *lutea*, the progeny come in interesting apricot shades. *P. d.* var. *lutea* hides its flowers beneath its foliage, whereas *P. d.* var. *ludlowii* (2m/6ft) shows them off well, in its brief season. After that, you have to be content, from late May on, with its foliage, which is pleasant enough but in only the largest gardens justifies the presence, at such an important time of the year, of a plant which may grow 4.3m/14ft across with ease. There are more inventive ways of gardening than with such as this.

Papaver

PAPAVERACEAE

Poppies of this type, whether annual, biennial or perennial, are just about as showy garden flowers as may be imagined and they are deservedly popular, combining bright colours and flamboyance with great delicacy of texture. A poppy flower is not expected to last for many days. With some, only for a morning, so you must be there.

Best known and most important are the oriental poppies, **Papaver orientale**, on which a lot of breeding work is currently being done, much of it in Germany, for these poppies are notably hardy. I wish I'd seen them in flower on the Anatolian plateau in eastern Turkey, but that was in May; the snow had only recently departed and the plants were still leafy clumps on stony slopes.

I like the typical scarlet oriental as much as any. It flowers, in late May, before most other perennials and is beautifully set off by surrounding green (or purple) foliage. However, there are many who hate it and for them there are plenty of pastel shades, like 'Cedric Morris', which is grey, with only a hint of pink and a black central blotch. 'Black and White', has more definite, punchy contrast than 'Perry's White'. The old 'Mrs Perry' is a charming pink, with just a hint of salmon, but that is now outclassed – for instance, by 'Turkish Delight', which is a good salmon and very free. 'Karen' is a nice compact variety, only 60cm/2ft tall with neat, round, bowl-shaped pink flowers, on the small side. If you like big and blowsy, there's plenty of that, too.

I think an oriental poppy flower should be in reasonably good condition for three days, and the old varieties are. Many of the modern kinds go all out for initial impact and become burnt and quite hideous from the second day. 'Beauty Queen' is an attractive soft orange, bleaching along the margins on Day 2, but not so as to be unsightly. The double orange poppy that you see naturalised along roadsides in Scotland, notably in Orkney, is 'Olympia'. Its thin stems twist in every direction and do not attempt to support the flower, but this does not matter, when all is surrounded in grass. I have even seen this poppy hanging out from a retaining wall.

37 The deep blood red 'Goliath', of upright habit to 1.2m/4ft, has huge blooms and is outstanding in every way. Good against the grey-green foliage of cardoons. It has sometimes been lumped with 'Beauty of Livermere', but is different and superior to that. Although, one has to add, not constant, as these poppies have often been propagated from seed yet been allowed to retain their cultivar name.

All are easily propagated from root cuttings, about 8cm/3in long and taken at pretty well any time of the year. After flowering, the plants can be cut right down, including the foliage, and be interplanted with summer bedding.

Of other perennial poppies, the one that will first come to mind is the Iceland (but it does not grow wild there), **P. nudicaule** (45cm/1½ft). It throws up naked scapes, which make it suitable as a cut flower. All the leaves are at the base. It is a short-lived perennial, typically orange, though yellow and white also come naturally its way. Further breeding has introduced other colours, including pink. Plants should not be in an exposed situation, as the stems are easily blown sideways.

Many poppies are naturally apricot orange. **P. rupifragum** (1m/3ft) is one of the best known – a great self-sower and a typical cottage garden plant. The loosely double form, 'Flore Plena', is even prettier and comes true from seed. **P. spicatum** (syn.

P. heldreichii) (30cm/1ft) has very furry foliage. The apricot flowers are borne close to the stem, the terminal one opening first. The buds are arranged in threes, the centre one opening first. This is a morning-only poppy.

Panicum

POACEAE/GRAMINAE

There are many species of *Panicum*, all North American, but the one that has been developed for garden and landscape use is **P. virgatum** (1m/3ft), called switch grass. It is clump-forming and non-invasive, coming into its own in autumn, wben the multi-branched inflorescences expand.

The flower heads are individually quite tiny, but so numerous that this cannot be described as a see-through plant; it becomes a dense cloud, blocking the view behind it, so is better as a background than a foreground. As the plants mature, they take on a range of bronze, reddish and plum-purple tints, gradually bleaching as winter approaches. Still the plant retains its shape, becoming a delightful vehicle for hoar frost. The two cultivars I grow are 'Hänse Herms' and 'Rubrum', both to be recommended (and both pretty similar).

Any grass that carries the garden gracefully forward from early autumn to late winter must be an asset, and this one such.

Paradisea

ASPHODELACEAE/LILIACEAE

St. Bruno's lily, **Paradisea liliastrum** (60cm/2ft), a European species long known in British gardens, is yet often difficult in cultivation. I have seen it flourishing effectively in a Scottish garden, where its loose racemes of white, lily-like trumpets were grouped in front of a bridal wreath *Spiraea* × *vanhouttei*. That was hung with wands of its little umbels of white blossom, down to ground level. May-June-flowering.

Much easier is the Portuguese **P. lusitanica** (1m/3ft). In damp soil, this makes a robust clump of lanky foliage. The flowering scapes are crowned by long racemes of white stars, in early summer, associating well with Siberian irises. It might also establish in meadow turf.

Paris

TRILLIACEAE/LILIACEAE

Paris quadrifolia (23cm/9in) is our native herb paris, of alkaline woodland. Although demure in colouring, the shape of the plant, which makes colonies, is always arresting.

How much more so **P. polyphylla** (60cm/2ft) from the Himalayas. It is a marvellously constructed plant for a damp, humus-rich position in partial shade. Above its scape is first a ruff of green leaves, then further ruffs of the perianth, followed by thread-fine yellow stamens. Finally a central knob, the ovary, with a purple stigma fixed on top of it.

This artifact expands in late May and remains, largely unaltered, into October, when the capsule is ripe and opens to reveal scarlet seeds. In time, you will be the proud owner of a clump of these inflorescences. The plant can be divided, but takes a long time to settle down again and should not be replanted in the same soil. I have not been successful in growing it from seed, yet I have a self-sown seedling.

Patrinia

VALERIANACEAE

A genus of hardy Asiatic species, with yellow flowers. The only one with which I am on intimate terms is **Patrinia scabiosifolia** (1m/3ft), and I rate that highly.

In habit it resembles its relation, valerian (*Valeriana officinalis*), being widely branched beneath loose corymbs of blossom. The leaves are deeply divided, not much in evidence at flowering. Its season, in our climate, is fairly late, August-October and the quite tiny flowers are cool yellow, with just a hint of green in them. It cohabits well with the purple *Verbena bonariensis*, whose growth is similar. Also with the light blue, late-flowering *Salvia uliginosa*.

Sometimes a not very long-lived perennial, this patrinia is most easily raised from seed, flowering from its second year. Seed, in our climate, is ripened only in hot years.

Pennisetum

P O A C E A E / G R A M I N A E

Most pennisetums come from warm-temperate or sub-tropical regions, which has two implications for us, in Britain. First, they cannot become pestilential weeds; second, they may not flower at all, our summers being too cool to bring them to this state. As their foliage is decent, at best, there remain only a few worth considering.

Pennisetum orientale (30cm/1ft) would be my first choice, although I have yet to grow it really successfully (that will surely come). It likes a hot position on light soil – chalk or sand will suit it equally. This is a grass to group at a border's margin. Its bottle-brush flower heads are soft pink, at first, in June, fading grey and lasting into October. They are especially attractive when laden with dew on autumn mornings.

It is easily raised from seed, as is *P. villosum* (45cm/1½ft), which is often treated as an annual. I have had the same path-side colony for quite a number of years, however, but you need to have nerves strong enough to leave the hideous dead foliage untouched right through the winter. Only cut it back in spring. Flowering, with near-white, rabbits'-tails, continues from late summer for nearly three months. Goes well with *Sedum* 'Herbstfreude' ('Autumn Joy') and a pale grey foliage plant such as *Senecio viravira*.

P. alopecuroides, making domes of dark, purplish bottle-brushes, is too late to flower properly, in Britain. The cultivar 'Woodside' is said to be more precocious, but its racemes are shorter; it is unexciting.

Penstemon

S C R O P H U L A R I A C E A E

This is a North American genus of subshrubby plants, some of them mat-forming, others of a rangy habit and up to 1.2m/4ft tall. Those we grow in our borders have loose racemes of more or less open funnel flowers, not unlike foxgloves, which belong to the same family.

I have always loved the freshness and generosity of penstemons, though they went through a long period out of favour, when much of my stock became infected with Leaf and Bud Eelworm (a nematode), *Aphelenchoides ritzemabosi*. The symptoms first appear as purplish, then brown patches on the leaves. They spread and kill the plant.

Watch out for this trouble – much the same as you find in chrysanthemums – and destroy infected plants. Propagate only from healthy shoots and don't replant for a few years on ground where infected plants were grown.

Otherwise, penstemons have a pretty clean bill of health, only their hardiness being, in many cases, questionable. The popular hybrids, with clonal names, tend to be short-lived perennials, anyway. Even if they survive several winters, they are best replaced with young stock frequently. In fact the professionals' way with them is to replace every year, for the sake of uniformity and predictability of performance. That way, they become bedding plants.

They root with great ease from soft, tip cuttings, made at any time of the year when suitable material is available. Normally, cold frame protection is all that's needed. Some plants produce a large proportion of non-flowering shoots, which are ideal for cuttings, but such plants may have a propensity to shy flowering, and this will be perpetuated in their progeny. I had this trouble with the tall pink 'Pennington Gem'. For stock, then, use plants that have flowered well, been cut back after flowering and thereafter made nice side-shoots. Or, in spring, use young shoots made from the base of the stock plant, generally after it has been cut back and has broken into fresh growth.

If your aim is for a display that will reach its peak in July, take cuttings the previous July, bring them on in individual pots, overwinter them in a cold frame and plant them out in April. If you have successfully overwintered old stock in a mixed border, it is likely to need pruning by shortening hard back, in late March. But for an early, June, display, you could go light on the pruning and do any cutting back that was needed in late July, after the main flush of blossom, thereby combining pruning and dead-heading in one operation. Penstemons lend themselves to quite a bit of manipulation. Although their principal flush of blossom may be in high summer, they will usually carry worthwhile aftermaths, deep into autumn.

Penstemon × **gloxinoides** is the outdated but descriptive name that was given to fairly tender hybrids with large, showy bells in a range of colours and raised from seed. Nowadays you find it in strains such as 'Large-flowered Mixed', from Suttons. The colours are varied, yet always compatible – white, pink, red, coral, mauve and purple. Mixtures are therefore a good buy. If seed is sown in early August, the seedlings being treated as for cuttings, the display will reach its peak in summer and autumn the next year. They will flower earlier from an earlier sowing, but the late display helps to freshen the garden at a time when decline is setting in.

At the end of their first season, you can cut back and lift all the healthiest of your seedlings, pot and overwinter them in a cold frame and plant them out again, next spring, to do a second turn, which will be earlier than the first. After that, it is best to start again. There is a tremendous range of named, hybrid penstemon cultivars. Forbes of Hawick was a nursery firm on the Borders, famed for its penstemons. A customer, contemplating two that were very similar, asked:

'Tell me, Mr Forbes, what is the difference between those two?'

'Sixpence'.

The judging committee for a huge trial that took place at Wisley in 1991 had many headaches over naming, so many of the same clone submitted having different names and so many different clones having the same name. One of the most per-plexing was 'Sour Grapes', the excellent selling name most commonly given to what, allegedly, should be 'Stapleford Gem', which is an uncharismatic name. The true 'Sour Grapes' seems to be a wan affair, with 'Stapleford Gem' (75cm/2½ft) a much more definite, acid mauve. As it is the flower that matters, customers will be well advised to choose by eye, whenever possible.

From my notes and personal experience, I give some of my recommendations. 'Chester Scarlet' (75cm/2½ft) seemed the showiest, to me, of the large reds (defi-nitely not scarlet). Other good reds with smaller funnels and more elegant foliage and presentation are 'Schoenholzeri' (75cm/2½ft) and 'Drinkstone' (1m/3ft), which I have long grown.

'Hidcote Pink' (1m/3ft) is tall and graceful. 'Apple Blossom' (75cm/2½ft) is all that its name could lead you to expect – pale pink and a white centre. 'Evelyn', quite a definite pink, is in a class of its own, only 45cm/18in high with fine leaves and small funnels in profusion. 'Alice Hindley' (1m/3ft) is the most striking of the mauves, large-flowered, the inside pale. Definitely tender. 'Snowstorm' (60cm/2ft) came to me as 'White Bedder' and leads in this field. 'Garnet' (1m/3ft) is one of the strongest growers, pretty hardy and long-lived. The colour is daringly bright purple, verging on magenta, but toned down by slender flowers and fine leaves. Its correct name is 'Andenken an Friedrich Hahn'. Of the species, *P. isophyllus* (1m/3ft) is a bit lanky, but with smallish, well spaced funnels, it is a pretty shade of coral. *P. barbatus* (1m/3ft), makes a basal mat of foliage. It flops around and is normally not worth it, even with coral flowers, but on a visit to Thompson & Morgan's trial ground, in July, they were growing a wonderful variant, 'Iron Maiden' (1.2m/4ft); very up-right, luminous coral, best in its second year from seed.

I had seed of *P. digitalis* 'Albus' (1.2m/4ft) from a friend in Minnesota, where it is entirely hardy. I liked it there, but not when I grew it. White and free-flowering with small funnels, the leaves are sometimes purple, which is an asset, but it flops.

P. heterophyllus 'True Blue' (60cm/2ft), has its admirers, myself not included. It has a long season, without ever making much impact, and it doesn't know how to hold itself. The colour is not true blue, whatever you may read.

You often read of a penstemon that is a good cut flower. Such has never been my experience. Condition it as you may, it will inevitably wilt on the third day. Perhaps that is good enough?

Pentaglottis

BORAGINACEAE

Pentaglottis sempervirens (1m/3ft) is a takeover perennial for damp shade where a colony of ground-cover vegetation is needed. It has mildly pleasing bluish, forget-me-not-style flowers in spring and coarse comfrey-like foliage all summer. The deep, fleshy roots regenerate if broken. It also self-sows. Make sure you want and can cope with it before introducing it to a new area. If you're desperate, pentaglottis can be eliminated with Roundup.

Persicaria

POLYGONACEAE

This formed a large part of the genus *Polygonum*, meaning many knees, which was descriptive of the swollen nodes that are typical, throughout. English: knotweed. The other part of *Polygonum* is now to be found under *Fallopia*.

Not all persicarias are coarse, but many are and for this reason best sited in the wilder parts of a garden (if such exist). They lend themselves to massive plantings, and often become massive whether you want them to or not. ***Persicaria amplexicaule*** 'Atrosanguinea' (1.2m/4ft), for instance, is just the sort of present that a friend will make you to start off a new mixed or herbaceous border. It has sterling virtues, bearing its upright, red pokers for a long, late summer and autumn season. To say that there is always too much of it is, of course, simply to say that the gardener is not exercising control, which shouldn't be too difficult in this case. The fact is that, when visiting gardens, I always see this plant in a huge patch, it having muscled out a large part of its neighbours' territory.

P. campanulata (75cm/2½ft) can be tedious in civilised company, too. Its leaves are better than most, with grooved veins. The sprays of small, bell-shaped flowers are often a too pale pink; one wishes they would either be white or deeper pink. Well, they sometimes are deep pink – particularly as I have seen them in Scotland, but I doubt whether this is a climatic factor. In a large setting, and given damp soil, it can do a splendid job in late summer and the whole of autumn. Its rootstock runs, but not alarmingly.

Most persicarias come from the Himalayas or further east, but bistort, *P. bistorta* (1m/3ft) has a very wide habitat range, including Britain, and it is a good sight to see colonising roadside ditches. It flowers in early summer with pink pokers, 'Superba' being the improved, i.e. showier, form for gardens.

P. virginiana (75cm/2½ft) (*Tovara* at one time) was a depressing plant in my garden, riddled with slug holes, which show on its large leaves. These, however, are supposed to be its principal asset, being blotched or variegated in varying degrees. This is most marked (even to the extent of being objectionable) in the cultivar 'Painter's Palette', which has a bold V mark, in brown, across the centre of each leaf. The rest of the leaf is more or less variegated, too; quite a feast. I soon threw it out.

So I did **P. affinis** 'Donald Lowndes' (23cm/9in). This is a mat-making, ground-covering plant with unspeakably boring leaves. It carries a succession of pokers that turn red as they age. Better, is 'Superba', in which the pokers are more substantial, anaemic pink at first but darkening to rich crimson. As it flowers over a long summer-autumn period, the mixture of old spikes and young is effective. Tony Schilling made a splendid sweep of it on a steep, damp slope at Wakehurst Place, in mid-Sussex. I still have 'Superba'; I don't know for how much longer.

I liked **P. milletii** (45cm/1½ft), for many years, but never gave it enough space. Eventually, it was crowded out. Its flower pokers are a rich shade of true red, but, although it flowered from May till autumn, there were never more than a few spikes at a time.

The gem in this genus is **P. vaccinifolia**, from damp rock faces and ledges in the Himalayas. You should see great pendent mats of it hanging in the way that aubrieta does. The leaves are small and neat, changing to warm brown in winter. It flowers in autumn, with pink spikes only a few inches above the mat. I use it to edge paving, with hedges of *Aster lateriflorus* var. *horizontalis* behind. They flower together and sometimes my intention is clear. At others, the persicaria suffers cripplingly from drought. We shall plant it again, after further enriching the soil with juicy, water-holding organic goodies.

I have been impressed, in Beth Chatto's garden, in mid-October, with **P. polystachya** (2m/6ft and a wider spread). It has lance leaves and terminal panicles of white blossom, honey-scented on the air. That was unexpected. While a willing grower, it does not appear to be a thug. (Further experience suggests that it is, quite).

Petasites

ASTERACEAE/COMPOSITAE

Large-, orbicular-leaved perennials, with an aggressively creeping, rhizomatous rootstock, forming massive colonies. Light-hearted insouicence is not the right mood for introducing them into the garden, but there are suitable places, even so. All like moist soils and are most often found in marshy ground or near to streams.

68 Largest is **Petasites japonicus** var. **giganteus** (2m/6ft), whose leaves are up to 1.5m/5ft across. They are rounded, kidney-shaped towards the stalk. Completely deciduous, the plant flowers before resumption of leaf growth, in spring, with dense clusters of white flowers, close to ground level and on their first appearance resembling an aristocratic cauliflower. I have recently planted the variegated-leaved form, which should be rather less vigorous, if it does not revert to the plain-leaved type-plant.

Butterbur, **P. hybridus** (1.2m/4ft), is native. It flowers in April and has no scent. Mauve (male) flowers, before any leaves, stiffly upright in dense columns. You may find it on taking over an old garden but there is no point in planting it.

Best known is winter heliotrope, **P. fragrans** (30cm/1ft), native of the Mediterranean but widely established in Britain along roadsides, railways and in old gardens. The loose clusters of pale mauve flowers appear at the same time as the young leaves, in January. Sickly-sweet scented, but welcome at that season.

Petunia

SOLANACEAE

Although petunias are generally treated as annuals, they are, in fact, perennial and can be overwintered only just frost-free. In fact, I have overwintered some in a cold frame.

Before seed strains became highly selected, named varieties of petunia were habitually propagated from cuttings. Even today, this method is practised, especially with the Surfinia, cascading types, used in hanging baskets. Cuttings are rooted in autumn. To save space and be sure of young, vigorous material, you can root a few plants in autumn, overwinter them under heated glass and then take cuttings from those plants in February.

But petunias are highly vulnerable to virus diseases. Vegetatively propagated clones will go down to these, sooner or later.

Phalaris

POACEAE/GRAMINAE

There are many cultivars of ribbon grass, **Phalaris arundinacea**, most of them variegated. Best and longest known is var. *picta* 'Picta' (1m/3ft), called gardener's garters. Deciduous, the white variegation is brightest and cleanest in early summer. When it runs to flower, the plant itself looks tired and the best policy, I find, in the south of England, is to cut the whole colony down. It will be refurbished from the base and, although only 23cm/9in or so high, will remain fresh into autumn. In colder districts, the response will be insufficient for this exercise to be worthwhile. It combines well with glaucous hosta leaves in front.

The plant is mildly invasive. I find it best to replant every season. In this way, you get the lushest foliage. 'Feesey' is a less vigorous clone with more of variegation and less of green. There is a broad white stripe down the centre of each leaf.

Gardener's garters is as happy in shallow water as in a border, and it does not get that tired look in these circumstances.

Phlomis

LAMIACEAE/LABIATAE

Shrubs or herbaceous perennials from the Old World. All are hairy.

Phlomis russeliana (1m/3ft) (syn. *P. samia*) is stiffly upright with large, heart-shaped leaves. The two-lipped flowers are borne in distant whorls, lending the plant an individual air of distinction, retained after the flowers have faded. They are dusky yellow, in July.

Not a plant I want to grow – it looks too grubby. But it has presence.

Phlox

POLEMONIACEAE

Border phloxes, derived entirely or mainly from the North American **Phlox paniculata** (long known as *P. decussata*), are the mainstay of many herbaceous and mixed borders throughout Britain, from early July to the end of August – well into September in Scotland. There the phlox season perfectly coincides with the brief return of largely absentee landlords and their retinue, for the stalking, fishing and

33

grouse (not to mention partridge) shooting. Many gardens were expected to reach their peak then, and relied on annuals, dahlias and phloxes for great splashes of colour.

For that is what the phlox is so adept at providing – soft eiderdowns, quilts, duvets of colour. But they are not entirely formless, for the domed panicle, which is the phlox's inflorescence, provides peaks and valleys within the overall mass. The other great phlox asset is fragrance – a warm, summery scent, borne on the air.

10 The colour range is mainly between white, pink, mauve, purple and magenta. Red is also approached. There are often two tones within a flower, which may have a dark centre, or a pale centre and a darker outside. Some look like old-fashioned cotton print frocks. I do not think that developments in phlox are likely to give us further improvements, if pursued along current lines. What we need is a vigorous, upstanding plant. Some newly bred varieties that I have seen in Holland had huge panicles on short stems, but even so, they lacked stability and flopped. Phlox should be bred to stand on their own legs.

In acquiring them, see the plant growing before you make a decision. Often it will be in a friend's garden, where you can immediately see how it performs and, very likely, be allowed to bear a piece away with you there and then – no point in waiting for 'the right time'. Now, is the right time.

The two cultural requirements of phlox are moisture in their growing season and loads of dung, or similar organic equivalent. They are greedy. They love heavy soils, like mine, but are difficult on sand. Miss Jekyll, on the acid, sandy fare of her Surrey garden, needed to replant her phlox on improved soil every year. Normally, they will need to be divided and replanted – using fair-sized pieces so as to give a good display in the first year – every third or fourth year. They are as happy in part-shade as in full sun, and will wilt less than when blazed upon in sunshine.

Phloxes are early into growth, their new shoots already prominent in February. These provide good material for stem cuttings. Ideally, division of clumps is best done in the autumn, but, if need be, you can still be doing it in May, when the young shoots (pinch out their tips) are already a foot long. Another way of propagating phlox is from root cuttings and it should be understood that, if you are moving phlox from one part of a border to another, some roots will always be left behind and will sprout into new plants.

This would have serious consequences if you planned to do some switching around of varieties, replacing one with another, in the same area. The one you intended to remove will be back, interfering with the new one you have introduced. Some gardeners, especially in Scotland, will devote a whole border entirely to different varieties of phlox. If you had second thoughts on how you wanted them placed, there would be a mix-up; not that that would necessarily be a serious matter.

Some of the earliest-flowering *P. paniculata* cultivars will often give a worthwhile repeat performance from side-branches made off the original panicle. Vigorous stock, not overcrowded and copiously watered, is most likely to do this. Overhead irrigation is fine until a colony is flowering, but should then be given a rest, as it tends to knock the flowers off prematurely.

The easiest way to remove the old stems of phlox is to wait until the New Year, when they are entirely sere and very light. Given a sideways knock, they will break off cleanly at the base, and far lower than secateurs would reach. We usually do this just as interplanted snowdrops are making their appearance. When the phloxes need replanting, the snowdrops will need lifting and replanting, too, and the best time for them will be immediately after they have flowered, in March. Return them in ready-made clumps between the clumps of phlox.

Phlox have two principal troubles. The first is from Stem Eelworm (a nematode). This is microscopic, but the effects are easily recognised by the reduction of leaves and stems to fine threads. The colony must be destroyed and no phlox returned to the same site for several years (three is usually long enough). The roots are unaffected, so you can save your stock by making root cuttings (wash the roots, first). This is another powerful reason for seeing the stock you are wanting to buy, or ask for, before adding it to your garden. Stem eelworm is bought with a plant, more often than not.

Powdery mildew is the other trouble, and has become more serious of recent years. It is quite crippling in many American gardens. I find that a couple of protective sprays against it, during the growing season, are sufficient to keep it at bay. It is always most prevalent in sheltered sites, which is where we are most likely to want to grow our phloxes, but if you were thinking in terms of an open field, you are unlikely to be bothered by mildew.

Most of the phlox I (and, perhaps, you) grow are unnamed, because they came that way from friends. However, I do have the wild type, *P. paniculata* (1.2m/4ft) itself, which is a nice, definite shade of mauve. The flowers are not well formed, by exhibition standards, but this matters not at all. Growth is slender and tall; we do give support to this one, with a cane and a tie for each clump (or with Link stakes). Var *alba* is a bit shorter, but also light and airy.

The variegated 'Norah Leigh' (60cm/2ft) is a beautiful foliage plant, with only a small patch of green in the centre of an otherwise white leaf. This makes it weak-growing, so it deserves the most generous cultural treatment. If it should sprout from the root, which happens when that is damaged, the leaves will be plain green, the shoot far more vigorous and likely to overtake the desired plant. Best to start again from stem cuttings, taken in spring and planted out on a new site.

'Norah Leigh' has sometimes been propagated from less variegated, but more vigorous stock, so you will be told that it is not weak-growing at all. The answer is that the best variegation occurs inevitably on the weakest clone. 'Harlequin' has sometimes been promoted as a more vigorous cultivar, and so it is, but its variegation is not up to much. The flowers of 'Norah Leigh' are quite small and pale mauve – entirely suited to the plant, in my opinion, but reviled by many, in which case they are removed before they can cause disgrace – for instance, in the white garden at Sissinghurst. Even the English know that *il faut souffrir pour être belle*, but are decapitated stems beautiful?

Phlox carolina 'Miss Lingard' (1m/3ft) is extremely handsome; blinding white (a trifle difficult to handle, in this respect), with a long, generously furnished inflorescence which is at its best mid-June to mid-July. If you don't want a passenger in your border after that, (and secondary flowering is not quite good enough), cut the plants back by half, water well and remove into discreet retirement for the rest of the growing season. In the border, they can be replaced with dahlias, cannas or some annual – African marigolds, maybe.

40   **P. maculata** (1m/3ft) is shapely, too, making a narrow cone, almost a cylinder, of blossom. 'Alpha' is pinky-mauve, with smallish but well-formed flowers; 'Omega' is white, with a pink eye.

Phormium

Agavaceae/Phormiaceae

Phormiums have become popular garden plants, in Britain, since the Second World War, largely promoted, in the first instance, by Alan Bloom. They took a beating in the 1963 winter, but some survived and anyway we have enough mild winters to make a good range of them worth growing.

This is New Zealand flax, whose fibre has long been used in the same ways as hemp and sisal. There are two species, endemic to New Zealand, and most cultivars have been bred in New Zealand from them. If you grow a batch of phormiums from seed (which needs to be sown fresh), it is easy to see, from the variability of the resulting seedlings, how successful a breeding programme would probably be.

Phormiums make fans, from ground level, of tall, evergreen leaves, slightly pleated along the main vein. **Phormium tenax** (3.6m/12ft) is the larger species, so bulky as to be an excellent first line of defence against strong winds along sandy coastlines. At the Logan Botanic Garden, in south-west Scotland, it has been found far more efficient for this purpose than (and has replaced) the hedging *Fuchsia* 'Riccartonii'. The loose panicle, which is the inflorescence, increases its height by several feet and is weirdly attractive, especially before the crane-like bud expands. The flowers are dull reddish.

P. cookianum (syn. *P. colensoi*) (1.2m/4ft), the other species, has yellowish flowers. Its leaves are lax, not straight, and its pendent seed-pods are spirally twisted. It is hardier – certainly a good garden plant but with the temptation, rather, to grow its variegated clone 'Tricolor' (1m/3ft), whose leaves, 7.5cm/3in across, are purplish red along the margins, then striped pale yellow alternating with green, then green to the centre. This is a beautiful landscape plant.

P. tenax 'Variegatum', which is yellow-variegated, is almost as vigorous as the type. On the other hand 'Nanum Purpureum' (or 'Alpinum Purpureum'), purple all through, is only a foot tall. It is a miserable plant, always emerging from or sinking into a state of squalid despondency, but never at its best. Some clones, especially in the Maori series, have brilliant red and carmine leaf colouring, but they are weak growers and too tender to be used in the garden except as pot plants for the summer.

Others, of the larger-growing types, have good prospects as permanencies, though time needs to be spent on them each spring, cutting out the dead leaves, which otherwise persist. 'Sundowner' (1.2m/4ft) is one that I find satisfactory, its leaves alternating pink with dusky green. In an exuberant planting, it combines well with a pink-flowered canna, like 'Louis Cayeux'.

The trouble with old phormium clumps that have continued to expand in bulk over the years, is that they become almost impossible to handle, so tough are their roots. Yet they continue to accumulate old leaves and flowering stems, so as to become an eyesore, even though of an unusual kind.

The normal run of phormiums can be divided in spring. Treat each fan of growth, with some roots attached, as a new plant, shortening the foliage by half, for the sake of stability and to cut down on transpiration until new roots have been made. The divisions will look as though they hate you for the first year, but will pick up in the second. Don't make the mistake of planting the units in a group too close, or they will soon interfere with one another. A yard between units of *P. c.* 'Tricolor' will work out right for a number of years. Double that for the larger kinds. You can always interplant with something temporary, for the early years.

Phuopsis

RUBIACEAE

Often used at the front of herbaceous borders, where, however, it soon spreads beyond its allotted area, **Phuopsis stylosa** (30cm/1ft) is a popular and long-flowerng perennial. It makes loose, untidy mats of straggling shoots, at the tips of each of which are carried umbels (rather in the style of woodruff) of murky pink cruciform flowers. The plant exudes odour of fox, far and wide, on the air. I don't mind the smell of a fox left behind by the animal when it has visited my garden but to have it all around me all the time would be intolerable. Many gardeners, it seems, feel differently.

Phygelius

SCROPHULARIACEAE

This genus is the South African equivalent of *Penstemon* in North America. It is sub-shrubby to 2m/6ft (more, against a wall where old growth may long be retained) but 1m/3ft is more normal where colonies have been cut to the ground in spring. The flowers are tubular in large panicles.

Commonest is **Phygelius capensis**, with open panicles of brick red flowers, mainly in June-July, onset of flowering being earlier if some of the previous year's wood has been retained. This has a running rootstock and makes a particularly handsome feature where allowed to run between the stones in dry-walling. The chief enemy of all phygelius is damage to the shoot tips by capsid bugs, and this can largely prevent flowering if unchecked. Early-flowering, lightly pruned colonies may escape relatively unharmed.

The other principal species is **P. aequalis**, with subtly coloured pinkish flowers and hints of green. The selection 'Yellow Trumpet' is pale yellow, but what usually spoils its display is a mass of over-luxuriant, coarse green foliage.

These two species have been hybridised (largely by Peter Dummer of Hilliers nurseries), the product being known as **P. × rectus**. There are some showy cultivars, of which 'Winchester Fanfare' is an excellent scarlet.

50 Cool shade with the Viridiflora tulip *'Spring Green'* running through *Epimedium pinnatum* subsp. *colchicum*. and the lime green, monocarpic *Smyrnium perfoliatum*, which self-sows.

51 *Stipa splendens* fluffed out at flowering time, with biennial *Salvia sclarea* var. *turkestanica* behind.

52 *Stipa splendens* in autumn, but it will retain this shape throughout the winter.

53 *Geranium endressii* clambering through *Hebe parviflora* var. *angustifolia*.

54 The pale yellow dahlia 'Claire de Lune', contrasting pleasantly with the soft purple *Verbena bonariensis*.

55 The michaelmas daisy, *Aster cordifolius* 'Little Carlow' and black-eyed *Rudbeckia fulgida* var. *deamii*, with tender, grey-leaved *Plectranthus argentatus* running between. ▷▷

57

58

59

⊲⊲ **56** From the front: non–climbing *Clematis* × *jouiniana* 'Praecox'; *Helianthus salicifolius* with narrow columns of foliage; the bamboo *Phyllostachys nigra* f. *punctata;* and *Buddleia davidii* 'Dartmoor'.

⊲ **57** One of the best hardy waterlilies, *Nymphaea* 'Escarboucle'. It is exceptionally long–flowering.

⊲ **58** Ornamental rhubarb, *Rheum palmatum* 'Atrosanguineum' and shuttlecock fern, *Matteuccia struthiopteris*.

59 *Veratrum album* stands up to be counted, retaining its presence even when fading to green.

Physalis

SOLANACEAE

From Japan came **Physalis alkekengi** var. *franchetii* (60cm/2ft), well known to cottage gardeners as cherry-in-the-lantern. It is grown for its fruits, the scarlet 'cherry' being totally enclosed by a persistent orange or scarlet calyx, beautifully shaped (and veined), coming to a point at the base. Of papery texture, it dries well. You can cut along the juncture of the sepals and bend them back so that the cherry is revealed with a frame.

The plant is hardy and has a running, rhizomatous rootstock. The flowers are of no interest.

Physostegia

LAMIACEAE/LABIATAE

The only species of note is **Physostegia virginiana**, from the eastern USA. The flowers are arranged in four vertical tiers, along a spike and a touch with your finger moves any one of them to right or left, where it remains, as though operating on a ball-and-socket joint. Hence the popular name, obedient plant.

The plant has a running rootstock (nothing serious) and makes a dense mat. There are many cultivars, one of the oldest and still most satisfactory being 'Vivid' (60cm/2ft). It flowers in autumn and never requires attention, being self-supporting. The colour is a fairly raw pinky mauve. 'Summer Spire' (75cm/2½ft) has longer racemes of a kindlier lilac shade, but it requires support. So does the pure white 'Summer Snow', and its dark green foliage makes a heavy impression. The cream-variegated-leaved 'Variegata' can look nice, its flowers rosy-mauve. All are autumn-flowering.

Phytolacca

PHYTOLACCACEAE

Virginian poke weed, **Phytolacca americana** (syn. *P. decandra*) (1.5m/5ft) is a coarse, weedy-looking plant that abounds in neglected gardens, where it is allowed to self-sow. From a thick, fleshy rootstock, it throws up stiff, densely-furnished spikes of nondescript flowers. The plant comes into its own (in so far as it is able) with the ripening of its purple, staining, five-parted fruits (succulent but poisonous), in autumn. But they don't quite add up, either, and the large oval leaves could scarcely be less appealing.

Some people like it.

Pilosella

ASTERACEAE/COMPOSITAE

Pilosella aurantiaca and **P. officinarum** (60cm/2ft) have been hived off from *Hieraceum*, the hawkweeds (q.v.). They have a running rootstock which, especially in the latter, can be a menace under border conditions. But they, especially *P. aurantiaca*, make a smashing display under meadow conditions in early summer, with heads of burnt orange daisies. This is an unusual and arresting colour. You see naturalised *P. aurantiaca* a lot in Scotland but I have so far failed to establish it in my own meadow areas.

Pimpinella

APIACEAE/UMBELLIFERAE

Native to England and most of Europe, **Pimpinella major** (1m/3ft) might well be overlooked in its normal, white-flowered form. But 'Rosea' is a first-rate garden plant for June flowering. The simply pinnate leaves are concentrated at the base of the plant, so that the sprays of lacy pink umbels are virtually untrammelled. The plant self-sows and seed is the easiest way to propagate it, but you do need to be selective about the flower colour, retaining only those plants whose flowers are a rich shade of pink. They, in their turn, will give rise to the highest proportion of well-coloured seedlings.

It is pretty with 'blue', June-flowering campanulas, such as *Campanula persicifolia* and *C. rapunculus*.

Plantago

PLANTAGINACEAE

The plantains are most generally recognised as weeds but they have their moments.

Plantago major has broad leaves and is one of the commonest weeds in lawns, where it thrives on mowing and forms conspicuous rosettes of foliage, tightly hugging the ground. It has two well-considered variants. In 'Rosularis' (23cm/9in), its normal inflorescence is transformed into viviparous, miniature-leaved green clusters whose shape earns it the name of rose plantain. These units drop off and make new plants.

'Rubrifolia' (23cm/9in) is the normal plant suffused with dusky, reddish purple pigment. It comes true from seed and can look pretty self-sowing in paving cracks or around a stone seat set in gravel.

The ribwort plantain, **P. lanceolata** (1m/3ft) is of rather upright habit with narrow lance leaves. It is one of the commonest mixed meadow ingredients and its dark inflorescences are a strong feature in the sward. It sometimes gives rise to variegated clones, with a broad white stripe running the length of each leaf. This is a beautiful feature but vegetative propagation is slow and reluctant.

P. media (1m/3ft) can be most attractive as a flowering plant, the central axis and the numerous stamens being in shades of lilac. But I have yet to see it used in a garden.

Platycodon

CAMPANULACEAE

The balloon flowers have inflated buds which open into campanula-like open bells. They are fleshy-rooted and need good drainage but are otherwise easy and hardy border perennials, coming from the Far East. Easily raised from seed, seedlings will even produce one bloom in the first year.

Platycodon grandiflorus is rather awkwardly tall at 45cm/1½ft, requiring support which is difficult to give discreetly, as the plants are by no means leafy. Better is the dwarfer 'Mariesii' (23cm/9in), of a rich campanula blue, flowering July on. The white form is nice, too, being a pearly grey-white.

Podophyllum

BERBERIDACEAE

A little grown genus, though popular in Scottish gardens, which suit a preference for cool, open-woodland conditions. There, they even complain of ***Podophyllum hexandrum*** (syn. *P. emodi*) (30cm/1ft) becoming a weed. It self-sows and also spreads by means of rhizomes. There are two, deeply lobed, peltate leaves to a stem, with the white flower between them, bowl-shaped, with six petals. That blooms briefly, in May, before the leaves have fully expanded. In autumn, a plum-like (and poisonous) red fruit, up to 5cm/2in long, ripens. It is this plant's chief claim for our attention.

Polemonium

POLEMONIACEAE

A boldly pinnate leaf is the reason for every *Polemonium* being nicknamed Jacob's Ladder, though this epithet is chiefly applied to **P. caeruleum** (60cm/2ft), the one we have always known since childhood. Its wide distribution includes the north of England and Borders and it is well established in meadow grass in a Perthshire garden that I know well. But it is also a cottage garden plant and a generous self-sower. In its early summer season, I like it with the scarlet *Lilium pyrenaicum* var. *rubrum*, but each of us will have a mental image of how and with what it grew, when we were close to it.

The plant's habit is upright. Its campanula-blue, open bells contrast strongly with bright orange anthers within. Sometimes reckoned to be short-lived, this may be so under border conditions, where division of clumps every third year would rejuvenate them, but many of us are content to allow seedlings to provide a continuing turnover. The white var. *lacteum* didn't like me but can be excellent. Then, there is the sharp variegaton of 'Brise d'Anjou', wherein every leaflet is margined with cream. A marvellous plant for the show-bench, before it runs up to flower, but none too successful a garden plant, so I am told. Perhaps just a question of learning how to handle it.

The low, bushy habit of **P. reptans** is probably responsible for 'Lambrook Mauve' (30cm/1ft), a thoroughly reliable spring-flowering perennial for a border's margin, with mauve blossom. I like it in front of the cool yellow racemes of pea flowers carried by *Thermopsis villosa* (60cm/2ft) at that season.

P. foliosissimum (75cm/2½ft) is blue-flowered but also making a particular virtue of its wealth of ladder-leaves. But there are a large number of polemonium cultivars, including some rather nasty, indeterminately-coloured between pink and yellow.

Polygonatum

<small>Convallariaceae/Liliaceae</small>

The common Solomon's seal of gardens has long been known as *Polygonatum multiflorum*, but that species, a native of Britain, is only one of its parents; the other (also a rare native) being *P. odoratum*. Result: **P.** × **hybridum** (1m/3ft). From fat, grey-green buds, it expands in May into an arching stem, clothed with leaves in two ranks, its bell-shaped, greenish flowers hanging in small clusters on the underside. Admirable for cutting.

However, it does suffer from one tiresome pest, its own sawfly, whose grey maggots feed in colonies and quickly strip every leaf to the bone. That happens in June, and almost always the damage is done before you notice what is happening.

Solomon's seal likes the same conditions as lilies-of-the-valley, and both are usually found in gardens, together, under a north wall or in some similarly shaded position, often in a vegetable garden where flowers for the house are also grown. *P.* × *hybridum* has a variegated form, 'Striatum' (60cm/2ft), but better is the variegated version of Japanese **P. falcatum** – 'Variegatum' (1m/3ft), with pinkish stems and rounded leaves that are neatly rimmed with a thin, cream border.

Specialists in *Polygonatum* cultivate many other delights, which I admire, though I have never joined the game, being short on the woodland conditions they prefer.

Polygonum – see Persicaria, Fallopia

Polypodium

<small>Polypodiaceae</small>

Polypodies are among our commonest native ferns. Being evergreen, they are ever before us. They will happily put up with much drier conditions than most ferns – being therefore one answer to the problem of dry shade. They like to grow in shallow, stony soils – or not in soil at all. Wherever moss or other organic debris has accumulated, they will colonise; sometimes, to charming effect, on the roof of a building where no one would have thought to grow anything. Often, they colonise tree trunks or their horizontal branches and their surface-running rhizomes enable them to spread easily, though they never become a problem like bracken. My healthiest colony started at the top of a shady, stone retaining-wall and has worked its way downwards, forming a curtain of fronds.

These, when healthy, are about a foot long and are divided only once. As the divisions do not quite reach to the main vein, the frond is described as pinnatifid, rather than pinnate. This is a characteristic of all polypodies. All, in Britain, were grouped under **Polypodium vulgare**, but chromosome counts reveal that this was an umbrella for three separate species, the other two being **P. cambricum** (syn. *P. australe*) and **P. interjectum**.

All have numerous named cultivars and are best selected by eye, which is easy, as hardy ferns are often brought to flower shows.

Polystichums can be cut back in the New Year or up to the end of March, when their young fronds start to expand. Polypodies are more evergreen than that, their young fronds not developing until the summer or, in the case of *P. cambricum*, not till autumn. A shearing off of old fronds is therefore not in order. You need to wait till they have withered, naturally; then run your fingers through a colony, when these fronds will break away cleanly from the base and be easily gathered.

Being freshly produced so late in the season, polypody fronds are among the brightest features of the winter garden. I would especially single out *P. interjectum* 'Cornubiense', whose fronds are often several times pinnate, giving them considerable depth. They vary, however, from frond to frond. Some come quite plain, and should be removed, to discourage the tendency. But 'Cornubiense' is a particularly bright, fresh green in winter. It makes a ground-covering carpet. But there are many other interesting shapes.

Polystichum

POLYPODIACEAE/DRYOPTERIDACEAE

The shield ferns are amazingly versatile – and hardy. Of the two British species, **Polystichum aculeatum** (60cm/2ft) is called the hard shield fern, on account of the harsh texture of its fronds. They are fairly narrow and parallel-sided for much of their length, and they glitter. On the level, they make a symmetrical funnel. In the wild, I most often encounter this fern on very steep slopes; the fronds adapt themselves accordingly, to receive as much light as they can, but they will thrive in quite deep shade. This species seems to have given rise to no variants.

The other British species, **P. setiferum** (1m/3ft), is the soft shield fern. It is easily picked out among colonies of *Dryopteris* in winter, by the fact of its being evergreen.

All the polystichums are just evergreen, their old fronds starting to die as the new ones start to unfurl, in early April. The epithet *setiferum* refers to the seta, or bristle, which every pinnule ends in and it is a good diagnostic feature. *P. setiferum* has given rise to more varieties than any other British fern.

61 Arguably the most beautiful, and found by a Somerset labourer in a hedgerow about 120 years ago, is 'Pulcherrimum Bevis' (1m/3ft), with elongated divisions, in-curving near to the frond tip. It is generally sterile, but makes a huge hummock, in a few years, which can be divided, though this operation is quite tricky, as the divisions are hard to make while retaining a piece of root on each.

Because there is so much variation even within named cultivars, they are often designated as belong to a group. The Acutilobum group makes an open fretwork of fairly hard texture and it has little bulbils along the centre of the rachis. When these are well developed, in autumn, fronds can be laid on the surface of a seed box full of a light compost, and pressed on to the surface with pieces of bent wire. In a close frame, not necessarily heated, they will root and can be cut up into numerous plantlets the next spring.

The same treatment works with the Divisilobum and Plumodivisilobum groups. These have very finely divided pinnules which, in the aggregate, compose a soft, mossy platform. These ferns like damp, humus-rich soil. If you have a shady bed that is slightly raised, one fern on a corner will make a projecting ledge of great distinction.

I use six or seven 'Acutilobum' to lead up to a couple of T-junction path corners, from both directions. Leave enough space between plants if you are doing this – a good three feet (one metre) – otherwise the plants will soon be interfering with one another and will need replanting. I cut them back in the new year, which is a little earlier than normal practice but gives light and space for a display of snowdrops, planted among the ferns.

There are foreign species of shield fern to be considered. **P. munitum** (1m/3ft), called the western sword fern, comes from the Pacific coast of the USA. Dark green, its fronds are once-pinnate. They look better under cultivation, with the old fronds removed, than in the wild, when the old fronds rather spoil the picture. Of course, local gardeners consider this a weed, being so familiar with it.

From the East Coast States comes the eastern sword fern, or Christmas fern, **P. acrostichoides** (60cm/2ft). In this, the fronds are held very upright and, because of heavy snows, they do not survive the winter. The fronds are sterile in the lower half, fertile in the upper, giving rise to a curious disjuncture, especially when the fertile half turns brown with the quantities of spores shed. This species looks best in spring and early summer and makes a nice contrast to bergenia foliage. Both species come from much wetter climates than we have in south-east England, and they grow better at home. Still, I like to have them.

Pontederia

PONTEDERIACEAE

Pickerelweed, **Pontederia cordata** (60cm/2ft), is disregarded in its homeland, on the east side of North America, but adds an original touch to our pond gardens in Britain. In shallow water, it gradually spreads by rhizomes to make a community. The leaves, and more particularly their stalks, are fleshy, the blade shape a sprightly heart, drawn to a point at the tip.

Dense spikes of small blue flowers are at their best in August. So for colour, presence and season, this is a plant that proclaims itself as different. If you are in the unhappy position of needing to use herbicide in the water to get rid of some invasive weed, pontederia will succumb, while nymphaeas will not.

Potentilla

ROSACEAE

With their interestingly divided, sharply toothed, strawberry-like leaves and brightly coloured flowers, usually yellow, orange or red, you would think that herbaceous *Potentilla* was well placed for widespread popularity. I no longer grow a single one.

Ideal for the messy type of cottage garden, they make unbearably stalky plants, this being the price of a long flowering season. 'Gibson's Scarlet' (1m/3ft) is an old favourite, flowering from May and clear, bright red in colour. I used to grow that. Also a hybrid called 'Monsieur Rouillard', which is bronze-red, semi-double, at its peak in July.

My third potentilla, **P. nepalensis** (30cm/1ft), I brought home from a meadow in Kashmir. That is pink and the best close derivative is 'Miss Willmott' (45cm/1½ft). Well, there are lots more.

Primula

PRIMULACEAE

Besides the primroses and polyanthus which are mainstays of our gardening lives, there are other *Primula*, mostly from the Himalayas, of great rarity. We occasionally see pot-grown examples of one or other of them, maybe at a specialist flower show or in the alpine section of a botanic garden. Our wonder and admiration is tinged with the thought that this beautiful specimen is so healthy that there seems no good reason for our not growing it ourselves. From a specialist source, we acquire a plant; within a year, it is dead. We have, in humility, to admit that what is well done has a way of looking easy.

With one exception, I shall not even mention such primulas as these, here. There is no reason why anyone of intelligence and understanding should not be successful with them, given time and application, but perhaps there is comfort in the thought that the specialists who achieve these wonderful results are often pretty poor gardeners in other respects, without a clue of what a garden can add up to as an environment in which to live and as a work of art in its construction and presentation. Each of us has our strengths, as well as weaknesses. It is demeaning to be envious, but a joy to admire hard-won achievement.

The primrose, **P. vulgaris** (15cm/6in), is often an eminently worthy garden plant. Liking rather heavy soil and partial shade, it may, for instance, be colonised on shady banks, otherwise the home of bluebells and ferns. Plant near to the top of the bank so that gravity may be harnessed to spread seed and seedlings over a wider area. You must plant at least two, preferably several specimens of different seedling origin, so as to achieve cross-fertilisation and further viable seed. In Scotland, primroses need no shade. On the west coast and in the Hebrides, they are to be found in sheets right out in the open, but always in wet places.

Another place that it is good to have primroses is along a hedge bottom. Often, they can be accommodated in the gap between a hedge and a path or lawn. Again, in the crutch of a deciduous shrub, primroses will flower before the shrub has come into leaf. In summer, it partially dies off and needs only a very little light to remain healthy.

Primroses in large areas of their natural habitats have white flowers. They also have very desirable double-flowered forms, of which the white is one of the purest, showing up far better in a shady setting than the double blue 'Bronwyn' (10cm/4in), for instance, although that commands instant sales should it ever provide spare stock. Named cultivars of double primroses (and of many others) can only be propagated by division. If infected by virus diseases, which is inevitable sooner or later, they are greatly weakened. Micropropagation, however, has enabled clean stock to be brought back into circulation. There are also seed strains, like the Barnhaven doubles, which give rise to a high proportion of double-flowered seedlings, though their colour and quality cannot be guaranteed. Those you like you can save and propagate vegetatively.

Another flower form, called hose-in-hose, has a coloured, enlarged calyx as well as the usual corolla, so that the bloom appears in two layers but not fully double.

Primroses have a delicious and characteristic scent, quite different from that of cowslips, though the latter is just as attractive. The cowslip, **P. veris** (23cm/9in), grows on open chalkland and limestone soils, in much drier conditions than suits most primulas. Its bunched, one-sided umbels are rich yellow in the wild, its petals incurved. Seed strains offering mixed cowslips will turn out to be red, orange and the normal yellow. The same plant will live for a long time, under meadow conditions, which is the best way to grow cowslips in the garden. They are a little later flowering than mainstream primroses (flowers of the latter may be found in every month of the year).

Where primroses and cowslips are found side by side in the wild, or in gardens, they interbreed, and the hybrid is sometimes called common oxlip. But the true oxlip, **P. elatior** (23cm/9in), is a species in its own right, with a wide natural distribution in woods and meadows. In England it replaces primroses in parts of East Anglia, growing in large quantities in ancient woodland, on alkaline soils. It is bunch-headed, the petals not incurved and not the deep yellow of cowslips.

Crosses between the deep pink **P. juliae** (5cm/2in), from the Caucasus, and **P. elatior**, gave us the popular old cultivar 'Wanda' (7.5cm/3in), which has flowers of vivid, unabashed magenta. In the early spring scene, I think this looks smashing with scarlet, multi-headed *Tulipa praestans* 'Fusilier'. Another small-growing and long-popular hybrid of modest growth that may be brought in here is 'Guinevere' (or 'Garryard Guinevere') (12.5cm/5in), with dark, purplish leaves, setting off much paler, mauvish flowers, borne in loose umbels.

Primroses and cowslips have always crossed, a property developed over the centuries to give us bunch primroses (bunches of flowers at the top of a common stalk), known in Britain as Polyanthus. Those that were used for bedding in my garden, before the First World War, were planted out in rough grass (by my mother), after they had done their stint, and have now survived for the best part of a century, the colours that were fashionable then making an interesting comparison with those on offer now.

All is not gain. The 'Munstead' strain, developed by Miss Jekyll and available as a seed strain till not so long ago, but now no longer, made exceedingly free-flowering plants, whose growth seemed to flow; whereas now, to take the Pacific Giants as typical of the sort of seed strains on offer for garden use, the umbel-bearing stems are fewer but far thicker, carrying a huge quantity of buds. To what purpose? The over-all effect is ungraceful and lumpy.

Miss Jekyll's 'Munstead' strain was all in shades of yellow and white. The centre of the flower is yellow anyway, come what may, so this was a well-integrated arrange-ment, going well, as I once had it in a damp, northwest-facing border, at the front of the single-flowered, yellow *Kerria japonica*. This yellow centre also goes well with orange and red-flowered strains, as also with blue, which is a deep indigo. It does not go well with a bright pink or magenta flower, such as you also find in mixtures. So, single-colour strains are the best choice.

Various breeders (the noted amateur Collingwood Ingram among them) finding the central yellow splash too domineering, have bred their polyanthus to eliminate it, with considerable success.

An F^1 hybrid strain, the Crescendo series, can be had through trade channels, in seven separate colour strains and I have found 'Crescendo Red', which is as much orange as red, particularly satisfactory, saving my plants from year to year. Their sea-son is on the early side, so they make a good carpet for the Fosteriana tulip hybrid 'Purissima' (38cm/15in) with glaucous leaves and large blooms, developing from cream to white.

Another popular strain, in this case because old-fashioned-looking, is 'Gold Laced', in which the flower is yellow-margined and yellow in the centre, but deep bronze in between. If grown from seed there will be some rogues, but they are easily eliminated.

The scent of polyanthus flowers is different again from that of primroses and cow-slips. The smell of the plant is also strong and personal, noticed when you come to divide your stock, which should be done immediately after flowering and before lin-ing it out in a cool spot for the summer.

Note well that all primulas suffer from replant disease. You may be able to get away with replanting them on the same site (for bedding, for instance) for two or three years but with an increasing and, in the end, overriding tendency for the replants to die. The notorious example of this occurred at Sissinghurst Castle, where there was a famous planting of polyanthus in the nut walk. The time came when they simply would not live, even for one season, and had to be totally replaced. The outcry from a conservative NT membership, who considered the polyanthus display as their right, lasted for the next twenty years at least, and photographs of the walk as it was in its heyday (though just as good and a lot more varied now) continued to be published as though nothing had changed. More trouble, from visitors who found that it had.

In respect of growing primroses, polyanthus or other primulas from seed, too high a temperature (higher than 68°F, 20°C), inhibits germination. 55-60°F (13-16°C) is quite high enough and March-April is a good time for sowing. Sow on the surface of the compost, which has been watered beforehand, and do not cover, except with milky polythene or with clear glass and a translucent paper covering. The idea is to allow light to reach the seed but no sunlight, and to cut down on water losses. These coverings can be removed when seed leaves have been made and most of the seed has germinated.

Auriculas, with their fleshy leaves and a large, pale eye to each flower, have long been treasured as florists' flowers for pot cultivation under glass. Dusty Miller is one of the names for those whose flowers and stems are coated with a farina. But those which do not depend on this as an asset are perfectly normal garden plants that can be used for bedding, though it will take two seasons to get large enough plants from seed, to be out-and-out effective. Buy what may be described as Alpine Mixed. If some of the colours are muddy, those plants can be discarded in their first season.

P. marginata (15cm/6in) belongs to the Auricula group, making a small shrub, which must be rejuvenated from time to time by rooting its rosettes separately. There are many cultivars, the best known being 'Linda Pope', with small heads of intense lavender flowers in spring, and mealy foliage.

Sometimes known as the drumstick primrose, **P. denticulata** (23cm/9in) is a most obliging species, flowering March to May. The globular flower heads are typically mauve but there are also white and pink seed strains and cultivars. Var. *alba* is pure white and a drift of it (if you have the space) is a great accompaniment to the yellow spathes of the aroid, *Lysichiton americanus* (q.v.).

Perhaps I should warn against primulas in the Petiolaris group – **P. whitei**, *P. w.* 'Sheriff's Variety', **P. boothii**. They are regularly on offer at the early spring RHS shows, in Westminster, and are irresistible, with their sessile cushions of blossom, surrounded by a ruff of immature, farinaceous leaves. Brought down from Scotland, they are destined for a near-certain grave in the south. In the coolth of Scotland it is another matter, although even there they will need regular waterings in time of summer drought.

P. rosea (15cm/6in) is none too easy in the south either, as it likes to grow in shallow, flowing water. A lovely thing with umbels of deep, true pink flowers. **P. sieboldii** (25cm/10in) can be treated as a normal border perennial, if frequently divided and grown in moist, humus-rich soil. It flowers in May and has bright green, frilly-margined leaves at that season. The flowers are distinctly large, each petal deeply notched, and with a white/mauve/pink colour range.

Quite late in the season, and flowering into August, comes **P. capitata** (15cm/6in), which is easily raised from seed. On a globular head, it carries drooping purplish bells. You may get a little bored with it, after a while. Never with **P. vialii** (syn. *P. littoniana*) (38cm/15in), also late-flowering and easy from seed. But for its primrose-like leaves, you might not think it was a primula at all. It makes a dense spike, red at first, this being the colour of the sepals, then lilac, from the bottom up, as the flowers open. With a reputation for being short-lived, that is not necessarily the case. It can build into good clumps.

There is a group of early-summer primulas called Sikkimensis. From primrose-like leaves, **P. sikkimensis** (60cm/2ft) carries a drooping cluster of scented, pale yellow bells at the top of its scape. Better known and more robust is **P. florindae** (1m/3ft), with large, heart-shaped leaves which look pathetic if allowed to go short of water. In July, it makes dense heads packed with yellow blossom, having a sweet/sharp scent in the evening. It will seed itself everywhere, crowding out its neighbours. There are strains with brownish orange flowers which I heartily dislike, as their colouring is so impure. A good, hearty primula with a long season.

In the same series is the early-summer-flowering **P. alpicola** (75cm/2½ft), a species which breathes refinement. Its heads of open bells are white or pale yellow or light purple, and they are wonderfully fragrant on the evening air.

Next to primroses and polyanthus, the most popular section of *Primula* is Candelabra. The flowers are borne in tiers of whorls. These are all easily grown in damp soil and are good border plants, but they do self-sow a lot and if this is allowed indiscriminately, the result can look like an invasion of weeds. Another point: when these primulas are going or gone over, they loll around in every direction and that looks sleazy. If you will take the trouble to dead-head them at this stage, while the pods are green, you will both restore neatness and forestall the weeding out of self-sowns at a later stage.

P. japonica (60cm/2ft) is already flowering in May. It is inclined to be muddy, pinky mauve, so be sure to get a strong, cleanly coloured strain like 'Miller's Crimson'. 'Postford White' is dirty white; I shouldn't touch it. This species is smooth and without farina, in all its parts, where **P. pulverulenta** (1m/3ft), as its name indicates, is powdered white all over, in contrast to its handsome magenta flowers. The Bartley Hybrids are pale salmon pink and very charming. They mix well with the typical magenta strain.

30

There are good magentas and bad, the latter having too much of blue in them. Two examples, here, are **P. burmanica** (1m/3ft) and **P. beesiana** (1m/3ft), both made even more aggressive by a bright yellow eye. When you buy mixed Candelabra Hybrids, these two play a large part in making the mixture altogether too hectic, combined with yellow and orange.

The most pleasing, soft orange is to be found in **P. bulleyana** (1m/3ft), and if you buy seed of Bulleyana Hybrids, they will come in a nice range of apricot and orange, sometimes with a trace of peach. **P. chungensis** (1m/3ft) is smaller-growing and smaller-flowered than most, a rich, deep orange. Crossed with *P. pulverulenta*, we have **P.** × **chunglenta** (75cm/2½ft), which is orange with a hint of pink in it. That works all right.

An astonishingly pure scarlet is the much-admired property of 'Inverewe' (75cm/2½ft), a sterile hybrid of disputed origin, but probably not from Inverewe in north-west Scotland. It can only be propagated vegetatively and is apt to go down with virus diseases. So can many of these primulas, one symptom being an unusually heavily serrated leaf margin, combined with reduced vigour.

One of the strongest growing candelabra primulas, with many whorls of pure, bright yellow flowers, is **P. helodoxa**, now subsumed into **P. prolifera** (1m/3ft). In open woodland, as at the High Beeches, in mid-Sussex, it is a great feature in June (when most Candelabra primulas are flowering), combining there with an azalea, 'Orange Beauty', which is a *Rhododendron kaempferi* hybrid.

Prunella

LAMIACEAE/LABIATAE

The self-heals are jumped-up weeds. The commonest, **Prunella vulgaris** features as an unattractive weed of lawns – unattractive because the oval leaves are lacking in style or personality, and this is a drawback to the entire genus.

The flowers are borne, during spring and early summer, in congested terminal whorls and are typically of violet colouring. **P. grandiflora** (23cm/9in) is the species that has been most developed for front-of-border planting, and it has quite a wide range of colour variants, including white. The pinkish-mauve 'Loveliness' is one of the oldest cultivars. If they appeal to you, good luck.

Pyrethrum – see Tanacetum

Pulmonaria

Boraginaceae

The lungworts are mostly European perennials, shade-loving, early flowering, many already at their best in March. They flower before their leaves are fully expanded. As in many members of the borage family, the colouring ranges between blue and pink; quite often a flower which opens pink changes to blue as it goes along, giving rise to the popular name of soldiers and sailors. Although there are good blues and good pinky-reds, many fall between these two colours and are muddy.

If they are grown notwithstanding, it will be for the sake of their handsome foliage, which is the other predominant feature in pulmonarias as garden plants. This may be covered with pale spots, giving the spotted dog epithet to ***Pulmonaria saccharata***, for instance. But the pale variegation may sometimes make a large, uniform area covering most of the leaf. As this is as bright in shade as in the open, it is fine for lighting otherwise rather dark areas (providing moisture is there) and pulmonarias are much used for ground cover. Although deciduous, their foliage should remain in good condition through to autumn. Unfortunately it is often subject to disfiguring powdery mildew.

All are easily divided or raised from root cuttings. If you move a colony, new plants will generally be made on the old site, where broken roots were left behind.

Height may be taken to be some 23cm/9in, unless otherwise stated, and plants develop quite a wide spread. The leaves are invariably hairy.

Among the earliest flowering is **P. angustifolia** 'Munstead Blue' (10cm/4in), a deep blue and still worthwhile, although Ernst Pagels's 'Blaues Meer' is even better. They spread slowly overground by short rhizomes.

The pinkish red **P. rubra** is at its best in very early spring, before its large, coarse leaves take over. However, this species has given rise to the cultivar 'David Ward', which is the brightest for its silvery foliage in summer and autumn. 'Margery Fish' also has excellent foliage of this type.

P. longifolia is our native species, rather late-flowering but with shapely lance leaves, excellently spotted. The flowers are not outstanding and the leaves may mildew seriously.

P. officinalis has given rise to 'Bowles's Blue, 'Blue Mist' and the Cambridge Blue group, all light blue and of clear colouring. They flower early and are effective, at a low level. 'Lewis Palmer', by contrast, is upstanding to 30cm/1ft, prolific and a strong mid-blue, usually best in April. 'Blue Ensign' is similar.

If you want an albino to lighten a dark place, *P. officinalis* 'Sissinghurst White' is one of the best.

Most pulmonaria cultivars have been named after people or places, which tells you nothing about the appearance of the plant. A little more imagination would be welcome.

Pulsatilla

RANUNCULACEAE

Once considered a part of *Anemone*, *Pulsatilla* has pinnate rather than palmate foliage, is generally covered all over with soft hairs which catch the dew, and has persistent, plumose styles, which elongate after flowering and are assembled into conspicuous, globe-shaped seed heads.

As a whole, the genus is better suited to cultivation by the alpine plant enthusiast than to be grown as an ordinary garden plant. Once seen in the wild, where its flowering quickly follows snow-melt in the alps, the cultivation of **P. vernalis** (15cm/6in) in a garden seems to me a paltry substitute.

Most pulsatillas are lime lovers, and such is our own native pasque flower (it flowers at Easter), **P. vulgaris** (syn. *Anemone pulsatilla*) (23cm/9in). If your garden includes thin turf overlying chalk or lime, this is the spot in which to naturalise it. The type-plant has purple flowers, which make a setting for the central cluster of yellow stamens. There are many cultivars, however, of varying colour – white, mauve, velvety red – often with quite large flowers and these are obliging border perennials, easily raised from seed.

Larger growing and calcifuge is **P. alpina** subsp. **apiifolia** (30cm/1ft), long known as *Anemone sulfurea*. When happy, as I have seen it in Scottish gardens, it makes a large, long-lived plant, best propagated from seed, though germination is not prolific. The colour is sulphur yellow.

R

Ranunculus

RANUNCULACEAE

Ranunculus is a fun genus, varied and showy. Our three commonest grassland buttercups are *R. bulbosus*, *R. repens* and *R. acris*.

R. bulbosus (30cm/1ft) is the first in flower, from the end of April. You can easily recognise it, not just from the swollen leaf bases, which form a sort of bulb, but from the fact of its green sepals being strongly reflexed, so that they lie against the supporting stem. For a long time, the double **R. constantinopolitanus** 'Plenus' was wrongly ascribed to *R. bulbosus*. This is the largest of the double buttercups, flowering in April, the centre of the flower green. Vine weevil larvae can decimate a colony, but it is otherwise easy.

R. repens (30cm/1ft) is the creeping buttercup, quite difficult to eliminate from lawns. It is extremely invasive in damp borders, always flourishing in the wet areas in meadows. This has a charming double version, *R. r.* var. *pleniflorus*, May-June flowering. Colonise it in an area of lawn that you do not mow after March or before September – keeping it separate from the single type-plant, of course.

R. acris (60cm/2ft) has the greatest presence of the three, widely branching, quite small-flowered but free. Its double version, 'Flore Pleno', May-June-flowering, is delightful. There is also a most robust cultivar, 'Stevenii' (1.2m/4ft), with a double row of petals. It looks well with the deep red oriental poppy, 'Goliath'. *R. a. citrinus* is pale yellow; definitely worthy of a border position. If allowed to self-sow, you may get the ordinary bright yellow species mixed in.

There is one other wild buttercup that you may find in your garden without having introduced it: **R. auricomus**, called goldilocks. Its first flowers come out in March and it is at its best in April. Liking damp turf, it is seen at its best in the company of mauve lady's smock, or cuckoo flower, *Cardamine pratensis*. Goldilocks is rich yellow but is sometimes missing a petal or two or even the whole lot. If introducing it to an area of rough grass, you want to be sure of a strain with its full compliment.

Our other spring-flowering native is the lesser celandine, **R. ficaria** (10cm/4in), whose shining petals can light up large areas of sward – unless there are pheasants

37

around. They will eat off every flower. Also, unless there is no sunshine, for celandines close demurely in dull or wet weather and at night. They give rise to a huge number of variants and there is quite a cult of collecting these.

One that I found myself in a nearby wood, and introduced to civilised society, I called 'Brazen Hussy'. Its brassy yellow flowers are highlighted by purple leaves. Sometimes its seedlings come green-leaved, but more usually not. The original colony has been pretty well overtaken by brambles. I do not have the collecting instinct, but I have bought a cream-white cultivar called 'Salmon's White'. A pity the eponymous Salmon's surname wasn't White. 'White's White' would have been so appropriate.

There are many double forms of celandine, none more beautiful than the semi-wild *R. ficaria* subsp. *flore-pleno*, which has a very tight rosette of yellow, green in the centre. It adapts admirably to lawn life. Celandines, however, can be ferocious weeds in flower borders and are hard to get rid of, once established. The whole contents should be turned out and the celandines treated, when growing lushly, with Roundup. Be careful what you plant back! They have tuberous roots, in clusters, and every tuber makes a new plant

Another tuberous-rooted buttercup is **R. gramineus** (23cm/9in). Its clear yellow flowers, in April-May, are set off by grey-green lance leaves. It looks good interplanted with *Omphalodes cappadocica* 'Cherry Ingram', which is deep blue and only a little shorter. Lesser spearwort, **R. flammula**, also has lance leaves. It is native, growing in marshes, boggy places and at pond-sides; beautiful when combining with water forget-me-not, *Myosotis scorpioides*, which is blue with a yellow eye. Both are summer-flowering. So is greater spearwort, **R. lingua**, grown in gardens in its 'Grandiflora' (1.2m/4ft) strain. Of upright habit, that will grow in a foot of water as well as less. It is a large-flowered, showy buttercup, but aggressive.

A buttercup that I should greatly like to succeed with (but it died on me quickly, without leaving an explanatory note) is **R. cortusifolius** (1m/3ft), from Madeira and Canary. It has shiny, orbicular leaves, 23cm/9in across, and compound panicles of clean yellow flowers, up to 5cm/2in across. A handsome beast. Said to like moisture in its spring growing and flowering season, but to have it dry, later on.

A hardy, white European species, **R. aconitifolius** (1m/3ft) is scarcely deserving of garden space but its neatly doubled 'Flore Pleno' (60cm/2ft) is a scintillating plant in late spring, for a damp, shady border in the south, but in Orkney you see it anywhere, in every garden. That has clusters of tuberous roots, easily divided. My plant was a victim to finger blight.

The florists' ranunculus, **R. asiaticus**, single or double, red, yellow, white, pink, and a long-lasting cut flower in its May season, comes from the Mediterranean. In the Levant, where I have enjoyed wild clumps of it in April, it is red, but it can be yellow or white, which contrasts well with the near-black centre. These are not easy plants in cultivation, though their tubers are on sale. Like *R. cortusifolius*, they need moisture in spring, when growing, but to be dry later on. Not being out-and-out hardy, they are most safely grown in a cold frame.

Finally, our native water crowfoot or water buttercup, **R. aquatilis**, which, however, is a complex group of subspecies and also of nearly related species. In a pond, it is a good under-water oxygenator, making a carpet of white blossom on the surface, in spring. This varies greatly in size and quality, so be sure to see what you are buying, in flower. The under-water leaves are generally thread-like, while those floating on the surface are orbicular.

Ratibida

ASTERACEAE/COMPOSITAE

A genus of American annuals and perennials with an obviously close relationship to *Rudbeckia* and *Helenium*. The brownish-orange rays are bent right back, almost parallel with the flower stem, while the disc is so prominent as to be columnar. It is a most attractive and unusual arrangement.

I brought seed of **Ratibida pinnata** (1m/3ft) back from Minnesota, where it is a prairie ingredient. After growing it on for a year till I had large plants, we planted them into a meadow area, where they flowered but were gone by the next year. In a border, they grow and perennate easily enough, but their stringy habit is against them. However, I feel there is a niche for them somewhere; perhaps in less dense turf than I was offering. The advantage of growing lanky plants in grass, is that they are held upright by the surrounding herbage.

Rehmannia

SCROPHULARIACEAE

Well known as a conservatory pot plant for early-summer flowering, **Rehmannia elata** (60cm/2ft), long known as *R. angulosa*, seems to have possibilities as a garden perennial. It makes a loose raceme of fair-sized, mimulus-like flowers, but pink. The leaves are pinnately lobed and rough. Definitely hardier – and I have brought it through several toughish winters – is **R. henryi** (15-60cm/6in-2ft), which has as much of yellow as of pink in its flowers and blooms for most of the summer. It has a running rootstock and makes a patch, but needs stronger soil than we have so far given it. Room for experiment, here.

Rheum

POLYGONACEAE

The ultra-hardy race of rhubarbs, with handsome, palmately-veined leaves. Edible rhubarb is now hedging its bets by calling itself **Rheum × hybridum** (at one time R. *rhaponticum*). Like most of the genus, it more than doubles its height at flowering, to 2m/6ft – a froth of white in late May, and if you catch it right, when the buds are just opening, it is a fine ingredient for a large floral arrangement. About a month later, when the seeds are ripening and still reddish, they can be dried for winter arrangements.

The ornamental rhubarbs, for use in the garden, are mostly derivatives of **R. palmatum** (1-2m/3-7ft when flowering) – 'Atrosanguineum' being the preferred cultivar. In practice, it is not one cultivar but many, and further selections have been given clonal names.

These rhubarbs have large, ground-covering leaves in the early part of the growing season. The leaves have deeply jagged margins and are purple or reddish all over, on first emerging. They retain much of this colouring on the underside of the leaf, as it expands. The inflorescence may be pink or white. Both colours are effective in their way, the white looking well above purple-suffused leaves, highlighted against a background still in shadow.

The snag with rheums is that while they require plenty of space, they largely vacate it and become dormant from midsummer. A position at the back of a one-sided border, works well if the plants in front are of a kind that will rise to conceal the hole in late summer and autumn. Japanese anemones would do this. In spring, plantings of red tulips, quite close to the rheum crowns, make an exciting combination.

The rhubarbs have tough, woody root/rhizomes, pieces of which can be chopped off, in late winter, to make new plants.

The smaller-growing hybrid, 'Ace of Hearts' is neat and only 1.2m/4ft tall at flowering. **R. alexandrae** (1m/3ft), from the Himalayas, is a beautiful and unusual-looking plant, but much easier to grow in Scotland than in the south. The rounded

58

leaves are small, the main point, in this case, being the narrow panicle, which is clothed along its length, with large, rounded, palest yellow-green bracts. They show up from a distance as something quite out of the ordinary. If your clump produces one panicle, you will be pleased; if three or more, you'll be really proud. If it dies, you are in my company.

Rodgersia

SAXIFRAGACEAE

Given rich, organic soil and plenty of moisture, rodgersias are wonderful hardy border perennials. They like the same conditions as hostas, with which they associate well, and seem as happy on alkaline as on acid soils. In most cases their leaves are thick-textured, with a rough, heavily veined surface. Mercifully, they seem impervious to the attentions of slugs or snails. All come from eastern Asia. They prefer the climate of Scotland to that of England, where a hot summer spell is apt to burn them up.

62   Particularly is this the case with **Rodgersia podophylla** (75cm/2½ft, so named because the palmate leaf is divided into leaflets the shape of a webbed foot). The leaves are reddish purple, on first appearing, become green but, around midsummer, begin to assume a reddish suffusion which gradually intensifies until, by autumn, it is bright carmine. These changes are much more pronounced in Scotland than in the south of England, where a dry spell will cause the leaves to shrivel. The white flowers, in open panicles, tend to be sparingly produced. They rise, as with all rodgersias, well above the foliage, almost doubling the plant's height.

R. sambucifolia (75cm/2½ft) has pinnate leaves, like an elder's. It looks good in its photographs, but mine has been slow to get going. I should lift and re-plant it in better-prepared soil. And I lost **R. aesculifolia** (75cm/2½ft) through negligence. Its palmate leaves have a particularly good texture.

This may be a parent of the plants we grow as **R. pinnata**. They are very variable, their leaves sometimes pinnate, sometimes palmate. The first clone I grew produced panicles of white flowers. Then I acquired 'Superba' (75cm/2½ft), which has a rather weak constitution but particularly rich, bronze-purple leaves, while the flowers, likewise, are a quite deep shade of red, becoming deeper as they fade. In this species, the inflorescence remains in perfect condition right into October, although it comes into flower in June. But the colour just keeps on deepening. It is the same with the clone I have named 'Maurice Mason' (1m/3ft), because he gave it me and it is quite distinct; much more robust than 'Superba' with plenty of rich pink flowers which, again, deepen as the season progresses.

As rodgersias do not come into leaf till May, they can be colonised with snow-drops, winter aconites and crocuses. They are propagated by division of the slowly-spreading rhizomes.

For *Rodgersia tabularis* see *Astilboides tabularis*.

Romneya

PAPAVERACEAE

The California tree poppy (not to be confused with Dendromecon) comes from the Santa Ana Mountains, south-east of Los Angeles. That is **Romneya coulteri**, but its variety, **trichocalyx**, till recently considered a separate species, continues south into Mexico. For garden cultivation, the clone 'White Cloud' (2m/6ft) (probably a hy-brid between the above) is the one to have, with the largest blooms.

At the height of its July season, this plant is a thrilling spectacle, carrying abun-dance of pure white poppies, up to 15cm/6in across and composed of five or six overlapping petals, and a central mass of bright yellow stamens. The flowers are set off by glaucous leaves of deeply jagged outline.

It is a suckering sub-shrub, best treated as a herb, cutting everything within sight to ground level in early winter. This will allow you to interplant an entire colony with winter-flowering bulbs. A notably successful association is of yellow winter aco-nites (*Eranthis hiemalis*) with mauve *Crocus tommasinianus*, the display being at its peak in February sunshine. The little blue, bulbous *Iris histrioides* 'Major' also succeeds in such a situation. At Denmans, in West Sussex, hybrids of *Narcissus cyclamineus* are used in combination with the monocarpic *Eryngium giganteum* (1m/3ft), whose pale, silvery inflorescences would coincide with the poppy's own flowering.

Another combination that intrigued me was in gravel at Hadspen, Somerset, where the equally suckering sub-shrub, *Clerodendrum bungei* (1.8-2.4m/6-8ft), was fighting it out with the poppy, on apparently balanced terms. The clerodendrum's season follows on from the romneya's, its dark oval leaves crowned by heads of deep pink, scented blossom. Where winters are mild and summers warm, you could cut the clerodendrum to the ground in the same way as the romneya, overplanting with winter-flowering bulbs and in this way achieving a triple display season from the one area of garden. But in most of Britain, with our cool summers, the clerodendrum needs to retain some of its old wood through to the next growing season, otherwise it does not flower in time before the onset of cold, late autumn weather. In that case, you would prune it in spring, back to 1m/3ft or so.

When well suited, romneyas will make huge colonies, and are apt to explore through shaky wall foundations, either in the garden or even into your kitchen. So long as their soil is well drained, they are not particular about acidity, and the best colony I have seen was on the chalk of the South Downs. They are also hardy and will flower well a long way north, in Britain, not only in Edinburgh but (as I have witnessed) at Drummond Castle, which is in the heart of Scotland. Such a climate suggests siting it near to a warm wall, where free flowering will be promoted by such sunshine as can be expected up there.

But romneyas are often tricky to establish in the first instance. The fleshy roots are extremely sensitive to damage and you should only acquire well-established, pot-grown plants. Being given a root division from their own colony by a friend, seldom results in success. But it does, occasionally.

Root cuttings should be taken from strong young pieces, each one inch long and a quarter inch thick, of young roots. Pot these pieces, each individually, in a vertical position in small peat pots, covering the top end of the cutting with an inch of compost. Do this in December or January and place the pots where the temperature will not fall below a minimum of 55° F (13° C). Pot on, pot and all, into a larger pot, in March and plant out, hardened off, in June.

Roscoea

Zingiberaceae

Belonging to the ginger family, roscoeas are yet of a somewhat orchidaceous appearance. They come from the Far East and are remarkably hardy, all things considered, giving an exotic flavour to their surroundings. They have fleshy, rhizomatous roots and deep planting in leafily organic-rich soil is recommended, though they are really not that particular. Single roots make no great impression and you need to have them building into sizeable clumps. These can be divided, for increase of stock.

The purple-flowered **Roscoea purpurea** (30cm/1ft) is one of the commonest in cultivation but more effective, in my opinion, is the pale yellow **R. cautleoides** (30cm/1ft) which, flowering in early summer, looks well in a sea of campanula-blue *Campanula portenschlagiana*.

Rudbeckia

ASTERACEAE/COMPOSITAE

The coneflowers are all North American, like the sunflowers. Many of the best are annual. They flower in late summer and into autumn. Usually, the cone is prominent, sometimes green, sometimes black. For those who like yellow daisies, there is excellent quarrying here.

Many grow tall and need support, especially under sheltered garden conditions, where they tend to get drawn. Paradoxically, on open sites they are better able to stand on their own legs.

Rudbeckia laciniata (1.5m/5ft) is not often grown and its cone is a rather nondescript feature. 'Goldquelle' (Golden Fountain) (1.2m/4ft) is a derivative and the best double – a bright, clean yellow. 'Herbstsonne' ('Autumn Sun') (2m/6ft) is a wonderful plant if you can cope with its height. As with most perennials that are liable to grow inconveniently tall, there are two routine methods of curbing this. Lift your clumps each early spring, and reset them. Breaking their roots acts as a growth check. When 60cm/2ft tall, pinch out the tips of all the shoots. 'Herbstsonne' has a prominent green cone and lax rays of a shining yellow, not a bit harsh but with just a softening hint of green. A good long flowering season.

R. maxima (1.2m/4ft) is the most desirable, quality species, though I have yet to see a sizeable patch of it looking really happy. Hardiness is no problem. It seems to dislike competition, so will resent border companions, requiring, rather, an open site. And also the best of growing conditions, in deeply dug, generously manured soil.

There are not many leaves; they are concentrated at the base, each simple, paddle-shaped, glaucous, on a long petiole. The stem is almost naked, the daisies few and widely spaced, each an individual, with very long, down-drooping rays – 'long, languid yellow petals', Beth Chatto describes – and a tall, thrusting black cone.

Any rudbeckia with a black cone is liable to be dubbed 'Black-eyed Susan'. Of the shorter, bushy and self-supporting kinds, the showiest is probably *R. fulgida* var. *sullivantii* 'Goldsturm' (45cm/1½ft), with long, rich yellow rays held horizontally. Brilliant for lighting up a somewhat shady place, but it must have plenty of rich living and moisture. In the US, where it self-sows, this clone has become adulterated. There is much inferior stuff going around as 'Goldsturm'. *R. fulgida* var. *deamii* (1m/3ft) is similar. However, the daisies are a little smaller, but prolific – a most cheering plant.

An oddity, recommended for flower arrangers (is this a nurseryman's ploy for selling it or do they really yearn for it?) is *R. occidentalis* 'Green Wizard' (45cm/1½ft).

55

Dispensing with colourful rays altogether, all that's left are the short green bracts, which stick out forming a frame for the black cone. It is miserably undistinguished.

S

Sagittaria

ALISMATACEAE

Arrowhead, **Sagittaria sagittifolia**, is a deep-rooted aquatic for up to 60cm/2ft of water, above which its growth rises another 60cm/2ft. It is a handsome plant but a rather ferocious and combative invader. The leaves are shaped like an arrow-head. Flowers white, with a purple basal blotch, in whorls, the males separate from the females. But in cultivation, it is generally the showier double-flowered form, 'Flore Pleno' that is grown.

Salvia

LAMIACEAE/LABIATAE

The genus of the sages is vast and includes a high proportion of rubbish, from the gardener's point of view, so don't be impressed when you meet a professed enthusiast for the lot. However, that still leaves a great deal to preoccupy us.

A trial of all but the bedding salvias, at Wisley, produced a satisfyingly large number of entries. It lasted for two growing seasons and, as one of the judges, I probably got more out of it than I contributed (not true; I was being modest and quickly recognise my mistake).

Many salvias – especially those from Mexico – are tender, but that in itself is no reason for shying off them. The majority of British gardeners have glass. Many salvias are shrubby; I shall mention the fact, when discussing them. Others are short-lived or biennial. I shall mention that, too. All like a position in full sun and not too rich feeding.

To start with culinary sage – ***Salvia officinalis***. Its flavour is pungent, so don't overdo it. I like a little, with onion and seasoning, to flavour apple sauce, with pork. The plant can be a boring, scraggy shrub, so you might just as well grow one of its nicer-looking cultivars. 'Purpurascens' is variable, always decent but unexciting. 'Icterina' is light green and yellow, seldom flowering, which is an advantage when the leaf is the main point. 'Tricolor' is variable and the AGM was given to a clone with less of pink in its grey, white and purplish variegation than can be the case, but this evidently made it a hardier plant, since it survived a toughish winter, whereas the most jazzily variegated clones are distinctly tender. It seldom flowers. 'Kew Gold' is very light yellow and can scorch, when hot and dry. 'Berggarten', with rounded grey foliage, makes a nice shrub to flow forward from a border margin.

I think highly of **S. lavandulifolia**, which has narrow, greyish leaves (this is the one I cook with) and masses of mauve blossom in early summer. The heights of all these sages varies according to how much you prune to keep them neat. Say, a foot; more with the coarser types and more if and when they flower.

S. blancoana is almost prostrate and its neat foliage looks pleasing from autumn to late spring. Its lavender flowers are pretty, in June-July, after which the plant needs tidying. The foliage smells of true sage and I suspect (though I haven't tested) that it could serve well for cooking.

There was a period when we had to call **S. candelabrum** S. interrupta, but we seem to be back where we started. It is a shrub with moderately large leaves, 60cm/2ft high when foliar, but rising to 1.5m/5ft or more, when flowering. It then becomes a stemmy, see-through plant, with bold purple flowers, in July. An excellent species on light soil (it loves chalk), but apt to die in winter on heavy fare.

In warmer climates than ours, **S. canariensis** is a splendid shrub of the same kind, rising to 2m/6ft or more when carrying its rosy-mauve flowers, in June. But it is tender here, a mere 60cm/2ft tall, flowering little and late. **S. leucantha** (1m/3ft) is the species for which I drool most heavily. Above veined leaves, it carries woolly spikes in which the calyx is rich mauve, the corolla white. In some forms, the entire flower is mauve. In California, where it can be grown as a low hedge, it is already in full bloom by early June, but in Britain it normally gets going only as the first frosts are about to nip it. Definitely tender, but if you can have decent-sized plants to put out even as early as late April, they may surprise you by flowering during the summer.

There are other late-flowering species that scarcely make the grade, in Britain, though it is tempting to toy with them. One called (possibly without justification) *S. vanhouttei* (75cm/2½ft) is much grown in East Coast US, and is a great sight in September, with long, loose racemes of pure red flowers, as though *S. splendens* had learned to be refined. *S. rutilans* (1m/3ft) has slender little red flowers, very late, but the main point of the plant is the pineapple smell of its leaves, when crushed. It must now be called *S. elegans* 'Scarlet Pineapple'.

It is tender and so is *S. fulgens* (1.2m/4ft), but that can make a handsome late display with loose racemes of sizeable, pure red flowers. Its shoots are often attacked by capsid bugs earlier on, which will ruin the display. *S. confertiflora* (1.2m/4ft) has spikes of tiny red flowers above a platform of large leaves – scarcely worth the effort, though occasionally it puts on a reasonable display. Although it got no award at Wisley, I fancied *S. elegans* (60cm/2ft), a tender species that put its best foot forward in October, with short spikes of scarlet flowers having very slender tubes. A nice habit, too, but admittedly not dramatic.

49   *S. coccinea* is a species that we grow as an annual, from seed, 'Lady in Red' (60cm/2ft) being the much improved version, excellent bedded alternating with the purple *Verbena rigida*. 'Pseudococcinea' (75cm/2½ft) is a tender clone having a good presence. Long racemes of well-spaced flowers in a strong shade of red.

S. discolor (60cm/2ft) is an oddball with a long summer season, the calyx pale green, but the corolla black. Totally ineffective, yet it has its appeal (not to me). *S. buchananii* (30cm/1ft) is a strong shade of reddish purple. A long summer season, tender, the plant on the thin side. One always has the feeling that it could be grown better, but could it?

We are on familiar ground with *S. patens* (45cm/1½ft), which is intense, pure Oxford blue. There are seldom more than two blooms flowering at one time on each spike, so the display can be a bit thin, albeit over a long season. Halfway through, it pays to clip the plants over. 'Cambridge Blue' is as good in its way, but 'Chilcombe' makes you wonder what is the point of a mauve *S. patens*, while 'White Trophy' is dirty white. This species is often raised from seed, but it makes tubers which can be overwintered in damp peat (they must not shrivel), and planted out again next spring or cuttings can be made from the young shoots. Plants are hardy enough often to survive winter outside.

S. cacaliifolia (38cm/15in) is as blue as the bluest, and its shovel-shaped leaves are attractive, but the flowers are on the small side and the habit floppy. Entirely tender, cuttings must be taken each early autumn.

To continue with pure blue salvias; 'Indigo Spires' (*S. farinacea* × *S. pratensis*)

(75cm/2½ft) is very deep blue, resembling its *farinacea* parent, as also in being tender, so you must take cuttings. **S. azurea** (1.2m/4ft) is a lovely colour but gets going too late and is too sparse in our climate. Excellent in New York.

With its sky-blue flowers, flecked white, in shortish racemes, **S. uliginosa** (2m/6ft) is a great favourite, flowering from late August, on. It makes a colony by suckering and contrasts well with the pale yellow of *Patrinia scabiosifolia* (1.5m/5ft), or with a pink or yellow dahlia, giving body to the planting. Hardiness is not altogether to be depended upon, so a root should be overwintered under glass. Cuttings root easily in spring.

As good in its much sturdier, upright way, is **S. guaranitica** 'Blue Enigma' (2m/6ft), with rich blue racemes from August, sometimes earlier. Be sure to get this clone; there are other, less good cultivars. 'Argentine Skies' makes a change, however. Its pale blue colouring contrasts kindly with the grey foliage of *Artemisia* 'Powis Castle' (60cm/2ft). But there is an unwelcome touch of mauve in it.

Of the hardy, herbaceous salvias, **S. pratensis** 'Haematodes' (1m/3ft) is a short-lived perennial, often best treated as a biennial and always raised from seed. With its open candelabra of pale lavender blossom, it is a wonderful sight for not much longer than ten days, in early June. There is scarcely any foliage in sight, the large leaves forming a rosette at ground level. *S. pratensis* 'Indigo' (1m/3ft) is less good than the last, at its best, but is a stayer, contributing over a long season.

A group of true hardy perennials starts with **S. × sylvestris** 'Mainacht' (75cm/2½ft) at the turn of May and June. But the purple colouring is too dark to be effective, except in specially contrived circumstances. 'Blauhügel' (75cm/2½ft) is a luminous shade of 'blue' (none in this section are pure blue), a month later.

Best is **S. × superba** (1m/3ft), whose first flush of purple spikes with reddish-purple calyxes, comes in July and contrasts effectively with the bronze daisies of *Helenium* 'Moerheim Beauty' (1m/3ft). Remove tired spikes in August and there quickly follows a crop of new side-spikes (the helenium also repeats). **S. nemorosa** 'Ostfriesland' ('East Friesland') (1m/3ft) is like a dwarf version, earlier in flower by a few weeks and less willing to repeat. It contrasts vividly with the bright orange daisies of *Anthemis sancti-johannis* (60cm/2ft). *S. n* 'Lubecca' (60cm/2ft) is much the same but a little taller, sometimes needing support.

S. nemorosa 'Porzellan' (38cm/15in) is a self-supporting white, which can be useful. *S. n.* 'Amethyst' (1m/3ft) is that colour. Good, not dim. *S. × superba* 'Rubin' (75cm/2½ft) is like 'Amethyst' but shorter.

The shrubby salvias largely derive from Mexican species. Given a sunny, sheltered spot, they will survive many winters, but are in any case easily kept going from soft cuttings, taken in summer. If lightly pruned by shortening old growths, in spring, flowering will often start before the end of May and continue into October. They are immensely generous.

S. greggii 'Peach' (75cm/2½ft) is soft red and free-flowering. 'Raspberry Royal' (75cm/2½ft) had lots of blossom in August and is hardier than some, surviving the winter in the open field. **S. microphylla** (1m/3ft) is a good, bright red, resembling the salvia we are no longer to call *S. microphylla neurepia*. *S. microphylla* 'Pink Blush' (1m/3ft) overwintered and flowered freely from early July on, with long, bright pink racemes. 'Pleasant View' is similar to it. *S. microphylla* 'La Foux' (1m/3ft) is intensely coloured, rosy red, but less free-flowering than its congeners. **S. × jamensis** 'Los Lirios' (1m/3ft) overwintered. It is a dusky, rather indefinite pink but showy. *S. × j.* 'Cienago de Oro' (60cm/2ft) is similar. Elizabeth Strangman liked it. The calyx is almost brown in contrast to the pale buff corolla. A little too subtle for me.

S. argentea is raised from seed and grown mainly for its low rosette of large, silky-grey leaves. It is best on really light soil. A panicle (60cm/2ft) of white flowers appears in its second year, after which it may die, or it may not. I even prefer the less known but similar **S. aethiopis,** which thrives on the driest roadside gravel, in Hungary. The first-year, basal rosette of grey leaves, which have deeply jagged margins, lies flat against the ground, rising to near 1m/3ft when flowering in the second year. This seems truly biennial.

So is the true clary, **S. sclarea** (the annual *S. horminum* is often given this name), often dubbed var. *turkestanica* in gardens. A nobly architectural plant (1.2m/4ft) making a bulky candelabrum with conspicuous rosy-mauve bracts. It smells strongly, when touched, and some find this disagreeable (what a fuss people make about perfectly harmless planty smells), likening it to tom cats.

51

Sambucus

Caprifoliaceae

In this woody genus, there are several herbaceous species of which by far the best known is Danewort, **Sambucus ebulus** (1.5m/5ft). It has a wide distribution in Europe and Asia, and in the Himalayas is often seen in the same role as bracken with us.

Its running rootstock allows colonies to build up and extend quite quickly and it is valuable for holding river banks together, for instance, and to use in many outlying areas where it looks beautiful, in the summer, without being a nuisance. Its white, or blush, corymbs of blossom are at their best in July-August and are followed by black berries. In all, an excellent plant in the right place.

Sanguinaria

PAPAVERIACEAE

One species, called Bloodroot, **Sanguinaria canadensis** (10cm/4in), from eastern North America. It is a woodland perennial preferring acid soil. The flowers, at first enclosed in an unfolding, glaucous leaf with wavy margins (resembling *Macleaya*), appear in March and are pure white. There are a dozen or so petals, the flower opening wide only when the sun is shining. A few days and they are finished. The leaves then develop to a height of 15cm/6in. Colonies are best divided at this stage. The rootstock is a thick rhizome which bleeds red latex when damaged. Not to worry.

Less graceful but having more substance, is the many-petalled double form, 'Plena'. Its appearance has been likened to a waterlily's. It lasts a couple of days longer than the type-plant. These plants are easy in cool, peaty leaf soil.

Sanguisorba

ROSACEAE

Our native salad burnet, **Sanguisorba minor** (syn. *Poterium sanguisorba*) (30cm/1ft), whose crushed leaves smell of cucumber, nearly always grows on rather dry, chalk or lime soils. But the other species are mostly moisture-loving.

46   **S. tenuifolia** 'Alba', clump-forming, with basal pinnate leaves, rises gracefully to 1.2m/4ft and carries fluffy racemes of white blossom in which (as with the others) the stamens are the most prominent feature. Generally best given low support. Flowers July.

S. canadensis (2m/6ft) flowers later and into October, in Scotland. It could be mistaken for a cimicifuga, at a distance. There are showy pink species, like **S. hakusanensis** (1.2m/4ft), also fairly late-flowering.

Saponaria

CARYOPHYLLACEAE

Soapwort, so called on account of soap-like frothing when crushed leaves are mixed with water, is **Saponaria officinalis** (1m/3ft). It is too invasive as a border plant and spreads readily, by its rhizomes, into any neighbouring lawn or turf. But it is pretty in flower, the double pink 'Rosea Plena' being most often seen, the flowers borne in panicles, July-August.

Far superior and non-invasive is *S.* × *lempergii* 'Max Frei' (30cm/1ft), which makes an excellent patch, at the front of a damp border, of double, soft pink blossom, at its best in August-September.

Saxifraga

SAXIFRAGACEAE

Not many saxifrages come within our orbit here. **Saxifraga granulata** (30cm/1ft), the meadow saxifrage, used to be locally common in permanent pastureland, especially on alkaline soils. It is still worth working up stock to introduce to your own meadow. It grows well at Hatfield House, Hertfordshire. This species becomes dormant in high summer and perennates by means of small, bulb-like tubers. The double form, 'Flore Pleno' is charming, too.

London pride is a sterile hybrid, **S.** × **urbium** (30cm/1ft), between *S. spathularis* and *S. umbrosa*. It makes a ground-hugging mat of fair-sized leaf rosettes, flowering in May with a haze of blush-pink panicles and deeper pink stems. Old-fashioned and still deservedly popular. It spreads by short stolons and can often be allowed to thread its way among other not too dense perennials. Good in front of deep, double red peonies, *Paeonia officinalis*. **S. umbrosa** var. **primuloides** (15cm/6in) has much smaller, neater leaf rosettes and a deeper pink inflorescence. It can be used as an edging to formal beds.

S. × **geum** (23cm/9in) makes fairly loose but dense ground cover in shade, as beneath a canopy of hydrangeas. A haze of small, blush-white flowers in May. **S. stolonifera** (23cm/9in) is another shade lover, spreading by means of quite long, flesh-pink stolons. As *S. sarmentosa* it was one of the most popular under-bench ground coverers in cool greenhouses. But it is a fine garden perennial with beautifully patterned, scallop-leaves in different shades of green. If not starved, it flowers abundantly in June, with multi-flowered panicles, the lowest two petals far longer than the rest.

S. fortunei (23cm/9in), a deciduous Chinese and Japanese species, has been much developed as a pot plant in Japan, with many cultivars, some of them a pronounced shade of pink. The flowers, which appear quite late in autumn, are usually white, zygomorphic (lop-sided), abundantly borne and nice combined with an autumn crocus, such as light blue *C. pulchellus*. The saxifrage leaves are scalloped and a feature has been made of them in some cultivars, such as 'Wada's Variety', wherein they are deep red. The flowering of this saxifrage always comes as a delightfully fresh-looking surprise.

Scabiosa

Dipsacaceae

The shape of the scabious 'flower' (really an inflorescence of numerous flowers) has always ensured its affectionate popularity. Pincushion flower is one of its names, referring to the central disc whereon the pin-like anthers are often prominent. In none more than the annual sweet scabious (a rather musty sweetness), **Scabiosa atropurpurea** (1m/3ft) from southern Europe, which, however, can give an even better account of itself in its second year if it has managed to survive the winter. It is usually offered in mixed – often washy – colours – white, pink, coral, lavender, but is always most dramatic when so dark a red as to be almost black (hence its specific epithet). A selected all-black strain has been named 'Ace of Spades', a particular attraction being the contrasting white anthers which form the pin heads.

S. caucasica (60cm/2ft) is a florists' flower with a long season. The flowering units are large and highly regarded when 'blue' (really lavender), as in 'Clive Greaves'. There are also good albinos, such as 'Bressingham White' and 'Miss Willmott'. Plants tend not to make a great show at any one time and are best suited to the cutting garden. Their somewhat sparse habit ensures considerable weed competition.

All scabious quickly disappear on heavy clay and are happiest on light, well-drained soils. None more so than **S. gramineus** (30cm/1ft), which also needs full sunshine. The fairly small, mauve flower heads rise above grass-fine, silvery leaves. Another charmer, in its modest way, is the very pale yellow **S. columbaria** var. **ochroleuca** (60cm/2ft). It makes a bush.

61

▷ **60** *Galax urceolata* (*G. aphylla*), a woodland plant for acid soils, can be shy-flowering but has great presence.

61 A most elegant fern, *Polystichum setiferum* 'Pulcherrimum Bevis', here with *Spiraea japonica* 'Goldflame'.

62 The boldly sculptured foliage of *Rodgersia podophylla*, which prefers cool half-shade.

62

63

63 A late summer jungle, mainly formed of tender perennials, though the banana, *Musa basjoo*, can be left outside in winter. It is best wrapped up for insulation.

64 The snowflake, *Leucojum aestivum* 'Gravetye Giant', will stand quite boggy conditions.

65 Waterlilies should neither be so crowded that their leaves hide the flowers nor conceal too much of the water itself. Front to back: 'Texas Dawn', 'James Brydon', 'Escarboucle', 'Rose Magnolia'.

▷▷

64

66 *Fascicularia bicolor* is one of the few members of the pineapple family hardy in most of Britain.

67 The South American *Senecio smithii*, hardy up to the Shetlands, loves moisture, even to be under water.

68 This waterside giant, *Petasites japonicus* var. *giganteus*, flowers in early spring before its leaves appear.

69 Best treated as a tender bedding plant, *Agastache* 'Firebird' has a very long summer flowering season. ▷

Schizostylis

IRIDACEAE

Known as Kaffir lilies in Britain but nowhere else, this is a South African genus flowering in late summer and autumn. In all cases, the spikes of blossom are about 45cm/1½ft tall on plants that spread by thin rhizomes into colonies. The flowers themselves are bowl- or star-shaped, red, white or some shade of pink. Narrow, sword-shaped leaves.

The plants are moisture-loving and may, if so desired, be grown emerging from shallow water. They detest dry conditions. Frequent division, even every year, and replanting in improved soil, is often beneficial but there is contrary evidence as to whether this promotes earlier flowering. In most cases, this would certainly be an advantage in the British climate. That said, the genus is surprisingly successful and prolific in the north of Scotland – in October.

All *Schizostylis* derive from **S. coccinea**, which is itself red, but much improved in the cultivar 'Major', which as well as being bigger and bolder, really is better. 'Alba' has small white, starry flowers. 'Pallida' is a very pale, perhaps too pale, pink. 'Viscountess Byng' is a more effective, clear pink but so late to start flowering that it will drift on into spring, if the weather is frost-free. Pretty, in November, with the small, mauve heads and dark, tangly foliage of *Serratula seoanei*. 'Jennifer' and 'Sunrise' are both popular with those who like salmon shades. 'Jennifer' has the clearer, cleaner colouring.

Scilla

HYACINTHACEAE/LILIACEAE

Best known is **Scilla siberica** (10cm/4in), synonymous in commercial terms with 'Spring Beauty'. Each fair-sized bulb pushes up several short, flowering stems, in succession, March onwards. Three or four bell-shaped flowers to a stem, of a rich blue. Increases quickly under border conditions but I have not been successful with it, over a period under meadow conditions.

S. bifolia (10cm/4in) is March-flowering, prolific and an excellent shade of rich blue. Looks good with the young yellow-green foliage of *Valeriana phu* 'Aurea'. Its pink-flowered cultivar, 'Rosea', makes a change.

The bulb marketed as *S. tubergeniana* (10cm/4in) has no right to adopt the nursery van Tubergen's name and should be called **S. mischtschenkoana**. For some mysterious reason, nursery catalogues, even of competing houses, are loath to make the change. It has wan blue flowers and is easy and obliging, in the *S. siberica* style, but hardly worth it.

S. peruviana (20cm/8in) comes from south-west Europe (make no mistake). As seen in cultivation, it is a stout, even coarse but showy plant, with large bulbs and thick pyramidal spikes of deepish blue flowers. Not to become blind, it requires frequent division.

We have two native species. **S. verna** (5-15cm/2-6in) is usually seen on sea cliff tops flowering in very short turf. This, on the Atlantic coasts of Great Britain. It is a delight to find in colonies in Orkney and sometimes, given richer conditions, clumps up like chives. The flowers are pale blue stars, May-June. **S. autumnalis** is rather similar but autumn-flowering, again most often seen on sea cliffs, for instance in Cornwall.

Scrophularia

SCROPHULARIACEAE

The plant first known to gardeners as *Scrophularia nodosa* 'Variegata', then *S. aquatica* 'Variegata', now **S. auriculata** 'Variegata' (1m/3ft), is a handsome perennial figwort for its foliage, when not decimated by slugs, mullein shark caterpillars or other predators. A widely branching plant, each leaf deeply margined with cream. Likes moisture.

Sedum

CRASSULACEAE

Sedums are something of a minefield, even excluding the rock-garden types. All are succulent and many do not fit easily into normal mixed borders. All require perfect drainage and they are ideally suited to the gravel garden, in which they stand out as primadonnas. A great asset in this genus is the persistence of their flower heads, in the larger types. They keep changing colour and often remain a feature throughout the winter.

The most familiar border *Sedum* in the past was **S. spectabile** (30cm/1ft), which is outstandingly popular with butterflies in its August season. It has slightly domed, quite large corymbs of light, but bright, clean pink flowers. There are several deeper-coloured derivatives, among them 'Brilliant'. This freely reverts to the lighter-coloured type-plant and if this does not annoy you, the mixture is enjoyable. 'Rosenteller' is a good deep pink, with large heads.

S. telephium (45cm/1½ft), called orpine, is a native, growing, as I meet it locally, on the margins of woodland. Rather a murky, dusty reddish-purple. Not glamorous but I like to have it self-seeding around the base of hydrangeas. It is an important parent of many hybrids, notably 'Herbstfreude' ('Autumn Joy') (38cm/15in), a very strong grower. It inherits some of the murkiness of *S. telephium*, but is a dominant border feature for many months, at first like heads of pale green calabrese, then a wan shade of pink as the flowers begin to open, but steadily intensifying through September to deep, dusky red; finally warm brown, retained through to spring. Old clumps fall apart from the centre. Replanting shortens the stem, so that this does not happen.

S. telephium subsp. *maximum* (1m/3ft) has an upright habit and large, well-spaced leaves. It is best known in its purple-leaved form, 'Atropurpureum', a splendid plant if not spoilt by slugs. The flowers are paler. This looks best set rather apart from other plants, other than carpeters, and with a gravel surround. Many modern cultivars have a purple suffusion through the plant. 'Ruby Glow' (15cm/6in) has a low, procumbent habit, with light purple leaves and reddish-purple flowers. 'Vera Jameson' is rather taller, still purplish. But there are many more.

Selinum

APIACEAE/UMBELLIFERAE

Selinum wallichianum (*S. tenuifolium*) (1.2m/4ft) is one of the most valuable perennial umbellifers for border use. It could probably also be naturalised in grass. Its season is long, starting in May with clumpy hummocks of very finely divided foliage. Umbels of white flowers follow, lasting July–September. The plant, albeit branching, is compact and needs no support.

Senecio

Asteraceae/Compositae. See also Ligularia, Sinacalia

A varied genus, even in what the botanists have left of it; still including two most familiar weeds, groundsel and ragwort.

Most have yellow flowers but exceptionally, **Senecio pulcher** (30cm/1ft) has fair-sized daisies, only a few to a stem, with bright magenta rays and a large yellow disc – quite a challenging contrast. A thrilling plant, but not easy. It dislikes any sort of competition and enjoys good living. Flowers late summer. Can be propagated from root cuttings.

67 **S. smithii** (1m/3ft), from the south of South America, is far easier in the north of Britain than the south and has naturalised near farmsteads in Orkney and Shetland, rather as might docks and with similar foliage. It likes abundant moisture and will grow in shallow water, but can be a prey to all sorts of leaf-eating predators. Large, rounded panicles packed with white daisies, yellow-centred. A striking plant. July-August.

10 **S. doria** (2m/6ft) is a handsome, July-flowering border perennial with wide platforms of ragwort-like yellow blossom above glossy, dark green, entire leaves. Self-supporting. Good near *Clematis* 'Jackmanii'.

Quite different is **S. scandens**, a scandent plant to 2m/6ft or more, which sometimes dies back in winter to ground level, sometimes retains a little old wood. Open panicles of small yellow daisies quite late, September-October.

Two semi-shrubby, grey-leaved species may be mentioned. **S. cineraria** (syn. *Cineraria maritima*) (30cm/1ft) has always been popular as an edging or dot plant in parks bedding, but is good at the front of a border, with white-felted, pinnate leaves. 'White Diamond' is less pinnate than most and moderately hardy. Should always be cut hard back in spring, to prevent flowering, since the yellow daisies are nothing in this case. **S. viravira** (syn. *S. leucostachys*) (60cm/2ft) has deeply pinnate leaves like a double comb. Its habit is somewhat rambling and against a sunny wall, with the help of some other shrub, it may rise to the second storey, but hardiness is not dependable, especially out in a border. If old growth does survive, flowering is abundant in early summer, with clusters of tubular, cream-coloured florets. Dead-heading must follow.

Serratula

ASTERACEAE/COMPOSITAE

Because it is pronounced the Irish way, **Serratula seoanei** (30cm/1ft) has often been misspelt *S. shawii*. It is a mini-knapweed, a tangle of finely dissected, purplish foliage being covered for a long while in autumn by small, mauve-purple thistle-heads. A charming plant, which people notice despite its modesty. The winter skeleton is good, especially on reaching drier weather in March, when the bracts of the old inflorescences open wide and look like fresh brown flowers.

Sidalcea

MALVACEAE

Obviously related to hollyhocks, sidalceas have the same spire-like habit but are much smaller-flowered. They are thoroughly hardy perennials from the west side of North America. **Sidalcea candida** is white, but rather too small-flowered to be effective. The rest, mainly derived from **S. malviflora**, are in some shade of pink. Pink is a difficult colour at the best of times and sidalceas do include some of the nastiest shades, as in 'Party Girl' – harsh pink with a good deal of mauve. But some are a delightfully clean, light pink, notably 'Sussex Beauty' (1.5m/5ft) and 'Elsie Heugh' (1m/3ft), which has frilly margins to its petals.

There are dwarf, self-supporting kinds like 'Oberon' (60cm/2ft) and 'Puck' (60cm/2ft) but they lack the grace of the taller varieties, all of which need support. They associate well with the kind of old-fashioned, once-flowering roses that peak in June-July.

Silene

CARYOPHYLLACEAE

Silene dioica (60cm/2ft) (syn. *Lychnis dioica, Melandrium dioicum*) is the red campion that flowers in woodland clearings and on roadside banks, alongside bluebells, in May. The brighter-coloured subspecies *zeylandica* is native to Orkney and Shetland and has found its way into gardens in the north. Also common, especially in the north, is the double-flowered 'Flore Pleno', which is an excellent spring bedding plant, as also is 'Richmond', another double. They go well with the May-flowering *Allium hollandicum*, better known as *A. aflatunense*. The doubles flower well into June.

Silphium

ASTERACEAE/COMPOSITAE

Not yet another lot of yellow, summer-flowering, American daisies! did I hear exclaimed? Yes, certainly, and none the worse for that. All are coarse-growing, moisture-loving prairie plants.

Best known in Britain is **Silphium perfoliatum** (2m/6ft). It has abundant foliage which is opposite on square, flowering stems, and encloses them at the base, forming a cup. The daisies are only 7.5-10cm (3-4in) across, but make a good display over quite a long period.

S. terebinthinaceum (not the easiest of names to remember correctly) is a fascinating species. It makes a few, very large, broadly elliptical basal leaves. The flowering stems soar, almost leafless to 2m/6ft or more and branch at the summit to quite tiny daisies. I am told that the cut-leaved **S. laciniatum** is a winner, but have yet to own it.

Sinacalia

ASTERACEAE/COMPOSITAE

Till recently known as *Senecio tanguticus*, **Sinacalia tangutica** (2m/6ft) is a handsome late summer-flowering perennial to use where its somewhat invasive habits will not be a worry. It spreads by tuberous rhizomes, not unlike *Helianthus tuberosus*, the Jerusalem artichoke. However, its deeply cut foliage is handsome, albeit pathetic in hot sunshine, the plant requiring heavy, moist soil. The stems are crowned, in August, by pyramids of small yellow blossom, which changes on ripening to fluffy, grey seeds. Good at all stages and combines well with some of the later-flowering forms of *Aconitum carmichaelii*.

Sisyrinchium

IRIDACEAE

Not unlike miniature irises. If they lack the iris panache, they compensate by having moods, closed by night and in dreary weather but opening to sunshine if the hour is right.

Sisyrinchium angustifolium (23cm/9in), called blue-eyed grass, never opens before midday, however sunny. It is a rather impure shade of blue. Freely self-sowing, like all the genus, and nice in paving cracks or edge-of-border positions where nothing else is going on. Native both in western Ireland and eastern USA. Hands across the Ocean.

15 Some sisyrinchiums are bright yellow, but one of the largest, **S. striatum** (1m/3ft) is very pale yellow, with iris-like leaves. Self-sowns, while still young, can make a delightful community, but they age badly, the foliage turning obtrusive black. **S. striatum** 'Aunt May' (or 'Variegatum'), is cleanly white-variegated.

Among the many species and hybrids, 'Quaint and Queer' (30cm/1ft) is arresting for its unusual *café au lait* colouring.

Smilacina

CONVALLARIACEAE/LILIACEAE

Closely related to *Polygonatum*, but flowering in a terminal panicle. The two cultivated species are woodlanders with a wide North American distribution. **Smilacina racemosa** (75cm/2½ft) makes dense rhizomatous clumps and carries dense sprays of tiny white, scented flowers in May. These can be followed by a handsome display of scarlet berries. **S. stellata** (1m/3ft) has a more suckering habit. The terminal panicle of flowers is sparser, each bloom clearly star-shaped. May.

Solidago

ASTERACEAE/COMPOSITAE

The golden rods are a generally despised genus, largely because of their rather brash yellow colouring. Also for the habit of **Solidago canadensis** (2m/6ft) to colonise waste places, though this should be welcome. Although prairie plants, I have not succeeded in establishing them in dense meadow turf. Most are late summer or autumn-flowering.

The solidago flowers are generally all tubular and borne in terminal, spraying panicles. Modern hybrids have been reduced in height. Thus **S. rugosa** 'Fireworks' is 1m/3ft or less and intense yellow. **S. sempervirens** (1.2m/4ft) is unusual in having an outer ring of rays and they are soft yellow, with quite a long season.

× Solidaster

ASTERACEAE/COMPOSITAE

A supposed hybrid between *Aster* and *Solidago*, × *Solidaster luteus* (1m/3ft) is summer-flowering with soft yellow daisies in panicles. It is not self-supporting and soon fades. 'Lemore' is a superior version, with the same faults.

Spartina

POACEAE/GRAMINAE

Spartina pectinata 'Aureomarginata' (1m/3ft) is the only current representative. It is a handsome, though invasive grass, with yellow-edged blades which arch over at the top. I grow it, to give height, in a colony of *Hakonechloa macra* 'Aureola'. It is easily controlled and the pairing works well.

Stachys

LAMIACEAE/LABIATAE

Some *Stachys* are grown for flowers, some for foliage. Of the latter, **S. byzantina** (syn. *S. lanata*) (1m/3ft in flower) is the best known with cosy names such as Jesus's blankets, lamb's ears and lamb's lugs. Elliptical, silvery-grey, furry foliage in loose rosettes at ground level. Sun-loving. Popular in white gardens and as a border edging, but liable to disfiguring mildew, which spots the leaves. The plant rises to flower in June and is beautiful at that stage, but becomes unsightly afterwards and must be cut down or, preferably, replanted forthwith with young, rooted shoots. 'Silver Carpet' flowers very little but mildews. 'Olympica' has imposingly large leaves – but mildews. This trouble is less prevalent in Scotland.

S. officinalis is our native betony of dry banks with shortish spikes of reddish-purple flowers. Improved cultivars include the pink 'Rosea Superba' (1m/3ft), making nice July-flowering clumps. It self-sows and seedlings may not be as good a colour.

S. macrantha (syn. *S. grandiflora*) (1m/3ft) is shorter with showy, thick, short spikes, a good shade of pinky-mauve in cultivars 'Superba' and 'Robusta'.

S. coccinea (30cm/1ft) has slender spikes of soft red flowers, like a refined salvia. A lovely thing but barely hardy and hard to keep unless the season allows it to ripen seed. Flowers late summer to autumn.

Hedge woundwort, **S. sylvatica** (1m/3ft), is a tiresome weed with a running rootstock, hard to extract when among other perennials. The foetid smell when bruised is unmistakeable. Dingy reddish-purple flowers, if it should reach that stage.

Stenanthium

MELANTHIACEAE/LILIACEAE

I fell for **Stenanthium robustum** (1m/3ft) in a Scottish garden more than thirty years ago but as with many plants that flourish there, I succeeded and was encouraged in the first year but then lost it. Not often seen in cultivation, it yet manages to flourish in the Edinburgh Botanic Garden.

It comes from woodland in central USA. The leaves are linear. The inflorescence, in early summer, is a branching, paniculate raceme, rather in the style of *Veratrum*, but the side-branches, each crowded with white star-flowers, are down-drooping in striking contrast to the plant's general upward thrust. Only for the daring.

Sternbergia

AMARYLLIDACEAE

Sternbergia lutea is a variable species, having a wide Mediterranean distribution. Some strains flower more freely in our climate than others. All like full sunshine and a good baking during their dormant summer season, but not starvation conditions, either.

The crocus-like flowers in September-October belie its relationship, but broken leaves smell of daffodils. Dark green strap-leaves appear at the same time as the flowers, which are brilliant chrome yellow. Sternbergias thrive on chalky soils. They can be a wonderful sight. Easily increased by division of the bulbs in spring, as the leaves are dying off.

Stipa

POACEAE/GRAMINAE

A genus of grasses that tend to dislike competition but anyway look best when standing above their neighbours or free of any.

Stipa barbata (1m/3ft) has great presence, with an arching habit and large, drooping awns. June-July. At the same time, the much larger **S. gigantea** (2m/6ft) comes into its own but lasts well into autumn if not destroyed by high winds. Clump-forming, it looks best as a solo feature (or several solo features), its oat-like panicles rising way above the undistinguished leaves. The colour is rose-tinted at first, maturing to pale fawn, the texture diaphanous.

51, 52   **S. tenuissima** (60cm/2ft) is highly regarded by those who grow it well, with fine, silken inflorescences that shimmer and gleam (or quickly subside into a depressing mush). **S. splendens** (1m/3ft), as labelled, is often the same as **S. calamagrostis** (*Achnatherum* and *Lasiagrostis* are other genera in which it has found itself). Flowering in July, the arching panicles are then green, open-textured and puffed out, but later close and become pale fawn, retaining a presence right through the winter.

S. arundinacea (60cm/2ft but more across) makes clumps of fine leaves and the airy panicles gradually develop through late summer and autumn, taking on rich autumnal tints. Excellent at its best but sometimes spoilt by rust disease. It self-sows freely and old clumps are anyway best replaced fairly frequently.

Stokesia

ASTERACEAE/COMPOSITAE

Named after an 18th century taxonomist, Dr Jonathan Stokes. Spare his memory the indignity of Stokeesia.

Only one species, **Stokesia laevis** (syn. *S. cyanea*), from the southeast USA.

Variable in height and colour, but usually a front-of-border, 30cm/1ft plant, summer-flowering and lavender blue, ('Blue Star'). 'Alba' is the white form. The largeish daisies, surrounded by a considerable involucre of bracts, have deeply cut rays. The central disc of tubular florets is somewhat enlarged. A decent perennial.

Stratiotes

HYDROCHARITACEAE

38 ***Stratiotes aloides*** is one of the best under-water oxygenators, where the water is not too acid, because it is not inclined to be invasive and is a handsome feature in itself. Making large rosettes of foliage that spread by stolons, the colour in winter is purple. In spring the rosettes rise to and partially above the water surface, where they turn green, sinking again in September. The leaves are saw-edged; hence, perhaps, the common name: water soldier. If flowers are produced, they are white. Stratiotes is hard to establish where there is undue disturbance by fish.

Strobilanthes

ACANTHACEAE

The only species likely to be seen in gardens is the hardy ***Strobilanthes atropurpureus*** (60cm/2ft), which self-sows freely and is quite nice poking through from the base of a shrub but hardly worth a position to itself. Tubular flowers in late summer with a kink in the middle (chronic stomach-ache, perhaps). Purple and looking their best when glistening in wet weather. In hot weather they quickly fall off.

Stylophorum

PAPAVERACEAE

A woodland plant from eastern North America, ***Stylophorum diphyllum*** (1m/3ft) has 5cm/2in-wide, yellow poppy flowers in spring, among deeply lobed, wavy-margined leaves. Comparable with but not quite so showy as *Hylomecon japonicum*.

Symphytum

BORAGINACEAE

Comfrey is our native ***Symphytum officinale*** (1m/3ft), a herb with many uses, both internal and external. It likes to grow in damp places and makes masses of lush stems and leaves. If these are cut down in June, as soon as the plants have flowered, a second crop, almost as vigorous as the first, will be produced.

The roots, also used medicinally, are fleshy and reproduce freely from root cuttings, if broken. Established colonies are therefore hard to get rid of, except with systemic herbicides. Leaves and stems are large, coarse and hairy. The flowers, as in all the genus, are tubular and borne in clusters. In this species they are either dull purple or dingy cream-yellow, but there are handsomely coloured forms, sometimes a lively red.

The plant widely grown for ground cover as **S. grandiflorum** should be known as **S. ibericum** (45cm/1½ft). Its leaves are quite small. The flowers are an impure cream-yellow. It has a spreading rootstock and does a good job but is otherwise pretty dim. The variegated form, which should be known as 'Goldsmith' (30cm/1ft), has a yellow leaf margin which looks well when fresh, but for most of the summer the plant is disappointing.

The vigorous plant once known as **S. peregrinum** should be **S. × uplandicum** (1m/3ft). The flowers, in May, are pale blue with some mauve but pretty until the plant collapses, when it should be started again by cutting it to the ground. The same treatment applies to the equally vigorous lime-green-coloured comfrey which Stephen Anderton introduced from Belsay, in Northumberland. This makes a lively foliage plant in spring but should not be overshaded. Its second crop of foliage will still be yellower than normal, though less pronouncedly and the leaves always become plain green on maturing.

At its best, *S. × uplandicum* 'Variegatum' is one of the handsomest of all variegated plants, with a bold white margin to its large leaves. Cut down soon after flowering, the second foliage display is even better than the first. When roots are disturbed or broken through cultivations, the subsequent foliage produced will be unvariegated, which is a considerable nuisance.

S. caucasicum (60cm/2ft) is a moderately spreading plant but flowers in a particularly lively shade of blue in spring.

T

Tanacetum

Most important, horticulturally, are the flowers we know as pyrethrums, once under *Chrysanthemum*, now **Tanacetum coccineum** (60cm/2ft). They are excellent cut flowers in early summer. Young and vigorous plants will continue flowering through to autumn. However, the display is generally over by late June, at which time the plants can be removed from beds where they are on display, split if necessary and lined out. They should not be moved, still less divided, in autumn, this job being delayed until new, mossy growth is evident, which may be as early as February. In a border setting, pyrethrums need discreet support, with twigs. Their colours, crimson, pink or white, are clean and bright, the disc being yellow. There are also named doubles. Pyrethrums can be raised from seed.

T. ptarmiciflorum (60cm/2ft) is a beautiful semi-hardy foliage plant, palest silver, its leaves quite small but finely divided filigree. It is really shrubby. Height depends on plant age. For bedding out, it is often best to raise young stock from seed the previous summer, overwinter it frost-free and plant out with summer bedding. Sometimes old plants survive the winter outside and will then flower profusely in May, with white daisies.

The highly aromatic feverfew is **T. parthenium** (height variable, to 1m/3ft), a crazy self-sower. Leaves pinnate, rays white, disc yellow. It is nearly always grown in some yellow-leaved form such as 'Aureum', the colour breeding near-true from seed, or in double-flowered forms, usually white, such as 'White Bonnet'. A popular bedding plant, usually grown as an annual or biennial.

Our native tansy, **T. vulgare** (1m/3ft) is no less aromatic. A vigorous and quickly spreading perennial, its finely dissected, pinnate foliage is a lively shade of green, especially in spring, when it makes a telling companion to Lenten-rose-type hellebores, but the tansy will need annually controlling. Flat-headed corymbs of mustard yellow blossom in August.

Telekia

ASTERACEAE/COMPOSITAE

Also known as *Buphthalmum speciosum*, **Telekia speciosa** (1.2m/4ft), from central and east Europe, is a tough, July-flowering border perennial with bold, ovate leaves and a branching inflorescence of yellow daisies. There are numerous green bracts, which look nice in the bud. Later, the flower heads turn near-black but look pleasing in a winter skeleton setting. In a wild garden, it self-sows enterprisingly.

Tellima

SAXIFRAGACEAE

Tellima grandiflora (60cm/2ft), from the west coastal regions of North America, is a woodland plant. Scalloped heart-leaves, often beautifully patterned. Slender flowering stems, in May, with loose racemes of tiny bells. Self-sows freely. There are variably purple-leaved forms. Nice with spring-flowering euphorbias, deciduous ferns in new leaf and tulip 'Spring Green'.

Thalictrum

RANUNCULACEAE

A deservedly popular genus of hardy perennials with charmingly divided foliage. Earliest in flower is **Thalictrum aquilegiifolium** (60-120cm/2-4ft), with mauve flowers in May on a rather stiff plant. The main distinguishing feature is that the pouffe of mauve stamens dominates. 'Thundercloud' is a recommended clone of rich colouring.

June is, perhaps, dominated by **T. flavum** subsp. **glaucum** (2m/6ft), with pouffes of pale yellow flowers above boldly glaucous foliage. The tall, widely branching **T. rochebrunianum** (2.4m/8ft) flowers then, purple with fairly large but coarse flowers. Definitely lacking in refinement.

T. delavayi (syn. *T. dipterocarpum*) (2m/6ft) is a most elegant July-August-flowering border perennial, liking moisture, as they all do. The compound-pinnate leaves are finely divided. Mauve, open-bell-shaped flowers with cream stamens. Needs support. 'Album', the white-flowered version, is good and so is 'Hewitt's

Double', with very neat but small, fully double flowers. This species is a modest self-sower but easily raised from seed.

T. diffusiflorum (60cm/2ft) is difficult but a triumph when grown well. Likes Scotland. Particularly large mauve bells on an airy substrate.

Thermopsis

PAPILIONACEAE/LEGUMINOSAE

A North American genus with lupin-like flower spikes but yellow. The May-flowering *Thermopsis montana* (75cm/2½ft) has the disadvantage that it won't stay put, but runs. A pleasing, not unduly bright shade of yellow, as is *T. villosa* (60cm/2ft), which is nice behind *Polemonium* 'Lambrook Mauve', perhaps pepped up with the near-magenta *Geranium macrorhizum* 'Bevan's Variety'. This is clump-forming and may be synonymous with *T. caroliniana*.

Thladiantha

CUCURBITACEAE

Seeing that it belongs to the cucumber family, *Thladiantha dubia* is an amazingly hardy perennial, herbaceous climber. It overwinters and rapidly spreads by tuberous roots. Small, yellow cucumber-like flowers appear from July on and reach a peak in early September. They make quite a show. The only clone I have seen in cultivation is male, so no fruit is borne. The additional weight of fruits might well make the species unsuitable for a range of supporting plants.

Tiarella

SAXIFRAGACEAE

A North American genus growing in woodland and closely related to *Heuchera*, with similar heart-shaped leaves. *Tiarella cordifolia* (30cm/1ft), called foam flower, makes colonies by stolons. Spring-flowering with loose racemes of white blossom. *T. wherryi* (30cm/1ft) is not stoloniferous. Somewhat later-flowering, again with white racemes. They like damp, organically rich soils and will disappear if not given them.

Tigridia

IRIDACEAE

A Mexican genus. **Tigridia pavonia** (1m/3ft) makes a wonderfully flaunting contribution to the summer garden. Above iris-like leaves, a succession of upright blooms divided into threes, cupped in the middle, which is often heavily spotted, flanged with a horizontal limb on the outside, is borne through much of the summer, although each bloom lasts only for a day. Overwintering corms are usually lifted and stored at the end of the season. They must be kept safe from mice. In a hot, protected position, corms will often survive outside and build into clumps. Seed is another easy method of propagation. There is an amazing colour range in any mixture, from white with red spots, pink, red, orange, yellow, all variously spotted or self-coloured throughout.

Tradescantia

COMMELINACEAE

The spiderworts that we understood to be *Tradescantia virginiana*, are really of hybrid origin and should be recorded as named cultivars under **Tradescantia × andersoniana** (60cm/2ft). They are popular, very hardy and easy border plants from the USA. The leaves are strap-shaped and lanky. Each cluster of flowers is also framed by three, leaf-like, horizontal bracts, giving rise to the name Moses in the bulrushes. Moses is a 3-petalled flower in a range of colours, some quite strong, like purple or magenta, others white or washed-out mauves, but cultivars allow you to make your choice.

They are open in the morning but crumple up in the afternoon if the weather is at all warm. The flowering season, from early June, is protracted but the plants become increasingly sleazy in appearance. These are not vital border occupants.

Tricyrtis

CONVALLARIACEAE/LILIACEAE

A strangely compelling genus from the Far East. Autumn-flowering, *Tricyrtis* tie in well with hellebores as regards cultural requirements (leafy, moisture-retaining but well drained soil) and for being in season when hellebores are out. And the two genera appeal to the same sort of people.

Most have upright or arching stems, clothed with pointed ovate leaves in two ranks, cordate at the base. The flowers are borne in the axils of the uppermost series of leaves. They usually face upwards, are in muted colours – subfusc mauves, yellows, off-white, purplish – and they are frequently spotted a darker purple. Toad lily is a name in common usage but does not help to sell the plants to toad-haters.

Commonest and easiest to grow is one or other form of **T. formosana** (75cm/2½ft), under whose umbrella are included those known as *T. stolonifera*, or Stolonifera group. The flowers are mauve-purple with darker spots. The rootstock is mildly stoloniferous and gradually builds into a colony. A long flowering season and nice to pick.

Very different from this type of tricyrtis, are **T. macrantha** and its subspecies **macranthopsis** (30cm/1ft). In these the drooping, quite strong yellow flowers are between a tube and a bell. Very exciting but having a death wish. If you want a challenge, here it is; if not, steer clear.

Trillium

Trilliaceae/Liliaceae

An almost exclusively North American, woodland genus, with fleshy, somewhat bulbous roots. All like deep woodland soil, so, simple as this sounds, it may take a bit of concentration to provide them with it in the average garden. They do not enjoy a lot of competition from neighbours.

The plants are distinctive in appearance, a more or less elongated stem supporting, first, three leaves, then the flowering parts, also in threes. The leaves are often beautifully marbled, as in **Trillium sessile** (30cm/1ft), whose flowers, with vertically pointing segments, are maroon red. The flowering time of trilliums varies, according to locality.

T. erectum (up to 1½ft) has spreading perianth segments, as have most of the genus. The colouring most often seen in Britain is maroon red, but this varies considerably in the wild. At the right season, say in early May, you are, in any American wood, likely to find two or three species, and they are often quite modestly green in flower.

T. grandiflorum (30cm/1ft or more) shows up at a distance on account of its white flowers. They fade to pale pink. The double-flowered kinds make a great display but are not easily come by.

A trillium that particularly struck me where there was a nice large patch of it in a hill garden in Victoria, Australia, was **T. luteum** (15cm/6in), with yellow flowers and marbled leaves.

Triteleia

ALLIACEAE/LILIACEAE

While *Triteleia uniflora* has been moved to *Ipheion*, *Brodiaea laxa* is now **T. laxa** (23cm/9in). Of the bulbs we plant in autumn, this must be one of the latest in flower, June–July. In a good strain the colouring is a quite intense shade of blue, in a trumpet-shaped flower. The flowers are borne in umbels. The bulbs increase quite quickly.

I find that this species flourishes in poor meadow conditions, where its colouring, quite unusual at that time of the year, is most welcome. Also good in borders, though the leaves have died off by the time the flowers open. I liked them with apricot-coloured pansies.

Trollius

RANUNCULACEAE

A genus closely akin to the buttercups. All are moisture-loving and flower spring to early summer. They are yellow-flowered, verging on orange in one direction, and on cream to white (in a few alpines) in the other. Always fresh and exciting to find in the wild.

The globe flower, **Trollius europeus** (30cm/1ft) typifies many trollius in having several rows of petals, which gives a double appearance. This is a common species in the north, on basic soils. Crossed with a couple of other species, it has given rise to a number of cultivars under the umbrella of **T. × cultorum**. In a border context, their one drawback tends to be a short flowering season.

A little later than most, we have **T. chinensis** (60cm/2ft), more familiar as **T. ledebourii**. 'Golden Queen' is the winner here. It is true orange. The central petals are spiky and form a crown. **T. yunnanensis** (1m/3ft) has a simple, single yellow flower of great charm and is happiest in Scotland as is the 15cm/6in **T. acaulis**.

Tropaeolum

TROPAEOLACEAE

A mostly southern South American genus of climbing or trailing herbs. The nasturtium, **Tropaeolum majus**, although generally treated as an annual to be lost in the first autumn frost, is actually perennial and needs to be propagated and overwintered from cuttings in clones, notably the double-flowered, non-seeding kinds, which cannot be elsehow reproduced. 'Hermine Grashof', makes neat double scarlet rosettes; 'Margaret Long' is double orange. The nasturtiums' main problems are from attacks by Large White butterfly larvae and by black aphids. Spray control often disagrees with the plant as well as the pest.

3   Many species grow in winter and aestivate in the hot months. **T. tricolorum** is one such and only occasionally gets away with it if left permanently out, though it can near a protecting wall. Generally best as a display pot plant, flowering March to May. Showy, with red, black and yellow in each pixie-hood flower. Tubers are freely produced.

T. polyphyllum is a beautiful trailing species, hardy and with glaucous foliage setting off yellow flowers in June. Needs perfect drainage, as on and in a retaining wall, but plenty of moisture when growing. Therefore easiest in Scotland, where also the famous **T. speciosum** predominates – a summer-flowering species with rich crimson red flowers (the seeds are blue). Often grown among rhododendrons and looks marvellous through a dark yew hedge. Its tubers are thin and vagrant, so it is not an easy species to market. Generally prefers acid soil but moisture is the main controlling factor.

T. tuberosum is generally grown against a wall. It is fairly but not dependably hardy and some tubers should be stored at the end of its season, which is generally at its peak in October. But there are early-flowering strains, from July on, notably 'Ken Aslet'. The narrow trumpet flowers are orange.

Tulbaghia

ALLIACEAE/LILIACEAE

A South African genus of which the showiest and most easily grown species for the garden is **Tulbaghia violacea** (38cm/15in). A clumpy plant, in the same way as chives, with narrow strap-leaves. The flowers, in umbels on naked scapes, are tubular, opening into rich mauve stars at the mouth. A long summer and autumn flowering season, albeit a trifle sparse at any one moment. Can often be treated as hardy, but some stock should be lifted in autumn for safety. The white-striped 'Silver Lace' (30cm/1ft) is a pretty thing but weaker-growing and less hardy.

Tulipa

LILIACEAE

Tulips are the essence of spring at its peak. In mood, they resemble crocuses – wayward and sulky in dim weather but gloriously expansive when touched by sunlight. Although they can be regimented in spring bedding to grand effect, their stems respond (unlike those of narcissi) to the forces of gravity, taking on sinuous curves as soon as placed in an oblique or horizontal position. They will turn to face upwards again.

This makes them tricky to arrange as a cut flower, but by no means impossible. On the contrary; they are wonderful cut flowers. If they turn the way you don't want them to face, on the second day twist their stems around to obey your intention, and they will not repeat their trick.

While narcissi are favourites with amateur breeders, and there is always a large section devoted to them in competitions at flower shows, tulips are little regarded (except around Wakefield, in Yorkshire, where they have their own show rules and traditions). There might not be more than a hundred blooms at an RHS spring show, in Westminster. And yet the tulip is tremendously susceptible to cross-breeding and to fresh development, with exciting prospects for anyone with the time and patience to experiment. The time factor is the snag. From an initial cross, it will take around nine years to produce and test a new cultivar of merit.

Like other florists' flowers, tulips are subject to fashion. Turkey, in the 16th and 17th centuries, saw a great flowering of tulips in art, particularly ceramics. Times have changed. The only cultivated tulips I saw there a few years ago were a present from Holland, in the centre of Istanbul. The tulipomania bubble in the Netherlands, in the 17th century was more of a gamble and an investment than a testimony of love for the flower, but the Dutch flower paintings, with all those beautiful striped Rembrandt tulips, are witness to a deep artistic appreciation and the Dutch do still hold fascinating collections of old tulips that were once in vogue.

Tulips in Holland are nowadays chiefly grown for the export market, traditionally by Roman Catholic families, many of which have emigrated to the Spalding area of Lincolnshire in England. Like hyacinths, they are accorded land with a high water table. Flower buds are removed in order to build up a large bulb and the result in many instances, especially with round-petalled, square-shouldered tulips, is an out-size, clumsy bloom. After a couple of years in the garden, however, their figures will fine down and may become tolerable, although the ordinary man's predilection for juxtaposing hard red with hard yellow tulips, presents this flower in its worst light.

The bane of the tulip market is unacknowledged substitution. In the year that I am writing, four out of the ten cultivars that I ordered have been a different tulip, and nothing admitted to that effect. The middle-man from whom you purchase makes his own purchases from, perhaps, half a dozen wholesalers. Accidents will happen, as we all know, but as a rule, tulips sold wrongly named have quite deliberately been substituted because stocks of the desired cultivar have run out but the merchant does not wish to lose his sale. Most often, another of the same colouring and flower type will be sold, and most of the time the customer either doesn't notice or can't be bothered to complain. Only greater vigilance and readiness to come back to the salesman, on the part of the customer, would remedy this situation. But accountability is often hard to trace.

Tulips, in Britain, are as popular for spring bedding as ever, and the climate suits them. In Australia and much of the USA, they are imported from the Netherlands and planted for a single display, tending not to be perennial. In areas of deep winter frost, deep planting is necessary.

The conditions that I can offer them in my south of England garden suit many tulips ideally, and they persist, in borders where they are undisturbed, indefinitely. These old colonies are a particular joy, because the bulbs, and hence the flowers they produce, are of differing heights and sizes, which makes for a relaxed appearance that is wholly suited to mixed border conditions.

Although tulips look wonderful in a meadow setting, I have yet to meet an example where they did not die out, after a while, so that topping-up on an annual basis is necessary.

Tulips for Bedding

6 For bedding out, tulips are generally underplanted or interplanted with a carpeter. Among the most popular are polyanthus primroses (which, for telling effect, should be of a single colour strain); *Bellis perennis* – double forms of the common daisy, again most effective if in single colour strains, red, pink or white, of which those with neat,

quilled rays are generally to be preferred; *Myosotis* – forget-me-nots, traditionally blue, but pink or white seed strains make pleasing alternatives; pansies, which offer a wide range of possibilities, though complete mixtures are unsatisfactory, because confusing to the eye.

There are less usual alternatives with which to experiment, such as bronze fennel seedlings, for their feathery leaves; doronicums, with yellow daisies at about the same height as the tulips (a mauve tulip goes well with these); *Primula denticulata*, the drumstick primula, generally mauve; *Erysimum linifolium*, from seed, is good but May-flowering, so its mauve flowers should be combined with a late tulip, like the orange 'Dillenburg'.

The carpeter is planted first; the bulbs then all set out at not less than 15cm/6in intervals. But first they should be rolled, in a plastic bag, with a tablespoon of fungicide powder, which will leave a coating over the bulb and protect it from tulip fire disease. Unless very severe winters dictate otherwise, shallow planting, no more than 5cm/2in deep, is normal and can be achieved at the approximate rate of one bulb every four seconds!

Provided they have been kept cool, in the run-up, and have not sprouted unduly, tulips can be planted quite late, November being normal, but into the new year, if planting conditions are not too sticky or frozen by then. I have even got away with planting in March, though there will be some failures, at so late a date.

After flowering, room will have to be made for the summer follow-on, while the tulips are still green and growing. It is pointless, because ineffective, to heel them into a trench to finish off growing, as is sometimes advocated. Lift and knock off the soil; then lay out on racks in a cool, airy shed. The nourishment still in stems and foliage will there be naturally withdrawn into the bulb. When all is sere, pull off the withered remains. You can either sort over the bulbs at this stage or before planting in the autumn, the idea being to separate those you think likely to flower in the next year, from those that are too small to do so. The former should be hung up (labelled) in string net bags from a cross beam or horizontal pole, away from the reach of mice, again in the cool, airy shed. The tiddlers can be similarly treated with a view to lining them out, in the autumn, to grow on for a year, at the end of which you will have many more flowering-sized bulbs. Alternatively, throw them away (shame on you).

It is worth remarking that, after flowering, a tulip bulb disintegrates entirely but, in doing so, re-forms into two or three new bulbs, the largest usually of flowering size, the rest, probably not.

Tulips as Border Perennials

A fairly stiff, well nourished soil is conducive to the persistence of most hybrid tulips as border perennials so that, left undisturbed, they will remain with you for many decades. They will build into clumps, in which some of the units will produce the single, broad leaf of the bulbs that will not flower in the current season, but probably will in the next; while others will flower this year. There tend to be shy-flowering and free-flowering years.

Weather plays a part in this. A cold, wet spring favours botrytis, causing tulip fire disease, which first spots and then rots petals, stems and foliage. The fallen spores will then attack the bulbs and will remain in the soil for further infections. Spray the growing plants with a protective fungicide if the trouble seems likely.

There are large, empty areas in borders, in April, largely occupied by plants that have not yet filled in their allotted space. Tulips can be planted into these gaps. Japanese anemones and sea hollies, like *Eryngium* × *oliverianum*, make very suitable hosts. We grow tulips among lupins, whose young foliage makes an excellent background, but this is, in fact, a form of bedding out, the lupins being discarded after they have flowered, and the tulip bulbs harvested, already dormant.

Clumps of *Inula magnifica* within a group can be spaced 1m/3ft apart, allowing ample scope for tulip inter-planting. The inula expands its young foliage quite slowly and late.

Among deciduous shrubs, whose lowest branches have been removed, is another suitable, permanent position. Such as summer-flowering tamarisk, *Tamarix ramosissima*, and a range of hydrangeas.

Types of Tulip

The classification of tulips is for our own convenience, but divisions are often more imagined than real, as tulips hybridise freely and are notoriously nonconformist. Not infrequently we change the rules.

The flowering season of tulips stretches from March to May, exact dates varying greatly in any year. It should be borne in mind that early-flowering tulips, unless given abnormal protection, are likely to be smashed to bits almost as soon as open, especially if their blooms are large. We must have some of them, but our main concentrations should be mid- and late-season.

Early-Flowering: Single and Double
Most of these are short-stemmed (30-38cm/12-15in), which is just as well for them.

28

They are suitable for pot and trough cultivation in sheltered places (though what might seem to be sheltered, close to a building, may be subject to nasty turbulence).

Many are amazingly sweet-scented. 'Bellona', a rich yellow single, is excellent (but I have twice been supplied the wrong thing). Double pink 'Peach Blossom' is another and 'Murillo' (orange), together with the many named sports to which it has given rise.

'Couleur Cardinal' is a rich, deep red single with a hint of pink on the outer segments, the leaves deeply glaucous. Dusky orange 'Princess Irene' is another early single that should not be missed.

Mid-Season: Triumph tulips and Darwin hybrids. Height 45cm/1½ft.
Triumph tulips are mainly used by parks and public gardens for bedding out.

Darwin hybrids are outsize – the largest of the large. That may sound dire but some are beautiful and exciting. 'Jewel of Spring' has yellow blooms with a fine line of red around the margin. When opened wide, it is an enormous bowl, with a dark, murky green centre. 'Red Matador' is among my most persistent tulips, after 25 years; strong red but with a pinkish flush on the outside and a dark green centre.

Single Late-Flowering (inc. former Cottage and Darwin tulips) 45-60cm/1½-2ft
This is an omnibus class. It includes 'Bleu Aimable', soft lilac with a blue centre; 'Greuze', deep purple with a smallish flower, probably surpassed by the silky purple 'Recreado'. These combine astonishingly well with the lily-flowered 'Queen of Sheba'. 'Dillenburg' – soft orange flushed pink – is my favourite latest tulip. 'Mrs John T. Scheepers', with long, egg-shaped yellow blooms, would formerly have been classified a cottage tulip. It stands out well, in my garden, against the purple foliage of a yellow loosestrife, *Lysimachia ciliata* 'Firecracker', a perennial which later takes over with its own yellow blossom, so there is no need to disturb the tulip.

'Halcro' has a similarly long bloom; red, with a pink flush – an invaluable late tulip. Demure 'Shirley' is white with a mauve rim and a blue centre, but generally outclassed by the similar, yet bolder 'Magier'.

The multi-flowered 'Georgette' (yellow, slowly changing to light orange) and 'Red Georgette' are placed in this category. From large bulbs, they bear one main, central bloom and, from side-branches, a couple of slightly later-flowering subsidiaries. Small bulbs will manage only one bloom. These are valuable bedders, with a long season.

Late-Flowering: Lily-Flowered — 60cm/2ft

This is the section of which I grow most varieties as they are invariably elegant, with markedly pointed segments, flared outwards. In 'West Point', which is a strong shade of yellow, the petals are drawn to fine points and this is splendidly highlighted by a background of blue forget-me-nots.

'Aladdin' is fine-pointed but a weak bronze with an uninteresting, pale centre. Utterly outclassed by 'Queen of Sheba' — rich bronzy-orange with a yellow margin and a sinister, dark greenish centre. Amazingly long-flowering, the blooms eventually open wide and stay that way.

Pink is apt to be a difficult colour to get right, but 'China Pink' is the best in this category and a universal favourite. Good underplanted with pink pomponette *Bellis*. And the best white tulip, in my estimation, is 'White Triumphator', though I have a feeling that stock is becoming weaker. Were it to become infected by virus disease, there would be no ready way to recognise the condition.

'Red Shine' is an excellent tall, late, soft red, toning well with the purple foliage of ornamental rhubarb, *Rheum palmatum* 'Atrosanguineum', or the young, orbicular leaves of *Ligularia dentata* 'Desdemona'. 'Dyanito' is brilliant scarlet; I like it near to the acid yellow-greens of *Euphorbia polychroma* and *E. × martinii*, with the softer orange lily-flowered 'Ballerina' in the same company.

Late-flowering: Parrot, 38-45cm/15-18in.

Parrots are my second most favourite class, but they seem to me to fall into two sections. All have quite deeply slashed petal margins, but what I would call the pseudo-parrots stand stiffly upright. Such are 'Blue Parrot', 'Black Parrot' and the abominable, dumpy 'White Parrot'.

True Parrots are the sexiest of tulips. Their stems curve and the young blooms are broadly streaked bright green. They include amazing colour contrasts. 'Texas Gold' and 'Texas Flame' are among the latest-flowering, the former starting yellow all through (with green thoughts early on), but developing orange at the margins, particularly; the latter, boldly flamed in scarlet and bright yellow — excellent scattered among blue forget-me-nots. 'Orange Favourite' is just about the prettiest orange tulip, its colouring subdued by a pink outer flush.

Other good Parrots would include 'Estella Rijnveld' — white, flamed red, and 'Flaming Parrot' — pale yellow and rosy red.

Late-Flowering: Fringed, Viridiflora, Late Double, 45cm/1½ft.

In Fringed tulips, the petal margins, albeit coloured, are like frost crystals. 'Fancy

Frills' sounds ghastly, but reminds me of the pink and white coconut icing that I loved as a child.

Viridiflora tulips have a lot of green in them, concentrated in a broad band along the centre of the outer segments. Some are good, some not. 'Greenland', pink and green, is a dull-shaped flower. 'Hollywood' is wonderfully sinister at its best, deepest red with a great deal of metallic green. But there is often so much of this that the **50** bloom never properly emerges from being a bud. Best is 'Spring Green' – gracefully shaped, with outwardly flared segments, these being white with a hint of green, and having a broad, central green bar. It goes tastefully with the green racemes of *Tellima grandiflora*, and the lime green bracts of *Smyrnium perfoliatum*, both flowering at the same time.

Late Double tulips, sometimes called Peony-flowered, are wonderful artefacts, the double white 'Mount Tecoma' especially good for picking, but their heads are so heavy that the slightest shower – even a heavy dew – will snap them off.

Broken Tulips

This is not a class but a condition brought on through the bulb being infected by virus disease, which can also be transmitted to lilies. Although it has a weakening effect, tulips can live with it and it creates very beautiful striped and flamed effects, always with the yellow or white basic colouring exposed that all tulips possess, although it is normally superimposed by some other colour.

These tulips were much prized, of old. Nowadays EC rules no longer allow them to be marketed, but they constantly turn up in the gardens of anyone who grows tulips for more than one year – in some varieties more than others (I have never seen a broken 'Red Matador' tulip).

These virus-infected tulips should not be confused with cultivars that are bicoloured by design – 'Flaming Parrot' for instance – and may not be infected at all.

Species and their Hybrids: Kaufmanniana

The demure, March-flowering **Tulipa kaufmanniana** (23cm/9in) is a frail little thing with long, pointed segments, dusky orange on the outside, the flower scarcely showing at all until opened out by sun. It then earns the affectionate name of waterlily tulip. It is pale yellow within. I find it far too prone to slug damage to be able to survive in my garden. But it is an important parent of many charming hybrids.

Species and their Hybrids: Fosteriana, 30cm/1ft

The flaming red **T. fosteriana**, best known in the clone 'Madame Lefeber' (or 'Red Emperor'), has a vast acreage of leaf and petal, totally unsuited to its early flowering season. The vermilion colouring and the flower shape are far from subtle. However, it has given rise to many wonderful large-flowered hybrids, all of them early-flowering. These include the Darwin Hybrids.

'Orange Emperor' is a soft shade of orange, with attractive green along the outer midribs of the young blooms. 'Purissima' (or 'White Emperor') has large, glaucous foliage supporting large, well-shaped blooms, cream at first, becoming white. I underplant it with F^1 'Crescendo Red' polyanthus, which are themselves early-flowering. 'Yellow Purissima' is similar apart from its soft yellow colouring; I like that.

Species and their Hybrids: Greigii, 30cm/1ft

The salient feature, here, is the longitudinal, chocolate striping along the leaves, but these will also be found in other classes where **T. greigii** has played a part in their parentage. Some Greigii's, like 'Pinocchio' and 'Red Riding Hood', are well-balanced and pleasing. Others, like the large-flowered, orange 'Compostella', are coarse and ill-balanced, the flower gross on a short stem.

Species: Miscellaneous

There are many delightful tulip species, although often tricky in cultivation for one reason or another. **T. sylvestris** (30cm/1ft), for instance, although naturalised and possibly a British native, is shy-flowering. It has a stoloniferous habit and will run happily about in meadow turf, but maybe never a flower in years. On the other hand I have heard of a case where it was allowed to run along paving cracks and flowered well. Sometimes this has to do with the strain acquired, sometimes with the amount of summer baking it receives. The flowers are yellow and sweetly scented.

I have had the same experience with the tawny red **T. orphanidea** (15cm/6in). It is still in my orchard turf but has given me two blooms in 60 years. **T. saxatilis** (15cm/6in), pink with a yellow base, is also apt to be shy. The red **T. linifolia** (10cm/4in), with narrow, keeled leaves, flowers well enough but is frail and liable to slug destruction, under ordinary border conditions. I have not grown the exquisite deep-pink-and-white-striped lady tulip, **T. clusiana** (30cm/1ft), but it is reputedly not easy to please.

T. eichleri (38cm/15in) is as easy as any garden hybrid and most rewarding. Fairly early-flowering, its glaucous leaves go well in an interplanting with border carnations and the crimson flowers with pointed segments are in handsome contrast. The centre of the flower is black, edged yellow.

T. batalinii 'Bright Gem' (10cm/4in), has sizeable buff-yellow blooms, and is charming at a border's margin, where it copes well. Some of the multi-headed species, like the green-and-yellow-striped *T. tarda* (10cm/4in) and *T. urumiensis* (10cm/4in), are easy if not exactly showy. By contrast, *T. praestans* 'Fusilier' (23cm/9in) is a knock-out, brilliant scarlet and just what we need to cheer us in its early season. Plant it among a carpet of magenta Primula 'Wanda' (5cm/2in) and see how you like it. I hope you do.

Finally, the latest-flowering tulip of all, *T. sprengeri* (45cm/1½ft). It is stoloniferous and awkward to market; therefore expensive. But once established, it not only spreads vegetatively but also, freely, by self-sowing. It is a charming accompaniment to bearded irises. The bud is buff on the outside, opening to a pointed bloom that is pure red. A lovely thing, albeit with a short flowering season.

Typha

TYPHACEAE

An aquatic genus, growing in moderately shallow water. The brown, club-like inflorescence of densely packed female flowers in *Typha latifolia* (2m/6ft), makes it popular with children and dried-flower arrangers. This is the reed mace, popularly known as bulrush. It spreads too rapidly, by means of its rhizomes, to be tolerated in polite ponds. *T. angustifolia* (1.5m/5ft), is more elegant, with narrower leaves and club-heads, but is still invasive and hard to control. The only controllable species is *T. minima* (60cm/2ft), which is indeed on a mini-scale, with short clubs. Not as exciting as the others.

U

Uvularia

CONVALLARIACEAE/LILIACEAE

5 This is a hardy, eastern North American genus of damp, deciduous woodlands and humus-rich soil. Best for garden purposes, because the showiest, is ***Uvularia grandiflora*** (38cm/15in), a fresh-looking, spring-flowering plant with smooth, perfoliate leaves and drooping clusters of narrow bells, the segments drawn to points, the colour a cheerful shade of yellow. In the wild, it will be found with ***U. sessilifolia***, with long, narrow, pale green flowers; also with *Trillium grandiflorum*, erythroniums, several species of *Osmunda* and many other delightful woodlanders.

V

Valeriana

VALERIANACEAE

Valeriana officinalis (1m/3ft) was so popular a herb for many medicinal uses in the Middle Ages, that it earned the name of all-heal. Bruised, the plant emits a strong odour, exceedingly attractive to cats and rats. Medicinally, it is the roots and rhizomes which are used. Often found in marshy places, in the wild. The corymbs of white or pale mauve flowers rise, June onwards, above a fairly sparsely clothed stem with pinnate leaves.

More often seen in gardens is ***V. phu*** 'Aurea' (1m/3ft), a similar plant but with basal leaves which, in March, are bright lime yellow. Being quite low at that time, their colour contrasts well with interplanted clumps of blue *Scilla bifolia*.

Vancouveria

Berberidaceae

Poor relations, from North America, of epimedium, and requiring the same conditions. Good in shade. ***Vancouveria hexandra*** (60cm/2ft) Has tiny white flowers, modestly looking down at the ground. Not worth while.

Veratrum

Melianthiaceae/Liliaceae

A hardy genus of tough-rooted, deciduous perennials, which enjoy moist leaf-soil and are happiest in partial shade, though not too particular. Their leaves, rounded and often heavily pleated, especially when young, are a particular asset. The inflorescence is a stately panicle of star-shaped flowers, up to 2m/6ft tall. Only three species are well-known in gardens.

A colony of any well-grown veratrum species, has me standing agape before it. Not so Reginald Farrer. 'These vast-foliaged portents are the curse of the cows in all the high meadows of the Alps'. He then compares its visual and toxic properties with those of *Gentiana lutea*. Next we have '… its stars of blossom which, in every form and every species, are in varying degrees of unmitigated dinginess, greenish, yellowish, or of a grubby brownish-black, which do not atone for the venomousness of all the plant, nor lead us to be tempted (even by its generous and statuesque port), to pine for Veratrum in the garden…'

Given the general enthusiasm that has developed of recent years for plants of good structure (largely, I believe, promoted by the flower arranging movement), veratrums would be popular garden plants were it not for the unavoidable slowness of their propagation. They do build into clumps and they can be divided, but they do not enjoy the experience (which can anyway only rarely be practised). Recovery is slow.

Seed is the only practical method and seed is generously ripened. But, from the time of sowing, it takes at least five years to produce a strong, saleable plant. The cost of this to the nurseryman is such as few customers are prepared to meet. It is ironic, that whereas they are prepared to pay the earth for a desirable shrub, herbaceous plants are seen as a lower form of life, because of their general reputation for being easily divided and swapped between friends. 'Don't buy that', one customer will say to another; 'I can give you masses of it'. When you buy a veratrum, treat it as an investment and expect to wait a while before it flowers for the first time.

Veratrum viride is the first to flower, in June or even earlier. The flowers are of a particularly luminous shade of almost fluorescent green. They show up to perfection against purple foliage, for instance of a cotinus or of Pissard's Plum (*Prunus cerasifera* 'Pissardii').

V. nigrum is early on the move in spring, with unbearably pristine bouquets of pale green, pleated foliage. Alas that they are a particular delicacy with slugs. Follows, in July, wide-angled candelabra wherein every branch is lined with deep maroon stars. These combine well, in dappled shade, with rich orange lilies, such as *Lilium pardalinum*. I have to admit, however, that in flower, this veratrum is too dark to be really effective.

59 Not so **V. album**, which is the sturdiest of the three. Its leaves (again, caviar to slugs) do not unfurl till May and it is then quite a long while before you can tell whether the shoot will flower or be blind. Blindness is a very common condition in this species – as common in the wild as in our gardens. Woods were full of it when I was in the Carpathians, one year, but I saw only two flowering plants. Obviously, it must at times flower freely to seed around so freely, but I had happened on an off-year. The richer soil conditions that we can provide in our gardens mitigates the frequency of this disappointment.

The white stars of *V. album* stand out well, in July, at a distance, combining nicely with the lavender bells or funnels of a hosta such as *H. ventricosa* or 'Tall Boy'. Later, the veratrum fades to green, but never becomes dowdy. A similar, white-flowered species that I admired in Washington state, in the Pacific North-west of the USA, was **V. californicum**. It was growing and flowering abundantly in large patches along the roadside when I was a passenger being driven by the typical man-at-the-wheel.

I begged to be allowed to stop, look and photograph. 'Not now', I was told, 'there'll be plenty more further on'. So there were, but we were climbing and they were only in bud. 'We'll stop on the way home', I was assured. By then, it was dark.

Verbascum

SCROPHULARIACEAE

A tremendously complex and naturally hybridising genus, most of whose species are biennial, providing some excellent garden material. **Verbascum dumulosum** (30cm/1ft) and a few others like 'Letitia' (30cm/1ft) are shrubby, requiring a baking position and perfect drainage. Grey, felted leaves and a mass of short, yellow flower spikes in early summer.

One of the most reliably perennial species is **V. chaixii** (1.5m/5ft). It has dull, dark green leaves but spikes of smallish yellow flowers with the central contrast of purple stamens. 'Album' has the same centre but white petals. Grown from seed, it will also produce a percentage of pale yellow-flowered plants. Persistent and easily propagated from root cuttings, as are the other perennial types.

V. phoeniceum (1m/3ft) has purple flowers, also mauve, white and intermediate shades. Charming and nice with *Viola cornuta* hybrids in May-June. Short-lived. This is one parent of the Cotswold series, which are handsome, June-flowering border perennials, some 1m/3ft tall. They are quite large-flowered and attractively coloured. 'Gainsborough' and 'Pink Domino' are two of the best. Root cuttings ensure continuity of stock.

Verbena

VERBENACEAE

Most verbenas are American in origin, especially South American, and many are tender, but excellent for bedding out. Those with cultivar names are the chief bedders and are sometimes loosely assembled as **Verbena × hybrida**. They naturally make loose mats with tillering side-shoots, and these are the best for covering the ground. Plant breeders, however, have selected seed strains of compact habit, which need to be planted much closer together. Although often treated as annuals, these verbenas, whenever a particular colour takes your fancy, can easily be maintained from autumn-struck cuttings overwintered under frost-free glass.

The flowers are borne in whorled heads and they tend to crumple after heavy rain, taking some time, like petunias, to recover their poise. In many, though never in the pure reds, the flowers are sweetly scented on the air, notably in 'Loveliness' (mauve), 'La France' (mauve), 'Lawrence Johnston' (rosy red) and 'Silver Anne', which is pink, not silver. Plants of certain varieties, notably 'Homestead Purple', often survive the winter and will then flower early in the summer but will lack the staying power of young plants, which are generally the best all-round performers.

One of the most popular parks bedding ingredients is ***V. rigida*** (38cm/15in) (syn. *V. venosa*), which has small, corymbose heads in brilliant purple. It spreads by underground rhizomes and may survive the winter but is better started again from seed. Germination from bought seed is often patchy and uncertain so it is better if you can save your own and sow in early March. The politely shaded ice-mauve strain 'Polaris' better suits those who are nervous of bright colours.

A brilliant, hard pink (odourless) mat-former, 'Sissinghurst' has its uses but is rather tiring. ***V. corymbosa*** (30cm/1ft) with lavender flowers, is hardy, but is a great traveller and tends not to be concentrated enough to make a reliable show. Best from young stock.

11, 14, 54 ***V. bonariensis*** (probably *V. patagonica*, correctly) (2m/6ft), is a stemmy plant with a succession of densely packed heads of small, light purple flowers and a protracted late summer to autumn season. Where seed is ripened, it self-sows abundantly and is a weed of cultivations in warm countries. A short-lived perennial. ***V. peruviana*** is a small perennial of creeping habit with brilliant, pure red flowers. Good in a trough, as is the mauve ***V. tenuisecta***.

The hardy, North American ***V. hastata*** (1.2m/4ft), has multiple flower spikes, mauve but better in the pink 'Rosea'. That is short-lived but self-sows.

Vernonia

ASTERACEAE/COMPOSITAE

A hardy North American genus, which they call ironweed. It is autumn-flowering and so late, in our climate, as to be almost too late. ***Vernonia crinita*** (2m/6ft) is the best known species, flowering in October and a rich shade of purple. Needs moist soil but sun to bring out the colour.

Veronica

SCROPHULARIACEAE

Commonly known as speedwell, *Veronica* includes a number of familiar weeds, the worst of which is **V. filiformis**, a creeping perennial with beguilingly innocent-looking pale blue flowers in spring. It quickly spreads across lawns and into borders and is hard to eradicate.

V. peduncularis 'Georgia Blue' (15cm/6in) (from the Caucasus) makes loose mats and is covered with deep flowers in April-May. Contrasts well with the miniature *Narcissus* 'Hawera'. In May comes **V. austriaca** subsp. **teucrium**, of which 'Crater Lake Blue' (30cm/1ft) is a really clear, intense shade. But its flowering period is brief. **V. prostrata** is rather similar as to inflorescence and flower colour but is a ground- or rock-hugger.

At the same time, **V. gentianoides**, which makes rosettes of leaves at ground level, but rises with its pale blue racemes to nearly 30cm/1ft. Briefly very charming as is 'Variegata', similar but with white leaf variegation.

V. spicata, with its grey-leaved subspecies *incana* (30cm/1ft), also makes loose mats, the spikes of flowers, over quite a long summer season, being long and densely packed. Blue is the basic colour but there are many named cultivars, including clear pinks.

V. longifolia (1m/3ft) is midsummer-flowering, never pure blue but a sound working perennial, apt to self-seed rather freely if not dead-headed.

Veronicastrum

SCROPHULARIACEAE

Veronicastrum virginicum (1m/3ft) is an American prairie perennial which establishes well in Britain under meadow conditions, flowering in late summer. Whorls of lance leaves, surmounted by branching spikes of small white veronica flowers. I have never seen a blue, but you can order *album* to be certain that white is what you get. This species is boldly upright and has presence.

Viola

VIOLACEAE

A complex genus of wide distribution. Any gardener will readily distinguish a violet from a viola, pansy and all the rest (although botanical differences are nice). Start with violets.

The native, spring-flowering scented violet is **Viola odorata**. It likes a semi-shaded position and is an excellent filler in borders, beneath deciduous shrubs, flowering before they come into leaf, and, like primroses, not resenting fairly heavy shade later on. Typically violet-coloured, there are many strains. 'Alba' is pure white, often seen in colonies on its own in the wild. There are some rich pink shades, the name 'Coeur d'Alsace' being given to one of them, but as they are often raised from seed, the name has little significance. The slightly later-flowering apricot-coloured violet should be called 'Sulphurea'.

The odourless violet that we most often find in woodland in April is **V. riviniana**. That, too, is a good border filler and nice poking out of hedge bottoms. It will also colonise in lawns where herbicides are not used. The Purpurea group, with purple leaves, has often been misnamed *V. labradorica*. It generally comes fairly true from seed.

The deciduous **V. septentrionalis**, from eastern North America, flowers, in 'Alba', before its young leaves have taken over and can make a great show with quite large white flowers pencilled purple at the centre. Will seed itself among other perennials. It has quite thick rhizomes.

V. hederacea is Australian and none too hardy, but can be bedded out for the summer, when it flowers. Called, by Lloyd, the chinless wonder, it has a receding lower petal. Coloured white shading to bluish at the centre. Quickly makes a low mat.

When we come to the so-called violas, violettas and pansies, I would be at a loss to sort t'other from which, since they seem to have distinctions without a difference. Violas do particularly well in the cooler climate of the north, being spectacular in Scottish gardens in June. The damp atmosphere suits them and they are there far less liable to go down to virus diseases than in the south.

V. cornuta is distinctive on account of its horned spur and of the gaps between its petals. It is one of the most persistent border plants, though all violas benefit from quite frequent splitting (or renewal from cuttings) and replanting. This one has a rich violet form which does not set seed. The Alba group are fertile and can be raised true from seed if segregated from coloured forms. The leaves are bright green, the flowers pure white. At their best in May, they are often attacked by aphids in

June but are anyway best cut to the ground then, so that their second flowering in autumn is on rejuvenated stock. Like many pansies and violas, they are adept at hoisting themselves through nearby, slightly taller plants, as do many cranesbills, thereby creating a tapestry effect.

There are many old favourites still current, such as the mauve 'Maggie Mott', the greeny-bronze 'Irish Molly', and 'Jackanapes', with violently contrasting bronze-purple standards against the remaining yellow.

A tiny-flowered pansy like 'Bowles's Black' is annual, but will, in an open position, maintain itself by self-sowing.

Excellent breeding work on violas, for winter or spring flowering in beds, window-boxes and other containers, has lately been done (with best results often emanating from Japan). These are sown in July but need cool conditions for germination. They flower from autumn till June, often without a break.

Pansies are generally larger-flowered, and have 'faces', rather than a plain bloom. The larger the flower, the fewer of them. Furthermore, a large flower is often unable to retain its shape without folding at the corners.

Pansies used for bedding may be short-lived perennials, but are usually treated as annual or biennial. As biennials is best, since their main flowering will then be in cool weather, which is what suits their metabolism. Sow in July for a spring display. Spring sowings will flower in summer, but there are many more suitable bedders for that season. Pansies detest heat and drought.

Waldsteinia

ROSACEAE

William Robinson's crushing dismissal tells us that 'not one (*Waldsteinia*) is ornamental enough for border culture' and recommends dry bank sitings. **Waldsteinia ternata** is an obliging, prostrate, evergreen ground-coverer with bright yellow, potentilla-like flowers in spring, but only at the margins of a colony. Established areas cease to flower.

Woodwardia

BLECHNACEAE/POLYPODIACEAE

A genus of magnificent, evergreen herbaceous ferns. They are of a drooping, decumbent habit, wide-spreading and rooting from a bulbil situated at the tip of each frond. Best known is **Woodwardia radicans** (30cm/1ft), which has a wide spread of 1.5m/5ft or more. Usually seen as a pot plant, it is often hardy if grown in a sheltered, wind-free spot. **W. fimbriata,** from western North America, extends quite far north and can sustain a modicum of frost. Luxuriant foliage, the pinnae drooping from either side of the rachis.

Yucca

AGAVACEAE

Natives of the warmer parts of North America. Some are woody, some spring from ground level, most are perennial but some are monocarpic. **Yucca whipplei** generally dies after flowering, though it is a widely distributed and variable species and there are perennial forms. Usually a crown of stiff, narrow leaves rises from ground level. Can be grown outside in a sheltered, well-drained spot. In its native California, it grows in grassy areas and flowers, dramatically, in early summer.

As with most yuccas, the flowers are borne in broad panicles, waxy, white and bell-shaped. In **Y. flaccida**, with limp leaves, and **Y. filamentosa** with thread-like filaments on the leaf margins, the crown is at ground level. After flowering at 1.2m/4ft or so, the flowered crowns are best sawn out, leaving room for the new crowns to develop. Both these species have excellent variegated forms, which flower well. 'Ivory' (1.2m/4ft) is a free-flowering clone of *Y. flaccida*, its flowers wide open at the mouth.

Y. recurvifolia (2m/6ft) is woody and dependable, if not one of the handsomest. **Y. gloriosa** (up to 2m/6ft or more,) is woody with large crowns of stiff, dark green leaves, making it suitable as a focal feature in any garden where something solid and shapely is needed. The cultivar 'Nobilis' has a bluish sheen on the leaf and is less stiff. 'Variegata' is stiff as they come and, like *Y. gloriosa* has an irritating way of deciding to flower too late in the autumn to succeed. Otherwise flowering is in July or August. Not to be missed. It helps the plants' appearance if an annual practice is made of removing old, dying or dead leaves. They pull off but the plant should be steadied with your free hand while doing this, or a large part of the plant may break adrift.

Propagation is from offsets or rhizomes, known as 'toes'.

16

Z

Zantedeschia

Araceae

18 The arum lily, ***Zantedeschia aethiopica*** (1m/3ft), called calla lily in America, comes from South Africa, where it grows in wet places. It is naturalised in similar places in other warm temperate parts of the world, like the North Island of New Zealand, where it is considered a weed. Flowering there in spring, its high season when grown outside in Britain is June-July.

Each bloom will last for three weeks unless burnt to a frazzle by direct, hot sunshine, for which reason there is reason for growing it in part shade. Moisture and rich living are essential for success. Given these, it will flourish equally under border conditions or in shallow water. *Z. aethiopica* will not stand heavy frosts but some clones are hardier than others. There has been no trial for hardiness, so the reputation of 'Crowborough' for especial hardiness is unproven. The flower consists of a broad white spathe and a club-like yellow spadix. In 'White Sail' the spathe is particularly broad.

In 'Green Goddess' the spathe is mainly green, which appeals to flower arrangers but does not distinguish it sufficiently from the foliage, on the growing plant. Seed is ripened outside even in Britain. If sown fresh, it will germinate in a few weeks even without heat and seedlings will initially have a clean bill of health from virus diseases, which can be a problem.

Handsome colourful arums have been bred, but are not hardy enough for outside cultivation in Britain.

Zauschneria

Onagraceae

A genus from California, where the botanists are in favour of subsuming it into *Epilobium*. This move is hotly resented and resisted by the rest of the world.

Zauschneria californica (15cm/6in) is the very variable species we grow. Basically, it has a running rootstock, a decumbent habit and thin stems. The flowers, borne in late summer and autumn, are a most cheering shade of pure scarlet; tubular, opening into limbs at the mouth, about an inch long. 'Glasnevin' (sometimes misnamed 'Dublin') is a recommended clone. Some clones, notably 'Olbrich Silver', have grey leaves but may not be as free-flowering as others.

A plant for hot dry ledges where it can poke out from the shelter of stones.

Zephyranthes

AMARYLLIDACEAE

A South American genus of which the hardy species, from the River Plate, is ***Zephyranthes candida*** (15cm/6in). A bulbous perennial with dark, rush-like evergreen leaves and a succession, August on, of pure white blooms shaped like crocuses. Can be very freely borne in good summers. Sun for preference. A good front-of-border plant.

Zigadenus

MELANTHIACEAE/LILIACEAE

Zigadenus elegans (1m/3ft) is a delightful perennial from the pine woods of North America. From narrow, basal strap-leaves, panicles of pale green star flowers stand poised and free. Elegant indeed. Flowers June-July. Easy from seed. Grow in cool, woodland soil.

GLOSSARY

aestivation: a summer resting condition or dormancy.

anther: upper part of stamen where pollen is produced.

AGM: the R.H.S. Award of Garden Merit.

Aroid: a member of the Arum family, Araceae.

axil: the juncture between a leaf or bract and the stem supporting it.

axillary: arising from the axil. e.g. an axillary bud.

bipinnate: of pinnae which are themselves pinnate.

bract: small leaf or scale below calyx.

bulb: underground storage organ consisting of swollen fleshy leaf bases or scale leaves.

calyx: outer whorl of a flower constituting the sepals.

cauline: adj., of leaves arising from the upper part of a stem.

close: as in close frame, close conditions, kept close - without air ventilation.

cordate: heart-shaped.

corm: a swollen underground stem, e.g. crocus.

corolla: inner whorl of a flower constituting the petals.

corona: an appendage coming between the perianth and the stamens, as the cup or trumpet of a narcissus.

corymb: an inflorescence in which the flowers are gathered into a flat-topped head, e.g. *Achillea filipendulina.*

cotyledon: seed-leaf, usually of a different shape from later leaves.

cruciform: cross-shaped.

cultivar: a cultivated variety.

decumbent: of plant habit. bent to the ground but rising from the stem tips.

dissect: dissected, finely cut.

dioecious: having the sexes on different plants.

dormancy: a state of living inactivity. adj. dormant - sleeping.

epicotyl: the part of the stem above the cotyledons.

fasciation: a deformed growth.

filament: stalk of the stamen.

foliar: of leaves; leaf-like

globular: globe-shaped.

hastate: of leaves, spear-shaped.

hibernation: a winter resting condition or dormancy.

inflorescence: flowering branch above the last stem leaves.

involucre (adj. **involucral**): a collection of bracts forming a structure at the base of an inflorescence, e.g. *Eryngium alpinum.*

Irishman's cutting: a cutting detached with some root already attached.

lanceolate: of leaves, narrow, lance-shaped.

linear: long and narrow, with parallel sides.

monocarpic: of plants which die after flowering.

monoecious: having unisexual flowers, but both sexes on the same plant, e.g. cucumber.

nectary: a nectar-containing organ.

obovate: of leaves, egg-shaped, broadest above the middle.

orbicular: rounded, with length and breadth approximately the same.

ovary: the female, seed-containing organ.

ovate: of leaves, egg-shaped, broadest at the base.

palmate: of leaves, with lobes spreading from a common axis like fingers on a hand. Compound palmate has the fingers separated.

panicle: a compound raceme, loosely branched, e.g. *Astilbe.* adj. paniculate.

pedate: shaped like a webbed foot.

pedicel: the stalk of a single flower.

peltate: of leaves in which the stalk is connected with

the centre of the leaf blade, e.g. *Darmera peltata.*

perennation: the condition that enables a plant to exist through the years. verb: perennate.

perfoliate: of leaves connected at their base around the stem, e.g. *Smyrnium perfoliatum.*

perianth segments: the separate units of which the perianth is made up, especially when petals and sepals cannot be distinguished, e.g. tulip (with three outer, three inner perianth segments).

perianth: the floral leaves as a whole, including sepals and petals.

petal: a member of the inner series of perianth segments, if differing from the outer series, and especially if brightly coloured.

petaloid: similar to, though not technically, a petal.

petiole: the stalk of a leaf.

pinna (plural **pinnae**): individual segment of a pinnate leaf.

pinnate: of leaves having leaflets on either side of a central axis.

pinnatifid: pinnately cut but not right back to the stalk, e.g. *Polypodium vulgare.*

pinnule (of fern fronds): secondary division of a pinna.

plumose: feathery.

raceme: inflorescence with separate flowers at equal distances along central stem (adj. racemose).

rachis: the central axis of a fern frond.

reflexed: turned back on itself.

reniform: kidney-shaped.

rhizomatous: having rhizomes.

rhizome: an underground modified stem, often swollen and fleshy.

rotate: of a corolla, with the petals spreading out at right angles to the axis, like a wheel.

R.H.S.: Royal Horticultural Society.

scandent: climbing, usually of plants that hoist themselves upwards without any specific climbing device.

scape: leafless flowering stem arising straight from the root, e.g. *Primula, Eremurus.*

scarious: dry and of papery texture.

sepal: part of the outer whorl or calyx of a flower, usually green.

spadix: closely arranged, club-like flower spike, frequently enclosed by a spathe, e.g. *Arum.*

spathe: a large, sheath-like bract, surrounding an inflorescence, e.g. *Arum.*

spike: a raceme of sessile flowers.

stamen: male, pollen-producing organ of flowering plant.

stigma (plural **stigmata**): upper part of female organ, receiving pollen.

stipule: a scale-like or leaf-like

appendage at the base of the petiole.

stolon: a creeping, overground stem capable of rooting at the nodes or tip.

stoloniferous: having stolons.

stop, stopping (of a shoot): a pinching out of the leading growth.

style: connecting link between stigma and ovary in female organ.

subsumed: taken into, amalgamated with or by, merged.

subtending: supporting.

tepal: one of many perianth segments wherein sepals and petals are undifferentiated, e.g. magnolia.

tillering: the habit of making tillers: prostrate, overground shoots.

trifoliate: of leaves having three leaflets.

tuber: a swollen root.

umbel: an umbrella-shaped inflorescence in which the units all arise from the same point on the main stem. In a compound umbel, the main division is further subdivided, e.g. the majority of Umbelliferae, such as cow parsley, *Anthriscus.*

viviparous: giving birth to live young.

whorl: more than two organs of the same kind (e.g. leaves or flowers) arising at the same level.

SOURCES OF PHOTOGRAPHS

We are most grateful to the following photographers

1	Jonathan Buckley	23	Andrew Lawson	47	Jonathan Buckley
2	Photos Horticultural	24	Marcus Harpur	48	Jonathan Buckley
3	Jonathan Buckley	25	Derek St. Romaine	49	Jonathan Buckley
4	Jonathan Buckley	26	Jonathan Buckley	50	Jonathan Buckley
5	Photos Horticultural	27	Jonathan Buckley	51	Jonathan Buckley
6	Garden Matters	28	John Glover	52	Garden Matters
7	Jonathan Buckley	29	Photos Horticultural	53	Jonathan Buckley
8	Jonathan Buckley	30	John Glover	54	Jonathan Buckley
9	Jonathan Buckley	31	Jonathan Buckley	55	Jonathan Buckley
10	Jonathan Buckley	32	Jonathan Buckley	56	Jonathan Buckley
11	Photos Horticultural	33	Jonathan Buckley	57	MAP (A. Descat)
12	Garden Matters	34	Photos Horticultural	58	MAP (A. Descat)
13	Derek St. Romaine	35	Jonathan Buckley	59	Garden Matters
14	Jonathan Buckley	36	Jonathan Buckley	60	Photos Horticultural
15	MAP (F. Didillon)	37	Jonathan Buckley	61	Jonathan Buckley
16	Jonathan Buckley (Beth Chatto's garden)	38	Jonathan Buckley	62	MAP (A. Descat)
		39	Jonathan Buckley	63	Jonathan Buckley
17	Jonathan Buckley	40	Jonathan Buckley	64	Jonathan Buckley
18	Jonathan Buckley (Beth Chatto's garden)	41	Jonathan Buckley	65	Jonathan Buckley
		42	Photos Horticultural	66	Photos Horticultural
19	Garden Matters	43	Jonathan Buckley	67	Photos Horticultural
20	Photos Horticultural	44	Oxford Scientific Films (Geoff Kidd)	68	Photos Horticultural
21	Jonathan Buckley	45	Jonathan Buckley	69	Jerry Harpur (Beth Chatto's garden)
22	Derek St Romaine	46	Jonathan Buckley		

INDEX OF PLANTS

References to photographs are by their numbers, and are printed in **bold** type